a beginner's guide to
RAG RUG
TECHNIQUES

a beginner's guide to RAG RUG TECHNIQUES

discover rag rugging methods from around the world to upcycle fabric into beautiful pieces for the home

Elspeth Jackson

CICO BOOKS

Dear Christian, you deserve a medal for putting up with the fabric explosion in our flat while I was writing this book. You're the salt to my pepper.

To my mum, dad, and brother, Ross—the best support network a girl could have.

To all the rag rug fans out there—may your days be filled with fabric and your bobbins always full.

This edition published in 2025 by CICO Books
An imprint of Ryland Peters & Small Ltd
20–21 Jockey's Fields   1452 Davis Bugg Road
London WC1R 4BW   Warrenton, NC 27589
www.rylandpeters.com
Email: euregulations@rylandpeters.com

First published in 2021 as *Rag Rug Techniques for Beginners*

10 9 8 7 6 5 4 3 2 1

Text © Elspeth Jackson 2021, 2025
Design, illustration, and photography © CICO Books 2021, 2025

The designs in this book are copyright and must not be made for sale.

The author's moral rights have been asserted. All rights reserved. No part of this publication may be reproduced, stored in a retrieval system, or transmitted in any form or by any means, electronic, mechanical, photocopying, or otherwise, without the prior permission of the publisher.

A CIP record for this book is available from the British Library. US Library of Congress CIP data has been applied for.

ISBN: 978-1-80065-414-3

Printed in China

Designers: Sally Powell and Geoff Borin
Photographers: James Gardiner and Penny Wincer
Stylist: Nel Haynes
Illustrators: Cathy Brear and Stephen Dew

Editor: Martha Gavin
Art director: Sally Powell
Production manager: Gordana Simakovic
Publishing manager: Penny Craig
Publisher: Cindy Richards

The authorised representative in the EEA is Authorised Rep Compliance Ltd., Ground Floor. 71 Lower Baggot Street, Dublin, D01 P593, Ireland
www.arccompliance.com

Contents

INTRODUCTION 6
Tools and Equipment 9
Techniques 10
Preparing your fabrics 10
Working with burlap 15

CHAPTER 1
SHAGGY RAG RUGGING 18
Tools and materials 20
Techniques 21
Checked Sari Rug 24
Joyful Mini Wreaths 26
Ragged Flower Bouquet 29
Moroccan Boucherouite-Style Rug 32

CHAPTER 2
LOOPY RAG RUGGING 36
Tools and materials 38
Preparing your burlap and fabrics 38
Techniques 40
Tranquil Triangles Rug 42
"You Are My Sunshine" Rug 45
All the Blues Blanket Box 48
Classic Christmas Stockings 52
Ocean Waves Pillow 56

CHAPTER 3
COILED ROPE 60
Tools and materials 62
Techniques 63
Gold Coast Rug 66
Let's Go to the Beach Basket 70
No-Sew Plant Pot Cover 74
Rag and Rope Rainbow Hanging 76

CHAPTER 4
PEG LOOM WEAVING 80
Tools and materials 82
Techniques 83
Highlands Rug 88
Toasty Fall Leaves Scarf 91
Knick-Knack Storage Bag 94
Pastel Paint Drip Pillow 98

CHAPTER 5
LOCKER HOOKING 102
Tools and materials 104
Techniques 105
Patchwork Rug 109
Domino Thread Catcher 112
"Ciao Bella" Wall Hanging 117

CHAPTER 6
TWO-STRING LOOM 120
Tools and materials 122
Techniques 123
Pink Ombré Rug 126
Eco-Friendly Gift Wrap Spirals 128
Christmas Tree 130

CHAPTER 7
STITCHED RAG RUGS 132
Tools and materials 134
Statement Boho Pillow 134
Stitched "Tapete de Retalhos" Rug 138
No-Sew Tulip Mirror 142
Swedish "Klackmatta" 146

CHAPTER 8
TWINING 150
Tools and materials 152
Techniques 152
Crafty Toolbag 160
Sunny Side Up Placemat 164
English Cottage Rug 168

Templates 172
Stockists 174
Index 175
Acknowledgments 176

INTRODUCTION

Hello there, I'm Elspeth Jackson, color lover, fabric hoarder, and chief rag rug designer and maker at rag rug one-stop-shop "Ragged Life." I've been cutting up my old clothing and making colorful rag rugs since the age of fourteen, which makes it surprising that I have any clothing left to wear! My aim is to get as many people as possible turning their fabric offcuts and material stashes into beautiful upcycled pieces for the home. Not only is it great for the environment, but also happiness.

Growing up in the UK, the types of rag rug that I came across were the sort my mum made—shaggy (proggy) rag rugs and loopy (hooked) ones. Both of these sorts of rug were made by hand using basic tools and a burlap (hessian) base. These techniques were so versatile that for my first ten years of rug making I didn't see the need to branch out—I had plenty to experiment with. So, I tried out different versions of the techniques, played around with every fabric under the sun, truly seeking to understand what makes a successful design and eventually wrote my first book which featured over thirty beginner projects made solely in those two lovely, traditional techniques.

As I traveled more, I discovered other ways of making rag rugs that I'd never come across before. It turns out that rag rug making exists in various forms all across the globe and there are dozens of different ways to make them. I've come across rug making in the USA, Denmark, India, Morocco, Sri Lanka, Thailand, and Tanzania.

It was these encounters that gave me the idea for this second book. I wanted to celebrate rag rug making from across the world and do my little part to help protect some of these traditional techniques so that they live on.

This is by no means all the techniques of rag rug making that exist—I'm sure there are plenty that I have yet to discover, but it'll give you plenty to sink your teeth into.

What are we covering?

This book covers eight different techniques of rag rug making, all of which are easy to learn and hard to put down. Starting with general techniques that are usefu for any budding rag rugger (deconstructing clothing, how to cut your strips quickly etc.), this book is then broken down into eight chapters—one for each separate rag rug technique. This means that you can drop in and out of the book, focusing on the technique that best suits you in the moment. Each chapter covers the equipment you'll need, a detailed run through of the technique including step by step instructions and illustrations, followed by at least three projects. These range in size from large rugs and a rag rug Christmas tree to beach baskets and rag rug flower bouquets. There's truly a project to suit everyone. This book is also full of useful design tips and tricks, so you can benefit from all my years of experimentation. Basically, after reading this book, you will have the know-how and confidence to turn any old fabric and clothing into any number of lovely rag rug projects.

What is a rag rug?

Hold your horses! Before we get started on the making, it's quite nice to know what exactly you're making… So, what is a rag rug? It may seem fairly obvious, but a rag rug is a rug or mat made from rags. That means old clothing, fabric offcuts, or any material that is no longer fit for its original use. Nowadays, rag rug making is a hobby, but historically rag rugs often grew out of poverty and necessity. In many cultures across the world, fitted carpets were an expensive luxury, so rag rugs were an affordable way to cover bare floors, an easy way to help warm homes in colder climates.

In some parts of the world, the patterns worked into the rag rugs were a form of artistic expression that reflected local traditions and cultures—Boucherouite rugs in Morocco are a good example. Here in the UK, historic shaggy rag rugs often featured a dark border, which was a practical way to help hide dust, and a diamond design to represent the hearth and home. Some even featured a red circle to ward off evil spirits. I like that tradition—we could all do with fewer evil spirits in our lives.

What rag rug techniques are in this book?

Below is a snapshot of the eight beginner rag rug techniques we'll be covering in this book.

Shaggy (proggy)

One of the easiest and most historic rag rug techniques. Great for using up small scraps of fabric.

Best for: amazing texture and foot feel.

Locker Hooking

A more hardwearing form of loopy rag rugging. Particularly beloved by crocheters, who pick it up very quickly.

Best for: neat designs with a linear pattern.

Loopy (hooked)

One of the neatest and most artistic techniques. Particularly great for wall hangings.

Best for: pictorial designs and detail.

Two String Loom Rag Rugs

One for working on in front of the TV. Great for mixing and matching small scraps of fabric.

Best for: 3D shaggy projects.

Coiled Rope

One of the simplest, yet effective techniques. Works very nicely for circular and oval projects.

Best for: gorgeous bowls and baskets.

Stitched

One for all you sewers out there! I like to think of it as stitched fabric origami from across the globe.

Best for: colorful doormats and practical patchwork rugs.

Peg Loom Weaving

One of the quickest and easiest ways to make a rag rug. Creates deep, cushy rugs that build in the blink of an eye.

Best for: simple striped designs and using thicker fabrics.

Twining

One of the most absorbing and addictive techniques in this book. Makes a satisfyingly neat woven-style rag rug.

Best for: dipping your toe into patterned weaving with rags.

TOOLS AND EQUIPMENT

EQUIPMENT

Below are some of the general tools which are useful for new rag rug makers to have to hand. Other equipment needed for the different rag rug techniques can be found in the relevant chapter.

Fabric or rag rug scissors

Rag rug making requires a lot of cutting of fabric, which is why it's worth investing in a good pair of fabric scissors. Rag rug scissors are designed to cut through lots of layers of fabric at once, saving you time and effort. Doing this with dressmaking shears can blunt them.

Marker pen

You can use any thick marker pen to sketch onto burlap, rug canvas, and even fabric warps. Any markings will be covered with rag rugging, so choose a color that is clearly visible and don't worry if you make a mistake.

Glue gun

Some projects require the use of a glue gun for finishing touches. Glue guns can now be bought cheaply in store or online. There is no need to buy an expensive model, as none of my projects require large amounts of gluing. It is, however, useful to buy transparent glue sticks so that the glue is less visible in your work.

Sewing machine or needle and thread

To hem burlap, secure rug canvas, or assemble some of the projects in this book, a sewing machine can save a lot of time. Your machine only needs two stitches—a simple running stitch and a zig zag stitch. If you do not have a sewing machine, there are plenty of projects that can be sewn by hand.

Rotary cutter, cutting mat, and ruler

If you have these three pieces of equipment, they can be used as an alternative to fabric scissors to cut strips of material for rag rugging. See the method on page 11.

MATERIALS

Burlap (hessian)

Burlap (also known as hessian), is the traditional base for both shaggy and loopy rag rugs. Rag rugs made using burlap last for years, as long as they don't get damp a lot, which can cause them to rot. There are a few things to look out for when you are buying burlap:

The weave of the burlap is the most important factor. If the weave is too tight then it is hard to pull the strips of fabric through, but if it is too loose then the rags won't stay in securely. All the burlap-based projects in this book have been made using burlap with a weave of 10 holes per inch (HPI). The weave can vary slightly from this, but is a good measure to aim for. Note: The weight and weave of burlap do not correlate, so a 10oz burlap is not the same as 10HPI.

Good quality burlap will make your rag rug last longer and will make the process of rag rugging much more pleasant. A little bit of variation is to be expected as it is a natural product, but you should avoid burlap that bunches in areas or is "hairy". Generally, the more golden in color the hessian, the better quality it is; the browner it is, the worse quality it is, and the more it will shed on you.

Where possible, buy your burlap in person (see Stockists on page 174), as it is very difficult to judge the quality and weave from pictures alone. When buying in person, we recommend taking a ruler with you to help you check it is the correct weave.

Always make sure to hem your burlap (whatever the weight and weave) before you begin a project, so it won't fall apart as you work. See pages 16–17 for how to hem.

Fabrics

All the rag rugging techniques in this book are great for using up old clothing and fabric scraps from other craft projects. Rag rug making is all about recycling, so first rummage in your closet or stash to source fabrics, or visit thrift stores. Remember, few items are too tatty to use! Stains can be cut out of clothing, and some techniques use fabric strips that are as small as 1½ x ⅝in (4 x 1.5cm) (see the Joyous Mini Wreaths on page 26), so even very small, oddly shaped scraps can be repurposed. Some techniques work better with longer strips of fabric—read the specific fabric notes in the Tools and Materials section of each chapter to understand what materials will work best for that particular technique.

I like to mix together different fabrics in my creations, as varied textures add interest. I use everything from cotton, lace, and sari silk ribbon to polyester, fleece, and blanket offcuts. Softer, smoother, more pliable fabrics, such as jersey, cotton, fleece, viscose, and velour are generally easier to work with. Thicker, stiffer, and more textured fabrics, such as denim or leather, can be harder work.

For most of the techniques in this book, when working with different thicknesses of fabric, it is important to balance the different weights by cutting your strips wider or narrower. If you don't do this, and cut all fabrics the same width regardless of weight or type, the project can end up looking unbalanced. Read the Techniques section in each chapter for how wide to cut your strips.

When making practical projects such as rugs, as opposed to a wreath for example, I tend to avoid using fabrics that "ravel" (fray) when you cut them into strips. Examples are thick upholstery fabrics and linen, loosely woven materials, and poor-quality polyesters. These fabrics will continue to shed over time, so can be a nuisance in certain projects. You can generally tell how a fabric will react after cutting just a few strips, so test a few pieces before cutting up a whole garment.

Knitted woolen fabrics, such as jumpers and tights, often ravel when you cut into them, but you can boil wash them beforehand to felt the fibers together. You can also cut fabric on the bias (diagonal to the weave of the fabric) to reduce fraying and raveling. This works particularly well for cottons and linens, so don't discount a fabric without trying this first. Most fabrics fray a little when you work with them as the edges get roughed up, but don't be deterred as this texture often adds interest. If you are worried about loose fibers on your rag rug, vacuum it to remove threads.

TECHNIQUES

The majority of projects in this book require breaking down fabric into either blocks or long strips of varying widths. I always try to get as much fabric out of one garment as possible. If you are using recycled clothing or offcuts, once you have run out of a fabric it is nearly impossible to find the same one again (particularly with patterned materials). Being clever with your cutting also avoids wastage. Below is how you deconstruct old clothing, and then different ways to turn these blocks of fabric into strips.

PREPARING YOUR FABRICS

DECONSTRUCTING CLOTHING

1 Choose the material to cut up—I recommend practicing with an old t-shirt first. Turn the item inside out so that any seams are visible. Cut along one edge of every seam, except the bottom hem and neckline, to separate the garment into its constituent pieces. For a t-shirt you will usually have four sections—front, back, and two arms. All the seams should be left on at this stage.

2 I sometimes use fabric seams in my rag rugging to add texture and avoid wastage. Always cut along the line of seams, never horizontally across them. For the shaggy and loopy techniques, cut strips ½in (1cm) away from the stitching of the seams. You may need to cut strips wider or narrower than this for other techniques (follow directions in each chapter). Strips containing seams are cut slightly narrower than usual to compensate for the added thickness of the stitching. Cut off and discard any parts of the t-shirt that cannot be used, such as stiff or thick collars and clothing labels. If you have any "lumps" at the end of your strips where two seams met, cut these off as they will show up in your rag rugging.

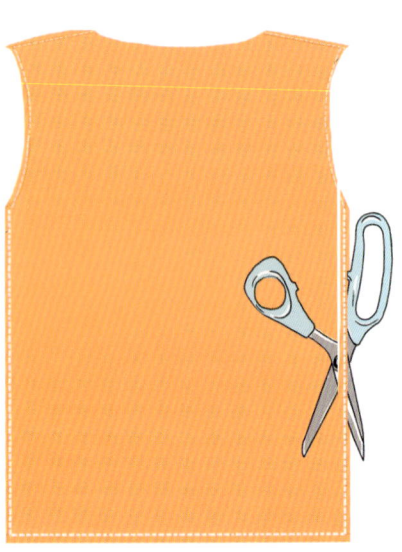

3 Cut a strip or strips from the bottom hem, if there is one. If the bottom hem is less than ½in (1cm) in depth, create one strip out of it by cutting above the hemming. If the bottom hem is more than ½in (1cm) deep, cut below the hemming so that the fabric opens up to create a normal strip. Create a separate strip from the seam left on the garment. You should now be left with blocks of fabric with no seams or lumpy bits left on. You do not need to remove pockets or darts.

CUTTING STRIPS WITH SCISSORS

It is important to use a sharp pair of fabric scissors for this technique of cutting strips, as you will be cutting through multiple layers of fabric at a time. Tougher materials, such as denim, can blunt dressmaking scissors—so if yours are your pride and joy, it may be a worth investing in a pair of rag rug scissors. Don't worry about cutting strips completely straight, as little kinks won't show up in your rag rugging.

1 Fold the fabric block in half across the width so that the top meets the bottom, then into quarters in the same direction, and then into eighths so that you have a tube. Remember to fold rather than roll, as thicker fabrics such as fleece become too thick to cut through when rolled. Folding across the width creates strips that are as long as possible.

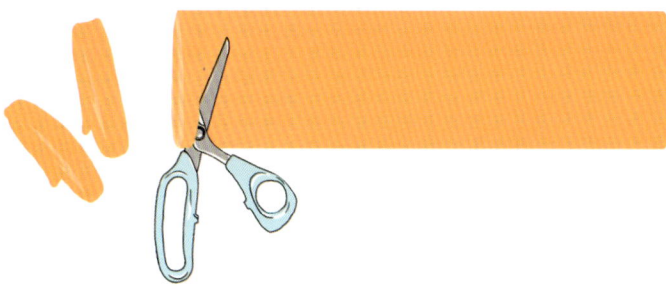

2 Cut the tube into rolls ¾in (2cm) wide (or whatever width the project requires). These rolls will unravel into long strips. Do not worry if the ends of the tube are uneven, as parts of these strips will be salvageable. Repeat this process on all the other fabric pieces. Remember to fold long sleeves across the width to get the longest strips possible.

CUTTING STRIPS WITH A ROTARY CUTTER

Many patchworkers or crafters own a rotary cutter, cutting mat, and transparent ruler. These are great for cutting large pieces of fabric (especially bed linen) into strips quickly and neatly.

1 Remove any seams or lumps from your fabric so you have a flat piece of fabric. Fold the fabric a maximum of two times (i.e. no more than four layers in thickness) and lay it flat on the cutting mat. Align the edge of the fabric with one of the printed lines on the cutting mat as best you can. Place the ruler on top of the fabric and align it with the same printed line. Hold down the ruler firmly, making sure your fingers aren't too close to the edge of the ruler where the blade will pass by.

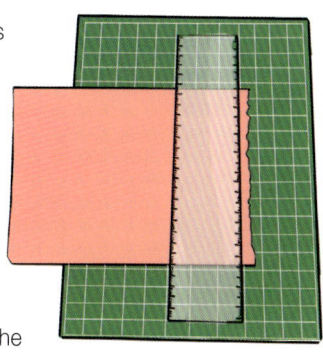

2 Using the blade of the rotary cutter, cut along the edge of the ruler, moving slowly away from your body. Apply even pressure to get a clean cut and keep going until you reach the other end of the fabric. Put this end piece aside.

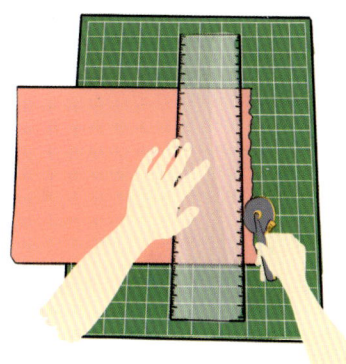

3 Move the ruler approximately ¾in (2cm) across the fabric (or whatever width you would like your strip to be) and cut another strip, using the rotary cutter as before. Continue cutting one strip at a time until you reach the end of the fabric.

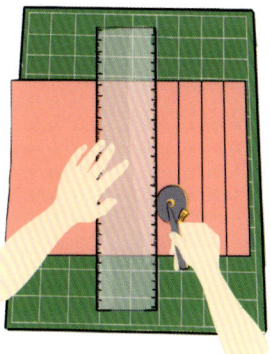

TECHNIQUES 11

TEARING STRIPS

This technique of creating strips can be used on light to medium weight woven fabrics, such as cotton, voile, chiffon, silk, and flannel. It can make the process of cutting strips slightly quicker, but bear in mind that the edges of the fabric strips will be frayed and sometimes curl, so this technique isn't for everyone.

1 Identify the grain of the fabric e.g. which way the horizontal and vertical strands that make up the fabric are running.

2 Snip approximately ¾in (2cm) (or whichever width of strip is required) in from the side of the fabric piece on its shortest edge, in the direction of the weave (this will create the longest strips possible). Hold the fabric on both sides of the cut and quickly tear the strip off. This will create a straight edge to your fabric block. If your fabric piece is very uneven, this strip may not be that long, but some of it will be salvageable.

3 Continue cutting ¾in (2cm) spaced snips at the end of the fabric in the direction of the weave as in step 2. The distance that you space out your snip marks to rip your strips depends on how wide your strips need to be.

USING A GAUGE

A gauge is a wonderful time- and effort-saving tool for turning longer strips into shorter ones for use in shaggy rag rugging (cChapter 1) and on the two-string loom (Chapter 6. Using a gauge creates a pleasingly consistent look, as it produces fabric pieces of a similar length.

1 Cut your fabric into long strips using fabric scissors or a rotary cutter (see page 11) or by tearing strips (see above).

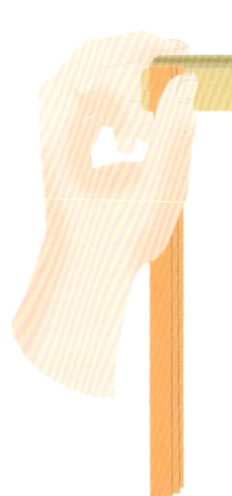

2 Hold a number of fabric strips together with the ends aligning (see box on opposite page for the number of strips to use for different fabrics). If any of the strips have a flatter end, hold that at the top. It does not matter if the strips are different lengths. Place the strips against the gauge, with the tops aligning with the groove.

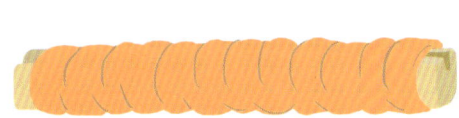

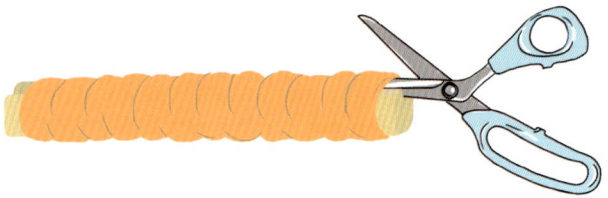

3 Wind the strips around and along the gauge until you reach the ends of the strips. Shorter strips can be secured into the gauge by wrapping the longer strips over them. Overlap the edges of your strips slightly as you wind so that you cross the groove at the top of the gauge vertically. Try not to pull the fabric too tightly as any material containing elastic will stretch, creating shorter pieces.

4 Use fabric scissors to cut along the gauge's groove. This will produce similar length, short pieces of material ideal for shaggy rag rugging. Discard any cut pieces that were too short to fit fully around the gauge.

How many strips can I use at a time?

The number of strips wound together on the gauge depends on the thickness of the fabric and the length of the strip. Assuming a strip length of approximately 20in (50cm), this is the number of strips I would usually wind on the gauge at the same time. Don't worry about following this guide exactly, as thicknesses can vary.

Denim: 3 strips

Fleece: 3 strips

Blanket offcuts: 3 strips

Thick jersey: 4 strips

Thin jersey: 6 strips

Cotton: 6 strips

Lining fabric: 8 strips

Chiffon/voile: 10 strips

JOINING STRIPS TOGETHER

Some of the rag rug techniques in this book work best with longer strips of fabric—for example peg loom weaving and locker hooking. Here are three ways in which you can join fabric strips together to make them longer.

Diagonal seam join

This is one of the quickest and cleanest ways to join, but it does require a sewing machine. It is particularly useful for projects where you want to make up extra-long, continuous strips of fabric before you begin making.

1 Place the "new" strip so that the end overlaps at right angles with the "old strip." Right sides should be facing.

2 Backstitching a few stitches at the beginning and end of the row, sew diagonally across the two strips. Pay attention to the diagonal direction.

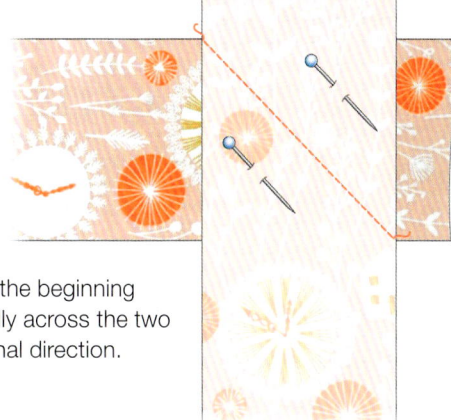

3 Cut the corner off, leaving a ¼in (0.5cm) seam allowance and trim any loose threads.

TECHNIQUES 13

Buttonhole join method

This method of joining strips is one of the quickest and most convenient techniques as it doesn't require any sewing and only requires scissors. However, the knots created can be quite chunky when working with thick fabrics, so it isn't appropriate for all projects, and it doesn't work particularly well for loosely woven fabrics, which can tear.

1 Align the tops of the two strips you want to join together, fold both tops over by about 1in (2.5cm), and cut a small slit through both layers.

2 Place the shorter strip on top of the longer strip so that the slits are aligned. If you taper the ends of the strips the join will be less bulky.

3 Pull the non-slit end of the shorter strip up through both the slits (from the bottom to the top) and pull tight to bind the two strips together.

Enclosed end join

The enclosed end join is the most time-consuming technique of joining fabric strips, but does give a nice smooth join.

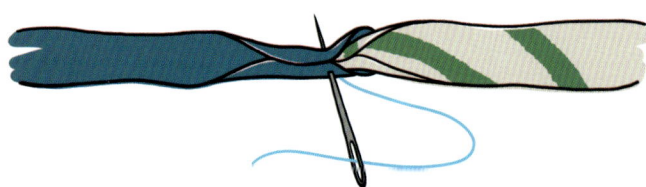

1 Starting approximately 1in (2.5cm) from the end of each strip, taper the ends slightly to remove some of the bulk. You should still have a flat end.

2 Enclose the "new" strip in the old "strip", folding the edges in twice to create a smooth join. Make sure that the right side of the fabric is facing outwards.

3 Hand sew the two strips together using color matched thread where possible.

WORKING WITH BURLAP

Both the traditional shaggy and loopy techniques of rag rugging are made using a burlap (hessian) base. Below are the tried and tested techniques on how to correctly hem it before you begin.

WORKING IN STRAIGHT LINES

To edge hem a square or rectangular rag rug, first you need to create straight lines for the edges. Hessian is an organic product, so simply sketching a line with a ruler doesn't always work. The technique below ensures that your lines are truly straight and that the rug you are planning won't taper out from one end to the other.

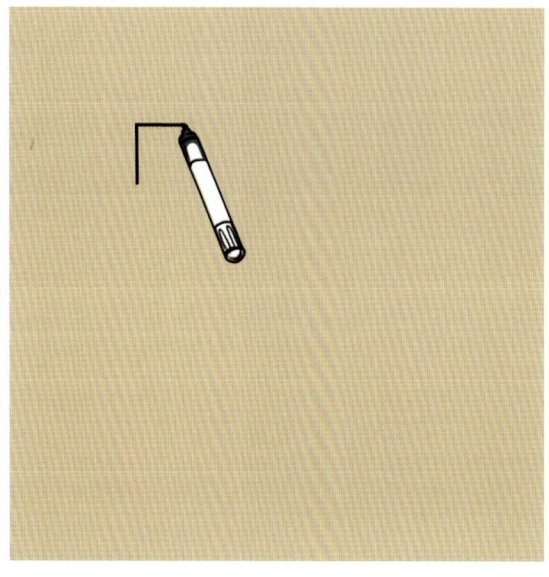

1 Using a marker pen, mark one of the corners of the square or rectangle on the burlap. Make sure you've positioned this corner so that there is enough space for the square or rectangle to fit onto the burlap.

2 Remove the vertical burlap strand at the marked corner by following the burlap strand you have drawn on top of to the frayed edge of the burlap and gently pulling it out. The burlap will bunch up as you do this, but do not worry. If the edge of the burlap is a selvage or already hemmed, you may need to make a small cut at the end of the strand so that it will come out. Pulling out the strand creates a gap in the burlap. This gap is in line with the weave and as straight a line as you will achieve. Use the same method to pull out the horizontal burlap strand at the corner.

3 Measure from your first corner along the gaps left by the missing strands and mark out the other corners of the square or rectangle. Pull out the vertical and horizontal strands at these corners to create an "invisible" square or rectangle. When you hem, use these gaps as guides to keep in line with the weave of the burlap.

HEMMING BURLAP

Burlap/hessian is usually sold by the yard or meter and cut from a large roll. This means that your piece will probably have two selvage/selvedge edges and at least two sides that are raw or cut. Rag rugging close to a cut edge will cause the burlap to unravel and any fabric pieces to fall out.

Hemming the burlap before you start rag rugging will protect your work. You do not need to hem selvage edges. There are two types of hemming used in this book—edge hemming and placeholder hemming. Edge hemming is the super-secure method used at the edge of rugs and wall hangings, as it will withstand a lot of wear and tear. Placeholder hemming is used to keep the burlap intact long enough for you to rag rug your piece and assemble it. It is traditionally used for decorative pieces such as wreaths and pillows, where there are further steps to assemble the project after the rag rugging is complete.

Edge hemming

It is generally easier to edge hem in straight lines, as opposed to curved or random shapes, as these can be prone to curling up on the edges. To see how edge hemming works for shapes other than squares and rectangles, see the "You are my Sunshine" Rug on page 45.

1 Mark out the size of rug or project you'd like to make on to the burlap. Every edge of the hessian that you edge hem will reduce the final size of the hessian by ¾in (2cm), so if you are making something where the precise size is important, take this into account. A stool cover or tray insert, for example, would need to be more precise than a large area rug. If your design is square or rectangular, first follow the "working in straight lines" method (see page 15) to ensure the marked out edges are in line with the weave of the burlap. Cut out the burlap so that the edges are clean cut without any loose threads.

2 Fold your first edge over by ½in (1cm), then fold it over again by ½in (1cm) to trap the frayed edge of the burlap underneath. Pin the edge in place.

Elspeth's tip

As you gain experience, you may no longer need to pin your hessian edges in place before machine stitching them. You can fold the hem under the sewing machine foot, and fold and stitch as you go.

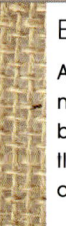

16 INTRODUCTION

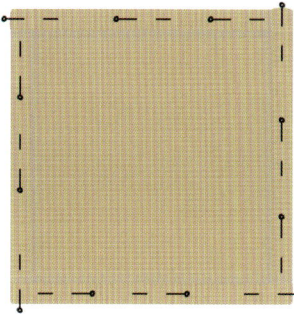

3 Repeat step 2 for each edge of the burlap to be hemmed. Corners can be quite tricky to pin as they are bulky.

4 Either hand sew or machine stitch along each of the pinned edges to secure them in position. If hand sewing, use a button thread for extra strength and baste (tack) a few extra stitches into each corner. If sewing by machine, sew a running stitch close to the inner fold of each hem in turn. When you reach a corner, manually lift your sewing machine foot onto the corner, as opposed to running directly onto it, as the added thickness in the corner can snap needles if you are not careful. Try to keep the folded hem even in width.

Placeholder hemming

Placeholder hemming is a less secure form of hemming used only for projects that require further assembling after they are fully rag rugged. Depending on the type of project, you may need either one or two rows of placeholder hemming (the instructions for each project will make this clear). The number of rows is determined by the rag rugging technique, the size of the project, and the way it is assembled. Some projects also require two rows of placeholder hemming stitch on top of each other for extra security.

1 Leaving at least 2in (5cm) between the frayed edge of the burlap and your design, draw your project on the burlap. If your design is a square or rectangle, first follow the "working in straight lines" method (see page 15) to ensure that the edges of your design are in line with the weave of the burlap.

2 Adjust the settings on your sewing machine so that the stitch width is at its widest setting (mine goes up to 6.0) and your stitch length is at its default setting (mine is 2.0). Zig zag stitch around the piece at least 1½in (4cm) away from the design to secure the burlap edge.

HOW MUCH FABRIC WILL I NEED?

Calculating how far your fabric will go is one of the hardest parts of rag rug making, as it depends on so many things—the technique used, the fabric weight and strip width, to the weave of the hessian (if using), and the particular way in which an individual rag rugs. What's more, projects are often made using hundreds of smaller pieces of fabric mixed together making calculations even harder. See each of the different techniques for tips on calculating how much fabric you will need for each one. If you are unsure whether a fabric will fill a space then mix together multiple fabrics from the beginning to avoid running out part-way through.

Right, that's it for the general methods section, let's learn some techniques…

WORKING WITH BURLAP 17

CHAPTER 1

SHAGGY RAG RUGGING

Shaggy rag rugging is one of the most popular and traditional rag rug techniques here in the UK. Confusingly, depending on where you are from in the country, it is done in different ways, with different tools and called different names. Shaggy rag rugs are sometimes called "proggy," "proddy," "clippy," "clootie," and "peggy" mats, and I'm sure there are other names that I haven't even come across yet!

All the projects in this chapter were made using a rag rug spring tool and burlap base. It's not the only way to make this style of rag rug, but it's certainly the easiest.

This rag rug technique is the ultimate scrap-busting craft, as the size of fabric pieces can be as small as 1½ x ½in (4 x 1.5cm), as used in the Joyful Mini Wreaths project on page 26.

Half the projects in my first book were rag rugged in the shaggy technique, showing the versatility of this gorgeous, textured technique.

TOOLS AND MATERIALS

Rag rug spring tool
Sometimes called a "bodger," this tool is the easiest and quickest tool to shaggy rag rug with. With the rag rug spring tool, you can work entirely from the top of the hessian, so you can see exactly how your rag rugging is looking as you do it. You do not need a frame to hold the hessian taut when working with the spring tool and it's great for joining pieces of hessian together. Over time, the spring can wear out, but it's easy and cheap to get hold of a replacement spring.

When purchasing a rag rug spring tool, ideally choose one with a thinner, less chunky end, as these will disturb the hessian less. The handles can come in different styles, but they all do the same job!

If you would like to try the shaggy technique without investing in a rag rug spring tool, a latch hook can also be used, but is not quite as easy to work with.

Gauge
A rag rug gauge is a time-saving tool that aids and speeds up the process of cutting strips of fabric to a similar length for shaggy rag rugging. Most rag rug gauges cut pieces to a length of approximately 3½in (9cm), but the exact length doesn't matter as long as they are vaguely consistent. For how to use the gauge, see page 12.

Other tools you may need
Fabric/rag rug scissors
Marker pen
Rotary cutter and mat (an alternative to fabric scissors)
Sewing machine/needle and thread (for hemming)
Pins (for hemming)
Tape measure/ruler

Burlap (hessian)
This material is the traditional base for shaggy rag rugs. See page 9 for more information on burlap.

Fabrics
Shaggy rag rugging is one of the best rag rug techniques for using up small fabric scraps. I like to mix together different materials in my shaggy rag rug creations, as varied textures add interest. I use everything from cotton and lace, to polyesters and fleece. When making projects that are practical, not decorative (a rug, as opposed to a rag rug wreath, for example), I tend to avoid using too many fabrics that "ravel" or fall apart. These fabrics will continue to shed over time, so you'll be forever vacuuming. Fabrics with elastic in can look particularly interesting when shaggy rag rugged as the fabric pieces will curl in on themselves and tube up. Thin, soft, and less textured fabrics are easiest to work with.

Preparing your burlap and fabrics
Before I begin shaggy rag rugging, I always hem my burlap (see page 16 for how to do this).

Shaggy rag rugging requires small pieces of fabric that have been cut to roughly the same lengths. Traditionally, these pieces are around ¾in (2cm) in width and 3½in (9cm) in length, but you can vary this to great effect.

To create small fabric pieces, first you create long strips of fabric. The precise length of the strips doesn't matter at this stage, but I try to make them as long as possible. You can cut or tear long strips using any of the methods on pages 11–12. The width that you cut these strips is dictated by the weight of the fabric you are working with. Thicker fabrics are cut narrower, while thinner fabrics are cut wider. For example, cut denim into approximately ½in (1cm) wide strips and cut chiffon into 2in (5cm) wide strips.

If you accidentally cut your strips too narrow, you can rag rug with multiple strips at once to bulk out the thickness. Sometimes I rag rug with seams of garments to generate less wastage and to add texture to a piece. These can be quite thick and stiff to work with, so I usually cut them ½in (1cm) in width.

Once you've created your long strips of fabric, you will need to turn them into shorter pieces, using a rag rug gauge (see page 12).

How much fabric will I need?
The shaggy technique of rag rugging is one of the more fabric-intensive techniques. To create a 40 x 24in (100 x 60cm) shaggy rug requires approximately 20 t-shirts. If you fold a piece of fabric in half four times, that will give you the rough area that that piece of fabric will cover when it is cut up and shaggy rag rugged.

20 SHAGGY RAG RUGGING

TECHNIQUES

Few things feel nicer than sinking your feet into a thick, shaggy rag rug. Here's how you make one.

1 Cut your fabric into long strips using any of the techniques on pages 11–12. Remember to adjust the width of the strips to compensate for their thickness. Next, cut them into short strips that are approximately 3 ½in (9cm) in length using a rag rug gauge (see page 12).

2 Keeping the spring tool closed, from the top of the burlap, weave the pointed end of the tool down into a hole in the burlap and up through a hole two strands away. You should now have two strands of the burlap on top of the lever of the tool.

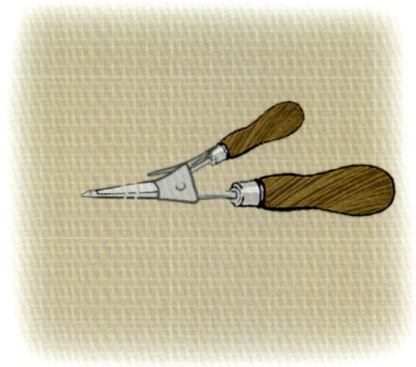

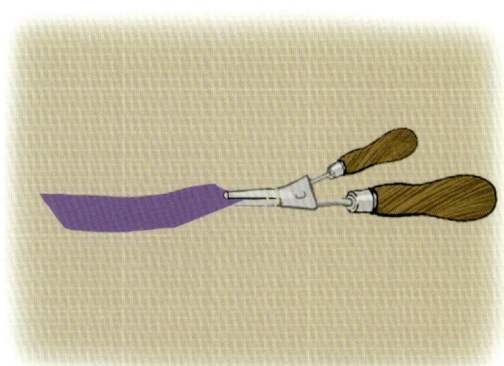

3 Squeeze to open the spring tool. Place the corner of the short edge of the fabric strip into the opening and release the lever to clench the rag.

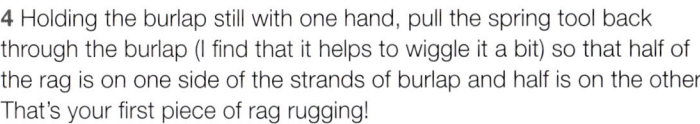

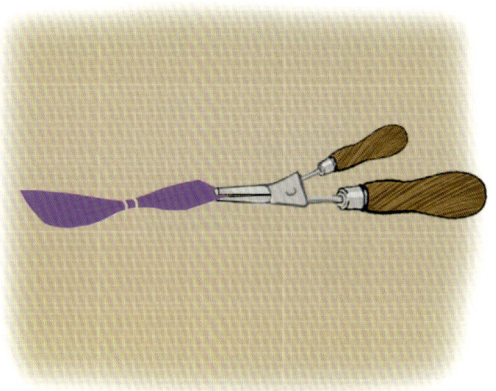

4 Holding the burlap still with one hand, pull the spring tool back through the burlap (I find that it helps to wiggle it a bit) so that half of the rag is on one side of the strands of burlap and half is on the other. That's your first piece of rag rugging!

5 Leaving approximately two or three strands between each rag and the next, repeat steps 2 to 4 to continue the method. You may need to miss out more or fewer strands between fabric pieces depending on how thick the fabric is. Miss out more strands between thicker fabrics, such as denim and blanket offcuts. You can weave diagonally across the burlap strands if it makes sense for the pattern you are following.

Elspeth's tip

With rugs, generally, you begin shaggy rag rugging on the inside of the hem, not through it. The long shaggy rag rug pieces fall over the edge to hide the hem.

TECHNIQUES 21

SHORT SHAGGY RAG RUGGING WITH THE RAG RUG SPRING TOOL

Short shaggy rag rugging is a technique that my mother and I have somewhat invented. We think it combines the best characteristics of both the shaggy and loopy rag rug techniques together. The shorter pile means that rag rug designs look clearer and more defined than they do with the shaggy technique, but you still get amazing foot-feel.

1 Cut your fabric into long strips using any of the techniques on pages 11–12. The width that you cut your strips should be roughly half the width you would usually cut that fabric. So, jersey would be about 1in (2.5cm) and voile, about ¾in (2cm). Next, cut them into short strips that are approximately 3½in (9cm) in length using a rag rug gauge (see page 12).

2 Keeping the spring tool closed, from the top of the burlap, weave the pointed end of the tool down into a hole in the burlap and up through a hole two strands away. You should now have two strands of the burlap on top of the lever of the tool.

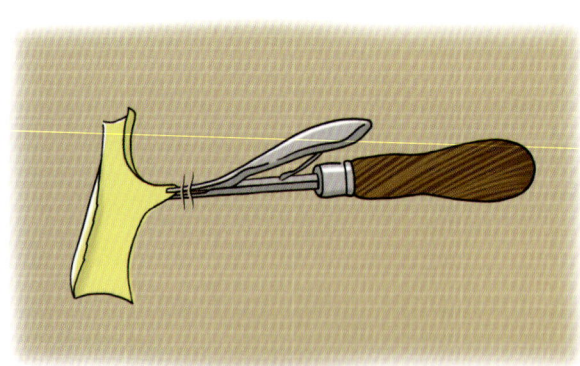

3 Squeeze the spring tool to open it, place the middle of the short strip in the spring tool opening, and release the spring lever to clench the rag.

4 Gently pull through, so that there is a loop of fabric on one side of the strands of burlap and two cut edges of fabric on the other side. The evenness of the two cut edges depends on how accurate you were in grabbing precisely the middle of the strip.

5 Leaving approximately 2 strands between each rag and the next, repeat steps 2–4 to continue. If you are struggling to pull the doubled over fabric through the burlap, try cutting your fabric strips narrower.

Elspeth's tip
It is important to cut strips a bit narrower than usual as the Short Shaggy Technique adds thickness to the fabric that can make it harder to pull through the burlap. When in doubt, it is better to cut your fabric slightly narrower as opposed to too wide.

COMMON MISTAKES

The hardest part of shaggy rag rugging is getting the spacing correct. It is much easier to see how your spacing is looking from the back of the burlap than it is from the front.

If you rag rug too far apart then you will see empty squares of burlap between your fabric pieces. The most common mistake beginner rag ruggers make, however, is rag rugging too close together. If you do this then the burlap will begin to warp and cave in around your rag rugging. This will create a rug that will curl on the edges.

If you begin to pick up too many strands of burlap onto the spring tool when you first weave across then it will create long loops on the back of the rag rugging. These can work themselves loose over time, particularly on rugs, where the back rubs against the floor.

SHAGGY-SPECIFIC DESIGN TIPS

The shaggy technique of rag rugging is all about texture, texture, and more texture! It makes the softest and coziest rugs, pillows, and more. Color is key for shaggy projects, so choose colors that you like and even the simplest of designs (stripes, polka dots, or checks) will look great.

However, as the fabric pieces have a life of their own and fall whichever way they please, the shaggy technique isn't really suitable for complex, pictorial designs with a lot of detail. Designs become blurry and indistinguishable if you're not careful.

If you want a line or feature to stand out, it needs to be at least three rows of shaggy rag rugging wide. Plain fabrics stand out better than patterned fabrics and can help to frame key design features. However, patterned fabrics add interest, so are a must-have in most classic shaggy rag rugs. When picking your fabrics, bear in mind that if your fabric has a right and a wrong side, some of both sides of the fabric will show. It is impossible to control the technique to show just one side of the fabric strip or the other. To understand how to build up large backgrounds of color, check out the Moroccan Boucherouite-Style Rug on page 32.

Checked Sari Rug

Checks are one of the simplest and most effective patterns you can create in rag rugging. The more defined you'd like the lines to be, the shorter the pile of the rug has to be, which is why we've used the short shaggy (rather than shaggy) technique here. The color scheme of this rag rug was inspired by Indian textiles and crafts. It even includes some recycled saris, which add richness and sheen.

You will need

Burlap/hessian: 40 x 23½in (102 x 60cm) piece

Tape measure/ruler

Fabric scissors

Marker pen

Sewing machine/needle and thread

Pins (optional)

Fabrics: I used approximately 15 full t-shirts in assorted shades

Rag rug spring tool

Rag rug gauge

1 Use a tape measure and marker pen to draw a 39½ x 23in (100 x 58cm) rectangle on to the burlap. Try to keep in line with the weave of the burlap as you do this (see page 15). Edge hem all around the rug (see page 16) using a sewing machine or needle and thread. This will reduce the size of the rug by ¾in (2cm) on each hemmed edge, so it measures 37¾ x 21¼in (96 x 54cm).

2 Mark dots every 2⅜in (6cm) along each edge of the rug to help guide your lines. Draw lines to join up the dots directly opposite each other to create a 9 by 16 grid of 2⅜in (6cm) size squares.

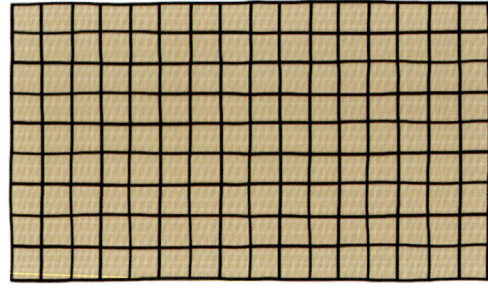

3 Prepare your first fabric for the short shaggy technique by first creating long strips, approximately ½in (1cm) in width (see page 11), then cutting these long strips into approximately 3½in (9cm) long pieces using a rag rug gauge (see page 12). Each square in this design was made up of one or two colors, but they repeated throughout the rug.

Elspeth's tip

Don't worry if your "squares" aren't completely square—mine certainly weren't! The rag rugging softens imperfections.

If you do not follow the color chart (step 4), I would recommend having one color that consistently appears in two or three squares every row. For me, that was pink.

4 Short shaggy rag rug (see page 22) one of the corner squares using the color chart on the left. I rag rugged each square in rows, leaving about three empty rows of burlap between each row of rag rugging and the next. Once you've filled your first square, move to the next one, working your way along the short edge of the rug. Work one row of squares at a time until you reach the far side of the rug. Only rag rug through the hem if it is visible.

24 SHAGGY RAG RUGGING

Joyful Mini Wreaths

For my first book I made a beautiful full sized festive wreath to adorn the front door in the lead up to Christmas. It got me thinking... wouldn't it be cute to have miniature versions to hang on the Christmas tree or to string up on garlands? And so, the Joyful Mini Wreaths were born. Each mini wreath only takes around half an hour to rag rug, so this is definitely one of the quickest and most satisfying smaller rag rug projects out there. Plus, as the fabric pieces used are so tiny, it's a great stashbuster.

You will need

Circular object, e.g. a cup or pillar candle, about 4in (10cm) in diameter

Burlap (hessian)

Marker pen

Sewing machine and thread (any color)

Ruler/tape measure

Fabric/rag rug scissors

Fabrics: I used red, green, and white for a traditional design

Rag rug spring tool

Ribbon/burlap strands to create a hanging loop

Glue gun

Felt

1 Take your circular object and draw around it onto the burlap, leaving at least 1½in (4cm) of burlap between each circle and the next (if you are making multiple wreaths), or between the drawn circle and the edge of the burlap.

2 Draw a second circle ¾–1in (2–2.5cm) inside of the first circle then zig zag stitch along both drawn lines to hem the burlap. Leave your stitch width at default, but adjust your stitch length shorter.

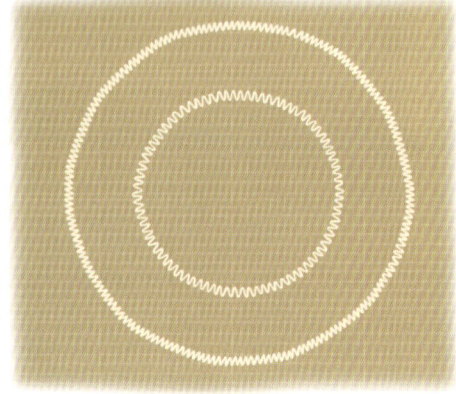

Elspeth's tip

These mini wreaths look best rag rugged in a mixture of plain and patterned fabric. You can even rag rug with other craft materials such as ribbon to add interest, or add mini baubles or bows to the wreaths at the end. The area to be rag rugged appears small at first, but the bushiness of the rag rugging makes them appear fuller at the end.

26 SHAGGY RAG RUGGING

3 Cut your fabric into approximately 1½in x ⅝in (4 x 1.5cm) size pieces. The strips must be long enough to cover the stitching, but short enough to leave a defined ring.

4 Leaving out approximately two strands of burlap between each fabric piece and the next, fill between the stitched lines with shaggy rag rugging using the technique on page 21.

5 Once you are happy with how your mini wreath looks from the front, cut away the excess burlap from around the outer stitched circle and from inside the inner stitched circle, making sure not to cut the stitching.

6 Plait together three strands of burlap to create a rustic twine or cut a piece of ribbon to length for the hanging loop. Shorter loops will be less visible, but will be harder to attach to a Christmas tree. My hanging loops are approximately 2¾in (7cm) long, so I cut my twine approximately 6in (15cm) long.

7 Choose which part of the mini wreath to have at the top and glue the hanging loop to the back of the mini wreath, making sure that the ends of the loop are not visible from the front.

8 Draw around the circular item from step 1 onto felt and draw a second line approximately 1⅛in (3cm) in from the first. Cut out the felt ring and glue it to the back of the mini wreath to hide your handiwork.

Ragged Flower Bouquet

These rag rug bouquets have fast become one of my signature makes at Ragged Life. They bring color to any room of the home and make a wonderful handmade gift. I made a particularly gorgeous bunch of colorful rag rug flowers for a friend's wedding. I like to make seven different sized flowers for each bouquet, but there's no reason why you couldn't supersize the bunch.

You will need

Round object of about 2in (5cm) in diameter

Burlap (hessian)

Marker pen

Sewing machine and thread (any color)

Fabric: I used fabrics that weren't too floppy, so the "petals" stood up well

Fabric/rag rug scissors

Rag rug spring tool

Twigs/wooden marshmallow or kebab sticks (12 x ¼in/30cm x 6mm diameter) for the flower stems

Glue gun

1 Place the circular object on the burlap and carefully trace around it to form a circle on the burlap. Move the object so that it overlaps the first circle by approximately ⅜in (1cm) and trace round it again, to form a figure-of-eight shape. Repeat 7 times, leaving at least 1½in (4cm) of burlap between each figure-of-eight and the next, and between the figures and the edge of the burlap.

2 Zig zag stitch around the drawn figure-of-eights to hem the burlap. Leave your stitch width at the default setting, but adjust your stitch length to be shorter.

3 Cut your fabric into strips that are approximately 2 x 3¼in (5 x 8cm) in size (you can vary the length and width of the strips for different effects). Lay 10 cut strips one on top of the other and use scissors to shape the ends of the bunch of strips so that they are either rounded, pointed, or heart-shaped. Different shapes will give different looks to your flowers.

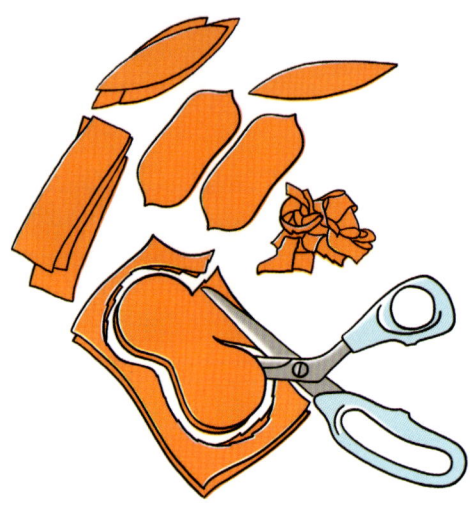

4 Leaving out approximately one strand of burlap/hessian between each fabric piece and the next, fill inside the stitched figure-of-eights with shaggy rag rugging using the technique on page 21. Fill the shapes in any order you would like (in lines or randomly, for example) but make sure to rag rug your pieces close together to ensure you get a nice full flower in the end. Rag rug all your flowers before cutting into the burlap/hessian as this helps to keep the strands intact.

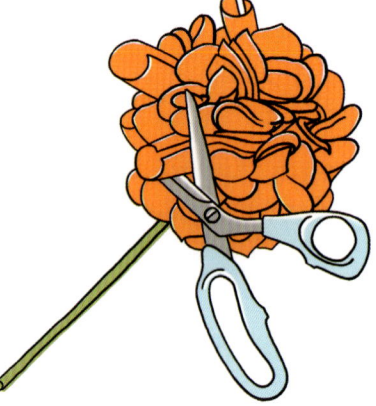

5 Once all the flowers are rag rugged, cut around the edge of the stitching of the rag rugged figure-of-eights to separate them from the sheet of burlap/hessian. Cut as close to the stitched hem as possible without cutting into it.

6 Lay the rag rugged figure-of-eights shaggy side down on a solid surface and place one of the wooden flower stems or twigs on, so the end is within the base of the figure-of-eight.

7 Glue around the edge of the stitching and around the wooden stick, then fold the figure-of-eight to sandwich the stick into the burlap/hessian. Press all the edges to secure them together and fluff up the rag rugging to cover the fold. Trim if necessary.

8 Arrange your jolly rag rug flowers in a vase. I like to cut some of the stems slightly shorter to create different heights within a bouquet.

Elspeth's tip

When choosing what fabrics to use for your flowers, think about how they will work as an ensemble. An easy trick is to take color inspiration from real-life floral bouquets.

Moroccan Boucherouite-Style Rag Rug

Morocco has long been known for its beautiful woolen rugs. However, during the mid 20th century, a new form of rug began to appear—boucherouite rugs. "Boucherouite" (pronounced boo-shay-reet) is a word derived from a Moroccan-Arabic phrase for torn and reused clothing. To make these practical and thrifty rugs, Berber women used old clothing, recycled carpets, cotton, nylon, and even the plastic from shopping bags. Nowadays, boucherouite rugs are often found in colorful and characterful homes across the world. The project I have designed is not a true boucherouite rug, as it hasn't been handwoven on a loom by a Berber woman in the Atlas Mountains, but it is an homage to the bright colors and abstract designs of these stunning rugs.

You will need

Burlap/hessian: 52¾ x 35in (134 x 89cm)

Tape measure/ruler

Marker pen

Template on page 172

Fabric scissors

Fabrics: I used approximately 40 t-shirts in shades of white, navy, blue, red, orange, yellow, purple, and pink—this is an excellent project for using up lots of scraps, which can be mixed together

Sewing machine/needle and thread

Pins (optional)

Rag rug spring tool

Rag rug gauge

1 Use a tape measure and marker pen to draw a 50½ x 31½in (128 x 80cm) rectangle on to the burlap. Try to keep in line with the weave of the burlap as you do this (see page 15). Fold the drawn rectangle in half lengthways twice and press, so you have sectioned the rectangle into quarters. Then fold it in half widthways and press. You should now have four pressed lines on the rectangle to help you place and draw the design onto.

Elspeth's tip

Boucherouite rugs are known for their asymmetry and free-form nature, so don't worry if your design is a little wonky or if your diamonds aren't exactly the same size as each other.

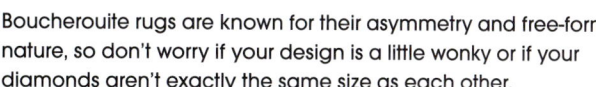

2 Using the template on page 172, draw eight diamonds including the grid pattern in the rectangle. The diamonds should be wider across then they are tall. The easiest way to do this is to pin the template to the underneath of the burlap and draw over the top. The squares on the points of the diamonds which touch the edges of the rug should overlap the edge by half (so you only draw half of that square onto the burlap). Each pair of diamonds should overlap on the central square on the center line (use the dotted lines on the template to help you line up the diamonds). After drawing the eight diamonds, extend the grid lines of each diamond towards the center of the rug, so that the three central diamonds and the two half-diamonds at the top and bottom are also split into squares. Use the color chart (right) as a guide for your design.

Elspeth's tip

To calculate roughly how far your fabric will go, fold the fabric in half four times. This shows the rough area that piece of fabric will cover.

3 Add ¾in (2cm) around the edge of the rectangle, and edge hem all around the rug (see page 16). This will bring the hem to the edge of the drawn design.

4 Using the color guide or your own color scheme, choose and prepare your fabric for the short shaggy technique by first creating long strips, approximately ½in (1cm) in width (see pages 11–12) then cutting these long strips into approximately 4in (10cm) long pieces using a rag rug gauge (see page 12).

5 Identify the rectangles along the four edges of each of the diamonds (purple in my rug) and fill them with short shaggy rag rugging (see page 22). Rag rug through the hem if it is visible to ensure it is fully covered at the end.

6 Leaving the middle three diamonds empty for the time being, fill in the eight outer diamonds in pairs with short shaggy rag rugging. Work one square at a time in rows from the purple inwards, changing color when you have completed four edges of the diamond. Label the squares with numbers or letters to make it easier to see where colors are repeated and remember to blend multiple fabrics together if needed.

7 Once each pair of diamonds is fully rag rugged, fill the edges of the rag rug with cream short shaggy rag rugging as well as the areas in the central diamonds. It doesn't matter what order you do this in, but I like to complete both edges before moving to the center. As it is a large area to cover, remember to blend together various shades of cream fabric before you begin, so you don't run out of one shade part-way through.

8 Fill the remaining empty squares in the central diamonds with short shaggy rag rugging. I prefer to leave these until last, so that I can get an idea of the final finished look before deciding on the final colors.

CHAPTER 2

LOOPY RAG RUGGING

The loopy technique of rag rugging, often called "rug hooking," "hooked rug making," or "hooky," is one of the neater and more precise forms of rag rug making. Although it looks quite impressive, it's still very easy to do with a bit of practice.

Loopy rag rugging is generally considered the best technique to use if you'd like to make something with a clear and detailed design. It can even be used to make pictorial artworks, which is why it's a favorite technique for making wall hangings. Don't believe me? Take a look at the beautiful work of rag ruggers Diane Cox, Sue Dove, and Victoria Goulden.

TOOLS AND MATERIALS

Rug hook/latch hook

The most specialized tool for making loopy rag rugs is a rug (or latch) hook. They can be bought in all different shapes and sizes, but all the projects in the loopy chapter have been made using a 6mm rug hook, which works well with a 10HPI weave hessian.

If you would like to try the loopy technique without investing in a rug hook, a latch hook or spring tool can also be used, but are not quite as easy to work with. Latch hooks have a deep hook to pick up the strips of fabric and a little metal "latch" to secure them in place.

A crochet hook can't be used to loopy rag rug as the groove is too shallow to cradle the strips properly and prevent them from falling off.

Other tools you may need

Fabric/rag rug scissors
Marker pen
Rotary cutter and mat (an alternative to fabric scissors)
Sewing machine/needle and thread
Pins
Tape measure/ruler

Burlap (hessian)

The loopy technique of rag rugging uses the same weave and quality of burlap as the shaggy technique, so see page 9 for more information on this material.

Fabrics

The good news is that you can use most fabrics to loopy rag rug with and, unlike some of the other techniques in this book, you don't need to work with very long strips, as stopping and starting a strip is very easy to do.

As loopy rag rugging requires working the fabric strips up and down through the burlap, it is considerably easier to do with softer, smoother, more pliable fabrics, such as jersey, cotton, fleece or lycra than it is with thick, stiff fabrics, such as canvas, denim, and upholstery fabrics.

Textured and loose weave fabrics, such as lace, woolen knits, and net curtains look lovely when loopy rag rugged, but are harder to work with as the rug hook can get caught in the fabric itself. Thick and stiff fabrics, including garment seams, are more difficult to use, but can be cut narrower to make them easier to pull through the burlap.

Although soft, thin, and smooth fabrics are easiest to work with, it's the variety of different fabric textures that will make your rag rug design look more interesting, so do try to include some slightly harder fabrics with an interesting texture once you get more confident.

As loopy rag rugging is done using longer strips of fabric than the shaggy technique (see pages 18–23), there are fewer cut ends, and therefore fewer issues with fabrics raveling and falling apart when you work with them. If you are unsure how much a fabric will shed and fray, loopy rag a small amount before committing to a lot.

PREPARING YOUR BURLAP AND FABRICS

Before starting any loopy rag rugging, I always hem my burlap (see page 16 for how to do this).

Loopy rag rugging doesn't have as long a pile as shaggy rag rugging, so will not cover and hide edge hemming. To disguise the hem, you can either rag rug through it, which is a little hard to do, but perfectly manageable. Or, alternatively, rag rug up to the hem, then at the end of the project, turn the hem under and stitch it to the underside of the rug.

To loopy rag rug, you need to create long strips of fabric to weave up and down through the burlap. The precise length of the strips doesn't matter as it's very easy to start a new strip without complicated joining, but the longer the strip is, the more of a rhythm you can get into. You can cut the strips using either fabric scissors or a rotary cutter and mat, or tear them (see pages 11–12).

The width that you cut these strips for rag rugging is dictated by the weight of the fabric you are working with.

I cut my strips slightly narrower for the loopy technique of rag rugging (as opposed to the shaggy technique) to make the fabric strips easier to manipulate through the burlap. However, if your loops are slipping out then cut your fabric strips wider or rag rug your loops closer together to tighten the burlap better.

Strip widths for different fabric weights

Light weight fabrics, e.g. viscose, chiffon, voile	1¼in (3cm)
Medium weight fabrics, e.g. cotton, jersey, silk	⅝in (1.5cm)
Heavy weight fabrics, e.g. denim, blanket offcuts	½ in (1cm)

How much fabric will I need?

To make a 40 x 24in (100 x 60cm) loopy rug requires approximately 10 t-shirts. If you fold a piece of fabric in half three times, that will give you the rough area this piece of fabric will cover when it is cut up and loopy rag rugged.

To use a frame or not to use a frame?

First, I'd just like to say that you don't need a frame to successfully rag rug and make beautiful pieces. Personally, I prefer the ease and portability of working with the burlap loose on my lap, for both the loopy and shaggy techniques. However, if you'd like to try a frame, first experiment with a small piece of rag rugging and an embroidery hoop. This pulls the burlap taut enough to see how a frame would work and is a cheap way to try it out. Bear in mind that a full-size rug frame takes up quite a lot of room at home.

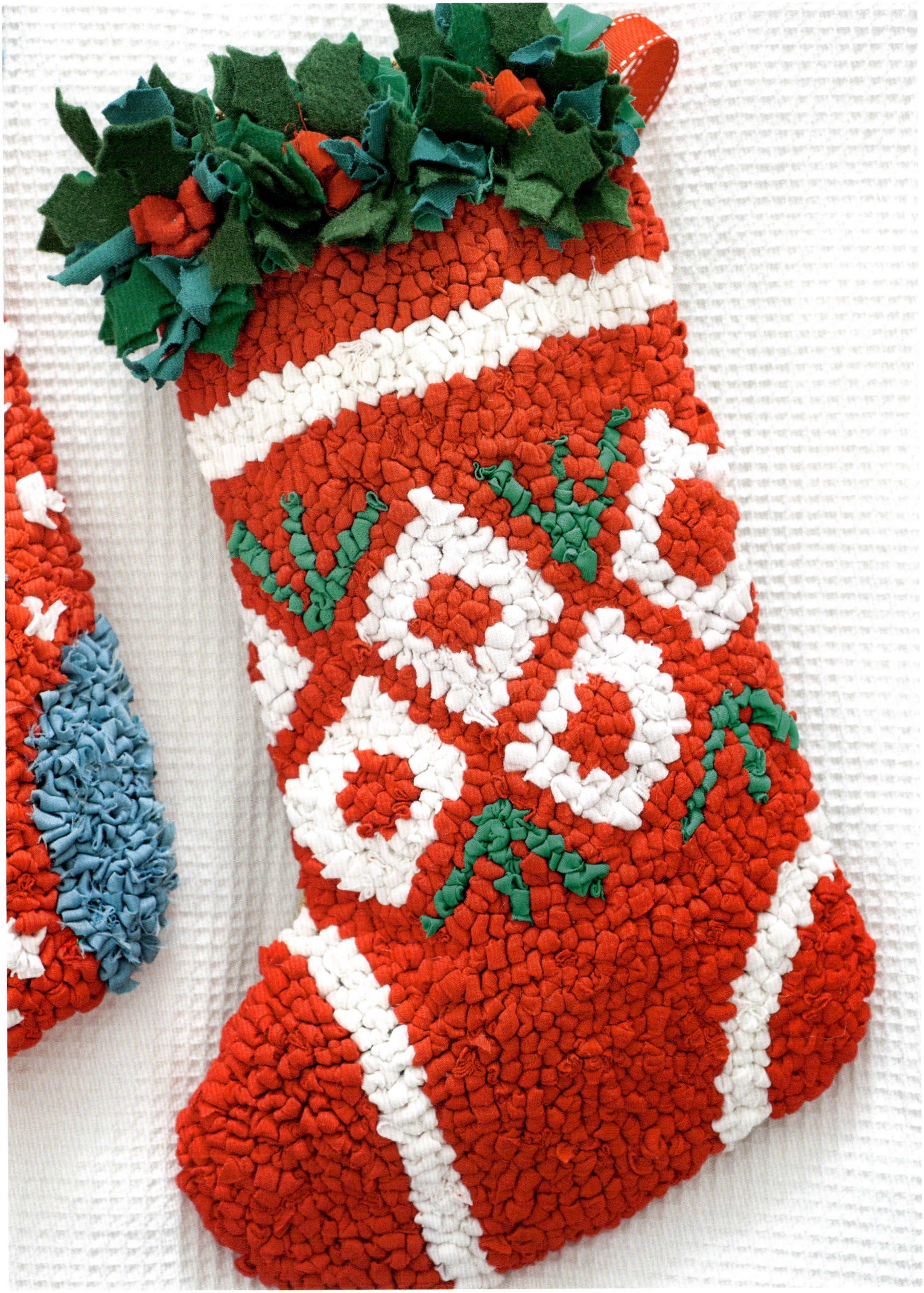

TECHNIQUES

The loopy technique has a beautiful, uniform appearance. Here's how you achieve it.

1 Cut your material into long strips, using any of the techniques on pages 11–12. Remember to adjust the width of the strips to compensate for their thickness (see page 38). The longer the strips, the better.

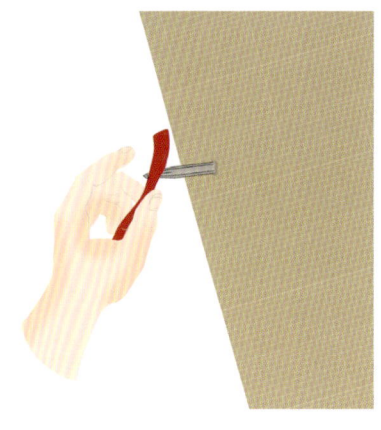

2 Hold the long strip of fabric under the burlap, and using either a rag rug hook or a latch hook, insert the hook into a hole from front to back and grasp near the top of the fabric strip with the hook.

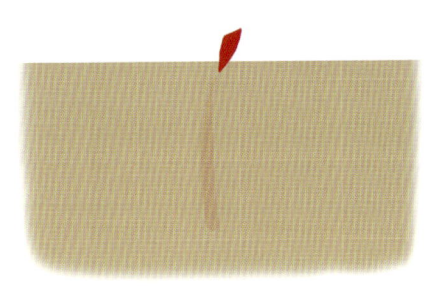

3 Pull the hook to bring the end of the strip to the top of the burlap. Adjust the height of the strip to how high you'd like your loops to be. A good height to practice at is approximately ½in (1cm).

Elspeth's tip
As a beginner, you may want to leave the first cut end of the strip slightly longer to prevent accidentally pulling it through to the underside when you are practicing. You can trim it at the end.

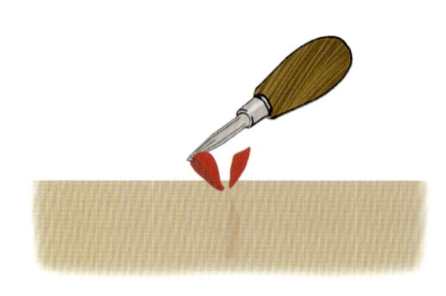

4 Miss out two strands in the direction you want to rag rug, insert the hook from front to back and hook the fabric strip to pull a loop up through the burlap. Try to make the loop the same height as the single end.

5 Repeat step 4 until you reach the end of the strip or until you would like to change color.

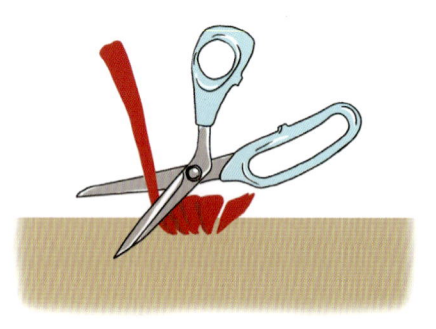

6 To secure, pull the loose end of the strip to the top of the burlap and cut it to the same height as all your loops. Trim the first end of the strip as well if needed. Ideally, start your new strip in the same hole as you ended in to double up single ends into the same hole. This makes them more secure.

Elspeth's tip
Do not leave ends of strips on the underside of the burlap, as these can easily work the whole row loose over time.

40 LOOPY RAG RUGGING

Loopy design tip

Loopy rag rugging works particularly well when you take a paint-by-numbers approach. You draw out a design and take it one block at a time. If one of these blocks requires more than one color then think carefully about the direction in which you loopy rag rug it, as it will become part of the design. For a large background of sea, for example, you may want to loopy rag rug in wave shapes with different blues, rather than straight lines.

COMMON MISTAKES

The back of my loopy rag rugging is lumpy

This happens when you grab too high up the strip, leaving a large loop of fabric on the back of the burlap. Try to grip the strip closer to where it comes out of the burlap and make sure any bagginess is pulled through to the front, not left on the back.

When I pull my loop up, it pulls my previous loop shorter

This happens when you pull the loop away from the previous loop. Try to pull the loop either towards the previous loop or straight up.

Burlap is showing between my loops

This means you need to adjust your spacing and miss out fewer strands between each loop and the next or between rows, or both. This sometimes happens when people try to make their loops too short as a beginner. It is the consistency of the height of the loops which will make the end project look neat, not the height that they're at.

My burlap is caving in and buckling

If your burlap is dipping in the area that you're working in, then you are rag rugging too close together or your fabric strips have been cut too wide. Either adjust your spacing to miss out more strands between one loop and the next or cut your fabric strips narrower.

Burlap is showing between my loops

My burlap is caving in and buckling

TECHNIQUES 41

Tranquil Triangles Rug

I designed this simple, geometric rug after I'd just finished a particularly colorful creation. I was looking to create a restful rug with a simple and neutral color scheme that would fit in almost any home. This rug is particularly cozy, as it's made from old blankets, but you could use any recycled fabrics as long as you have enough of them. Old duvet covers are a great source of large amounts of material, for example.

You will need

Burlap/hessian: 55 x 55in (140 x 140cm)

Tape measure

Marker pen

Fabric/rag rug scissors

Sewing machine/needle and thread

Ruler

Fabrics: I used approximately 1¼ x 7⅜yd (1 x 6.7m) of both the blue (B) and cream (C) fabric for this project, but it does vary based on the thickness of the fabric and how close you rag rug

Rug hook

Pins (optional)

1 Use a tape measure and marker pen to draw a 52¾ x 52¾in (134 x 134cm) square onto the burlap. Try to keep as in line with the weave of the hessian as possible (see page 15). Edge hem all around the rug (see page 16). This will reduce the size of the rug to 51 x 51in (130 x 130cm).

2 Mark out each edge of the rug to break it into six sections (see the black dots on the diagram, right—mine were spaced 8½in/21.7cm apart). Draw lines to join up the dots on two opposite sides of the rug (the pink lines on the diagram). Then draw lines to join the black dots together to form triangles, following the blue lines on the diagram. Label the triangles with Bs or Cs using the photograph opposite as a guide, to make it easier to remember which triangles should be what color.

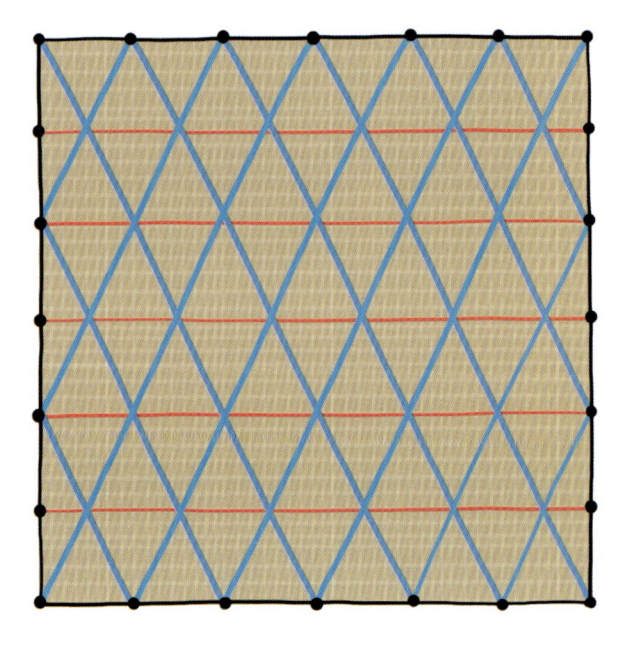

42 LOOPY RAG RUGGING

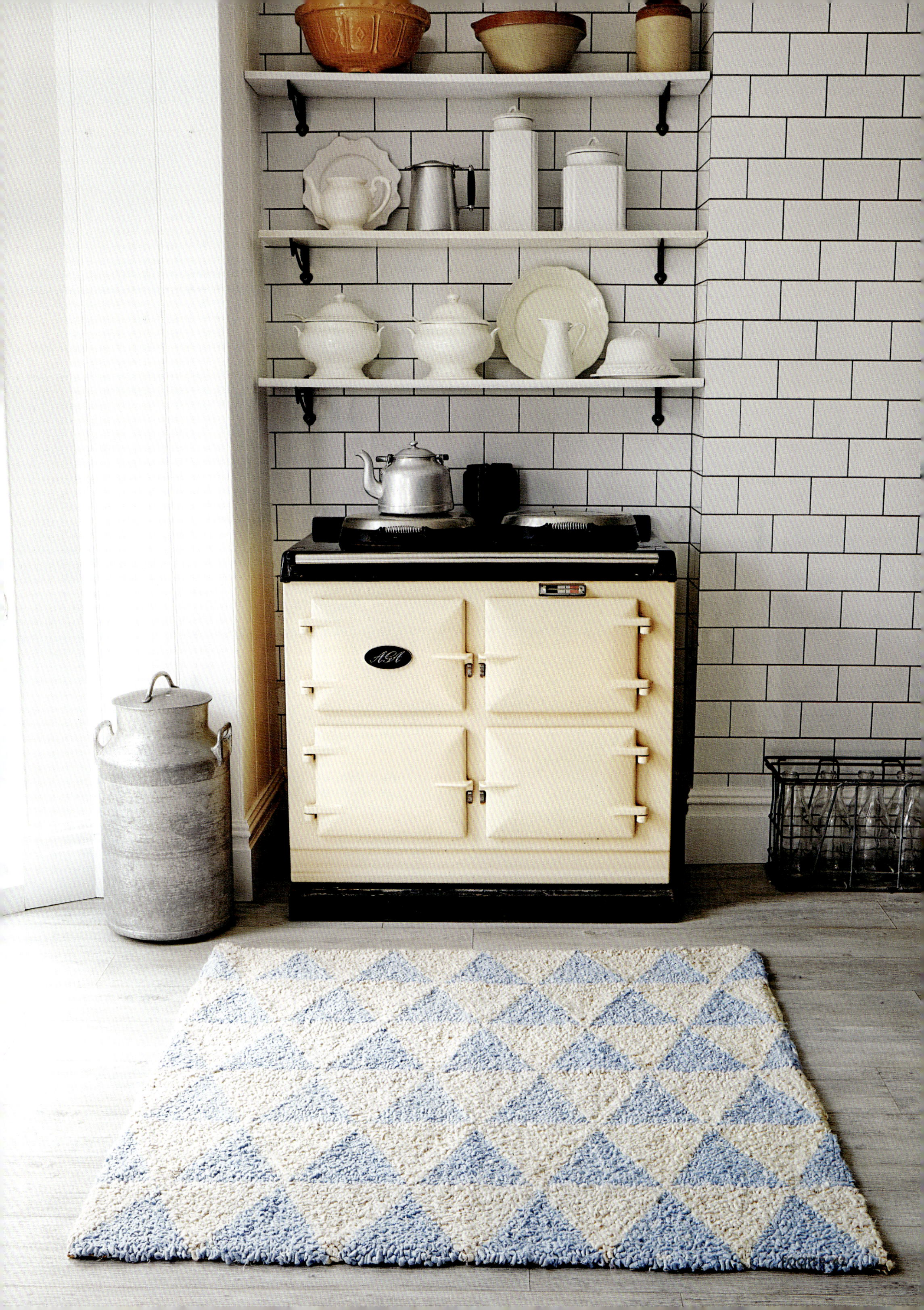

Elspeth's tip

As this design uses only two colors, there is a risk of running out of fabric part-way through. Either blend together similar shades from the beginning of the project and make it part of the design, or ensure you have plenty of your chosen fabrics (or a source to find more of each) before you start.

3 Prepare your cream fabrics for loopy rag rugging by cutting them into long strips (see pages 11–12), approximately ⅝in (1.5cm) in width. Adjust the width you cut your strips to the thickness of the fabric (see page 38).

4 Starting in one corner of the rug, loopy rag rug (see page 40) one cream triangle (marked with C) at a time, working from the outside of the triangle inwards. Complete one row of cream triangles before moving on to the next. Your loops should be approximately ⅝in (1.5cm) in height to make a thick, cozy rug. Rag rug through the hemming to ensure that none of the burlap is visible.

5 Once the cream triangles are complete, prepare your blue fabric and completely fill the remaining triangles (marked B) with blue loopy rag rugging. If you think that you are going to run out of a fabric, fill random triangles across the rug to distribute the color evenly or outline all the triangles in one fabric before moving onto a similar shade for the next row. This is called "working in the round" and makes changes in color part of the design.

Elspeth's tip

You can write the numbers and letters on to the hessian to make things easier as any markings will be covered by the rag rugging eventually.

Large rugs become heavier and more unwieldy to work with as you progress. Some rag ruggers roll up and clip the bulk of the rug together to concentrate the weight in one area.

"You Are My Sunshine" Rug

I made this colorful rug in the middle of winter here in the UK, when I needed a little bit of sunshine in my life. Yellow is such a cheerful and invigorating color that it just brings a smile to my face. Freehand sketching is what makes this rug characterful, so don't be afraid to embrace wonky lines and asymmetry.

You will need

Marker pen

String

Burlap/hessian (minimum 55 x 55in/140 x 140cm)

Rug hook/latch hook

Fabrics: yellows in shades of sunshine and golden honey, white patterned fabric with flecks of yellow, and mixed blues and turquoises. I used approximately 51 x 51in (130 x 130cm) of the white patterned fabric. You'll need approximately 2 or 3 times this amount for the scraps of yellow and blue fabric

Needle and thread

1 Tie a marker pen to a piece of string. Measure 23½in (60cm) from the tied pen and cut the string to length. Firmly hold the end of the string without the pen in the centre of the burlap and, holding the marker pen as vertically as possible, sketch a circle on to the burlap. You may need to do this in smaller arcs, rather than one continuous line.

2 Use a placeholder hemming stitch (page 17) to stitch 2½in (6cm) outside of the drawn circle to create a rudimentary hem. This stops your burlap from falling apart.

Elspeth's tip

Mix small amounts of patterned fabrics into large blocks of solid color to make them look more interesting. Use patterned fabric that features some of the color you're looking to blend into.

3 Sketch your design within the drawn circle, starting with four circles drawn from the center of the rug. The first circle should be drawn 5in (13cm) from the center point of the rug (10in/26cm in diameter), the next should be 1¼in (3cm) outside the first circle (it will be 12½in/32cm in diameter), the third circle approximately 2¾in (7cm) from the second circle (approximately 18in/46cm in diameter) and the fourth circle should be drawn 1½in/4cm from the third circle (approximately 21in/54cm in diameter).

4 Next, sketch the wonky sunbeams coming out from the fourth circle, reaching to the very edge of the outer sketched circle. I drew eleven. Draw eleven small arches between the second and third inner drawn circles. These arches start and end roughly in the middle of each sunbeam. Draw five small arches inside the smallest circle in the center of the rug.

5 Sketch a circle approximately 1½in (4cm) in from the outer sketched circle of the rug. This will be how far your sunbeams will protrude out from the edge of the rug.

6 Cut long strips of fabric that are approximately ⅝in (1.5cm) in width using any of the methods on page 11. Adjust the width you cut your strips to the thickness of the fabric (see page 38).

7 Loopy rag rug (see page 40) the rug using the color chart (see right). Your loops should be approximately ½in (1cm) in height. For this project, it is generally easiest to work from the center outwards. Leave the outer ring of the burlap empty, so that your sunbeams will poke out beyond the edge of the rug once you have finished hemming.

8 Once the design is complete, fold the excess burlap to the underside. Fold the stitched edge under twice to "edge hem" the burlap (see page 16) and pin it in place. Around the pointed ends of the sunbeams, you will need to overlap the hems before pinning. Once the edge is fully pinned, make sure that the hessian is still lying flat on the floor. If any areas are coming up from the floor, adjust the pinning on the back. Hand stitch the hem in position using a hemming or overcast stitch.

Elspeth's tip

When you rag rug the sunbeams, I like to work on all the sunbeams at once, working from the outside of each shape inward. This means if you run out of a certain color, the rug doesn't look unbalanced.

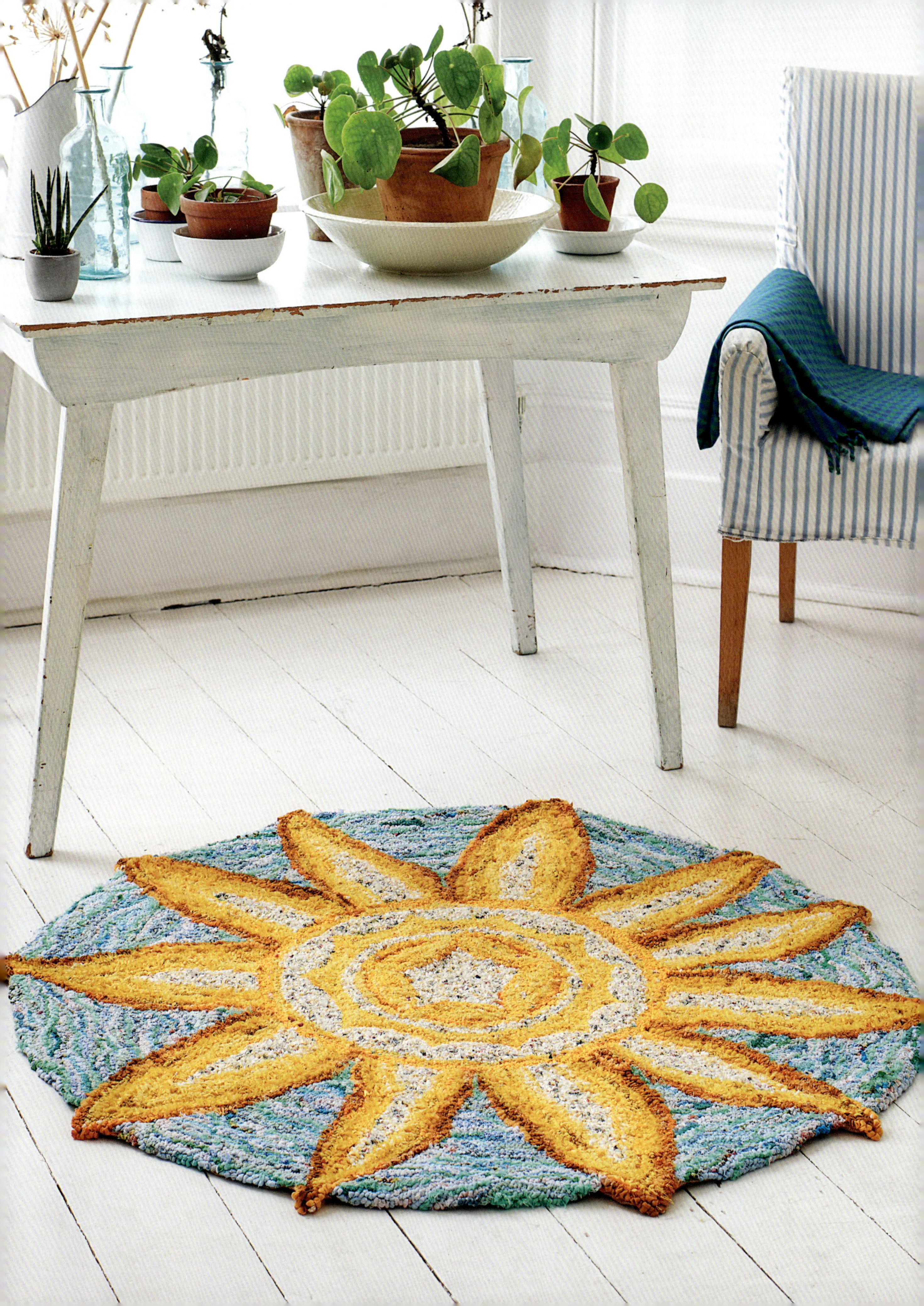

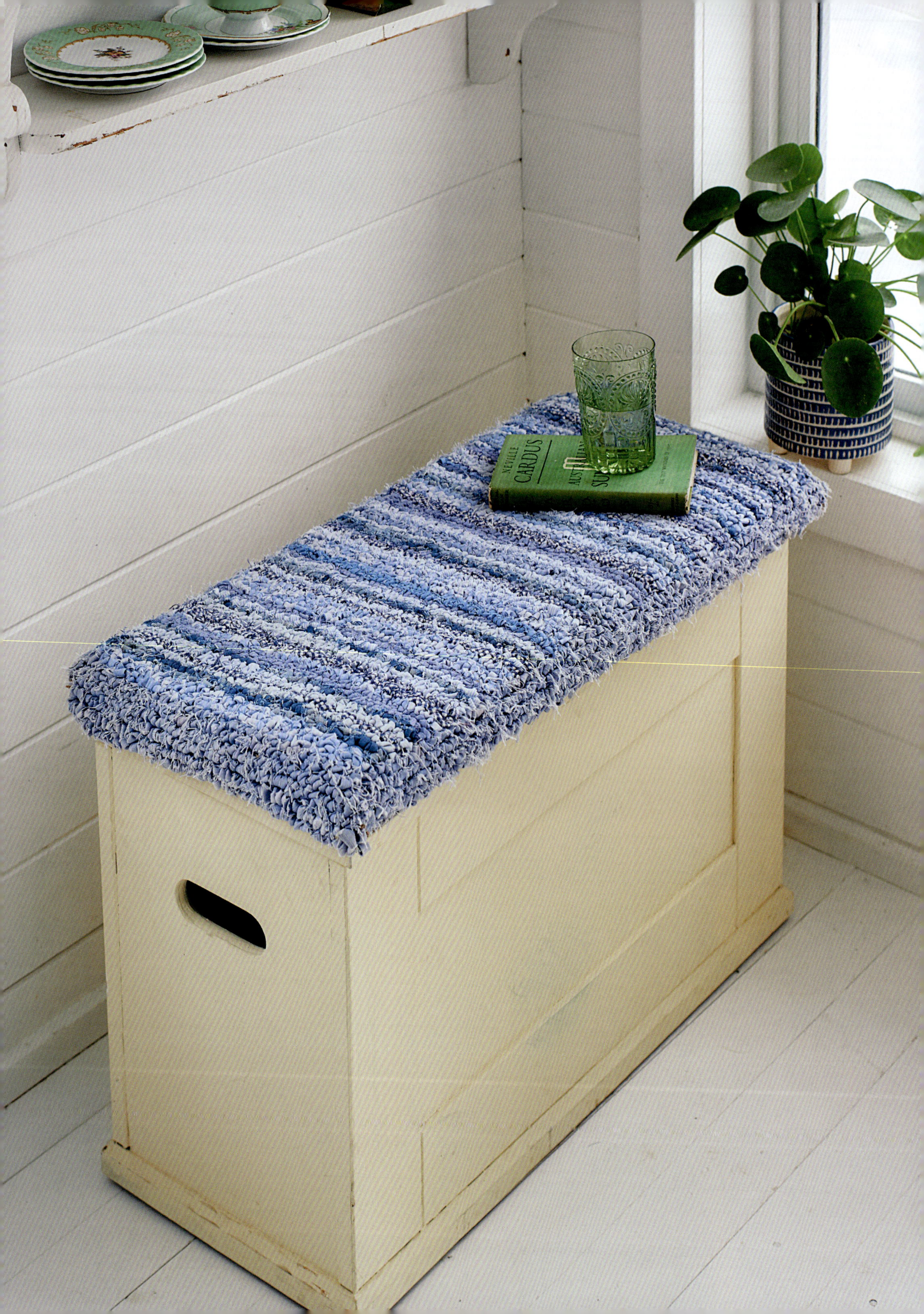
NEVILLE
CARDUS

All the Blues Blanket Box

I found a tired, old pine blanket box in my local bric-a-brac market and decided to give it a makeover. The loopy rag-rugged pillow pad I created for the top made the blanket box dual-purpose—now, I can store mess and clutter in it, and use it as versatile seating as well. It would be perfect in a narrow hallway.

You will need

Wooden blanket box

1in (2.5cm) thick high density upholstery foam

Bread knife (optional)

Burlap (hessian): 10HPI weave

Marker pen

Tape measure or ruler

Sewing machine and thread

Fabrics: I used seven shirts to make my 27½ x 12in (70 x 30cm) seat pad

Fabric or rag rug scissors

Rug hook

Spray adhesive

Backing fabric: this won't be visible, but tidies the project up

Needle and thread

2 x 4in (10cm) long pieces of velcro tape

1 Measure the length and width of the top of your blanket box. Subtract 2in (5cm) from both measurements and cut a piece of high-density upholstery foam to size. This is best done carefully with a bread knife. The top of my blanket box measured 27½ x 12in (70 x 30cm), so I cut my foam 25½ x 10in (65 x 25cm). Round off the corners of the foam rectangle slightly, so they aren't quite so sharp.

2 Place the foam on the burlap and draw around it with a marker pen. Leave at least 12in (30cm) between the foam and edge of the burlap. The rectangle you have drawn will be the top of your blanket box seat pad.

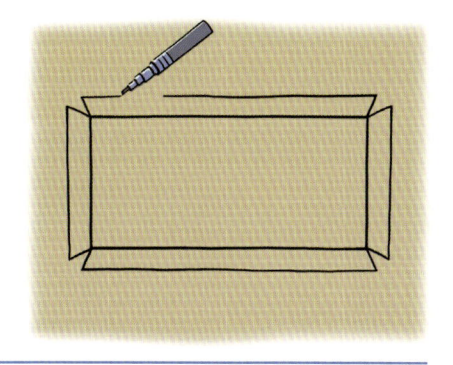

3 Draw 1½in (3.5cm) deep tabs on each side of rectangle. Creating these tabs will ensure that the sides of the upholstery foam are fully rag rugged.

Elspeth's tip

Include at least two patterned shirts in your design to make it look more eye-catching. I included a blue gingham and a light blue striped shirt for interest.

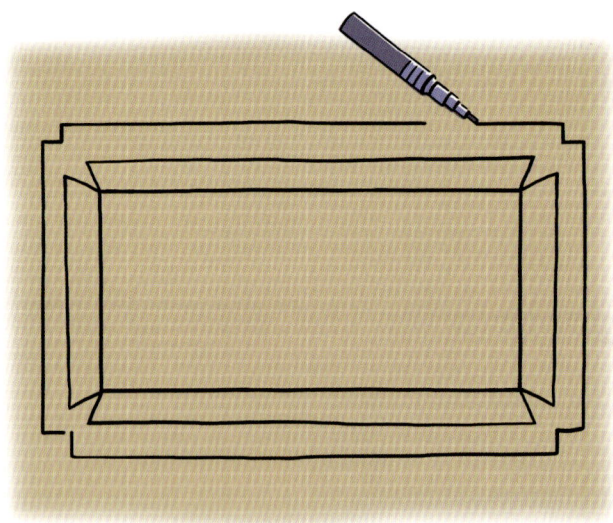

4 Draw a hem around the edge of the seat pad and tabs, approximately 2in (5cm) from the edge of the tabs.

5 Sew along all the drawn lines using placeholder hemming stitch (page 17). This will hold the shape of your pillow pad and stop the burlap from falling apart later in the project.

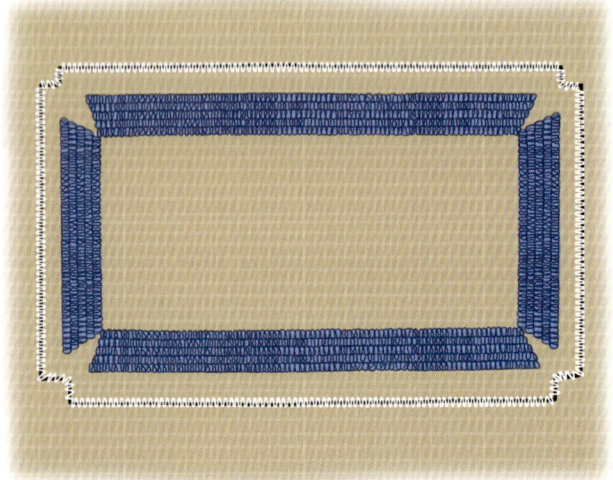

6 Rag rug the side tabs and the first row around the top of the seat pad in the same fabric using the loopy technique (page 40) to frame the design. I used a particularly large shirt to do this, but if your seat pad is larger than mine, you may need more fabric.

Elspeth's tip

To see roughly what area your fabric will cover in the loopy technique, fold the fabric in half three times.

50 LOOPY RAG RUGGING

7 Fill in the rest of the pillow pad one row at a time from one short end to the other. I changed fabric every 1–3 rows for my striped design.

8 Cut away the excess burlap from around the outer hemming, outside of the white zig zag stitching. Lay the burlap with the rag rugging face down and place the foam on top, aligning all four edges with the loopy rag rugged rectangle. Fold the outer burlap border onto the back of the foam and use spray adhesive to keep it in place tight around the foam.

9 Cut a piece of backing fabric 1½in (4cm) longer and wider than the base of the seat pad. Fold each edge of the backing fabric under ¾in (2cm) (press if needed) to disguise the raw edge of the fabric. Pin the backing fabric onto the base of the seat pad (the hem should be hidden underneath) and hand stitch in place to cover your burlap and work.

10 If you would like, hand sew two 4in (10cm) pieces of Velcro to the back of the seat pad and glue the corresponding pieces of Velcro to the top of the wooden blanket box so that they align. This will prevent the seat pad from falling off.

Classic Christmas Stockings

This jolly, festive project is actually a mash-up between the loopy and shaggy techniques of rag rugging. However, if you don't own a rag rug spring tool for the shaggy technique (see page 21), you can loopy rag rug the shaggy trim with long loops, which you can cut at the end or leave as they are. This contrast in textures is what makes these stockings look so appealing.

You will need

Burlap/hessian: approximately 19¾ x 15¾in (50 x 40cm)

Marker pen

Template on page 173

Tape measure/ruler

Sewing machine (ideally with zipper foot) and thread

Needle and thread

Pins

Fabrics: I used one red t-shirt and one white shirt to make one stocking

Rug hook

Rag rug spring tool (optional)

Rag rug scissors or fabric scissors

Medium weight backing fabric e.g. cotton: approximately 19¾ x 15¾in (50 x 40cm)

4oz-batting (wadding): approximately 19¾ x 15¾in (50 x 40cm)

Medium weight lining fabric e.g. cotton: approximately 31½ x 19¾in (80 x 50cm)

Wide ribbon or fabric for a hanging loop

1 Copy the Christmas stocking template on page 173, enlarging it to the correct size. Cut the template out and draw around it onto the burlap with the design face-up. Leave at least 2in (5cm) between the stocking and the edge of the burlap. Then draw the heel, toe, cuff, and snowflake onto the stocking. You can do this by placing the template under the burlap and tracing through.

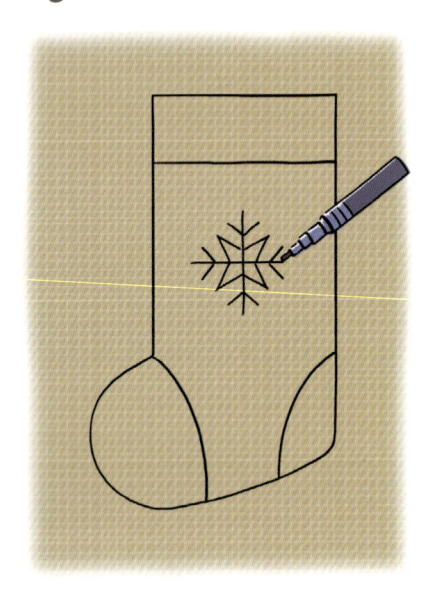

2 Sew a placeholder hemming stitch (see page 17) on both the drawn stocking outline and 1¼in (3cm) outside the stocking shape.

3 Removing all the seams and hems from your shirt first, cut half your white shirt into approximately 2 x ¾in (5 x 2cm) pieces (see pages 11–12). Use these pieces of fabric to shaggy rag rug (see page 21) the cuff of the stocking. I did this in rows, missing out two strands between each piece of fabric and three strands between each row.

> **Elspeth's tip**
>
> The steps for this project are for my classic red and white snowflake festive stocking, but you can experiment and play around with the design. You could customize your stocking with a loved one's initial, for example, or choose colors to match your Christmas décor.

52 LOOPY RAG RUGGING

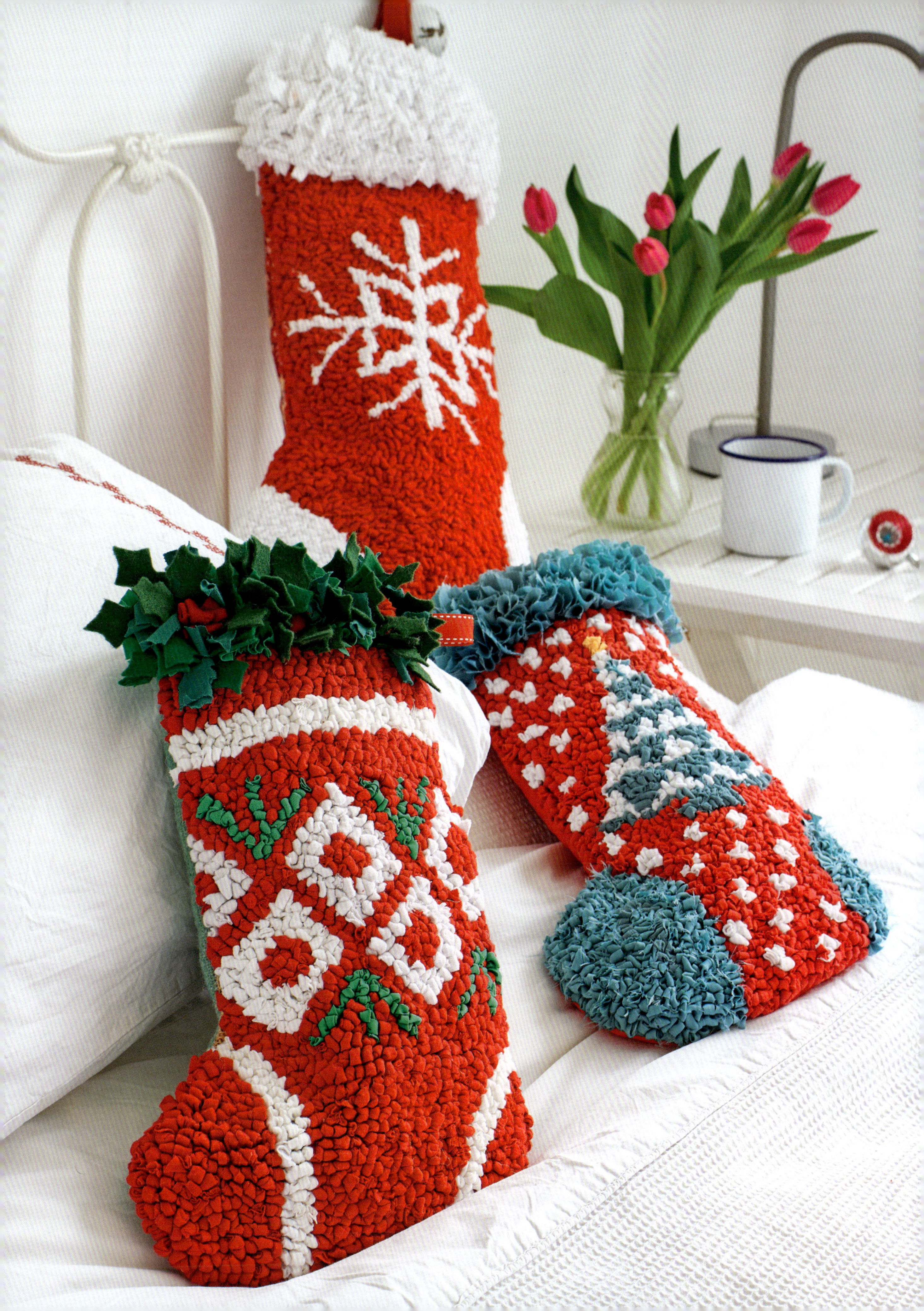

4 Prep the second half of the shirt into long strips that are approximately ⅝in (1.5cm) wide (see page 11). Loopy rag rug (see page 40) the heel, toe, and snowflake. Your loops should be approximately ½in (1cm) in height. I prefer to work my way from the outside of the heel and toe inwards.

5 Prep your red fabric into long, ⅝in (1.5cm) wide strips. Fill the rest of your stocking in red loopy rag rugging. I filled the stocking from the outside edge inwards, but you can fill the body of the stocking in any direction.

6 Place the Classic Christmas Stocking template with the design face-up onto the wrong side of the backing fabric, pin in place if necessary and draw around the template. Draw a second line approximately 1in (2.5cm) away from the edge of first line. Repeat this process on the batting and cut both pieces out.

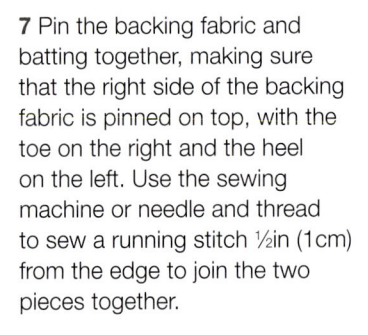

7 Pin the backing fabric and batting together, making sure that the right side of the backing fabric is pinned on top, with the toe on the right and the heel on the left. Use the sewing machine or needle and thread to sew a running stitch ½in (1cm) from the edge to join the two pieces together.

8 Cut away the excess burlap from around the stocking up to the placeholder hemming stitch.

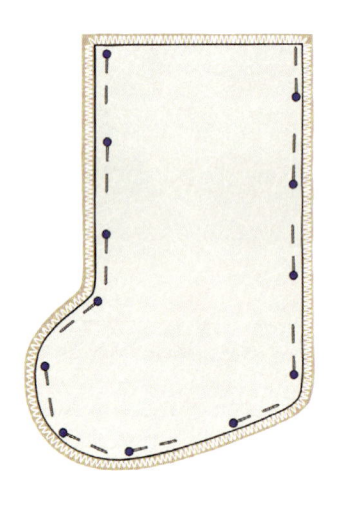

9 Pin the rag rugged stocking and backing piece right sides together, leaving the top edge of the stocking unpinned. Make sure to pin as close to the rag rugging as possible so no burlap will be visible around the edge.

10 Sew the two pieces together, leaving the top edge open. You can do this either by hand or machine (using a zipper foot). Trim any excess batting from around the stocking to remove unnecessary bulk. Turn the stocking right way out.

11 Draw two stockings onto the lining fabric using the template, adding 1¼in (3cm) to the top edge of the stocking. If your fabric has a right side and a wrong side, draw around the template once with the template face-up and once with the template face-down.

54 LOOPY RAG RUGGING

12 Pin the two pieces of lining fabric right sides together and sew a running stitch ½in (1cm) in from the edge around the stocking, except for the top edge.

13 Fold the burlap and excess backing fabric in the top right corner of the stocking in on themselves and hand sew a sturdy hanging loop in place. Wide ribbon or plaited fabric works nicely here. The sewing doesn't have to be perfect, as it won't be on show.

14 Push the lining fabric inner down into the rag rugged stocking. Fold the rest of the burlap and backing fabric down into the stocking and pin it to the lining, while turning under a small allowance of the lining to make sure that the raw edge of the fabric isn't exposed. Hand sew all around the opening of the stocking to complete your project. I used ladder stitch to hide the stitching better.

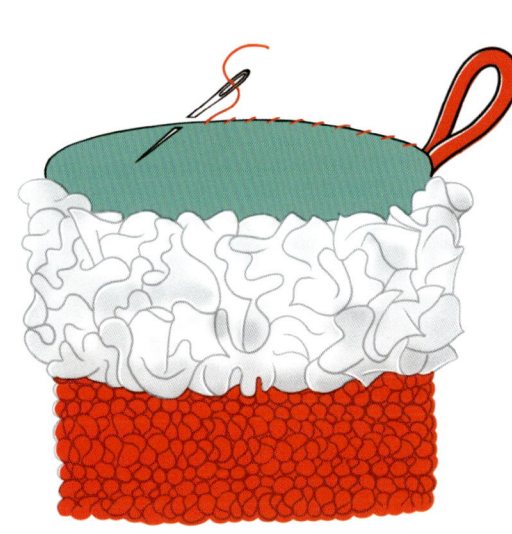

CLASSIC CHRISTMAS STOCKINGS 55

Ocean Waves Pillow

We all go through phases of loving certain colors and at the moment I'm head over heels for blues and pinks. To me, those colors evoke coral reefs and sparkling oceans, which immediately transports me to warmer climates. This particular pillow has a lot of texture as I used a mixture of chenille, which frays a fair bit, woolen offcuts, and the odd bit of denim. The loopy technique works well for fabrics that fray, as there are fewer cut edges to shed.

You will need

Burlap/hessian: approximately 19¾ x 19¾in (50 x 50cm)

Tape measure/ruler

Marker pen

Fabric/rag rug scissors

Sewing machine

Fabrics: I used chenille, woolen offcuts, and scraps of denim, all in shades of blues, pinks, and off-whites

Rug hook

Backing fabric (I recommend thick cotton): approximately 20 x 15in (51 x 38cm)

Pins

Iron

Zipper foot (optional)

16 x 16in (40 x 40cm) pillow pad

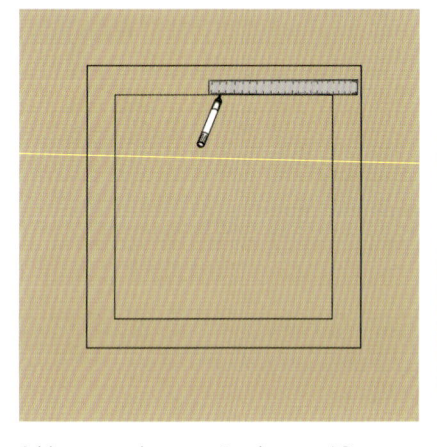

1 Use a marker pen to draw a 16 x 16in (40 x 40cm) square on the burlap, making sure to leave at least 3¼in (8cm) between each side of the square and the edge of the burlap. Draw a second square 1½in (4cm) outside the first square. Stitch along the four sides of the outer drawn square using placeholder hemming stitch (see page 17).

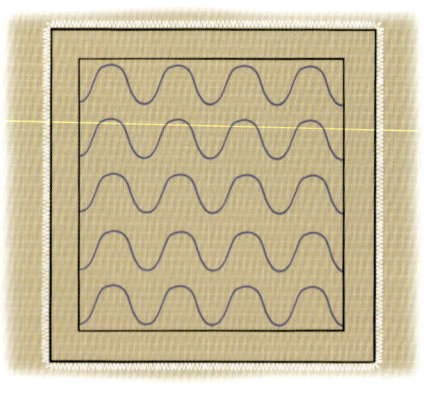

2 Sketch five wave patterns across the 16 x 16in (40 x 40cm) sketched square with each wave peaking four times. They do not have to be perfect.

3 Prepare your navy and light blue fabrics for loopy rag rugging by cutting them into long strips (see pages 11–12) approximately ½in (1cm) in width. Adjust the width you cut your strips according to the thickness of the fabric (see page 38).

> **Elspeth's tip**
> Fill in odd gaps with "rogue" scraps you have lying around. I had a small amount of orange, burgundy, and pink fabric that I used to plug any gaps.

56 LOOPY RAG RUGGING

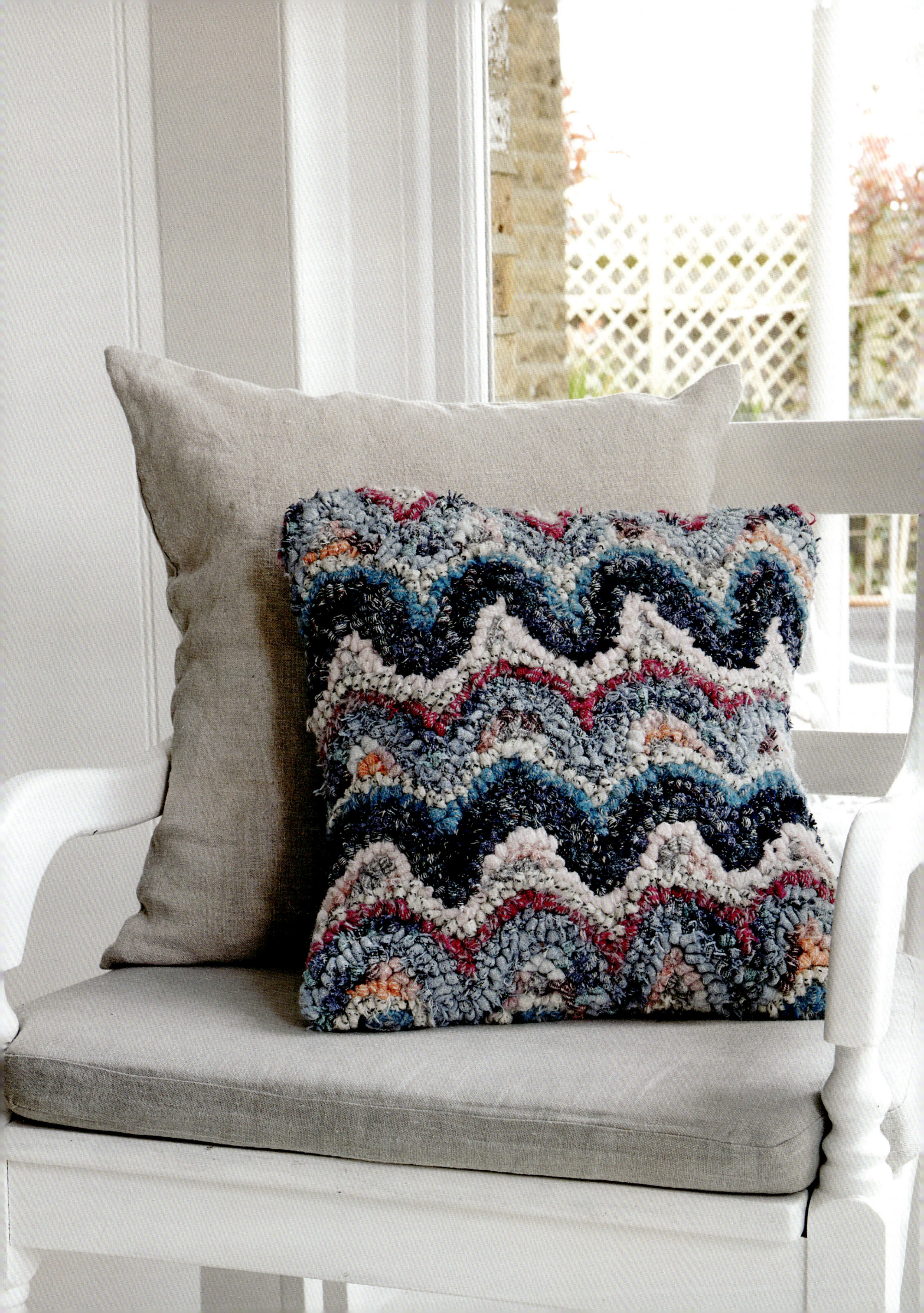

4 Starting with your light blue fabric, do three rows of loopy rag rugging (see page 40) starting on the first drawn wave at the top of the pillow. Your loops should be approximately ½in (1cm) in height. Repeat this for each drawn wave, alternating light blue and dark blue for each wave.

5 Loopy rag rug one row of fuchsia pink above each of the light blue waves, turquoise above each of the navy waves, and light pink below each of the navy waves.

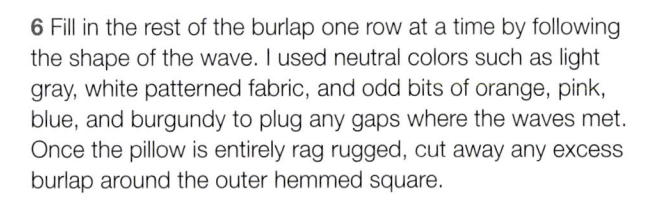

6 Fill in the rest of the burlap one row at a time by following the shape of the wave. I used neutral colors such as light gray, white patterned fabric, and odd bits of orange, pink, blue, and burgundy to plug any gaps where the waves met. Once the pillow is entirely rag rugged, cut away any excess burlap around the outer hemmed square.

7 Cut out two rectangles of fabric each measuring 19 x 14in (48 x 36cm) for the back of the pillow. I used a blanket which had tassels, and kept the tassels on one of the short edges of my backing pieces to add to the design, but you can use any material—a thick cotton would work well.

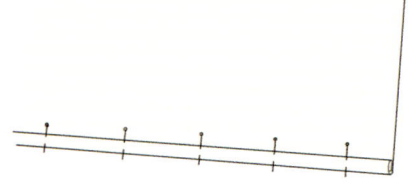

8 Hem along one of the longer edges of each backing piece. Do this by folding the raw edge over twice by about ½in (1cm), then press with an iron. Pin if needed, then machine stitch in place using straight stitch. Cut off any loose threads and press both pieces of fabric.

Elspeth's tip
You can always pull out any rag rugging from the back of the burlap, so don't hesitate to experiment.

9 Place your rag rugged square face up on a table. Lay one of the backing pieces on top of the square. The hemmed edge should be nearest the center of the pillow and the rough side of the hemming should be facing up.

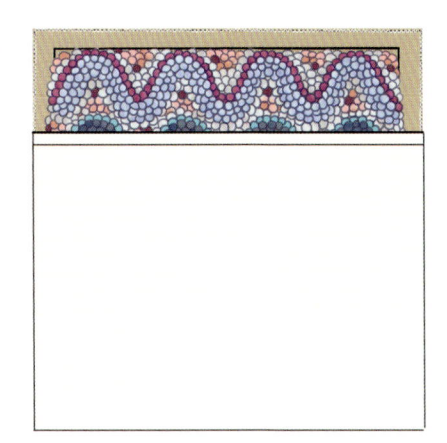

10 Place your second backing piece on the pillow. As before, the hemmed edge should be nearest the center of the pillow and the rough side of the hemming should be facing up. The backing pieces will overlap.

11 Pin the layers in place. Pin as close to the rag rugging as possible, but try not to trap any of the rag rug loops or you will end up sewing over them.

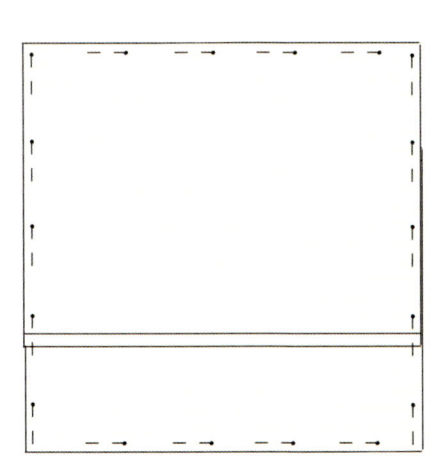

12 If you have a zipper foot for the sewing machine, now is the time to use it as it helps you to stitch a little closer to the rag rugging, giving a neater finish. Machine stitch all around the pillow using straight stitch. Stay as close to the rag rugging as possible.

13 You now have a fully sewn-up pillow cover, but before you turn it right side out, diagonally cut off all the corners (being careful not to cut any stitches) and trim away some of the excess burlap and backing fabric from around the edge of the cover. This will remove some of the bulk from inside the pillow.

14 Turn the pillow cover right side out and insert the pillow pad through the overlap opening in the back.

OCEAN WAVES PILLOW 59

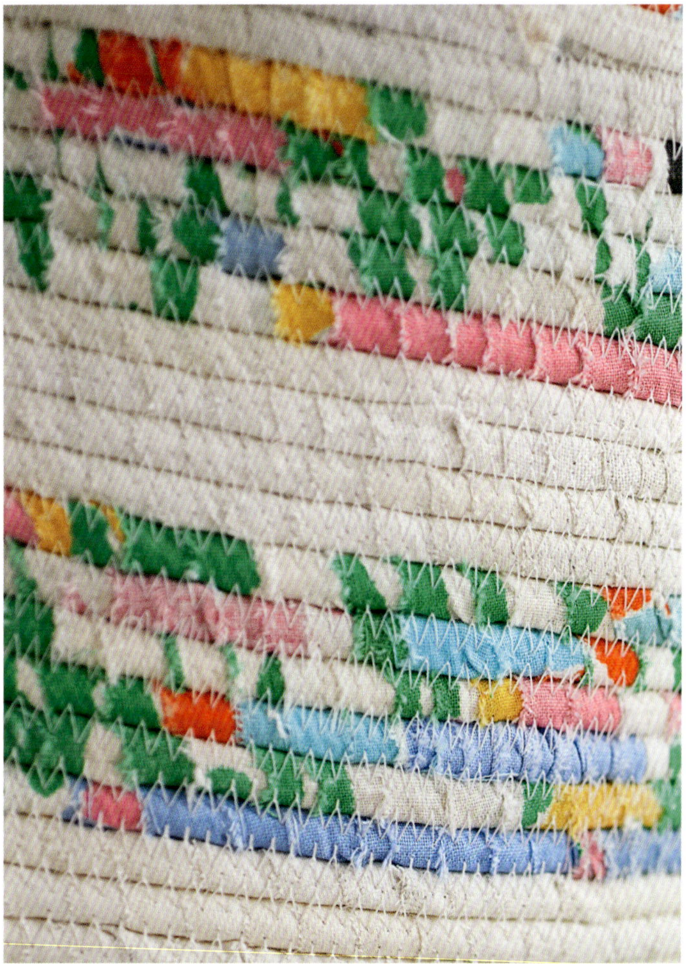
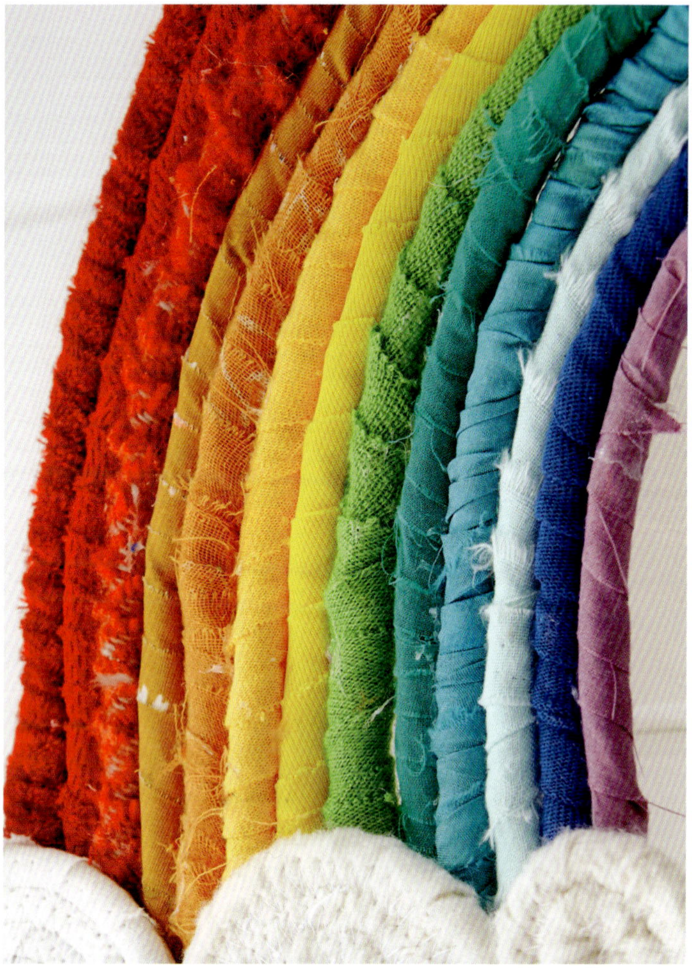
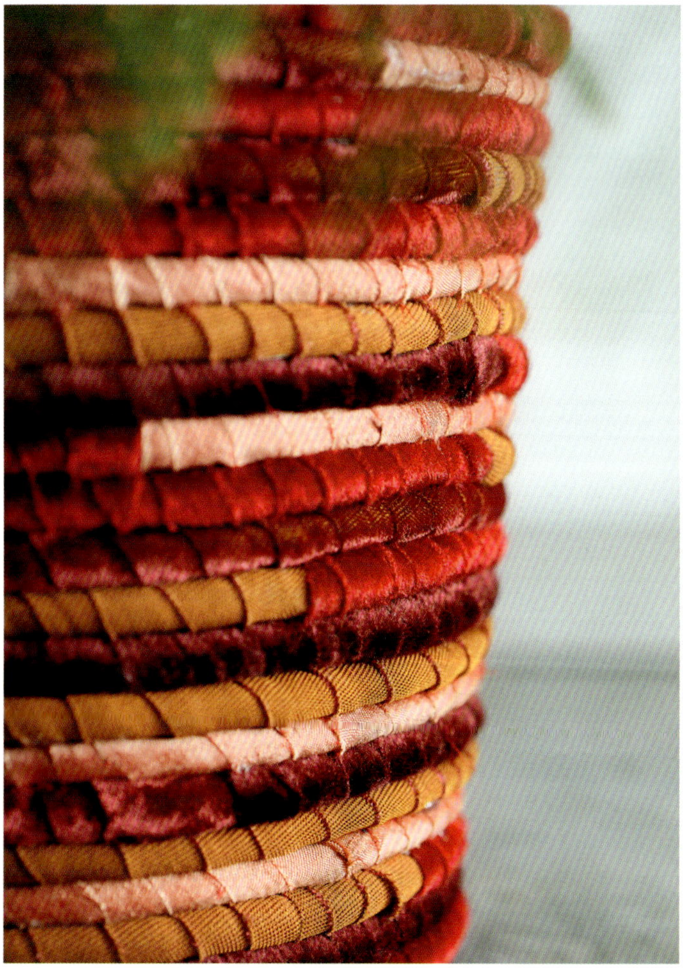
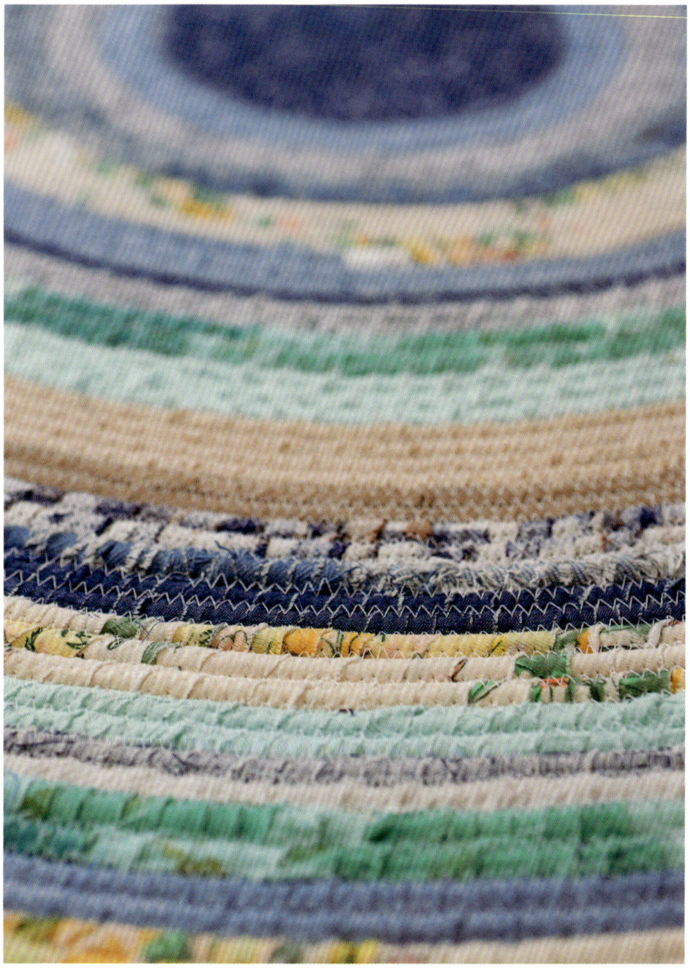

CHAPTER 3

COILED ROPE

Before writing this book, I'd come across coiled rope bowls and storage caddies, but had never considered scaling the technique up to a larger project like a rug. Well, shame on me as this wonderful technique is now one of my favorite ways to make a rag rug! Coiled rope rag rugs are not only beautiful, but are also very practical. They are flat, compact, and surprisingly hard-wearing, they look fabulous under a dining room table, and they work beautifully on hard wood floors, as they don't move around much.

TOOLS AND MATERIALS

Sewing machine and thread
The coiled rope projects on pages 66–79 were constructed using a sewing machine. For this, you need a sewing machine capable of doing a zig zag stitch. You can hand stitch your coiled rope projects together, but this is much more time-consuming and requires a good deal of patience. For a no-sew version of this technique, take a look at our No-Sew Plant Pot Cover on page 74.

It's worth noting that in coiled rope projects, the zig zag stitching becomes part of the design, so make sure to use thread that complements or contrasts with your fabrics. If in doubt, use white thread, as this goes with most designs. Coiled rope projects take a lot of thread, so you will need multiple spools of your chosen color(s). Choose good quality thread to make sure your stitching is as strong as possible. A denim needle is good to work with if you have one.

Glue gun or fabric glue
You can make coiled rope projects without glue, but it does help to secure joins and make adding fabric pieces that little bit easier.

Other tools you may need
Fabric scissors/rotary cutter and mat
Pins/plastic sandwich clip
Masking tape (for joining cord together)

Cord or rope
Cord or rope forms the base or "core" for this style of coiled rag rug. Choose cord or rope that is even in thickness (the thicker the cord, the chunkier your rug will be) and soft so that you can stitch into it easily. Do not use anything too plasticky as this can damage your sewing machine. I use ¼in (5.5mm) diameter cotton washing line, but you can experiment with other cores, such as t-shirt yarn, rope, and macramé cord. Cotton washing line generally comes in 65ft (20m) lengths, but you can join pieces of cord together to make it as long as you need. If you are unsure how much cord you will need for a project, ensure you can get hold of more of the same cord before starting. If your cord comes in a hank, it helps to re-wind it into a ball before you start working to prevent it getting twisted and tangled, particularly when working on larger projects.

Fabrics
Coiled rope rag rugs are made using strips of fabric. You can prepare strips using any of the methods on pages 11–12. Cut strips as long as possible, but don't worry too much about their exact length as you can join pieces together easily (see page 64) and cut strips to length based on the design as you go.

You can use any fabric, however lightweight materials are easier to work with. Fabrics that ravel and fray will look more distressed, so avoid these types of fabric (loose weave cotton, linen, rayon etc.) if you prefer a cleaner look. Frayed fabrics become less wild once they are zig zag stitched into position. For best results, concentrate on the colors in your design as opposed to the textures.

For coiled rope projects, the width of the fabric strips is very important. Cut them too thin and the fabric won't cover the cord very well, cut them too thick and the fabric will not lie flat against the cord and will bunch up. Cut medium and light weight fabrics such as jersey, cotton, and chiffon approximately ⅝–¾in (1.5–2cm) wide and cut heavy fabrics such as denim, fleece, and woolen fabrics approximately ½in (1cm) wide. If in doubt, test a small amount of fabric by wrapping it around the cord and see how it lies, before committing to cutting up a whole garment.

TECHNIQUES

Coiled rope projects are made by wrapping fabric strips around cord, coiling the cord into a shape of your choosing, and stitching it into position. In this way you can create striking rugs, homewares, and more.

WRAPPING THE CORD IN FABRIC

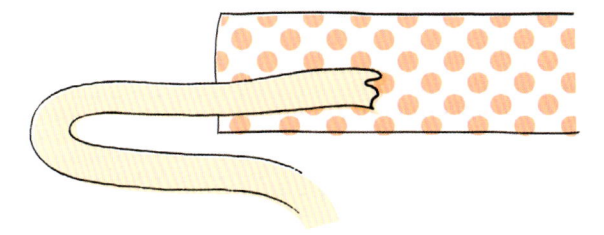

1 With the wrong side of the fabric face-up, place the end of your cord on to your fabric strip as illustrated. The ends should overlap by at least 1¼in (3cm).

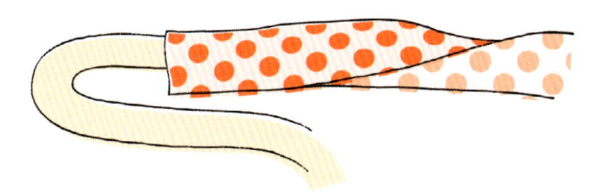

2 Apply a small line of glue around the sides and end of the cord then press the fabric edges together around the cord.

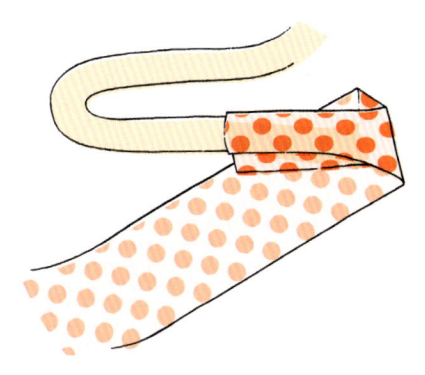

3 Fold the fabric strip back on itself to cover the end of the cord as illustrated.

Elspeth's tip

Struggling to wrap the cord? Weigh down the end of the cord with something heavy or use the sewing machine foot and needle to keep the cord taut while wrapping it with fabric. Secure the wrapped cord with a pin or plastic sandwich clip to prevent it coming unraveled when you are not working on it.

4 Carefully wrap the fabric strip diagonally around the cord, completely covering the cord as you go, using pins if necessary. Tuck in the fabric corners at the end of the cord as neatly as possible. Slightly overlap the edges of the fabric strips as you wrap.

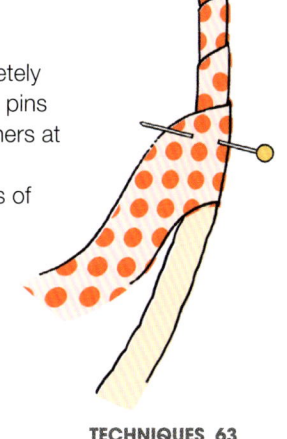

JOINING STRIPS

When you reach the end of a fabric strip, dab a little glue at the end, place a new strip wrong side up on top, overlapping approximately 1¼in (3cm), and continue wrapping the old and new strips together around the cord. If the join looks a little clunky, taper the end of the new strip to disguise the join better. Any imperfections will be smoothed out during the stitching.

For coiled rope projects, you can either wrap all your cord in fabric first before stitching it together, or wrap and stitch as you go along. For larger projects, I prefer to create the fabric cord beforehand, so that it doesn't occupy the sewing machine for days on end. However, for 3D projects, such as the Let's Go to the Beach Basket on page 70, I prefer to wrap the cord and stitch it together as I go, so I can see how the design is developing. This allows you to change colors exactly where you want to. For flat projects like rugs, you can lay the fabric-covered cord out roughly as you go to see how big it is getting and understand how much more cord you will need to cover in fabric.

STITCHING THE CORD TOGETHER

Coiled rope projects can be stitched or glued together into various shapes—circles, ovals, rectangles, squares, and 3D objects. Although you can hand stitch the cord, it is far easier to use a sewing machine. To use a sewing machine, adjust your stitch width one or two points wider than default. It should be wide enough to capture the outer edges of neighboring cords as you stitch. Bear in mind that the wider you set the zig zag stitch, the more of the stitched thread will show in your final design. Use the first few rows of stitching in any project to find the right balance of stitch width and length.

Stitching a circular coiled rope project

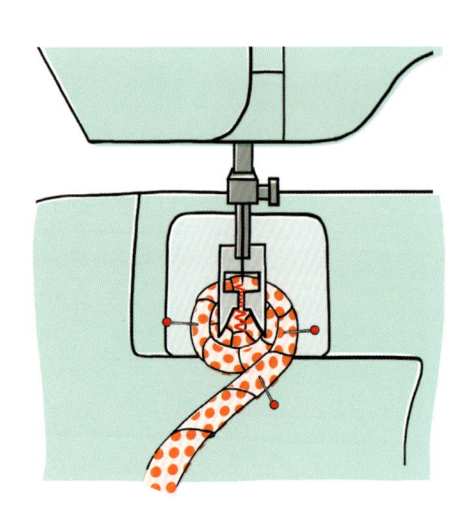

1 Coil the end of the fabric-covered cord into a spiral. Pin in position if needed. Place the spiral under the sewing machine foot, so that the cord spirals clockwise and the loose tail comes round to the front. This ensures that the stitched coil will build to the left of the sewing machine, rather than underneath it.

2 Starting in the center of your coil, make a few securing stitches. Keep the center of your foot in line with the line where two edges of cord meet, and stitch around using a zig zag stitch that catches the fabric-covered cord to either side. Continue spiralling and zig zag stitching around each "round." It can help to use the blunt end of a pencil to press the coil tightly together under the sewing machine foot when you first start stitching. The first stitches are the hardest, so take it slowly to begin with.

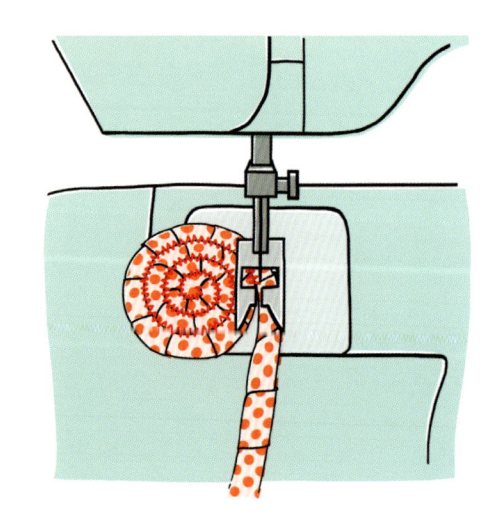

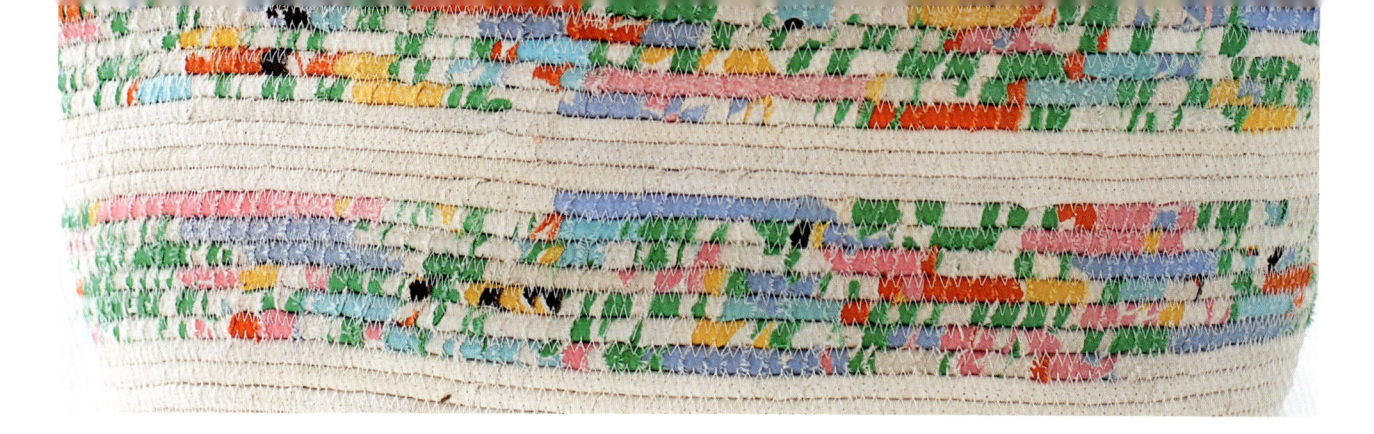

Joining new cord

Continue zig zag stitching the spiral together. When you run out of cord, use masking tape to attach the new cord to the old cord. Continue wrapping your fabric strip around the joined ends and zig zag stitch as normal. The join may be slightly chunkier than elsewhere, but will be pretty well disguised.

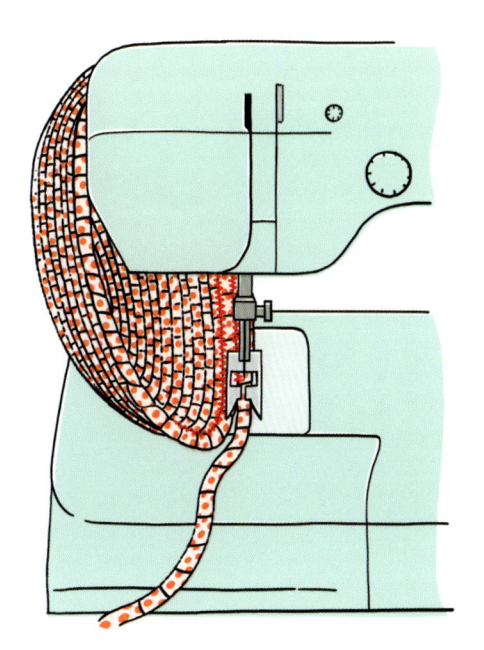

Creating 3D objects

To create bowls and bags, like the Let's Go to the Beach Basket on page 70, you will need to angle the coiled spiral as you zig zag stitch it together. Lift the left side of the spiral up and support it angled toward the head of the machine. The more sharply you angle the stitched coil towards the head of the sewing machine, the steeper the walls of your bowl or bag will be.

Neatly finishing the coil

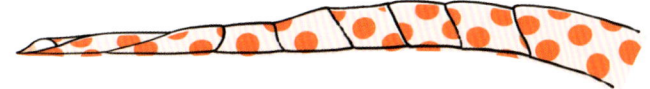

1 When you are reaching the end of your project, you will need to secure the end of the cord in position neatly. Leave approximately 4¾in (12cm) of fabric strip past the end of the cord (trim to length if necessary). Dab a little glue around the end and sides of the cord, as well as inside the fabric strip. Wrap the fabric strip around the end of the cord then twist the remaining fabric strip to a taper. Pin if necessary.

2 Zig zag stitch the tapered cord in position, creating a gentle join. Press the tapered fabric to the neighboring coil tightly using the blunt end of a pencil to hold it in position as you stitch. End your cord in as unobtrusive a place as possible, e.g. on the side, as opposed to on the front.

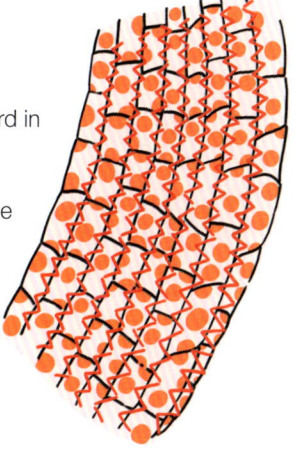

TECHNIQUES 65

Gold Coast Rug

The colors in this coiled rag rug were inspired by a holiday my friend and I took on the Gold Coast in Australia a few years ago. The combination of subtle blues and sandy neutrals is immensely calming and brings back fond memories of sun, sand, and salty waves. I may have got a bit sunburnt that holiday, but for me this rug has nothing but good vibes.

You will need

Fabrics: I used blues, blue gray, turquoise, duck egg blue, patterned cream, and camel

120¼yd (110m) of ¼in (5.5mm) cotton washing/pulley line or cord

Fabric or PVA glue/glue gun

Clothes pins

Sewing machine and matching thread (I used white thread for the body of the rug and blue thread for the small outer circles)

Flattened cardboard boxes/foamboard and a stack of books (optional)

Masking tape to join cord (if needed)

1 Cut or tear your fabric into approximately ⅝in (1.5cm) width strips that are as long as possible using any of the methods described on pages 11–12. If you tear the fabric then remove any loose strands from the selvage edges as you go.

2 Glue and secure the first fabric strip to the end of the cord as described on page 63. Wrap your first fabric strip diagonally around the cord (I used blue), making sure to overlap so that none of the cord is visible. When you reach the end of a fabric strip, glue the next strip in place and continue wrapping and joining (see page 64).

Elspeth's tip

You can adjust this design to whatever size rug works for you by using more or less cord. Use whatever fabrics you like for this project, but thinner fabrics tend to be easier to work with. I combined cotton, ribbed jersey, denim, polyester lining fabric, and linen. I recommend a relatively plain fabric for the smaller circles around the outside of the rug, as this will help to frame the rug better.

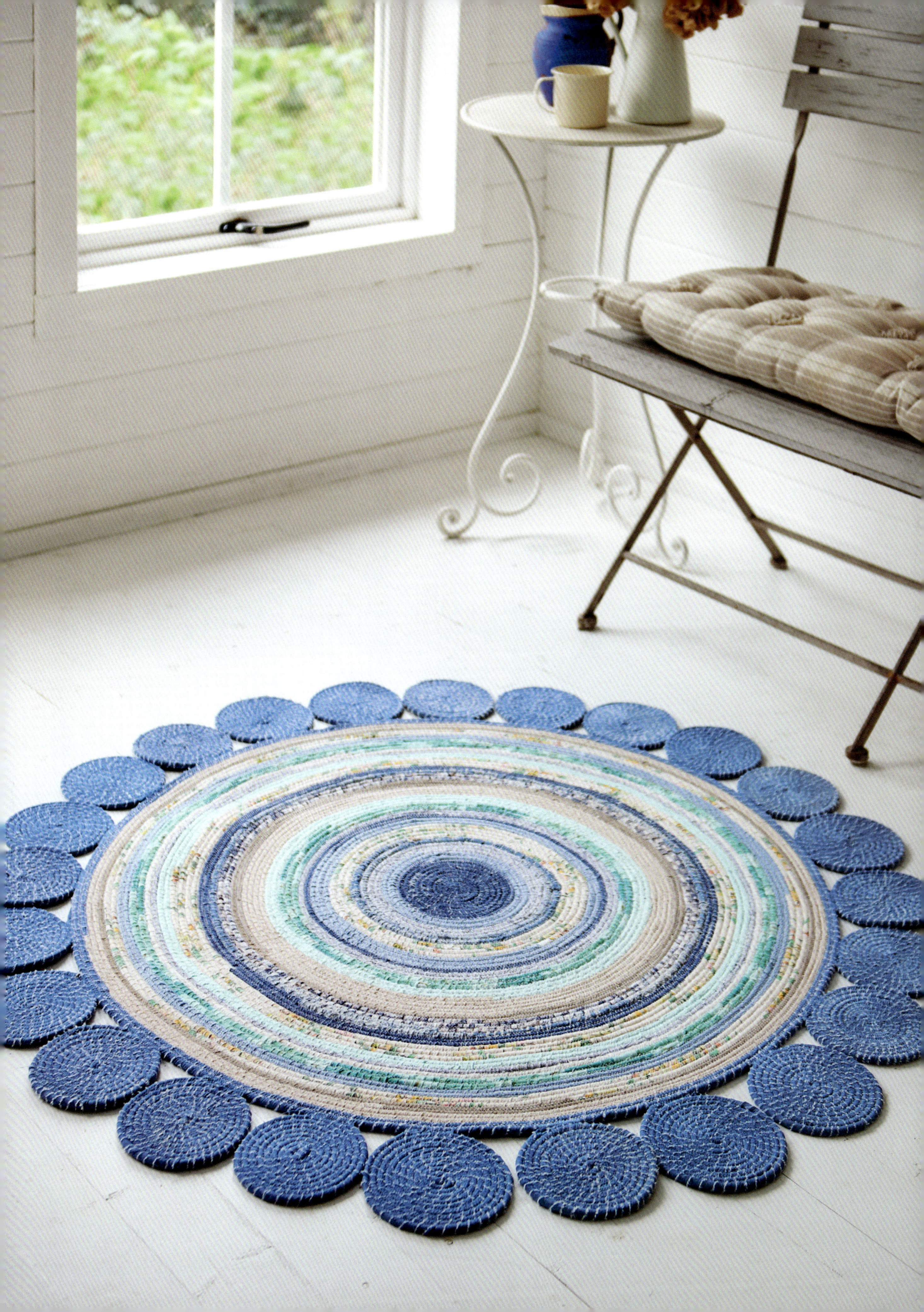

Order of fabrics from center out

9 rounds dark blue

2 rounds medium blue

2 rows gray blue

2 rows denim (right side and wrong side combined)

3 rows patterned cream

2 rounds medium blue

1 round dark blue

1 round gray blue

3 rounds patterned turquoise

2 rounds duck egg blue

4 rounds camel

2 rows tan

2 rows patterned blue/brown

1 row denim

2 rounds dark blue

3 rounds patterned cream

2 rows duck egg blue

1 round gray blue

1 round cream

2 rounds turquoise

2 rounds medium blue

2 rounds patterned cream

1 round tan

2 rounds camel

2 rounds outside blue (I used the same color for the last two rows of the rug as I did for the small circles around the outside to give it a smarter finish).

3 Once you've covered at least 39in (1m) of cord in fabric, roughly coil the cord in a circle to get an idea of how much you've done and to see how it is looking. Pin in place if preferred. Ideally the color changes should not all align in one area of the rug. Continue wrapping and gluing fabric along the cord, building up the design however you please. Alternatively, use the color chart (see right) to match our Gold Coast color palette.

4 Once you have laid out the coiled cord and are happy with the approximate size of the rug (mine was 35½in/90cm diameter), zig zag stitch the coil together in a circle (see pages 64–65). It is important that you keep the circle as flat as possible to avoid the rug's edges curling up. When it becomes large and unwieldy, support its weight next to the sewing machine using a raised surface, to give you more surface area on the table or desk where you are sewing. I used a sheet of foamboard and stacks of books, but you could also use flattened down cardboard boxes.

5 Once you have finished stitching the coil of the rug together, cut the cord, twist and taper the fabric end and stitch it to the outside of the rug as described on page 65.

6 Wrap, coil, and zig zag stitch together twenty-four 5⅛in (13cm) diameter circles to attach to the outside of the main rug. Each small circle took approximately 78¾in (200cm) of coil to create and the twenty four circles took 59 x 39½in (150 x 100cm) of fabric, so be careful not to run out. Do not stitch the ends of the small circles in place until you have laid them out around the large circular rug to check the sizing and to ensure that there will be no gaps between them. You may need to create more or fewer circles depending on the diameter of your central rug. Leaving the ends loose allows you to adjust accordingly.

7 One by one, stitch the edges of the small circles to the edge of the large circular rug using two rows of zig zag stitching.

Let's Go to the Beach Basket

I made this colorful coiled beach basket from my friend Claire's childhood bedroom curtains. Her parents were doing a proper clear-out, so I swooped in to rescue what I could fabric-wise. The cream part of the basket is made using the thick lining of the curtains, while the colorful fabric is an animal scene, made up of lions, elephants, giraffes, monkeys, and more... although you wouldn't know it. It just goes to show that in rag rugging, the colors are far more important than the pattern, so get creative!

You will need

Fabrics: One plain and one patterned, each a minimum of approximately 56 x 48in (142 x 122cm) in size

Fabric or PVA glue/glue gun

43¾ yards (40m) of ¼in (5.5mm) cotton washing/pulley line or cord

Clothes pins

Sandwich bag clip (optional)

Sewing machine and matching thread (see design tip below)

Stack of books (optional)

Pencil

Masking tape to join cord (if needed)

1 Cut or tear your fabric into approximately ½in (1.5cm) width strips that are as long as possible using any of the methods described on pages 11–12. If you tear the fabric then remove any loose strands from the selvage edges as you go.

2 Starting with the plain fabric, glue the first fabric strip to the end of the cord as described on page 63 and begin wrapping the fabric strip diagonally around the cord, making sure to overlap so that none of the cord is visible. After wrapping at least 12in (30cm) of cord or more in fabric, pin or sandwich clip the fabric in place so that it does not come unraveled.

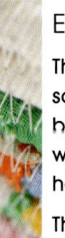

Elspeth's tip

The thread you use for sewing will be an intrinsic part of the design, so choose a shade that works with the colors in your fabrics. It could be a complementary or contrasting color. If in doubt, white works with most fabrics. This project uses a lot of thread, so be sure to have a few spools of your chosen color.

Thin fabrics work best for this project.

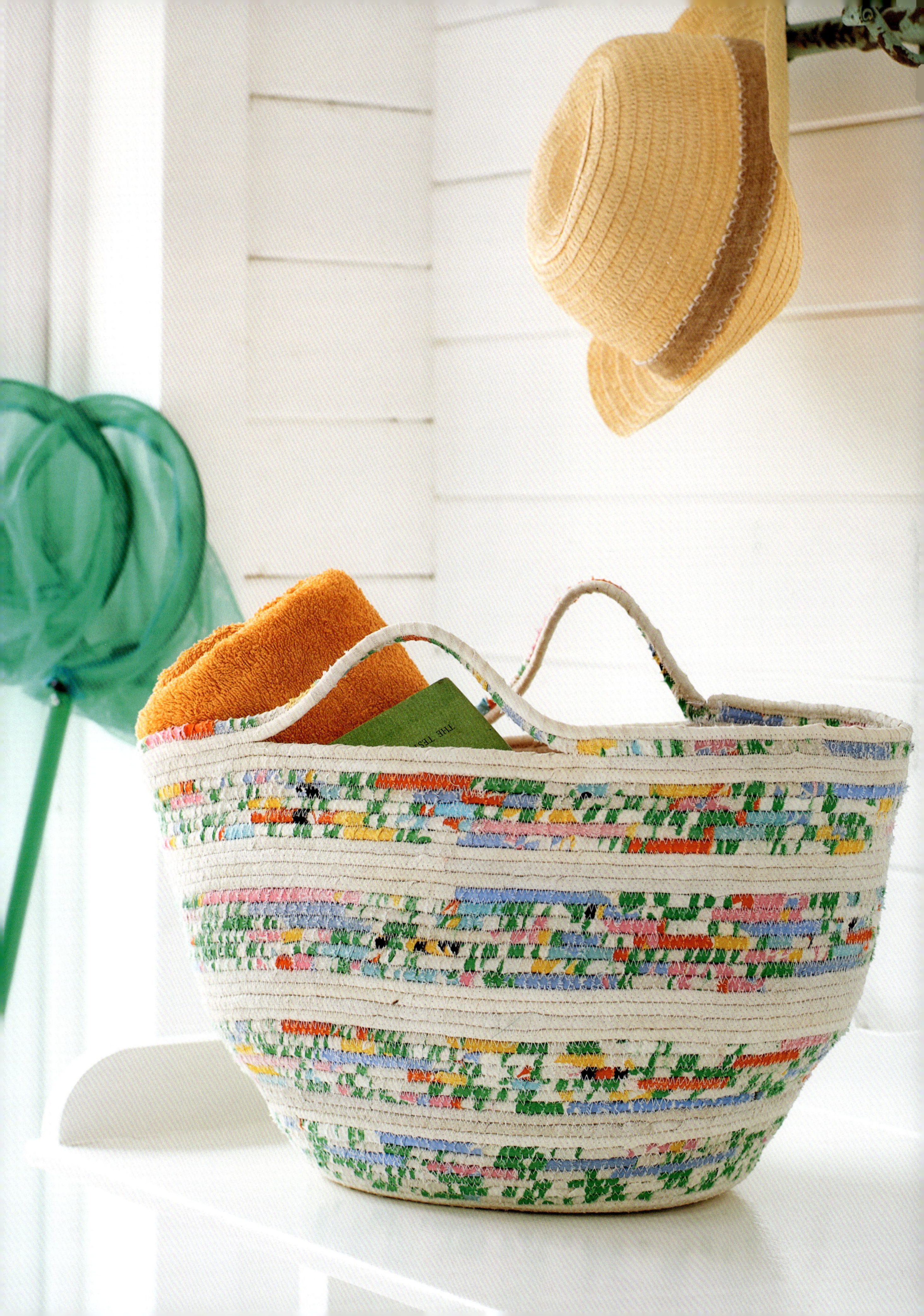

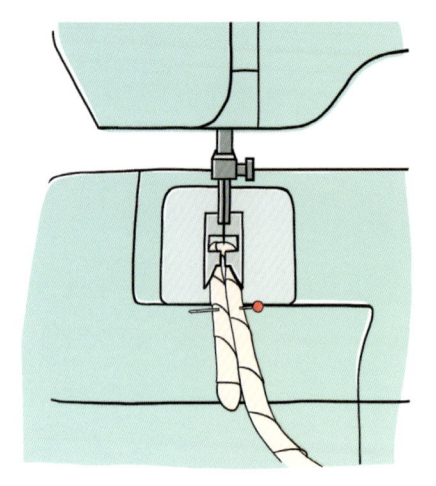

3 Fold the fabric-covered cord back on itself to create a "U," that measures approximately 3¼in (8cm) in length, pin in place to keep the edges together and place the bend of the "U" under the sewing machine foot. It is important that the continuous tail is to the right and coming towards you, as this will ensure that your coiled basket will build to the left of the sewing machine.

4 With your stitch width slightly wider than normal (I used 6.5) and your stitch length at default (2), zig zag stitch the two edges together. As it is less visible than other parts of the project, use this starter section to make sure that your zig zag stitch is catching both edges of the coiled fabric and adjust your stitch width or length accordingly.

5 When you reach the end of the "U," turn the stitching around to continue stitching the cord together in an elongated spiral. Keeping the oval as flat as possible, continue wrapping and stitching the plain fabric strips and cord into a coiled oval (see pages 64–65). Continue until your oval measures approximately 10in (25cm) in length. This took me fourteen rounds of cream fabric. This will form the base for your basket.

6 Once the stitched oval measures 10in (25cm) in length, start wrapping the cord with the patterned fabric, and begin to slightly angle the stitched oval, so that the stitched coil begins to curve upward in the beginnings of a bowl shape (see page 65). The angle that you tilt at will dictate how steep the walls of the basket will be. At first, the aim is to create a shallow angle to increase the capacity of the basket.

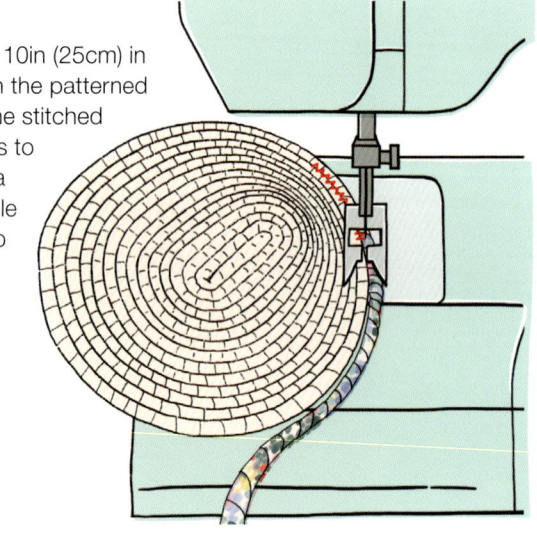

7 Continue wrapping and stitching the coil together. When you run out of cord, join more using the method on page 64. Once you are happy with the width of the basket, begin to angle the sides of the basket to make them less shallow. Do this by raising the left side of the basket sharply toward the sewing machine as you sew. You can raise it using a stack of books. After the initial 10in (25cm) oval base, I stitched 6 rounds of patterned fabric, 3 rounds cream, 6 rounds patterned, 4 rounds cream, 6 rounds patterned, 4 rounds cream, 5 rows patterned, 1½ rounds cream, making sure to change colors on the short edges of the basket where possible to make them less visible.

8 Once you are happy with the height of the basket, cut the cord and cocure the loose end to the rim of the basket using the method described on page 66. It should be tapered to blend well and ideally be positioned on a short edge of the basket.

9 You are ready to make the handle. Find the midpoint of each long edge of the basket and using a pencil, mark 3½in (9cm) away in each direction to demarcate a 7in (18cm) section. This indicates where the handle will loop up from the basket.

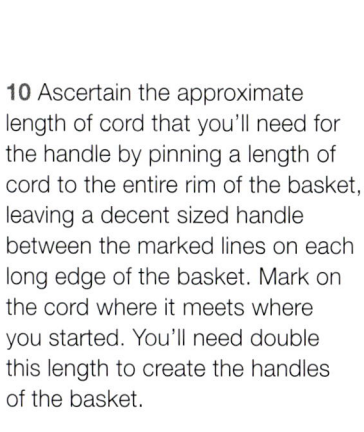

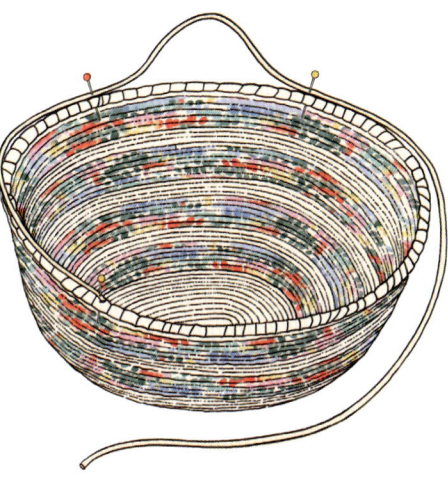

10 Ascertain the approximate length of cord that you'll need for the handle by pinning a length of cord to the entire rim of the basket, leaving a decent sized handle between the marked lines on each long edge of the basket. Mark on the cord where it meets where you started. You'll need double this length to create the handles of the basket.

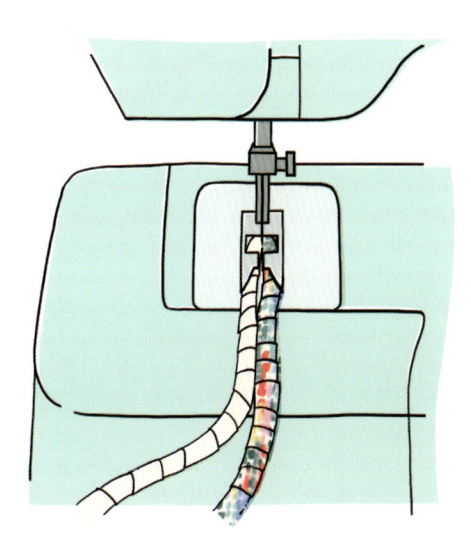

11 Unpin the cord and wrap it in plain fabric (as before) until you reach the marked halfway line, then swap to patterned fabric and wrap until you have the same length of cord wrapped in plain and patterned fabric. Secure the end with the sandwich clip.

12 Starting where the cream covered cord meets the patterned fabric covered cord, zig zag stitch the plain and patterned lengths of cord together.

13 Starting at one of the "handle position" pencil marks and working towards the short edge of the basket first, pin the double thickness cord to the top rim of the basket. When you come away from the rim to form the handle, twist the cord once. This means that half the basket will have the plain cord on top and half the basket will have the patterned fabric on top.

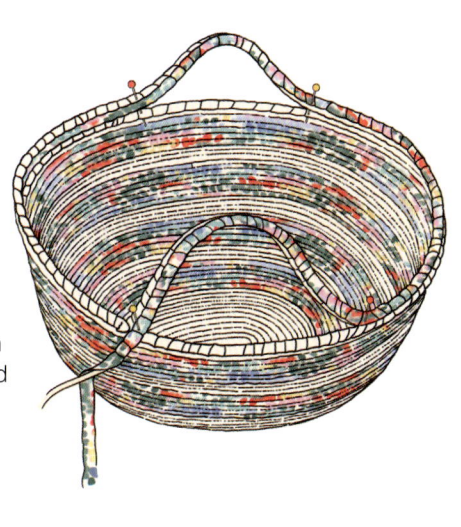

14 Once you are happy with the positioning of the handle, zig zag stitch it to the main body of the basket, making sure to backstitch at the beginning and end of the cord to reinforce it. Glue and taper the final cut end of fabric to the basket smoothly before stitching it in position.

LET'S GO TO THE BEACH BASKET 73

No-Sew Plant Pot Cover

With this project, I really wanted to give a no-sew option for anyone out there who, like me, isn't the most enthusiastic of sewists. The nice thing about this project is that the principle can be applied to so many other objects. You could cover an old lamp stand, a laundry basket, or little pots and cans to have as pen holders. There are so many possibilities, so get your thinking cap on.

You will need

Fabrics: I used red, orange, and burgundy velvet, which gives a nice sheen

¼in (5.5mm) cotton washing/pulley line or cord: enough to cover your plant pot (I used about 27⅜yd/25m to cover a 6¾in/17cm pot)

Plant pot

Glue gun

Masking tape (to join cords if needed)

1 Cut or tear your fabric into approximately ⅝in (1.5cm) width strips that are approximately 9¾–13¾in (25–35cm long using any of the methods described on pages 11–12. We use shorter lengths for this project to give more variation in color over a smaller area.

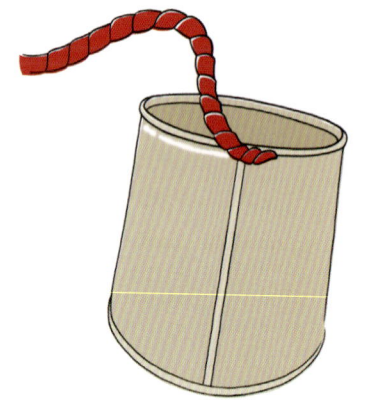

2 Leaving at least 2½in (6cm) of excess fabric at the beginning of the cord, wrap your first fabric strip diagonally along the cord (see page 63) and glue the end in place. Twist the first end of fabric at the beginning of the coil and glue it to the bottom edge of the plant pot to create a tapered start.

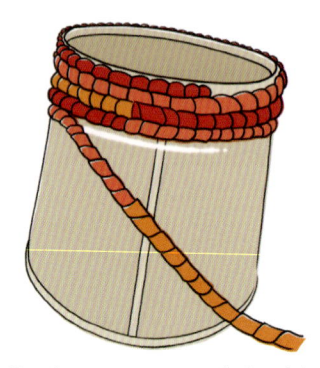

3 Continue to wrap and glue fabric strips around the cord using techniques from page 63, alternating colors. Every now and then, glue the fabric covered cord to the plant pot making sure that the rows of cord are pushed up close to each other and no gaps show through. Do not use too much glue, as it may seep through between the coils.

Elspeth's tip

For this project, you do not need to work with only fabric. To make the plant pot cover more waterproof, you could easily substitute plastic bags or other materials as long as they are flexible and can be cut into strips.

4 Continue wrapping the fabric and gluing the cord in place until you reach the top rim of the plant pot. To better disguise the inside of the plant pot, create one last coil on the inside edge of the pot. To finish the project, leave at least 3¼in (8cm) of excess fabric, cut the cord, twist the fabric strip to create a taper and glue it to the inside edge of the coil as you did at the beginning.

74 COILED ROPE

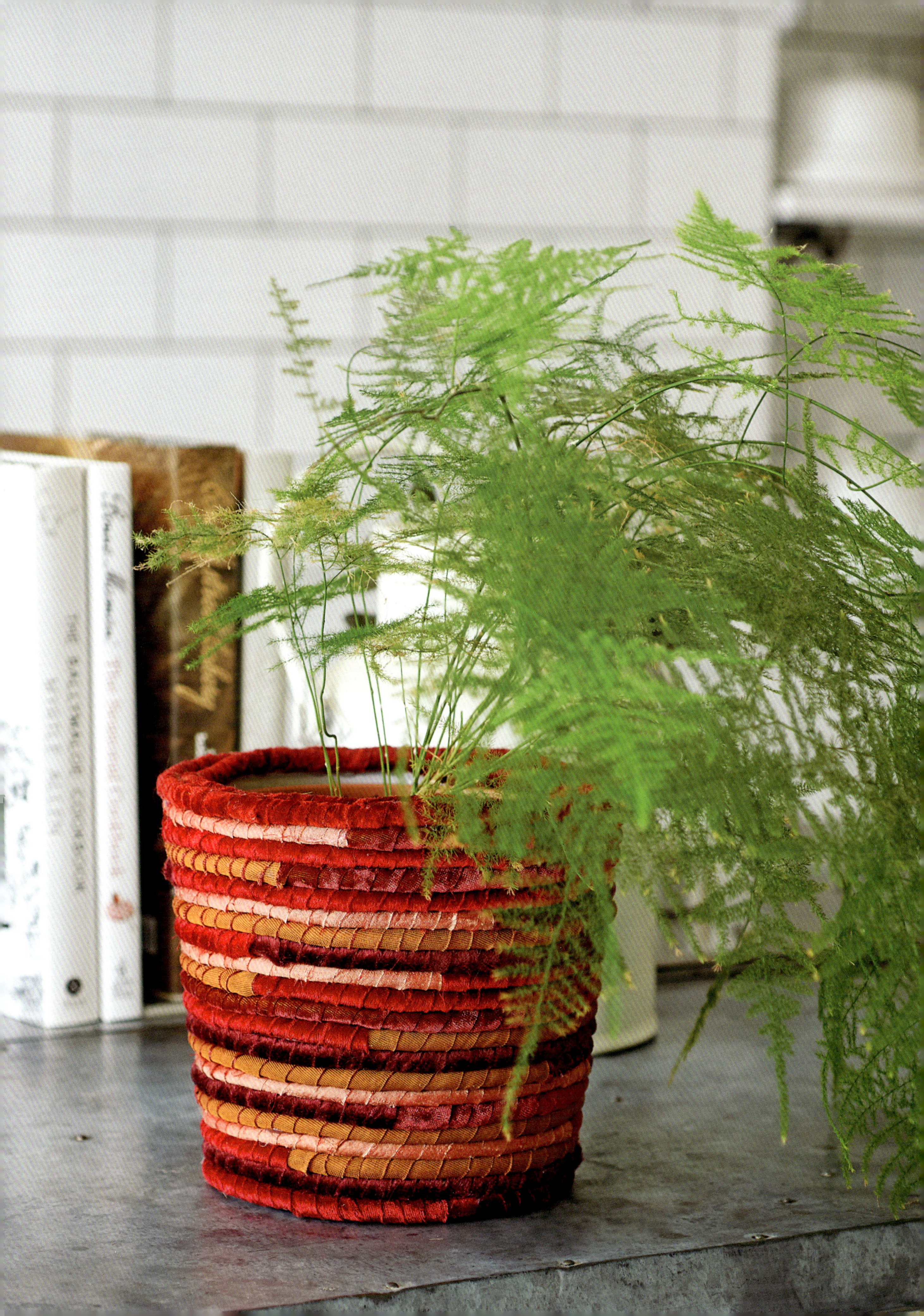

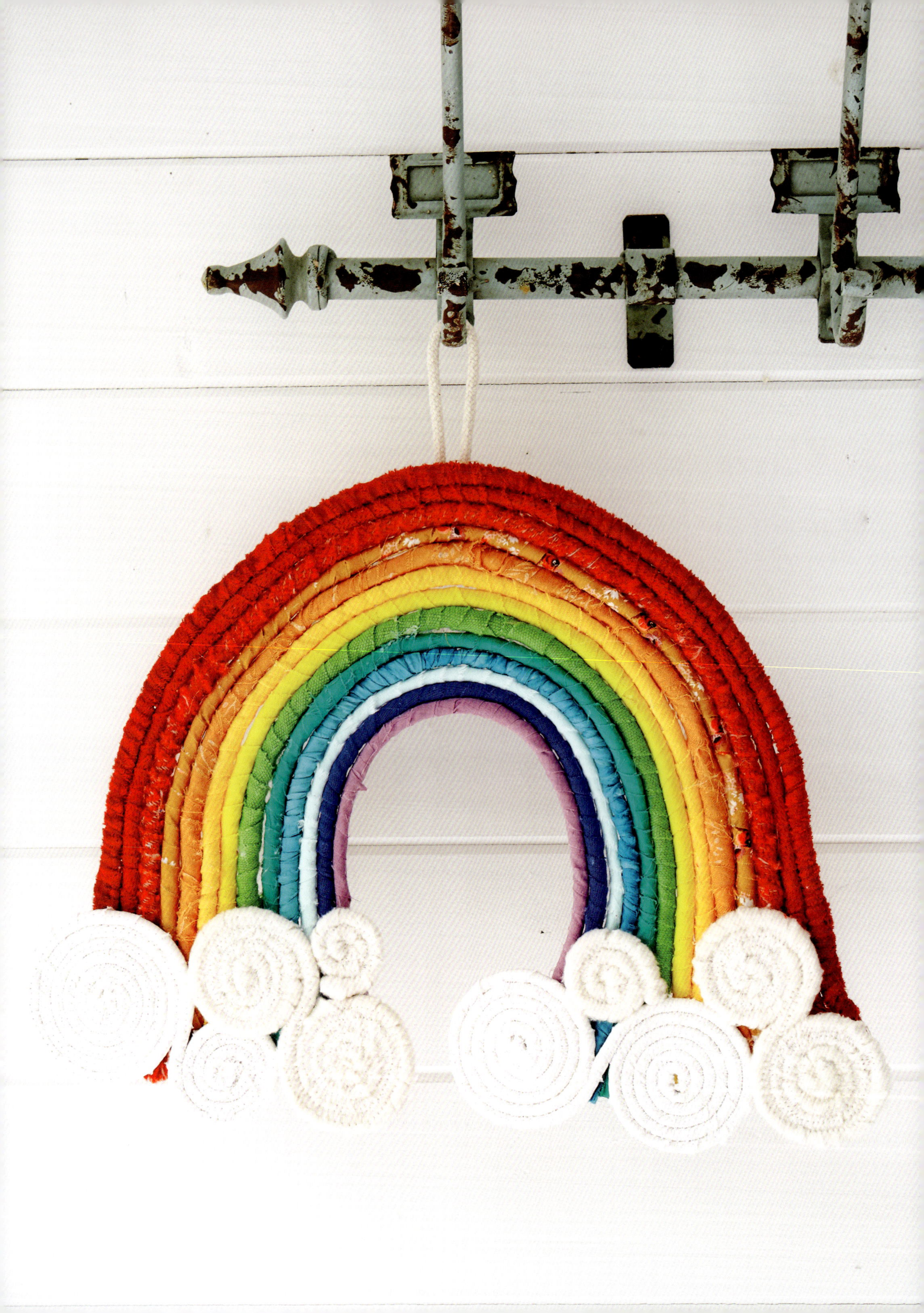

Rag and Rope Rainbow Hanging

This colorful rag rainbow would brighten up any dull day. It's a great way of using up small, colorful scraps of fabric that you have lying around, and would look great in softer shades too—pretty Liberty print rainbow anyone?

You will need

13yd (11.9m) cotton washing line (I used ¼in/5.5mm diameter)

Fabric scissors

Fabric/rags: two or three long strips for each color. You will need thirteen rainbow colors, plus white or cream for the clouds.

Glue gun

Two metal coat hangers or approximately 61½in (156cm) of floristry wire

Wire cutters (optional)

Tape (optional)

Sewing machine and white thread (optional)

Elspeth's tip

As it is so easy to join strips together in the coiled technique, you can use small pieces of multiple fabrics for one arc of the rainbow to use up scraps. Feel free to use a mixture of plain and patterned fabrics to add interest.

1 Cut your first piece of cotton washing line cord to approximately 26in (66cm) in length. This will be the outer arc of your rainbow. Trim the ends of the cord if they are very frayed.

2 Remembering to compensate for the weight of the fabric, cut your red fabric into ½–¾in (1–2cm) wide strips that are as long as possible (see pages 11-12). You will not need much fabric to cover one arc, so only cut a couple of strips to start with.

3 Glue the end of the red fabric strip over one cut end of the cord before wrapping and completely covering the cord (see techniques on page 63). If necessary, join pieces of fabrics together using the technique on page 64.

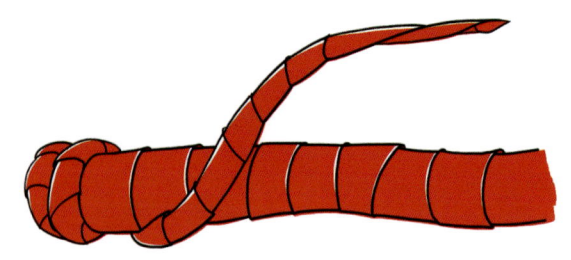

4 Trim the fabric strip you've been wrapping so it measures 2in (5cm) beyond the cut end of the cord. Taper the fabric strip to a point (see page 65). Wrap and glue the tapered end of the fabric strip up and around the base of the cord. The end may be slightly chunkier than higher up the cord.

5 Lay out the cord you've just wrapped in an arc shape and place the next piece of unwrapped cord on the inside edge. Cut it to length so that the cut ends are in line with those in the first arc. For each new arc, the length of cord decreases in size by about ¾in (2cm), but it is best to measure and cut each arc after completing the previous one.

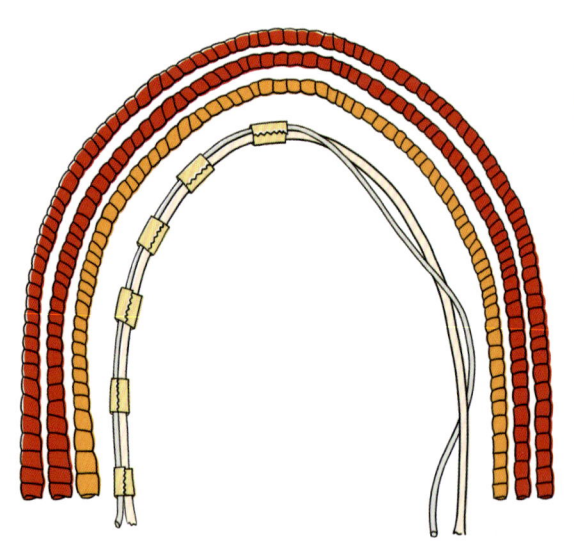

6 Repeat steps 1–5 to create thirteen arcs in total—two red, two orange, one ochre, two yellow, two green, two blue, one indigo, and one violet. To add structure to the rainbow, incorporate half a metal coat hanger or some floristry wire into the fourth, eighth, and twelfth arcs. Cut the wire slightly shorter than the arc, shape the wire to the approximate shape of the arc, then wrap the fabric around the cord and wire as one. It sometimes helps to tape the wire to the cord before wrapping it in fabric.

Elspeth's tip

If some arcs look skinnier than others, you can wrap a second layer of fabric over the first to make it thicker and balance out the weights.

7 Starting from the outside and working your way inwards, glue the arcs tightly together to form a rainbow. Be careful not to use too much glue as this can seep out and show. Don't worry if the ends of your arcs don't perfectly align as these will mostly be covered by the clouds.

8 Cut six pieces of cord to make up the clouds. Four of the pieces of cord should be approximately 43¼in (110cm) in length and two should be approximately 9¾in (25cm) in length. Wrap and glue each length of cord in white or cream fabric strips using the same technique as used in steps 2–4. You do not need to taper the ends, just make sure that both ends of the cord are completely covered in fabric.

9 These next steps can be done using either a glue gun or sewing machine. I used a sewing machine and a zig zag stitch on my clouds. Stitch or glue the 9¾in (25cm) lengths of white cord into circles using the technique on page 64.

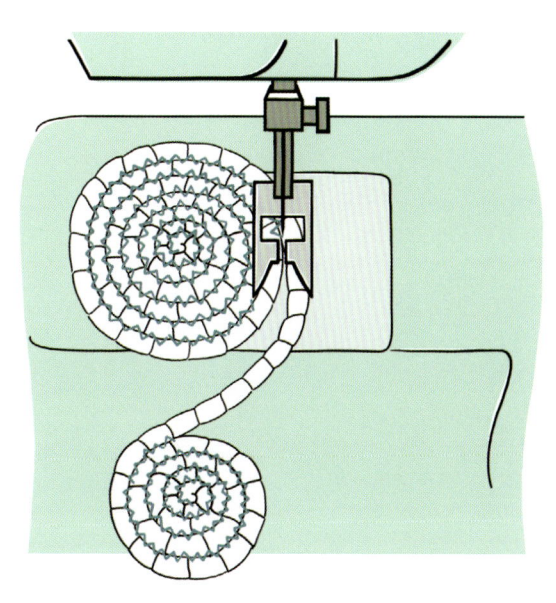

10 Starting with one of the 43¼in (110cm) lengths of cord, coil and stitch (or glue) together one half into a circle using the technique on page 64. Once you've stitched together approximately half the length of cord, flip the cord circle over, and stitch the other end of the fabric-covered cord into a circle.

11 Position the clouds at the bottom of the arcs wherever you would like them before gluing them in position. Glue a hanging loop in the top center of the back of the rainbow. This could be more fabric-covered cord or a ribbon.

RAG AND ROPE RAINBOW HANGING

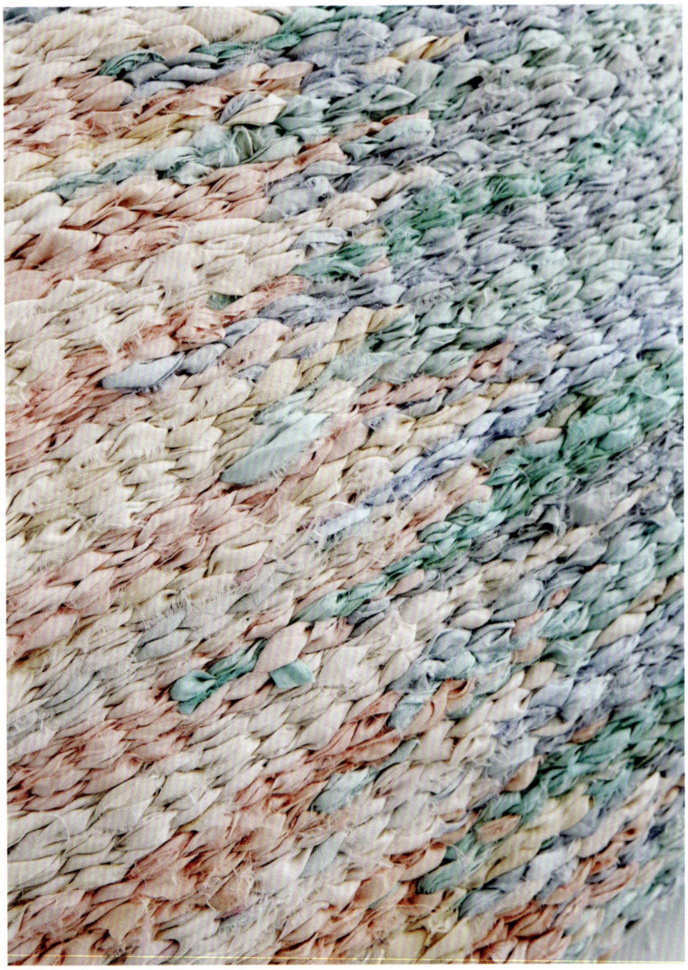
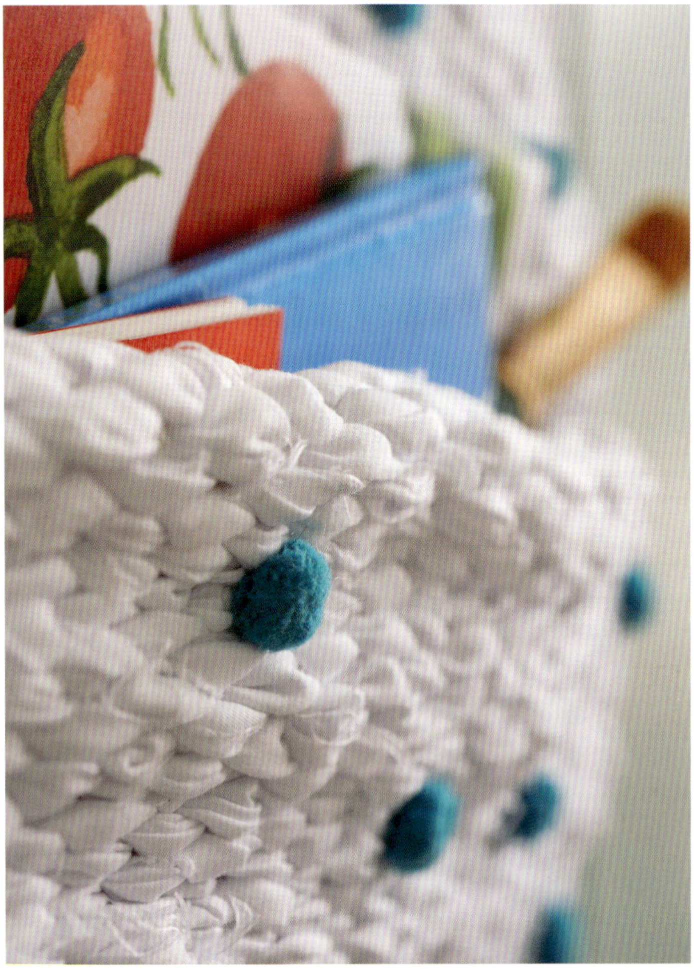
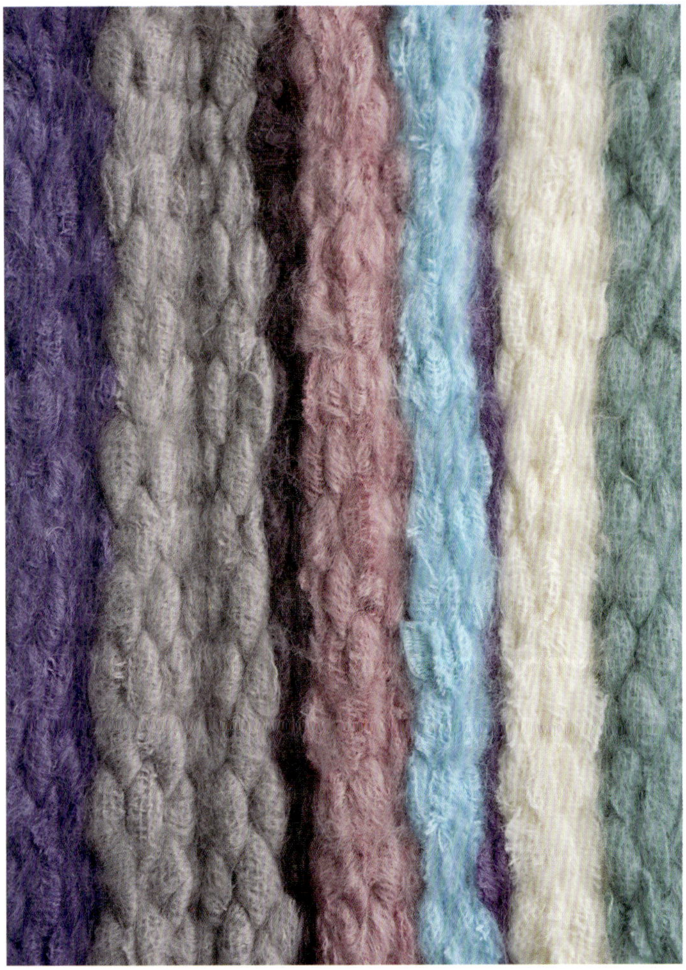
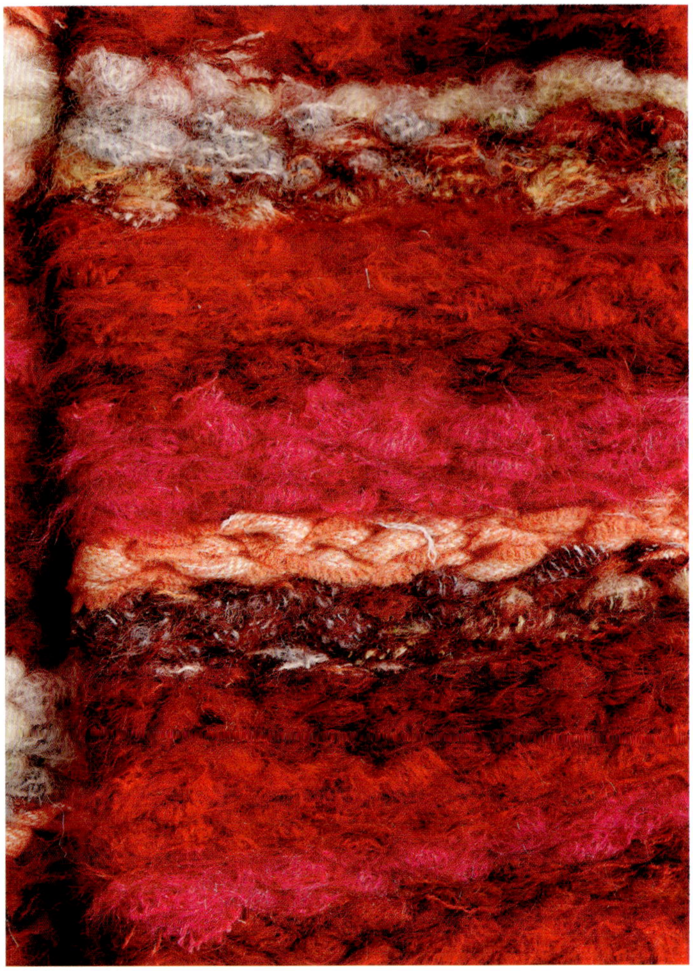

CHAPTER 4

PEG LOOM WEAVING

Peg loom weaving is a basic form of weaving where rags, wool, or even untreated fleece are woven back and forth between wooden dowels to build up cushy rugs, pillows, seat pads, and more. This is probably the fastest-building of the rag rug techniques in this book. In fact, the Highlands Rug on page 88 only took me a day and half to make, which is the fastest I've ever made an entire rug!

TOOLS AND MATERIALS

Peg loom

A peg loom is a heavy block of wood with holes drilled at regular intervals across its length. Each hole supports a removable "peg" with a small hole near its base. These pegs are usually wooden or plastic and the warp is passed through the small hole in each peg (see page 83 for how to warp the peg loom).

Peg looms can be bought in different lengths. Regardless of the peg loom size, you can make your weaving as long as you would like, but the length of your loom dictates the maximum width your woven piece will be. For example, a 24in (60cm) peg loom will make rugs that are a maximum of 24in (60cm) wide, but as long as you would like. You can work part-way across a peg loom if you would like to make narrower pieces, so you can make smaller items on a larger loom, but not the reverse.

As well as coming in different lengths, peg looms are sold with different sized pegs, spaced at different intervals. Generally, thinner and closer-spaced pegs are used for finer materials, such as yarn and lightweight fabric, and thicker, wider-spaced pegs are used to weave with chunkier materials. Typically, when working with lightweight fabrics, the pegs are around ¼in (6mm) in diameter and spaced ½in (12mm) apart. When working with thick fabrics, the pegs are around ⅜in (9mm) in diameter and spaced approximately 1in (25mm) apart. However, the precise size and spacing of the pegs isn't crucial as you can cut fabric wider or narrower to compensate.

If you want true flexibility, you can buy peg looms with multiple rows of holes. These come with different sets of pegs that fit into corresponding rows. This means that your peg loom can be used for all weights of yarn or fabric without the need to buy multiple looms. See each individual project for the details of how far my pegs were spaced apart. The spacing depends on the thickness of fabric I was working with for that particular project.

Other than the size and number of pegs, choose a peg loom with a heavy base so that it doesn't move or get dragged off the table as you weave. Be extra careful when working with thin wooden pegs as they can snap. Ideally you should buy from a supplier who offers spare pegs, just in case.

Wire threader or needle threader

Threading the warp through the tiny holes at the base of each peg can be quite tricky. I like to use a wire threader or needle threader to make it easier. These often come with your peg loom.

Other tools you may need:

Fabric scissors/rotary cutter and mat
Latch hook/darning needle/crochet hook (to sew in ends)
Ruler/measuring tape
Sewing machine/needle and thread

Cotton string, twine, or thin macramé cord

When choosing a string or cord for the warp (the vertical strands that hold together your weaving), use a material that is strong, but thin enough to easily pass through the small holes at the base of each peg. I prefer to work with sturdy cotton twine, but have used yarn, thin macramé cord, and other materials too. You won't see any of the warp in the body of your peg loomed project so the color doesn't matter. Feeling creative? You can add extra length to your warp and knot the warp strands together macramé-style to create more intricate fringes on your creations.

Fabrics or yarn

The good news is that just about anything can be used to weave on a peg loom. If it can be made into strips (and even sometimes when it can't, like natural fleece) then it can probably be used. If working with fabric, you can prepare strips using any of the methods on pages 11–12. Cut strips as long as possible, but don't worry too much about their exact length as you will need to join pieces together into one long strip. You can mix fabrics together in one piece, but as with many of the techniques in this book, it looks better when you balance the weights of different materials so they compress to approximately the same diameter when rolled up into a tube. For example, a thick fabric like fleece should be cut narrower than a fabric like sari silk, as it is much finer. The width that you cut fabric strips is determined by the spacing of your pegs and how dense you'd like the weaving to be. Fabric strips should generally be cut narrower when working with pegs that are spaced closer together and if you would like your weaving to be less dense. The table at the top of the page opposite gives you a rough idea of how wide to cut your strips based on two commonly spaced peg looms.

Fabric	Pegs spaced ½in (12mm) apart	Pegs spaced 1in (25mm) apart
Light weight fabrics, e.g. viscose, chiffon, voile	strip width: 1½–2½in (4–6cm)	strip width: 5½–6¼in (14–16cm)
Medium weight fabrics, e.g. cotton, jersey, silk	strip width: 1¼–2in (3–5cm)	strip width: 3¼–4in (8–10cm)
Heavy weight fabrics, e.g. woolen jumpers, mohair, blanket offcuts	strip width: ⅜–¾in (1–2cm)	strip width: ¾–1½in (2–4cm)

TECHNIQUES

Peg loom weaving is one of the easiest and most accessible forms of weaving. I like to work with my peg loom on an ironing board, so it's the perfect height to stand and work at. I prefer to have the warp dangling away from me, but as a beginner you may prefer to have dangling toward your body. Here are the basics of how peg loom weaving is done.

WARPING THE LOOM

Before you get started, you will need to warp up the loom. First, make sure that the pegs are positioned in the loom with the holes near the base.

1 Decide how wide you would like to make your peg loomed piece. Remember, you don't need to work across the full length of the loom. Measure the width across the peg loom and count how many pegs you will need to warp to achieve that size. In this example, I'd like to create a 15¾in (40cm) wide piece. 15¾in (40cm) covers approximately 32 pegs on my ½in (12mm) spaced peg loom, so place that many pegs into the loom.

2 Choose how long you would like to make your piece. To make a 19¾in (50cm) length of weaving, you need to double that measurement and add 15¾in (40cm) (to allow for knotting the warps and any adjustments at the end), which comes to 55in (140cm). This means that each of the 32 pegs will need to be threaded up with a 55in (140cm) length of warp, so you need to cut 32 pieces of twine or string to this length.

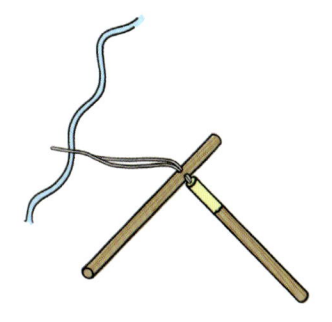

3 Thread a warp strand through the hole in the base of each peg with a wire threader or needle threader. You can take the peg out of the loom to do this.

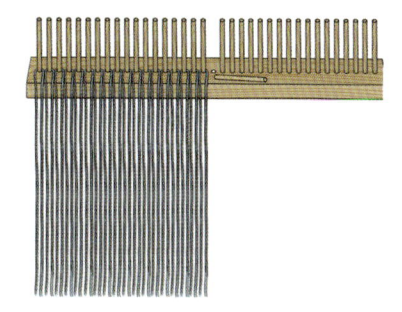

4 Replace the pegs into their holes and pull the warp strands, so that they are approximately the same length on each side of the hole.

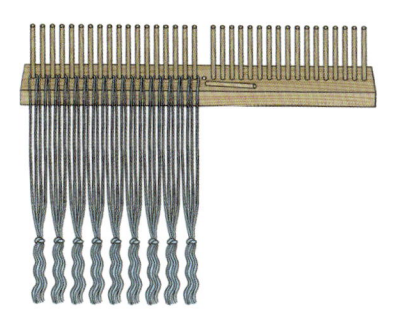

5 Starting from one side of the loom, loosely knot together neighboring warp threads into bunches of four (threads from two pegs) or six (threads from three pegs) depending on how many pegs you have warped and whether that number is divisible by four or six. Some projects (those that use a number of pegs not divisible by either four or six) will need a mix of bunches of four and six. Try to make the knots as equal in length from the pegs as possible, approximately 6in (15cm) from the cut ends of the warps. The excess warp and knots will be sewn in at the end and will not show.

PREPARING YOUR FABRICS

Once your peg loom is warped, prepare your fabrics for weaving. Use the chart on page 83 to determine roughly how wide to cut your strips for your particular loom before cutting strips of fabric that are as long as possible using any of the methods on pages 11–12.

Once you have created long strips of fabric, join strips together into one long continuous strip using either the diagonal seam join on page 13 or the enclosed end join on page 14. The buttonhole join (page 14) is an option, but it can make the weaving a bit lumpy, particularly when working with thick fabrics.

If you don't mind where your color changes will be in your design, join together different colored fabric strips to self-pattern as you weave. If you would like more control of your design, only stitch together same color strips so you change color where you like.

PEG LOOM WEAVING

Once your warp is in place and your fabric is prepped, it's on to the actual weaving. As a beginner it's often easier to have the warp coming towards you, so you can see what you're doing.

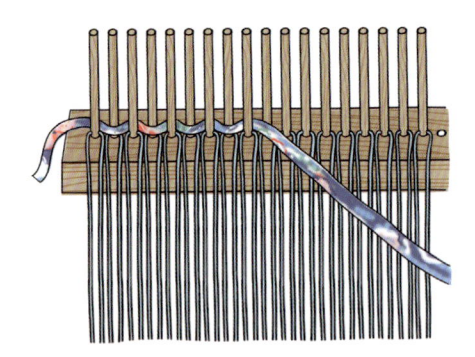

1 Leaving around a 2in (5cm) tail of fabric, weave in and out between the pegs from one side of the loom to the other. This involves alternately passing in front then behind neighboring pegs. Only weave onto pegs that have been warped.

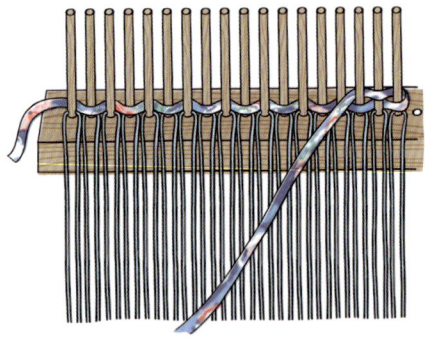

2 When you reach the final peg, pass around it and continue weaving the opposite direction. It should always alternate between in front and behind the peg from one row to the next. You've gone wrong when you pass on the same side of the peg as the row below.

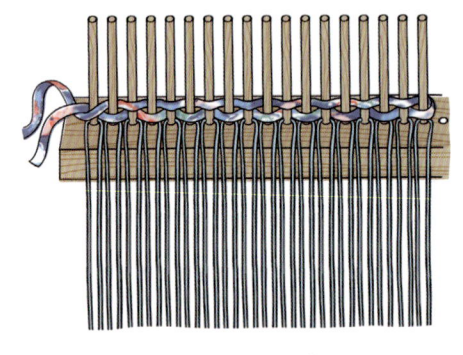

3 When you reach the original first peg, pass around the tail end to catch it up the side of the weaving so it doesn't come undone. Pass around the end peg and continue weaving.

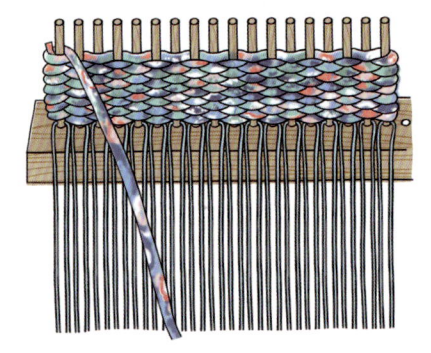

4 Catch the original tail end every time you reach the first peg to secure and hide it. If your fabric is relatively thick, it helps to cut this tail end narrower to make it less chunky and easier to disguise.

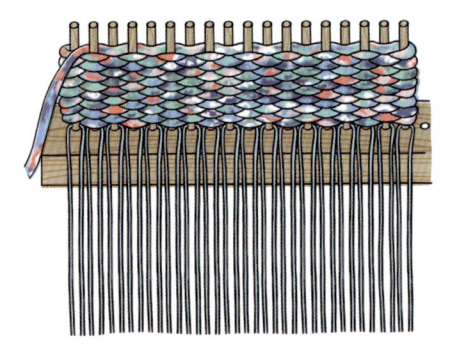

5 Continue building the weaving up the pegs one row at a time. When you have about ¾in (2cm) of empty space at the top of each peg, you will need to advance the warp.

Advancing the warp

Eventually your weaving will reach near the top of the pegs and you won't have enough space to continue. This means you need to "advance the warp."

1 I prefer to advance the warp when I've just completed a full row of weaving. Make a note of which direction you need to pass around the outer peg to continue weaving.

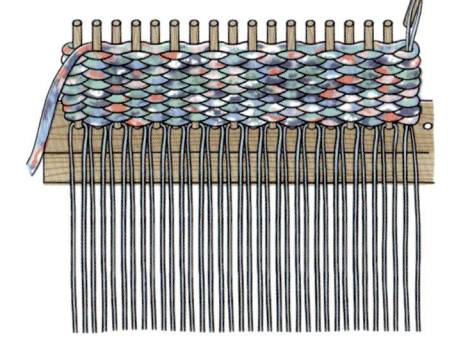

2 Starting at the end of the loom furthest from where you have just stopped weaving, lift the end peg from the hole, so the weaving moves down the warp.

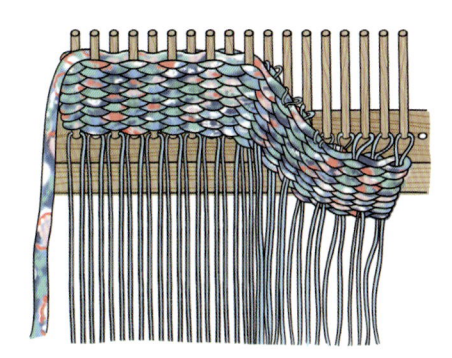

3 Replace the peg into the hole behind the weaving and repeat with all the pegs one by one. Be careful not to trap any of the fabric or warp under the peg when you replace it and be particularly careful not to let go of the peg when you remove it from the hole as it can get sucked into the weaving if the project is particularly heavy. If the holes are a bit loose, the pegs can slip out, so make sure they are firmly wedged in.

4 When you reach the final peg, make sure you are clear whether you need to pass in front or behind the next peg to continue weaving before you take the peg out and replace it.

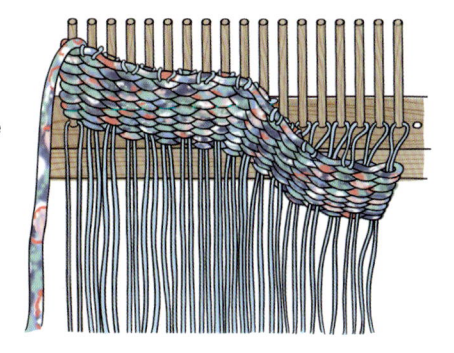

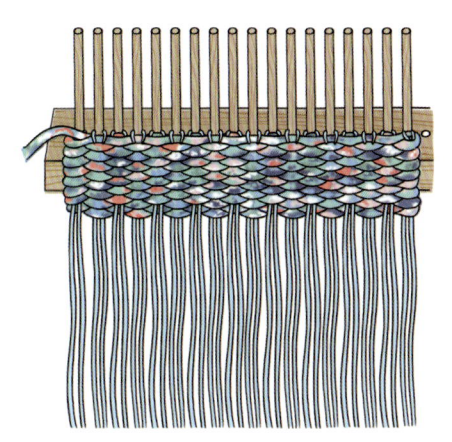

5 Once you've advanced the warp, tighten the weaving by gently tugging the dangling pairs of warp strands so that the weaving compacts up and sits closer to the pegs.

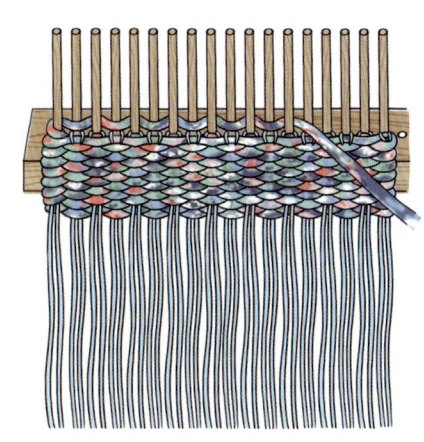

6 Starting with the turn you were about to do, continue weaving.

Your work will build down the warp strands. To get an accurate measurement of how long your weaving is, you may need to compress it up, as it will be tightest closest to the pegs and looser further down.

TECHNIQUES 85

Joining strips and changing color

In peg loom weaving, the longer your strips are, the more of a rhythm you can get into with your weaving. That is why, ideally, I prefer to join lots of my strips together into one long strip before I start a project (particularly if the design isn't complex—simple stripes, for example). In the Knick-Knack Storage Bag project on page 94, as the base was entirely one color, I sewed together one long strip of white cotton using the diagonal seam join on page 13 before I started weaving. Without a sewing machine, this can be done by hand using the enclosed end join or the buttonhole join, both on page 14. If using the buttonhole join method, try to push your knots to the back of the weaving as you work.

With these simple designs, every time I reach the end of my long strip, I sew together another large batch of strips, which I then join to the tail of the weaving.

Where you'd like to change colors on the edge of the weaving without sewing (as in the Pastel Paint Drip Pillow on page 98), you can follow the steps below:

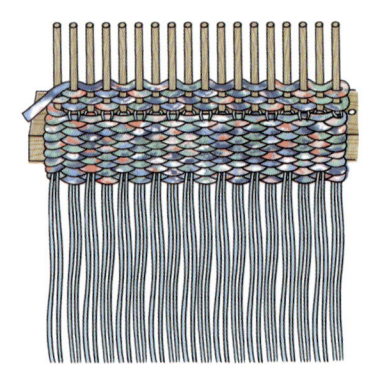

1 Weave to the edge of the loom and cut the tail of the fabric strip to approximately 2in (5cm) in length.

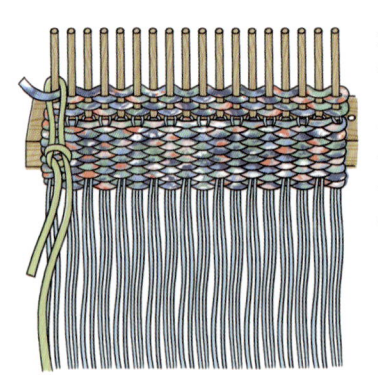

2 Create a slip knot near the end of your long fabric strip. Place the slip knot over the first peg, pass the tail end of the previous color through the loop and tighten the loop on to the peg.

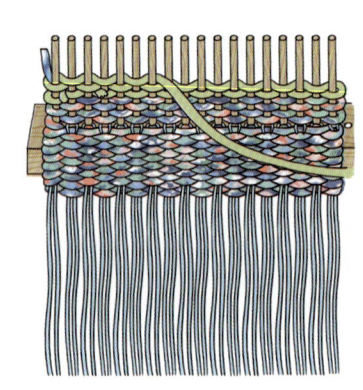

3 Continue weaving with the new strip and the tail of the slip knot as one. If the knot appears very chunky, undo it and cut the fabric strip narrower before creating the knot. Every time you come back to the peg with the knot, wrap around the tail end of the previous color to gradually work it into the weaving. Or you can leave tail ends to sew in later.

How to make a slip knot

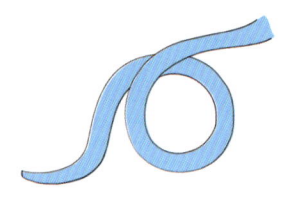

1 Taper the end of the fabric strip to a point. Make a loop with the tail-end of the fabric strip on the bottom.

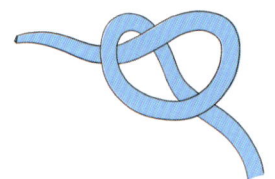

2 With your thumb and index finger, pass through the loop, and pinch the longer fabric strip that isn't a cut end.

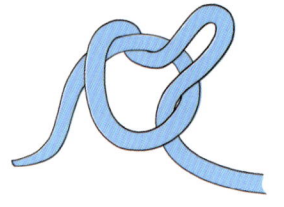

3 Pull it through the loop.

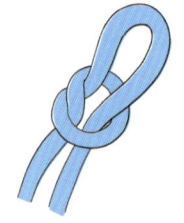

4 Pull to tighten the knot. Pulling the cut end of fabric tightens the loop at the top.

FINISHING YOUR PEG LOOM WEAVING

Measuring the length of your peg loom weaving can be a little tricky. Advance the warp (see page 85) and even up the tension of the weaving by sliding it up and down the warps before measuring to get the most accurate reading. You want to loosen up the weave closest to the pegs (which will be very tight) and tighten up the weave near the knotted ends of the warp. The weaving furthest down the warps may be too loose where it has traveled down the warps with gravity, so take that into account when measuring.

1 After advancing the warp, cut the strip of fabric you were weaving with and loosely tie the end to the final warp strand.

2 Starting at one end of the loom, push the weaving nearest the pegs down the warps to expose at least 2½in (6cm) of warp. Two pegs at a time, carefully cut the warps and tie them off to the neighboring pair. Make sure to tie the knots at the same length down the warp to create a flat edge to the weaving.

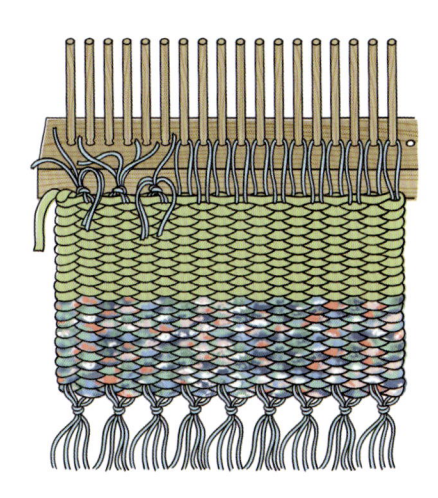

3 Tidy up the other end of the weaving if needed. Untie or carefully cut each knot one by one and re-knot the warps further up so the end of the weaving is level. You may need to tighten and re-weave in the first row of weaving before doing this if the tail end has come a bit loose.

Elspeth's tip
Do not cut the warps all at once, as they can get sucked down into the weaving. Hold firmly onto the warp strands when you do cut them.

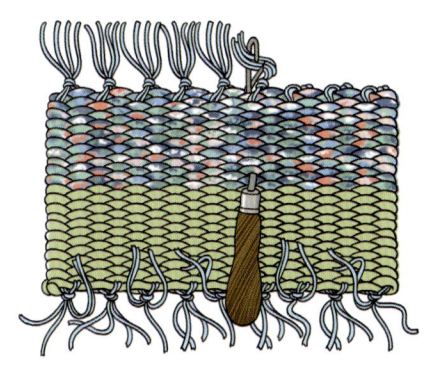

4 Trim the warp strand ends to approximately 2in (5cm) in length and use a threader, latch hook, darning needle, or crochet hook to pull the warp ends up through the weaving in the direction of the warp threads. Repeat the process with any loose weft strands (the ones that go from side to side) in the same way to secure them.

5 Choose a right side to the piece and poke any imperfections through to the wrong side of the weaving. If you've used the buttonhole join method, these could be the slightly chunky knots.

Peg loom weaving design tips

Peg loom weaving lends itself nicely to simple striped designs, so color choice is key. Fabrics with a design will self-pattern across the weaving, whilst plain colors will stand out boldly. Peg loom weaving doesn't have to be perfect as you can manually tighten or loosen the weaving to your taste. For rugs, I prefer to create a chunkier, denser weave (use thicker fabrics or cut wider), but for practical items I prefer to create a thinner, more flexible weave (use light fabrics or cut narrower). For successful stripes, you do not necessarily need to join colors on the edge as the rows compress up and it becomes hard to see where one color ends and another begins. Peg loom weaving looks neatest when you balance out the weights of your fabrics. The edges of peg loom weaving will never be as neat as in other forms of weaving, but that's part of its charm.

Highlands Rug

The colors in this rug were inspired by the beautiful heathers, grasses, and wildlife of the Scottish Highlands. I used cosy mohair fents for this project, but you could use thick, soft materials like fleece, woolen jumpers, and blankets.

You will need:

66½yd (60.8m) of cord/string

Peg loom (my pegs were spaced approximately 1in/2.5cm apart)

Fabric/rags: I used just over 2lb 3oz (1kg) of fabric, but the quantity you will need depends on the thickness of the fabric

Sewing machine/needle and thread

Darning needle/latch hook/crochet hook/wire threader

1 Prepare your warp by cutting the string to length for the rug. This should be the length you would like your rug x 2 + 16in (40cm). For me, this was 55in (140cm) (the length I wanted the rug) x 2 = 110in (280cm) + 16in (40cm) = 126in (320cm). Cut one warp string for each peg you plan to use. I used 19 pegs to create a 22in (55cm) wide rug, so cut 19 pieces of 126in (320cm) long string.

2 Warp up the peg loom (see page 83), making sure that the knots joining together neighboring warps are as level as possible, approximately 6in (15cm) from the bottom of the strings.

3 Cut long strips of fabric. I was using thick mohair and my pegs were spaced quite far apart, so I cut my strips 1½in (4cm) wide. If you were working with cottons, you may need to cut your strips 3¼-4in (8–10cm) in width for a chunky rug. If in doubt, cut up and try a little of the fabric first before cutting up the rest.

4 Stitch together your strips of fabric into one long length using either a sewing machine and the diagonal join method on page 13 or by hand using the enclosed end method or buttonhole join on page 14. First, create a length of approximately 33yd (30m), joining together different colors. For wider stripes of color, sew together multiple strips of the same color one after another. Try to vary the size of the stripes of color across the rug and repeat contrast colors at fairly even intervals.

Elspeth's Design Tip:

If you are mixing different fabrics together, try to balance the different weights (thicknesses of the fabric) by cutting your strips narrower or wider to compensate. It is easier to peg loom weave using similar thicknesses.

88 PEG LOOM WEAVING

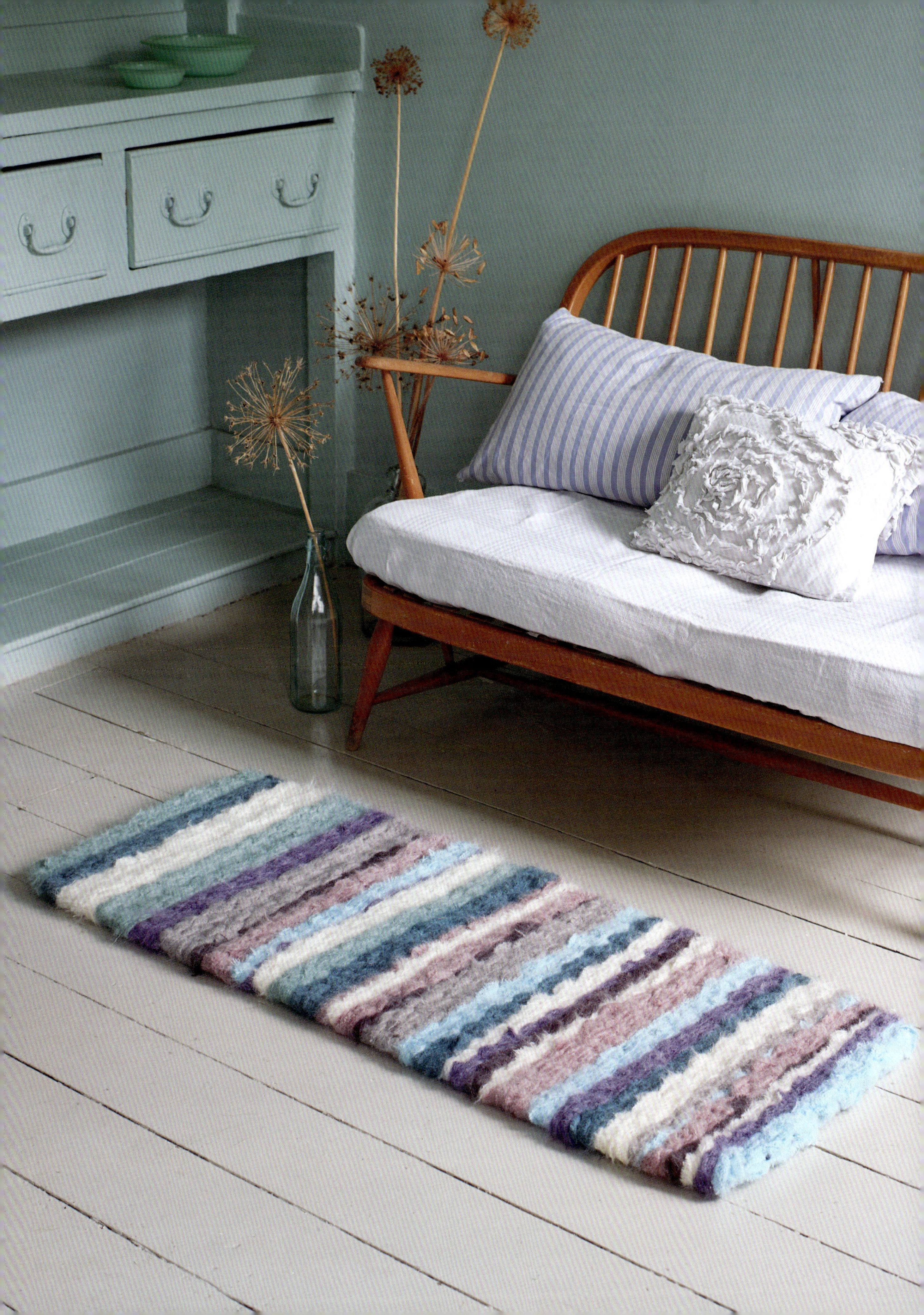

> **Elspeth's tip**
>
> When weaving a long project, I like to work on an ironing board with the warp strands trailing away from me. They get less tangled this way.

5 Using the technique on pages 84–85, peg loom weave the rug until it measures approximately 55in (140cm) in length. When you run out of your 33yd (30m) of fabric, create another long strip as in step 4. Either stitch this strip directly to the end of the previous long strip to keep weaving or create a slip knot at the end of the new strip, pass it over the first peg and continue weaving, trapping the end of the previous strip underneath. See page 86 for more details.

6 Push the weaving nearest the pegs down the warps to expose at least 2½in (6cm) of warp. Two pegs at a time, carefully cut the warps and tie them off to the neighboring pair (see page 87). Make sure the knots are spaced an even distance down the warp to create a flat edge to the rug.

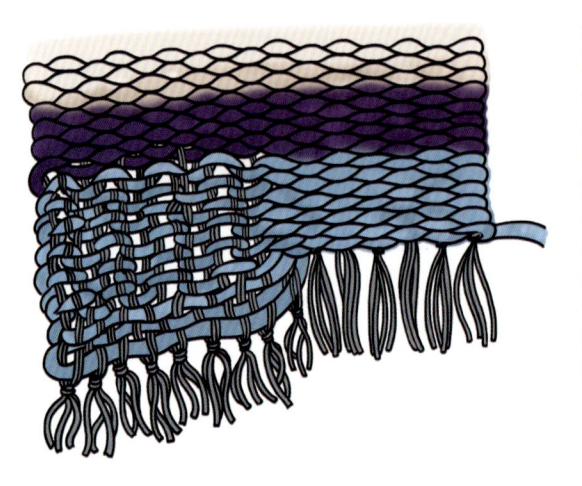

7 When the warp strands are very long, it is difficult to knot the warp strands together perfectly aligned in step 2, so you will probably have to level out the end of the rug where you started. Cut the warp strands (see tip below) near each knot and re-knot the warps together so the end of the rug is level. You may want to tighten and re-knot the first row of weaving before doing this if it is looking a little slack.

8 Trim any loose fabric or warp ends to approximately 2in (5cm) in length and weave them into the rug (see page 87). I like to pull the warp strands up where the warp runs. Push any imperfections through to the underside of the rug.

> **Elspeth's tip**
>
> Do not cut the warps all at once, as the pegs can get sucked down into the weaving. Hold firmly onto the warp strands when you do cut them.

90 PEG LOOM WEAVING

Toasty Fall Leaves Scarf

A warm, chunky scarf is a must-have in most people's wardrobes. On a cold day, accessorising with a warm pop of color can really brighten my mood. As you'll be wearing this gorgeous rag rugged project, choosing soft fabrics is key. I used old woolen jumpers, fleecy blankets, and mohair offcuts to add coziness to the scarf.

You will need:

50yd (45.6m) of string

Peg loom (my pegs were spaced 1in/2.5cm apart)

Fabric/rags: I used about 18oz (500g) of fabric, but the quantity you will need depends on the thickness of the fabric

Sewing machine/needle and thread

Latch hook/rug hook/crochet hook

1 Prepare your warp by cutting the string to length for the scarf. This should be the length you would like your scarf x 2 + 16in (40cm). For me, this was 59in (150cm) (the length I wanted the scarf) x 2 = 118in (300cm) + 16in (40cm) = 134in (340cm). Cut one warp string for each peg you plan to use. I used 12 pegs to create an approximately 8in (20cm) wide scarf, so I cut 12 pieces of 134in (340cm) long string.

2 Warp up the peg loom (see page 83), making sure that the knots joining together neighboring warps are as level as possible, approximately 6in (15cm) from the bottom of the strings.

Elspeth's design tip
Planning to use old woolen sweaters? Wash them at a high temperature to tighten the weave, so that they hold together better when you cut into them.

3 Cut long strips of fabric. I was using thick fabrics but didn't want the scarf to be too dense so cut my strips ¾in (2cm) wide. If you were working with thinner fabrics such as cottons, you need to cut your strips wider, approximately 3¼in (8cm) in width. If in doubt, cut up and try a little of the fabric first before cutting up the rest.

4 Stitch together your strips of fabric into one long length using either a sewing machine and the diagonal seam join on page 13 or by hand using the enclosed end method on page 14. I prefer not to use the buttonhole join as this will create knots that are less comfortable to wear and harder to disguise in a scarf. First, create a length of approximately 33yd (30m), using strips of fabric that are about 35½–59in (90–150cm) in length. Changes in color will create different width stripes across the scarf so try to repeat contrast colors at fairly even intervals.

Elspeth's tip
For a less chunky scarf, this pattern would work well 6in (15cm) in width.

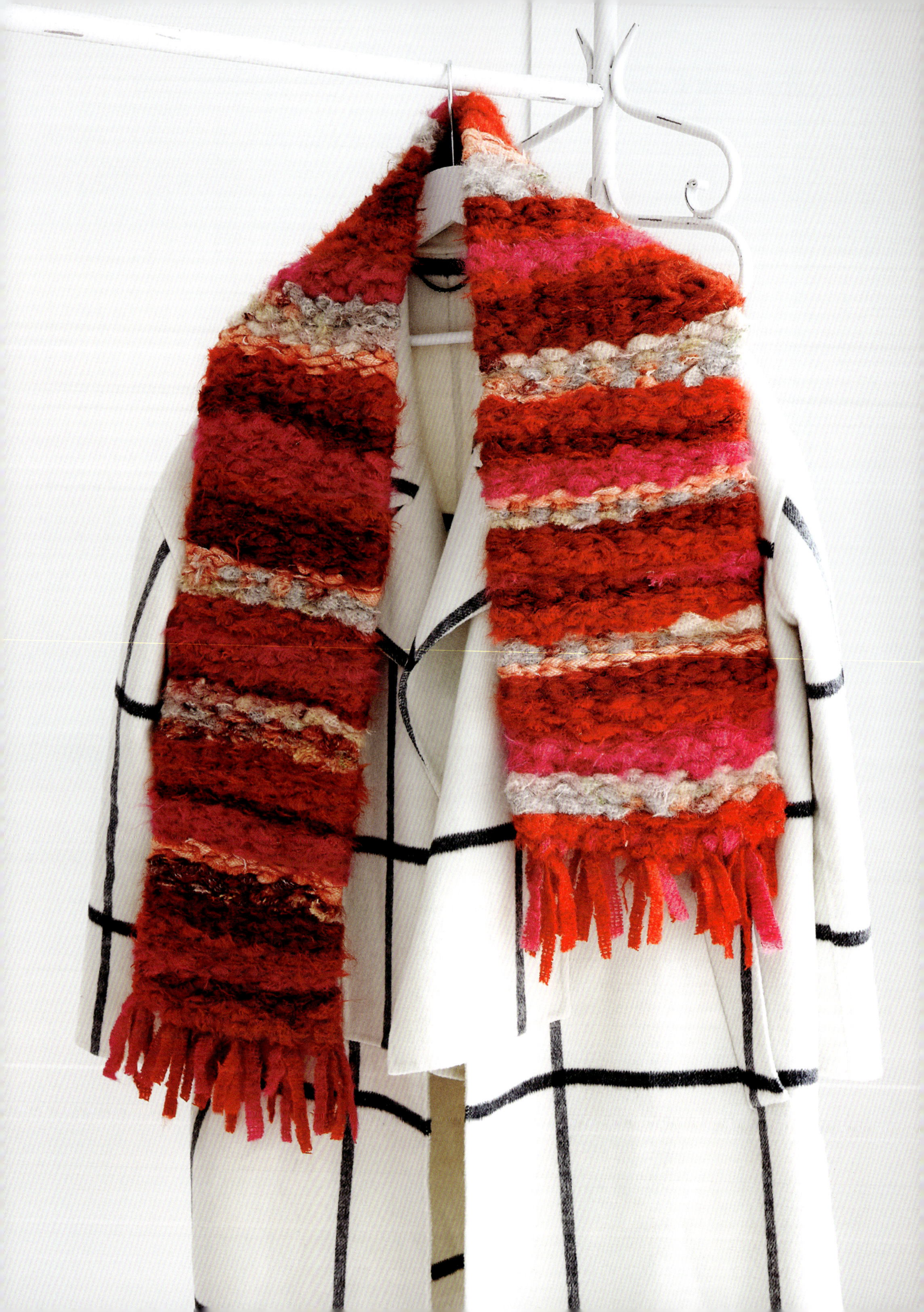

5 Using the technique on page 84, peg loom weave the scarf until it measures approximately 59in (150cm) in length. Before measuring the length of the scarf, loosen the weaving nearest the pegs by pushing rows down the warps. You want the weaving to be as loose as possible without showing the warps. If you leave the weaving too tight when you tie it off, the scarf will not bend comfortably around your neck. The weaving furthest down the warps may be too loose where it has traveled down the warps with gravity, so take that into account when measuring—it will compress a little.

Elspeth's tip

When you run out of your 33yd (30m) length of fabric, create another long strip as in step 4. Either stitch this strip directly to the end of the previous long strip to keep weaving or create a slip knot at the end of the new strip, pass it over the first peg and continue weaving. See page 86 for more details.

Elspeth's tip

Do not cut the warps all at once, as the pegs can get sucked down into the weaving. Hold firmly onto the warp strands when you do cut them.

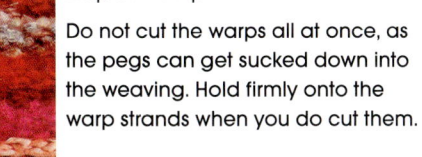

6 When your scarf measures approximately 59in (150cm) in length, push the weaving nearest the pegs down the warps to expose at least 2½in (6cm) of warp. Working with the warps from two pegs at a time, cut the warps to remove them from the pegs and tie them off to the neighboring pair of warps (see page 87). Make sure the knots are spaced an even distance down the warp to create a flat edge to the scarf.

7 Make sure that the weaving is not too dense across the length of the scarf before tidying up the other end of the scarf. If it is too tight it won't sit comfortably around the neck. Cut the warp strands (see tip above) near each knot and re-knot the warps together so the end of the scarf is level. You may want to tighten and re-knot the first row before doing this.

8 Sew in any tail ends of fabric and weave in the warp strands carefully at the top and bottom of the scarf (see page 87).

9 Cut thirty-six ½ x 10in (1 x 25cm) fabric strips to make the fringe of the scarf. I used three fabric pieces per tassel (six tassels per each end of the scarf) as my fabric was quite thick, but you may need more fabric pieces if you are working with a thin, fine fabric.

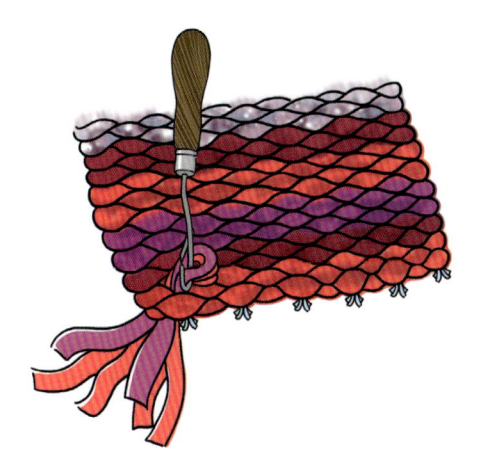

10 Push your hook through the weave of the scarf about ¾in (2cm) from the bottom. Try to align each tassel with the warp strand knot, as this will allow you to disguise them well. Place the middle of three fabric strips into the hook and pull the fabric strips part way through the weave of the scarf to form a large loop.

11 With either your fingers or the hook, pull the ends of the fabric strips through the loop and pull the cut ends to tighten the loop against the weave of the scarf. Adjust one or two of the fabric strips loops to cover any visible warp. Repeat until you have six tassels at each end of the scarf and your warp ends are totally disguised.

TOASTY FALL LEAVES SCARF 93

Knick-Knack Storage Bag

My rag rug studio is full of tools, fabric, half-finished projects, and many an unusual craft item. That's why it's good to have versatile storage caddies that I can use to tidy up in a hurry. This storage bag looks great hanging on the back of a door and would be perfect in a pretty guest room or craft room.

You will need:

61¼yd (56m) of string

Peg loom (my pegs were spaced approximately ½in/1.2cm apart)

Fabric/rags: I used a 3 x 3yd (275 x 275cm) white cotton sheet, but the quantity you will need depends on the thickness of the fabric

Coat hanger

Needle and white thread

Latch hook/rug hook/crochet hook/wire threader (for sewing in your ends)

Pom poms: I used 21 small pom poms from a ⅜in (10mm) wide pom pom trim

Glue gun (optional)

Pins (optional)

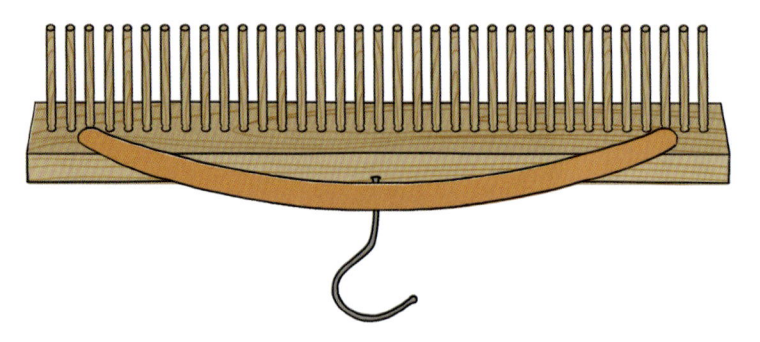

1 Measure the width of your coat hanger to determine the number of pegs you will need to warp up. My coat hanger was 15⅜in (39cm) wide and I added approximately 2in (5cm) to allow for a bit of wiggle room, so I needed to warp up 35 pegs (a width of approximately 17⅜in/44cm).

2 Prepare your warp by cutting the string to length for the hanging storage container. For me, this was 23½in (60cm) (the length needed) x 2 = 47in (120cm) + 16in (40cm) = 63in (160cm). Cut one warp string for each peg you plan to use. I used 35 pegs, so cut 35 pieces of 63in (160cm) long string.

3 Warp up the peg loom (see page 83), making sure that the knots joining together neighboring warps are as level as possible, approximately 6in (15cm) from the bottom of the strings.

Elspeth's tip

This is a good way to prettify unattractive coat hangers from stores. Only the metal hook at the top will show.

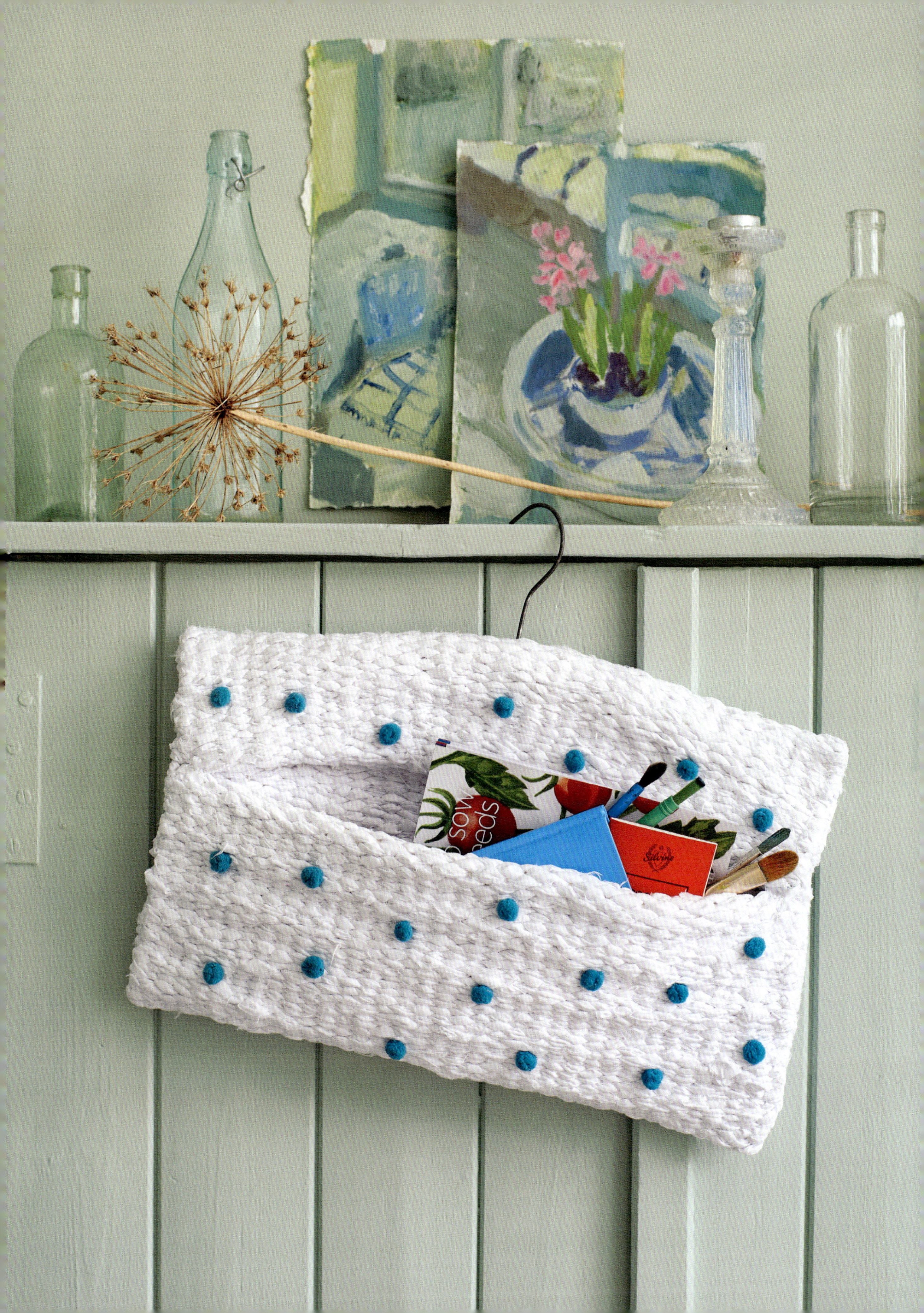

4 Cut your white cotton sheet into long strips that are approximately 2in (5cm) in width (see page 11). Cut your strips narrower if working with thicker fabrics. If unsure how wide to cut your strips, cut up and weave a little of the fabric to try it first before cutting up the rest.

5 Stitch together all the strips into one long continuous strip using either a sewing machine and the diagonal seam join on page 13 or by hand using the enclosed end method on page 14. Ball up the length of fabric to keep it neat.

6 Peg loom weave (see technique on page 84), until your piece of weaving measures approximately 23½in (60cm) in length. Before measuring the length, even out the density of the weaving along the warp strands. None of your warp should be visible except at the top and bottom. If you run out of fabric part way through the weaving, join new strips using either of the techniques on page 86.

7 When your weaving measures approximately 23½in (60cm) in length, push the weaving nearest the pegs down the warps to expose at least 2½in (6cm) of warp. Working with the warps from two pegs at a time, cut the warps (see tip, below left) to remove them from the pegs and tie the pair of warps to the neighboring pair of warps (see page 87). Make sure the knots are spaced an even distance down the warp to create a flat edge.

8 Even up the other end of the weaving if needed. Cut the warp strands one by one near each knot and re-knot them to create a level edge. You may want to tighten and re-knot the first row of weaving before doing this.

Elspeth's tip
Do not cut the warps all at once, as the pegs can get sucked down into the weaving. Hold firmly onto the warp strands when you do cut them.

96 PEG LOOM WEAVING

9 Choose which side of the weaving will be your front and push any imperfections through to the back. Weave in any tail ends, before cutting your knotted warp strands to only ½in (1cm) in length.

10 Fold both edges with the knotted warp over ¾in (2cm) to the wrong side of the weaving and hand sew them in position using white thread. This hem will create a cleaner edge to your hanging storage bag.

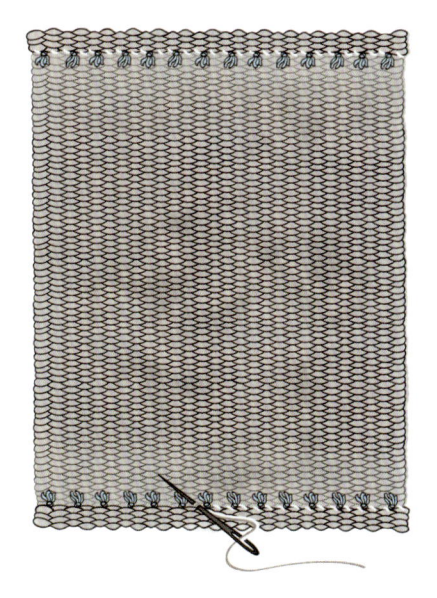

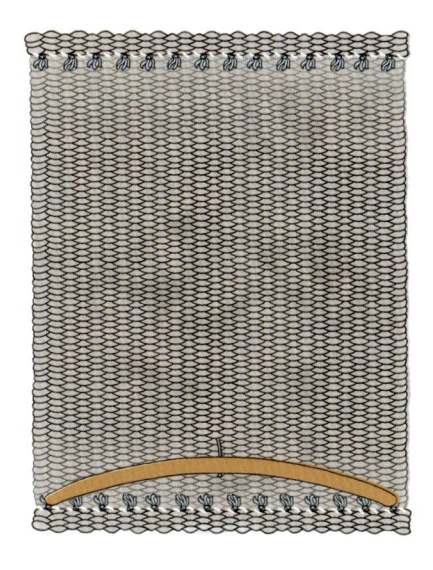

11 Lay out the weaving with the wrong side facing upwards. Push the hook of the hanger through the weaving approximately 4in (10cm) up from one of the hemmed edges in the center of the weaving.

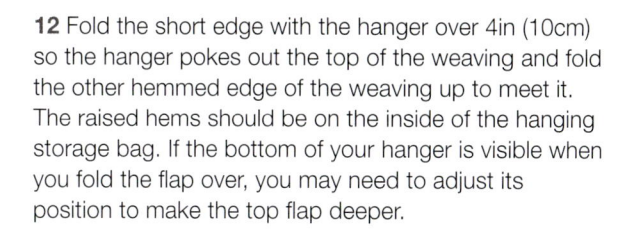

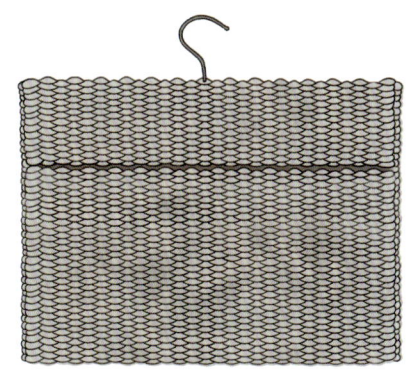

12 Fold the short edge with the hanger over 4in (10cm) so the hanger pokes out the top of the weaving and fold the other hemmed edge of the weaving up to meet it. The raised hems should be on the inside of the hanging storage bag. If the bottom of your hanger is visible when you fold the flap over, you may need to adjust its position to make the top flap deeper.

13 Hand stitch both sides of the hanging storage bag together before stitching the top and bottom flap together 2in (5cm) on each edge to reduce the size of the bag opening. Don't worry if your stitching isn't perfect as the texture of the weaving will hide imperfections.

14 Cut the pom poms off from the trim and lay them out across the front of the knick-knack storage bag. When you are happy with the distribution, stitch or glue them in position.

KNICK-KNACK STORAGE BAG 97

Pastel Paint Drip Pillow

I'm a firm believer that you can never have enough pillows and I'm sure there are some other avid pillow fans out there. This particular design was inspired by paint drips, but rather than using bright saturated colors, I decided to go a more subtle route with toned-down pastel shades. This project is great to learn how to go beyond simple stripes on a peg loom.

You will need:

39⅜yd (36m) of string

Peg loom (my pegs were spaced approximately ½in (1.2cm) apart)

Fabric/rags: I used about 13oz (380g) of cream, pink, blue, and green fabric, but the quantity you will need depends on the thickness of the fabric

Sewing machine/needle and thread

Latch hook/rug hook/crochet hook/wire threader (for sewing in your ends)

16 x 18in (36 x 46cm) of thick cotton backing fabric

12 x 16in (30 x 40cm) pillow pad

Elspeth's tip

Don't worry about any imperfections in this design as any lumps and bumps can be pushed through to the inside of the pillow cover.

1 Prepare your warp by cutting the string to length for the pillow. This should be the length you would like your pillow x 2 + 16in (40cm). For me, this was 12in (30cm) (the length I wanted the pillow) x 2 = 24in (60cm) + 16in (40cm) = 40in (100cm). Cut one warp string for each peg you plan to use. I used 36 pegs to create an approximately 17in (43cm) wide piece of weaving to make a 16in (40cm) wide pillow (I added 1in/3cm seam allowance). So, I cut 36 pieces of 40in (100cm) long string.

2 Warp up the peg loom (see page 83), making sure that the knots joining together neighboring warps are as level as possible, approximately 6in (15cm) from the bottom of the strings.

3 Cut your four fabrics into long strips (see page 11). As the pegs were spaced quite close together on my loom, I used a thin fabric and cut strips approximately 1¼in (3cm) in width. If you were working with thicker fabrics, you would need to cut your strips narrower to create a less dense pillow cover. If in doubt, cut up and try a little of the fabric first before cutting up the rest.

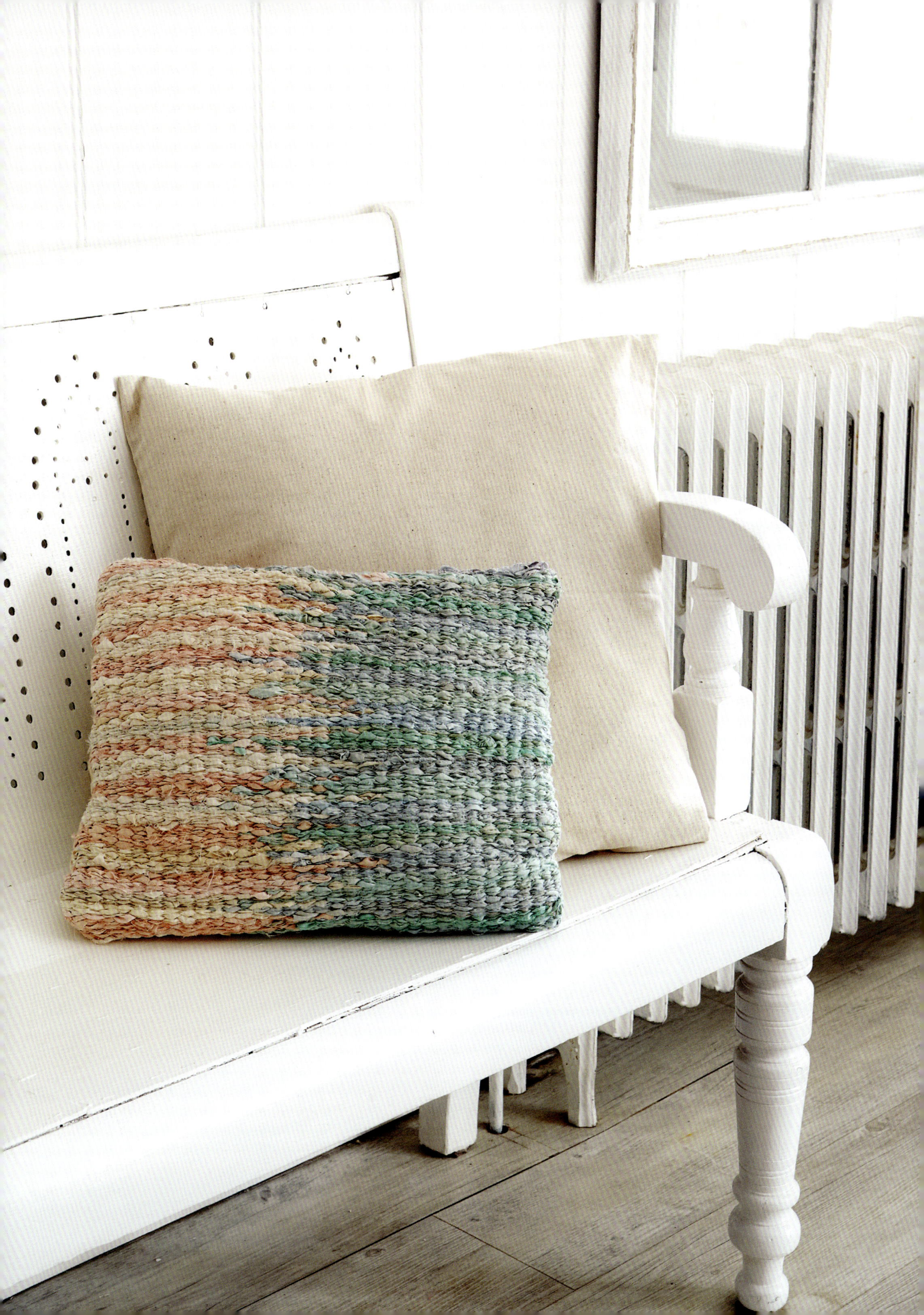

4 Stitch together the strips of each color into one long continuous strip using either a sewing machine and the diagonal seam join method on page 13 or by hand using the enclosed end method on page 14. To start off with, create a length of approximately 21 yards (20m) for each color. You will probably have to add to this later on, but it's a good start.

5 Take your first color (I used duck egg blue), leaving a 2in (5cm) tail, working left to right, weave in and out between the pegs until you reach the central peg (see technique on page 84). Take your second color (I used cream) and repeat the process, weaving from right to left. Both fabric strips should come forward into the same gap between the pegs near the center of the loom.

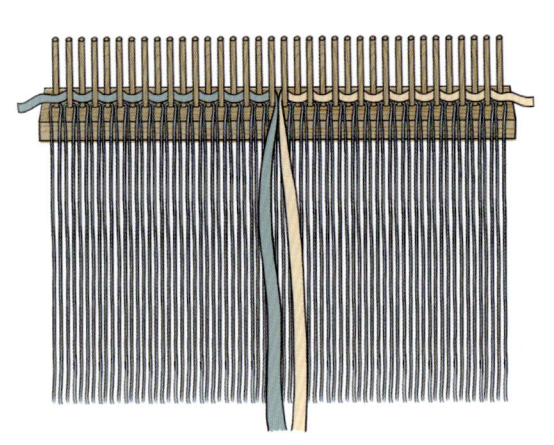

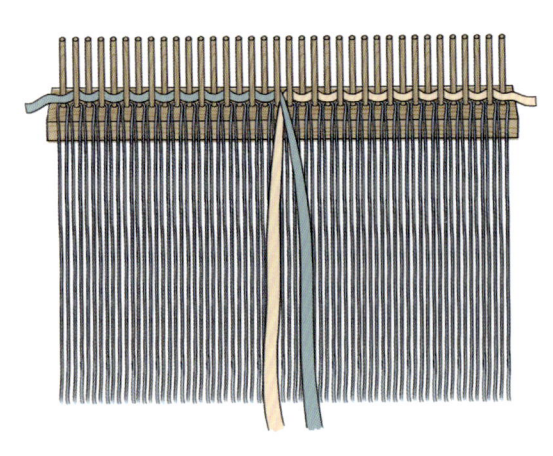

6 Pass the blue strand over and around the cream strand to twist the fabric strips together.

Elspeth's tip
You've woven incorrectly when the fabric passes around the same side of the peg as the row below it. The weaving should alternate in front and behind as you work up the peg.

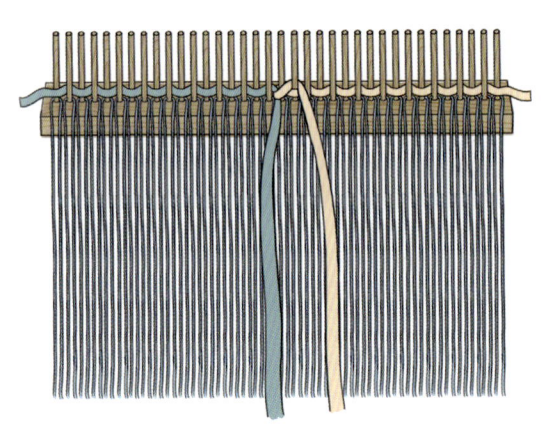

7 Continue weaving in the direction you came from with both fabric strips.

8 Continue peg loom weaving from both sides of the loom, twisting to join the two colors in different locations across the loom to create shorter and longer drips of color. The precise location of the joins does not matter, as long as they vary. Every seven rows of weaving, I joined a strip of cream to pink and blue to green (see changing color technique on page 84). If you are planning to weave in your tail ends at the end of the project, rather than catching them in as you weave, you can loosely tie together tail ends on the edge to secure them as you weave.

9 Continue to peg loom weave the pillow until it measures approximately 13¾in (35cm) in length (this is to account for the seam allowance and a bit of a buffer). Before measuring the length, even out the density of the weaving along the warp strands. The weaving furthest down the warps may be loose where it has traveled down the warps with gravity, so tighten it up. It is better to have a bit too much weaving, as opposed to too little.

100 PEG LOOM WEAVING

10 When your weaving measures approximately 13¾in (35cm) in length, push the weaving nearest the pegs down the warps to expose at least 2½in (6cm) of warp. Working with the warps from two pegs at a time, cut the warps (see tip at bottom of page) to remove them from the pegs and tie them off to the neighboring pair of warps (see page 87). Make sure the knots are spaced an even distance down the warp to create a flat edge.

11 Even up the other end of the pillow if needed. Cut the warp strands near each knot (see tip below) and re-jig them to create a level edge. You may want to tighten and re-jig the first row of weaving before doing this.

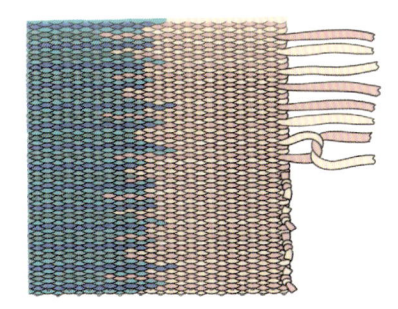

12 Choose which side of the weaving will be your front and push any imperfections through to the back. Knot any tail ends on the edge and cut them short (these will be hidden inside your pillow cover). Weave in any loose ends of fabric in the body of your weaving and weave in the warp strands carefully at the top and bottom of the pillow (see page 87). You may need to cut the warp strands shorter to do this.

13 Follow steps 8–9 on page 137 to create a simple pillow backing or create an envelope back to your pillow cover by following steps 7–13 on pages 58–59.

Elspeth's tip

Do not cut the warps all at once, as the pegs can get sucked down into the weaving. Hold firmly onto the warp strands when you do cut them.

PASTEL PAINT DRIP PILLOW 101

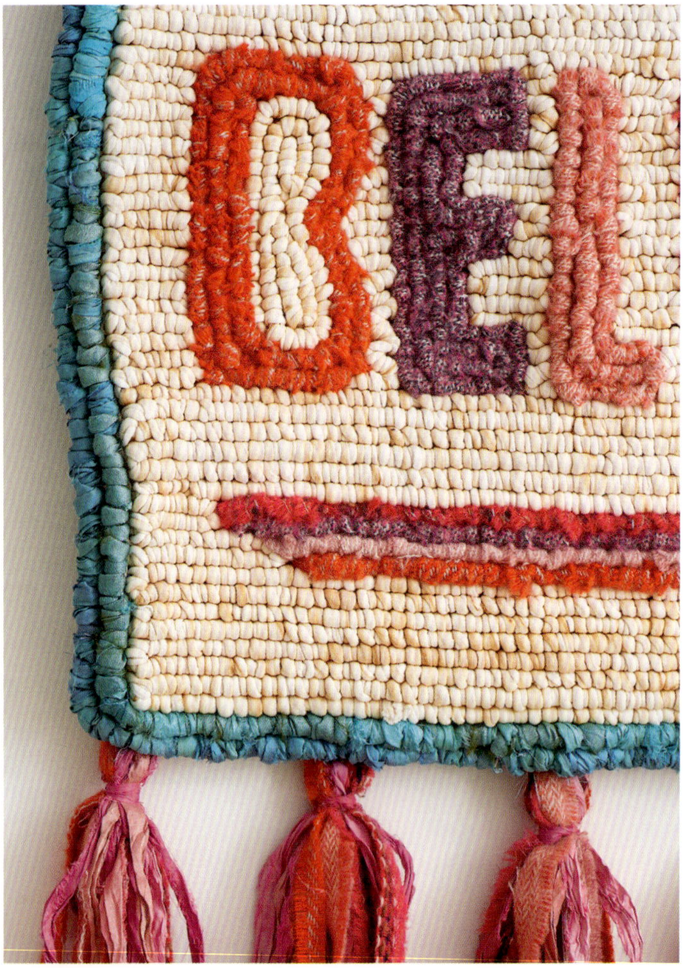
BEL
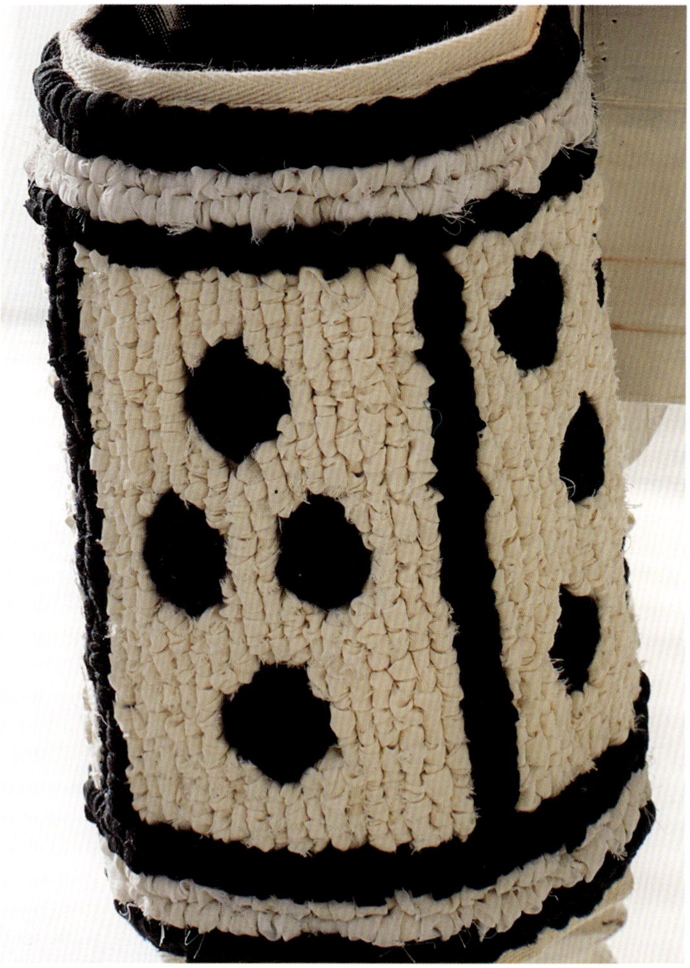
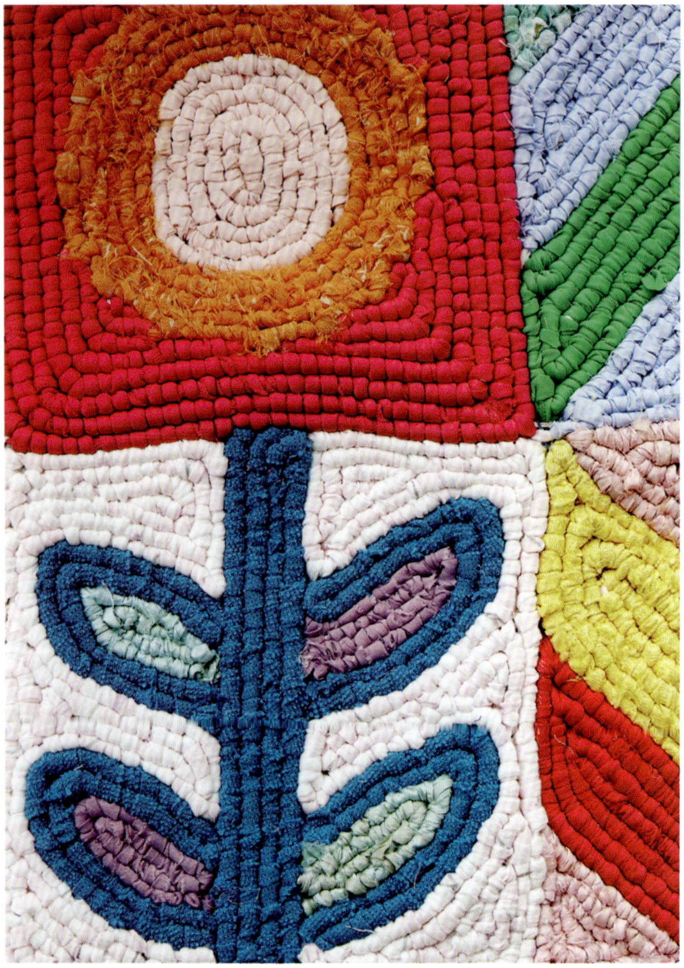
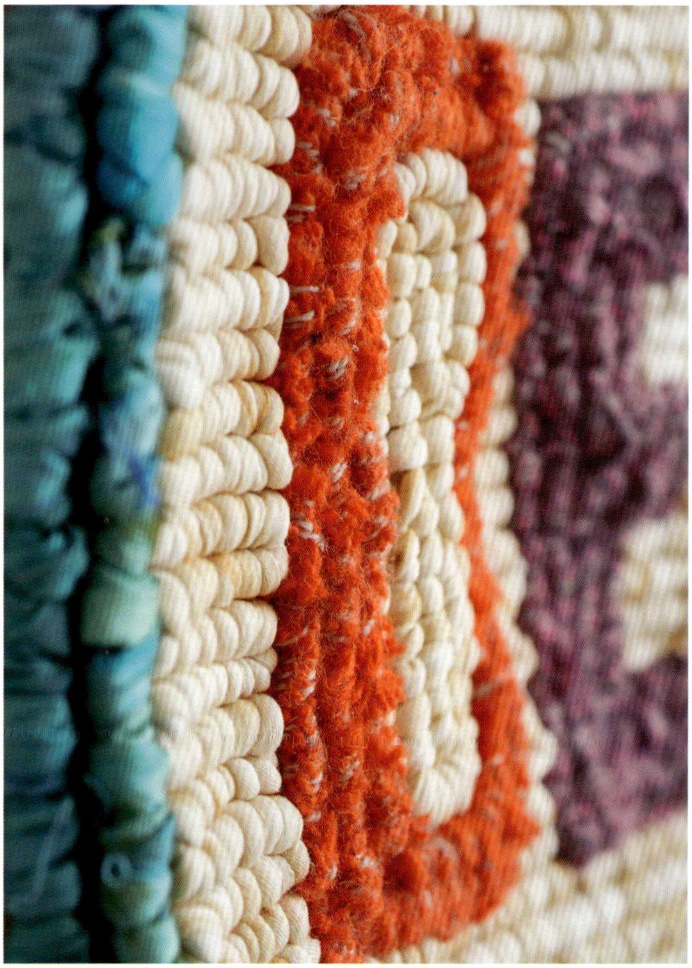

CHAPTER 5

LOCKER HOOKING

Locker hooking is definitely one of those techniques that it is very easy to get hooked on (pun intended!) Loops are threaded through an open-weave canvas before being locked in place with a fabric, cotton, or yarn core. Although some may think that this technique appears to be a lot like the loopy technique of rag rugging, it looks very different on closer inspection as the loops form little tunnels that twist and turn across the canvas. What's more, the locking process means that it's extremely difficult for loops to be pulled out of position by excited pets or daily wear and tear, which makes locker-hooked rugs very sturdy.

Locker hooking has become increasingly popular in recent years as it is mindfully repetitive and grows quickly right before your eyes. The square mesh works particularly well for linear designs and bold blocks of color.

TOOLS AND MATERIALS

Locker hook
This is a specialized tool with a deep hook at one end and an eye at the other end. Locker hooks come in different sizes, but we recommend using a ¼in (4mm) diameter locker hook, with a large eye to work with rags. Locker hooks are generally steel or aluminum. Aluminum hooks are lighter.

Other tools you may need
Fabric scissors/rotary cutter and mat
Masking tape (to prevent edges unravelling)
Darning needle (if you'd like a wrapped fabric edge)
Ruler/measuring tape
Marker pen
Needle and thread/sewing machine
1in (25mm) width cotton tape (for finishing edges)
Pins

Rug canvas
Rug canvas is a rigid square or rectangular mesh made up of vertical and horizontal fibers woven together. You can buy it in cotton or cotton/plastic blends. Generally, rug canvas comes with a pre-marked out grid. A blue line is woven into the mesh every ten threads, which makes it easier to count your "stitches" and follow patterns.

Burlap (hessian) can be used for locker hooking, but the weave needs to be relatively loose and it can be trickier to work with, so isn't recommended for beginners.

The most important part of buying rug canvas is choosing the correct gauge. This means how open or loose the weave is. To work with rags, as opposed to wool, the rug canvas should have about 3 holes per inch (HPI). However, if you'd like to build more detail into a design, you can work with a 5HPI rug canvas and narrower strips of fabric.

Generally, rug canvas is sold cut from a roll. This means that at least two edges are cut and the remaining edges are "selvage," or machine bound. Cut edges of rug canvas will unravel a bit when you are working on a project, which is why they need to be secured using either of the two methods on pages 105–106.

Locking medium (core)
Macramé cord, strips of fabric, twine, or t-shirt yarn can be used as the "locking medium" or "core" to hold your loops in position. However, it is quicker and easier to use a long, smooth continuous strand that can be cut into approximately 79in (2m) lengths. Any longer and the strand is prone to getting tangled and takes too much time to pull through the loops.

When you want your loops to be taller than ¼in (0.5cm) (for a thicker rug), use a thicker core like t-shirt yarn, whereas with shorter loops (as in the Domino Thread Catcher on page 112) use ⅛in (3mm) macramé cord or yarn. If in doubt, try it out first, as the locker hooking can always be pulled out without damaging the canvas.

Whatever you use, the locking medium must be strong, so it doesn't break and thin enough to pass through the eye of your locker hook. If you plan to join together fabric strips to make the core, the joins must be stitched and smooth, so they do not catch as you thread through the loops. The locking medium should be completely covered by your loops of fabric, so the color doesn't matter too much, but given a choice, try to use a color that doesn't stand out too much against the colors in your design, just in case it isn't covered as well as you'd hoped.

Fabrics or pre-cut fabric strips
As a form of rag rugging, locker hooking can be done using most old clothing and fabric. However, it is easiest to do with long, continuous strips, so short strips of fabric will need to be joined together using any of the techniques on pages 13–14. You can do this as you work or all together at the start before you begin locker hooking. If you do not mind about the pattern, you can stitch together one long length of different colored strips, which will self-pattern as you work. If you want to save time, you can work with sari silk ribbon, t-shirt yarn, or even very chunky wool, all of which come in one long strip. You should balance out different weights of fabric by cutting your strips wider or narrower as otherwise the rug canvas will not lie flat. As a general rule of thumb, you should cut fabric around three times the width of each small square on the canvas. However, if your fabric is particularly thick, cut one square smaller, and for thinner fabric, cut one square wider. Remember, the texture of the fabric will show up in your piece, so fabrics that fray will look more distressed, particularly if you have torn your strips, as opposed to cutting them. Plain fabrics will stand out strongly (as in the Patchwork Rug on page 109), whereas patterned fabrics will look more dappled.

TECHNIQUES

PREPPING YOUR RUG CANVAS

Once you've decided on a design and have sketched it onto the rug canvas, choose one of the two methods below to secure the edges of your rug canvas. You can choose to create a wrapped fabric border or simple folded over edge. Below are the steps for both methods.

Wrapped fabric border

1 Sketch your design on to the rug canvas, leaving either a margin of 3 empty holes around each edge for a thin border or 4 empty holes for a wider border. Cut the canvas to size, including the margin.

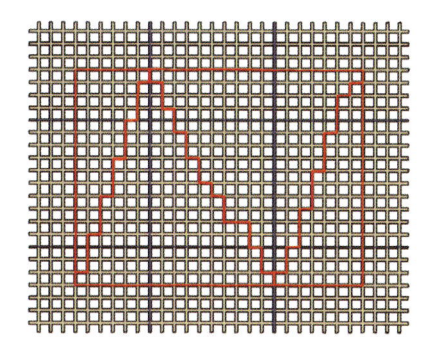

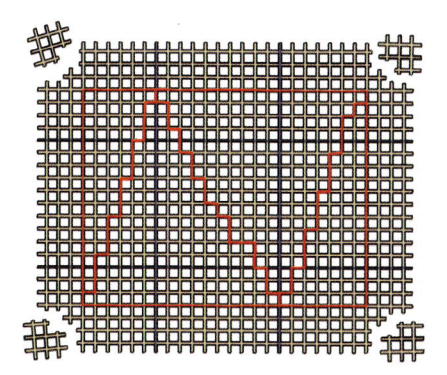

2 Cut away the corner squares to make them less bulky when folded.

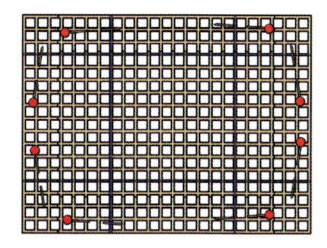

3 Fold two squares of the border to the underside of the rug canvas, making sure to align the squares one on top of each other. Pin each edge in position, making sure to pin through the cross sections of the threads so the pins don't slip through. Depending on whether you left 3 or 4 empty holes on each edge, you will be left with either one row of empty holes, or two.

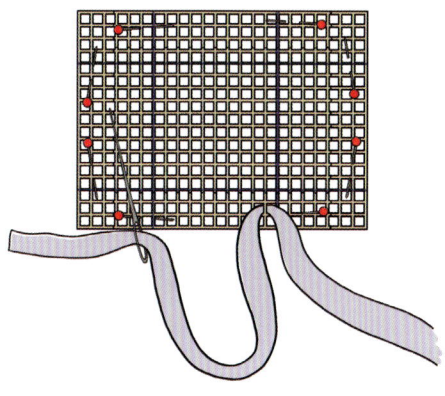

4 Thread a long strip of fabric through the eye of a darning needle (I like to use approximately 39in/1m long pieces, as longer strips fray a lot as you work) and whip stitch around the edge in either the second row of holes for a thin border or third row for a wider border. I like to start halfway up an edge and leave a 1½in (4cm) tail, which I catch inside the loops of the whip stitch as I work.

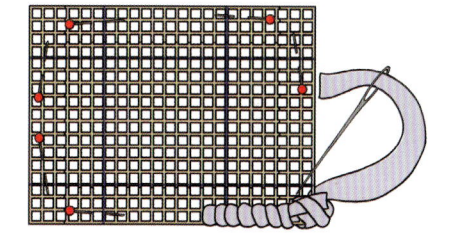

5 For the cleanest look, adjust the fabric loops to overlap each other before tightening them and look on the front to make sure all the canvas is covered fully. You will need to pass through the squares at the corners a few times to completely cover them.

Elspeth's tip

Put paper underneath the rug canvas when you are sketching out your design so that the worktop is not marked.

6 When you reach the end of a strip, pass the darning needle through a few of the previous loops and trim off the excess strip. Start a new strip and repeat steps 4 and 5 until you have completely covered the raw edge of the rug canvas.

Folded over edge border

I prefer to complete this border at the end of the project, rather than at the beginning, but you still need to follow steps 1 and 2 before starting to locker hook your design!

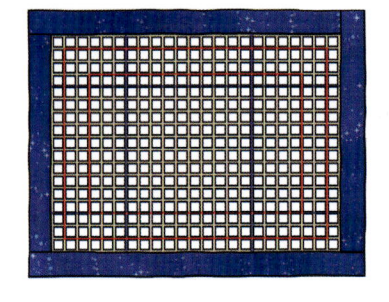

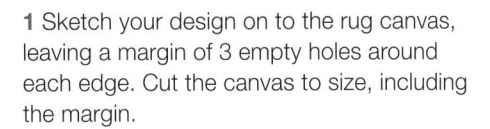

1 Sketch your design on to the rug canvas, leaving a margin of 3 empty holes around each edge. Cut the canvas to size, including the margin.

2 Masking tape the raw edge of your rug canvas to protect it as you work. You will need a fairly sturdy tape for this.

3 Once your design is fully locker hooked, remove the masking tape and cut away the corner squares to make them less bulky when folded.

4 Fold each raw edge of the rug canvas to the underside and pin 1in (25mm) cotton tape just inside the locker hooked edge to hide the rug canvas fully. Pin through the cross sections to prevent your pins slipping. Miter the corners of the cotton tape and fold the raw edge of the cotton tape under to prevent raveling and give a cleaner appearance.

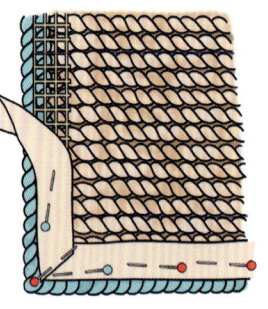

5 Hand stitch the outer then inner edges of the cotton tape to the rug canvas. It does not matter if you stitch through the loops on the back of the locker hooking as this will not show from the front. Stitch through crosses of the rug canvas itself to make things even more secure. Color match your thread for a more professional look.

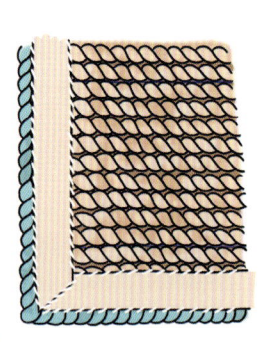

HOW TO LOCKER HOOK

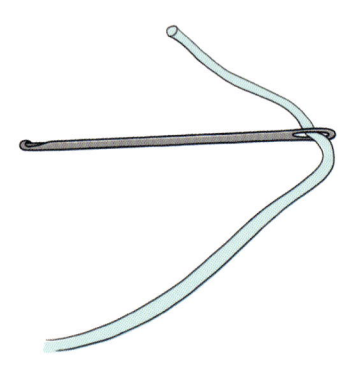

1 Choose your "locking medium" or "core" (blue in the illustrations) and cut a length of approximately 79in (2m). Any longer and the strand becomes harder to pull through the loops and prone to knots. Thread the locking medium through the eye of the locker hook.

2 Cut your long fabric strips using any of the methods on page 11. As a general rule of thumb, you should cut fabric around three times the width of each small square on the canvas. However, if your fabric is particularly thick, cut one square smaller, and for thinner fabric, cut one square wider. If you are planning to locker hook a large area in one color, it pays to join your strips together into one long one before you begin. Use any of the methods on pages 13–14.

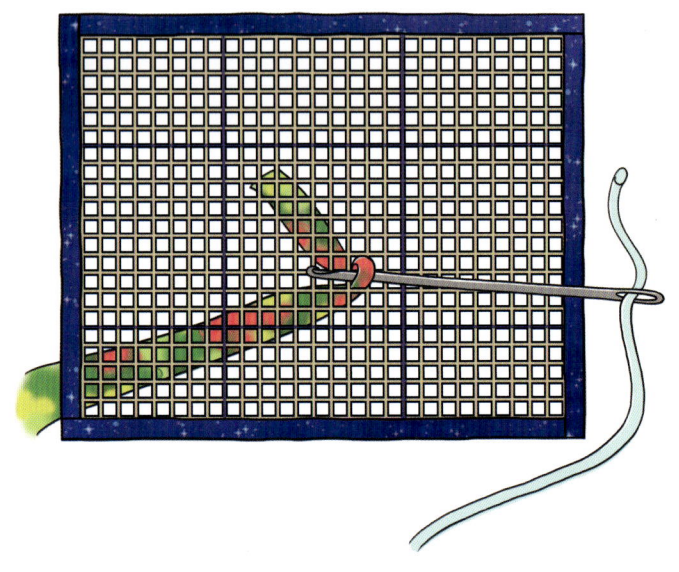

3 Choose where on the rug canvas you would like to begin and from the front of the rug canvas use the hook to bring a loop of fabric through from the underside of the rug canvas to the top. Adjust the loop to the size you would like and keep it on the neck of the locker hook. A good height for your loops is approximately ¼in (0.5cm). There should be at least a 2in (5cm) tail of fabric.

106 LOCKER HOOKING

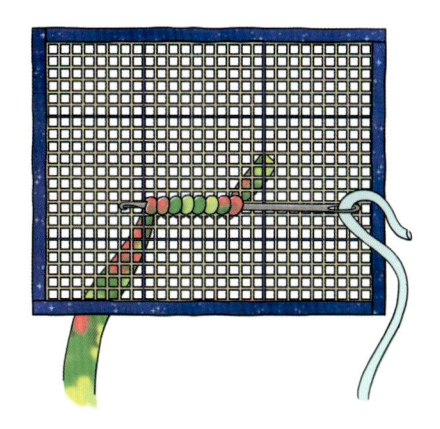

4 Move to a neighboring hole and repeat step 3. Try to keep your next loop approximately the same height as before. Continue hooking one loop after another in adjoining holes in whichever direction the design dictates, catching the loops on to the neck of the locker hook.

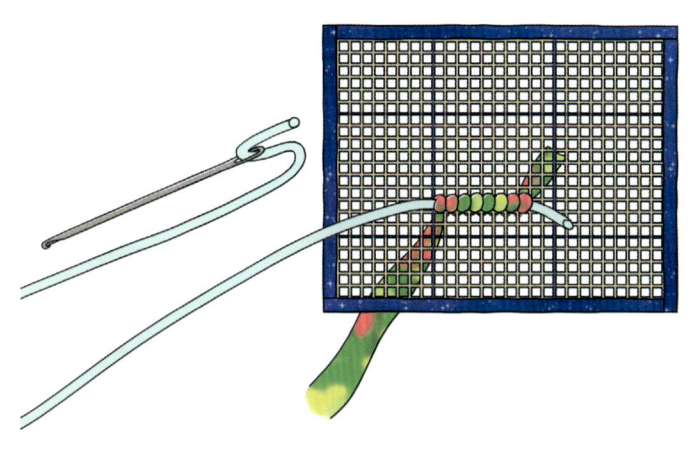

Elspeth's tip

If you can see your locking medium between your loops, cut your strips wider to cover it fully. You can even locker hook with multiple strands of thin fabric at once when you get more confident. This is a good way of using up finer yarns.

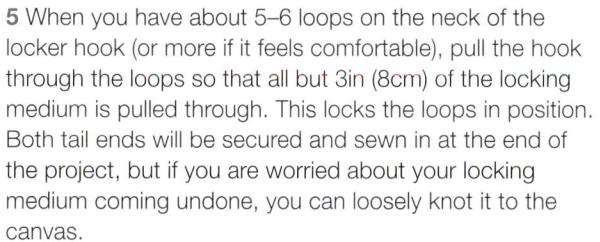

5 When you have about 5–6 loops on the neck of the locker hook (or more if it feels comfortable), pull the hook through the loops so that all but 3in (8cm) of the locking medium is pulled through. This locks the loops in position. Both tail ends will be secured and sewn in at the end of the project, but if you are worried about your locking medium coming undone, you can loosely knot it to the canvas.

6 Repeat steps 4 and 5 to continue this method. You can move in any direction you please (up, down, left, right, diagonal), as long as you work into neighboring holes. When you run out of locking medium, knot pieces together if you are working with a thin strand or leave a 3in (8cm) tail and start again as if you're starting from scratch.

Joining strips

When you want to change color, trim your fabric strip to leave at least a 2in (5cm) tail on the underside of your work and start a new fabric strip as in step 3. There is no need to cut off the locking medium if you are continuing in the same area of the rug canvas.

Sewing in your ends

When the rug canvas is fully locker hooked, there will be fabric tails through to the underside of the canvas and locking medium strands through to the front. If the back of your project does not have to be particularly flat and will not be on show (as in the "Ciao Bella" Wall Hanging on page 117), the quickest way to secure these ends is to thread the locking medium strands through to the underside of the rug canvas (making sure to pass through a neighboring hole so as not to undo your first loop), before tying them off to the fabric strip tails in a knot. Sometimes I dab a bit of glue on the knot to make it even more secure.

However, these knots are not ideal and would be uncomfortable to walk on, so below is the more professional way of securing these ends which gives a clean back and front to your piece.

1 Use the locker hook, latch hook, or a darning needle to bring up all your fabric strip ends from the underside of the rug canvas to the front. You will need to come through a neighboring hole (not the one the fabric strip starts in) to avoid undoing the first loop in the chain.

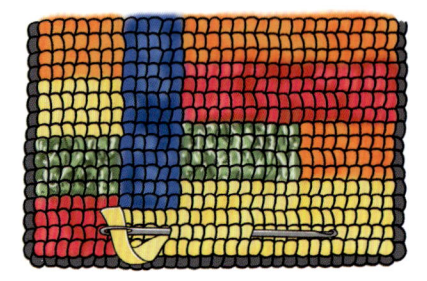

2 Carefully pass the locker hook back through at least four loops so the eye is nearest the fabric strip tail. Thread the fabric strip through the eye of the locker hook and pull it through the four loops. Trim the end off. Repeat the process with all your fabric strips and locking medium ends.

Locker Hooking Design Tips

The easiest way to transfer designs to the rug canvas is to print or draw out your design, go over it with a dark marker pen, then place it under the rug canvas to trace on to the mesh. Sometimes designs don't show up very well, particularly on the blue strands, so you may want to use different colored pens or go over a line more than once.

With the locker hooking technique, each "stitch" generally covers one square of the canvas. This means that locker hooking lends itself very well to linear designs involving straight lines and angles. When locker hooking designs involve circles and curves, you may need to locker hook into the same hole twice—when you come back to locker hook the next row—as this ensures that no gaps will show in your piece.

With locker hooking, you will always see the direction in which the piece has been rag rugged, so bear that in mind when you are filling in backgrounds or shapes and make it part of the design.

It is more time-consuming to change colors in specific places on the rug canvas in locker hooking, so if you are looking to create a very detailed design with lots of color changes, you may prefer the loopy technique (pages 36–41).

Locker hooking looks best when you keep your loops consistent in height and when the locking medium is fully covered, so make sure your fabrics strips are cut the correct width to make this easier.

Patchwork Rug

This rug was a lot of fun to make as each separate square felt like a smaller project in itself. The way in which all the squares build up together to form a final colorful piece is what made me think of beautiful patchworks, hence the name. There's so much scope to play around with this design, swapping out squares, mixing up colors, and changing directions.

You will need

40 x 40in (101 x 101cm) piece of 3HPI rug canvas.

Marker pen

Scrap paper/newspaper

Masking tape

Fabric/rag rug scissors

Fabric/rags (I used scraps of various fabrics I had to hand)

Locker hook

Approximately 5yd (4.5m) of 1in (25mm) width cotton tape

Needle and thread

Darning needle (optional)

Elspeth's tip

Designs like this work brilliantly for locker hooking as the rug canvas that we work on already has a grid marked out. This makes measuring out and sketching designs nice and easy. Build the design up one square and row at a time, so you can choose colors that work with the neighboring squares.

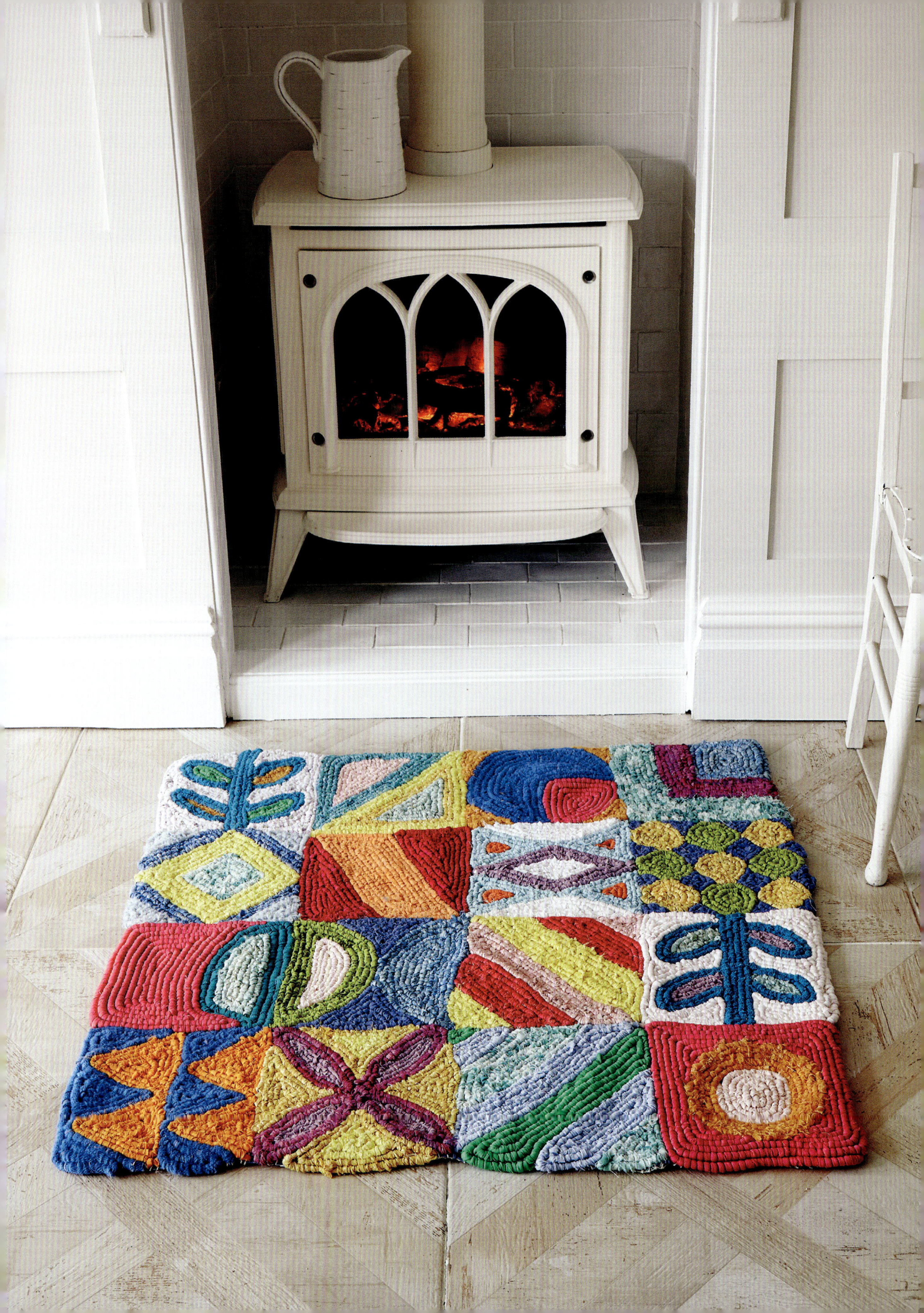

1 Cut out a 40 x 40in (101 x 101cm) piece of rug canvas. If you have selvage edges on the rug canvas, these can be kept for one or two edges. Masking tape any non-selvage edges (see page 106).

2 Using the dark blue grid lines as a guide if you have them, sketch out a 36in (92cm) square. This will be the size of your rug. Divide the square up into sixteen 9 x 9in (23cm x 23cm) squares. There should be an allowance of approximately 2in (5cm) around each side of the 36in (92cm) square to protect your rug canvas as you work. Larger projects get more wear and tear on the edges as they take longer to complete so this extra margin is a precautionary measure.

Elspeth's tip

Sketched lines don't always show up very well against the dark blue lines of the rug canvas, so sometimes I use thin washi tape to mark out areas before sketching my design on. These are only a temporary aid as they do come unstuck.

3 Sketch the individual designs into each of the sixteen squares using the design template, left. I sketched around different sized plates and jam jars for the circular elements of the design. Make sure to put scrap paper or newspaper underneath when you do this to prevent marking your floors or worksurface. You can play around with the order or orientation of each of the designs for variety. Use the grid to help space the designs into the squares.

4 Cut your first fabric into ¾–1¼in (2–3cm) wide strips that are as long as possible. Remember to cut thicker fabrics narrower and thinner fabrics wider. Locker hook each square one by one, working one row at a time. With most of the design elements in this rug, I outlined the shape first before filling in. Remember, you can locker hook diagonally across the weave.

Elspeth's tip

Locker hook with two different fabrics into the same hole to cover joins and gaps if necessary. I often did this where the corners of the different squares met.

5 Sew in all the visible tails using the technique shown on page 108. This involves pulling all your fabric strip ends through to the front and passing them through at least four loops to secure them. The same method is used for the locking medium strands left on the front of the piece.

6 Once your canvas is fully covered in locker hooking and your tails are sewn in, follow the steps for a folded over edge border on page 106 to secure your rug canvas border to the underside of the design. Or follow the steps on page 105 to create a fabric wrapped border for a slightly different look. You may need to trim away a couple of rows of the empty rug canvas to reduce bulk before doing either of these methods.

Domino Thread Catcher

A lovely Ragged Life customer called El sent me a handmade thread catcher in the post a couple of years back and I can't even begin to tell you how incredibly useful it has been, particularly during the making of this book. Whenever I'm crafting, I hang the thread catcher over the edge of the table to tidy away small fabric offcuts, loose threads and general crafty clutter. Plus, the weighted pin cushion on top is excellent for keeping pins and needles at the ready when you're completing sewing projects. I think that every crafter needs one of these thread catchers in their life!

You will need

18 x 10½in (45.5x 26.5cm) piece of 5HPI rug canvas.

30 x 20in (76 x 51cm) cotton lining fabric

Marker pen

Fabric scissors/rotary cutter and mat

Fabric/rags in shades of black and white, I used 1 t-shirt/shirt of each

Locker hook

Approximately 33yd (30m) of yarn or string for the locking medium

Tape measure/ruler

36in (91.5cm) length of 1in (25mm) white cotton tape

Needle and thread

Sewing machine

Iron

Rice, sand or crushed walnut shells, to fill

Darning needle (optional)

1 Iron the lining fabric and cut out a 10 x 3½in (25 x 9cm) piece of fabric for the strap and a 9 x 4½in (23 x 11.5cm) piece of fabric for the pin cushion. Leave enough fabric to cut out a 16 x 10in (40.5 x 25.5cm) piece of fabric for the lining in step 16.

2 Create the hanging strap that attaches the pin cushion to the thread catcher. Right sides facing, fold the strap fabric in half lengthways, so your fabric measures 5 x 3½in (12.5 x 9cm). Stitch down both 5in (12.5cm) edges, creating a ¼in (0.5cm) seam. Leave the short edge open.

3 Turn the strap right sides out and carefully push the corners out (the locker hook works well for this).

Elspeth's design tip

Making 3D projects is slightly harder than flat ones, so I recommend choosing a fairly simple design with few color changes while you are getting used to the locker hooking technique.

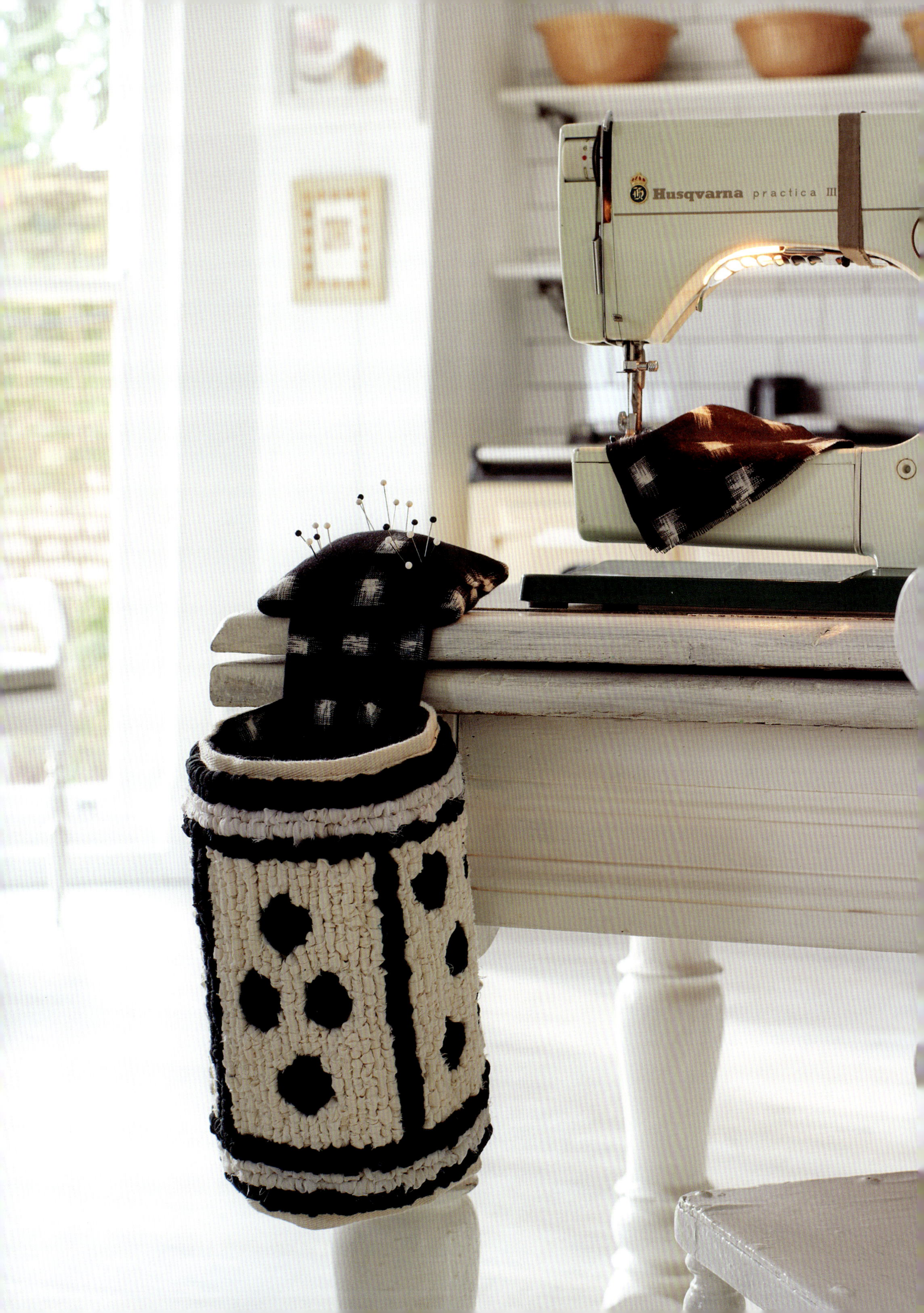
Husqvarna practica III

4 Position the strap on the right side of the pincushion fabric as illustrated. B is the folded end of the strap and A is the open end. Fold the pin cushion fabric in half right sides facing to enclose the strap. It should measure 4½ x 4½in (11.5 x 11.5cm). Adjust the position of the strap so it is centralized then fold the folded edge of the strap (B) inward to prevent it getting caught in the stitching coming up next. Pin all the layers together and stitch ¼in (0.5cm) in from the top and bottom edges and down ½in on the top and bottom of the right edge, leaving an opening, so you can turn your pincushion right sides out to fill it.

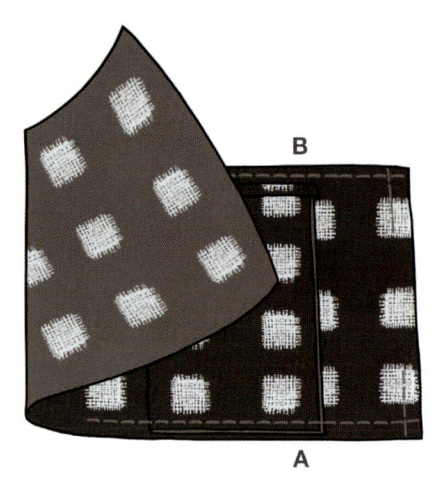

IMPORTANT: Only catch the non-folded short edge (A) of the strap fabric in the stitching. Do NOT catch the folded end of the strap (B), as this will create a bracelet.

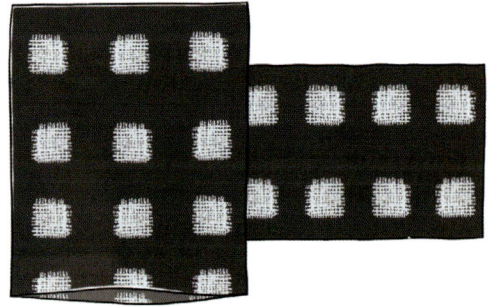

5 Turn your pincushion right sides out, so it looks like the diagram, left. Press with an iron.

6 Next fill your pincushion with either rice, sand, or crushed walnut shells.

7 Fold in the raw edges of the opening and stitch them together to close up the pincushion. Set it aside.

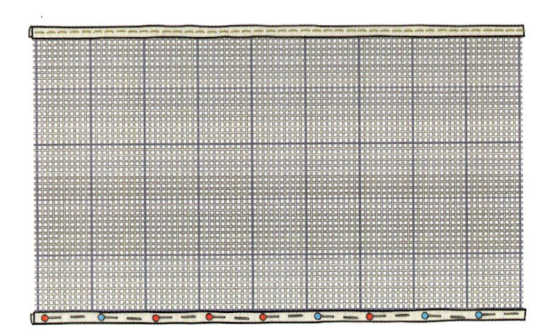

8 Cut out a piece of rug canvas measuring 18 x 10½in (45.5x 26.5cm), you should have 53 x 90 small holes. Centralize the larger blue squares to make counting easier. Cut two 18in (45.5cm) lengths of 1in (25mm) width cotton tape. Fold the first piece of cotton tape in half over the 18in (45.5cm) edge of the rug canvas, pin, then stitch in place on the sewing machine. Repeat with the other length of cotton tape on the other long edge.

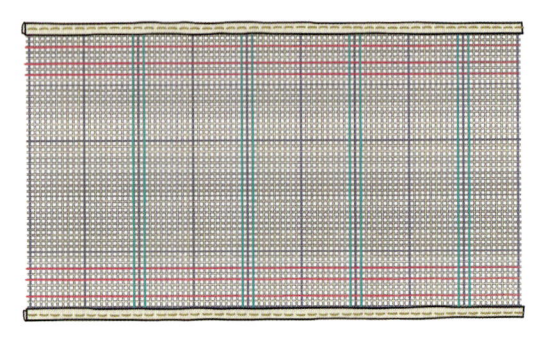

9 Sketch the grid lines for the domino design onto the rug canvas as follows. Draw three horizontal lines at the top of the canvas, the first is two squares down from the cotton tape, the second is three squares down from the first line, and the third is two squares down from the second line. Do the same at the bottom of the canvas. Then draw four pairs of vertical lines either side of the blue pre-marked grid lines, to create four sections that are 18 holes wide.

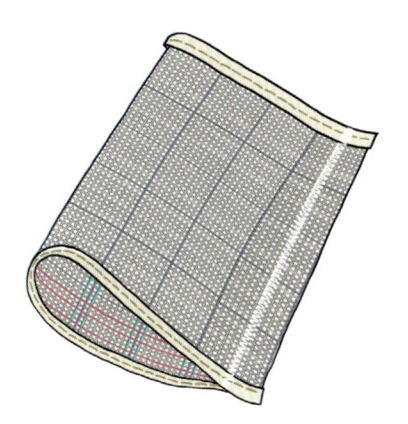

10 Fold the rug canvas in half widthways, with the drawn design on the inside of the fold. Pin the 10½in (26.5cm) edges together so that they overlap by four small squares. Use a wide, but short zig zag to stitch them together securely. You may need to stitch over the same area twice.

11 Turn the tube inside out so that the seam is hidden on the inside.

12 Sketch domino spots in the rectangular panels, leaving a margin of at least three holes, approximately ½in (1.5cm) around each edge of the rectangle, so the black elements in the design do not blur together.

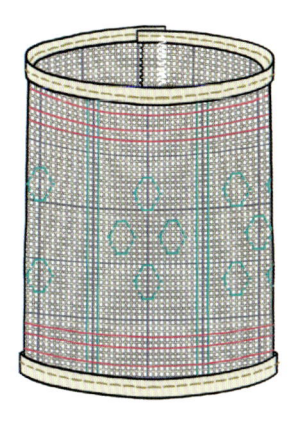

13 Cut your black and white fabric into ½in (1.5cm) wide strips that are as long as possible using any of the methods on page 11. Starting with the horizontal lines, locker hook (see page 106) the vertical and horizontal lines you sketched onto the thread catcher as illustrated. You will need to work with one hand inside the tube.

14 Locker hook the spots in black before filling in the background in white. There is no right way to do this, but I like to work in vertical rows for the background. When you reach the seam, locker hook close by to cover it fully.

15 Sew in all the visible tails using the technique on page 108. This involves pulling all your fabric strip ends through to the front and passing them through at least four loops to secure them. The same method is used for the locking medium strands left on the front of the piece.

16 Cut and press a 16 x 10in (40.5 x 25.5cm) piece of fabric for the lining. With the wrong side of the fabric face down, fold one long edge over 1in (2.5cm) to the wrong side of the fabric and press in position.

DOMINO THREAD CATCHER 115

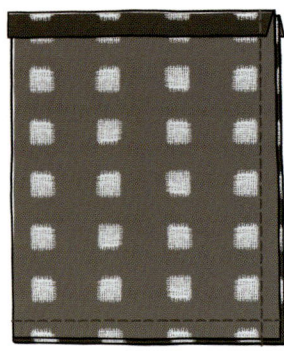

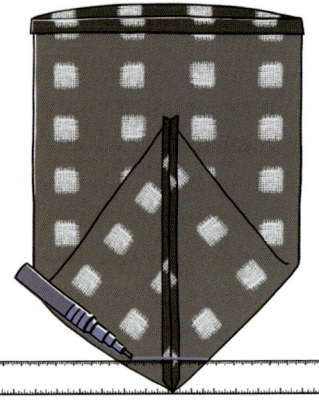

17 Fold the piece of lining fabric in half widthways right sides together with the pressed hem on the outside. Pin in position then stitch ½in (1cm) in from the long and bottom edge, leaving only the top edge with the pressed hem open.

18 Press the lining fabric as illustrated so that the base of the lining creates a square. Mark approximately 1½in (4cm) up from all four corners and draw a line straight across Sew along each line in turn, refolding as necessary. This will make the base of the thread catcher flatter and more bin like.

19 Pin the strap of the pincushion to the cotton tape at the back of the locker hooked thread catcher. Hand stitch the strap in position.

20 Pin the thread catcher lining inside of the locker hooked tube with the raw hems facing towards the back of the locker hooking. Hand sew the folded over hem to the cotton tape using color matched thread.

"Ciao Bella" Wall Hanging

My mum bought me a "Ciao" necklace for my 30th birthday and it fast became one of my favorite things to wear. It's that necklace that inspired this jolly wall hanging. However, there's no reason why you couldn't change the message to something else: "Happy Place," "Coffee Corner," a loved one's name... The sky's the limit.

You will need

3 HPI rug canvas

Scissors

Masking tape

Marker pen, I used three different colors to make the different design elements stand out better

Macramé cord/thick twine/t-shirt yarn (for the inner channel of the locker hooked loops)

Fabrics: I used a turquoise sari silk ribbon, pink, orange, and purple blanket offcuts, and cream t-shirt material

Fabric/rag rug scissors

Approximately 2¾ yd (2.5m) of 1in (25mm) width cotton tape

½ x 24in (1cm x 60cm) wooden dowel/pole for hanging

Glue (optional)

1 Cut the rug canvas so that it measures 79 x 83 squares. Stick and fold masking tape around each edge of the rug canvas to prevent the cut edges of the rug canvas from falling apart as you work. Fully cover the three squares nearest each edge to later create a secure hem. Stick multiple layers of tape if it feels loose.

2 Sketch your design onto the rug canvas. First draw a line two squares in from the masking taped hem. This area will be your border. Then, draw a line 6 squares in from your border. This shows where the first letter should start and last letter will end. Count how many squares are left between these inner lines. Accounting for a minimum of two empty squares of background between each letter, divide the remaining number of squares by the number of letters. This gives you an approximate width for each letter, although letters like "I" take up less space than "C," "A," or "O," so you can adjust accordingly. I left 11 empty rows between "CIAO" and "BELLA." I then drew 4 decorative lines 6 rows below "BELLA," the top one being the same width as the words, with the lines decreasing in length.

Elspeth's design tips

To create the cream color for the background of this wall hanging, I dyed white t-shirt material with teabags. This gave the fabric a slightly rustic, aged feel.

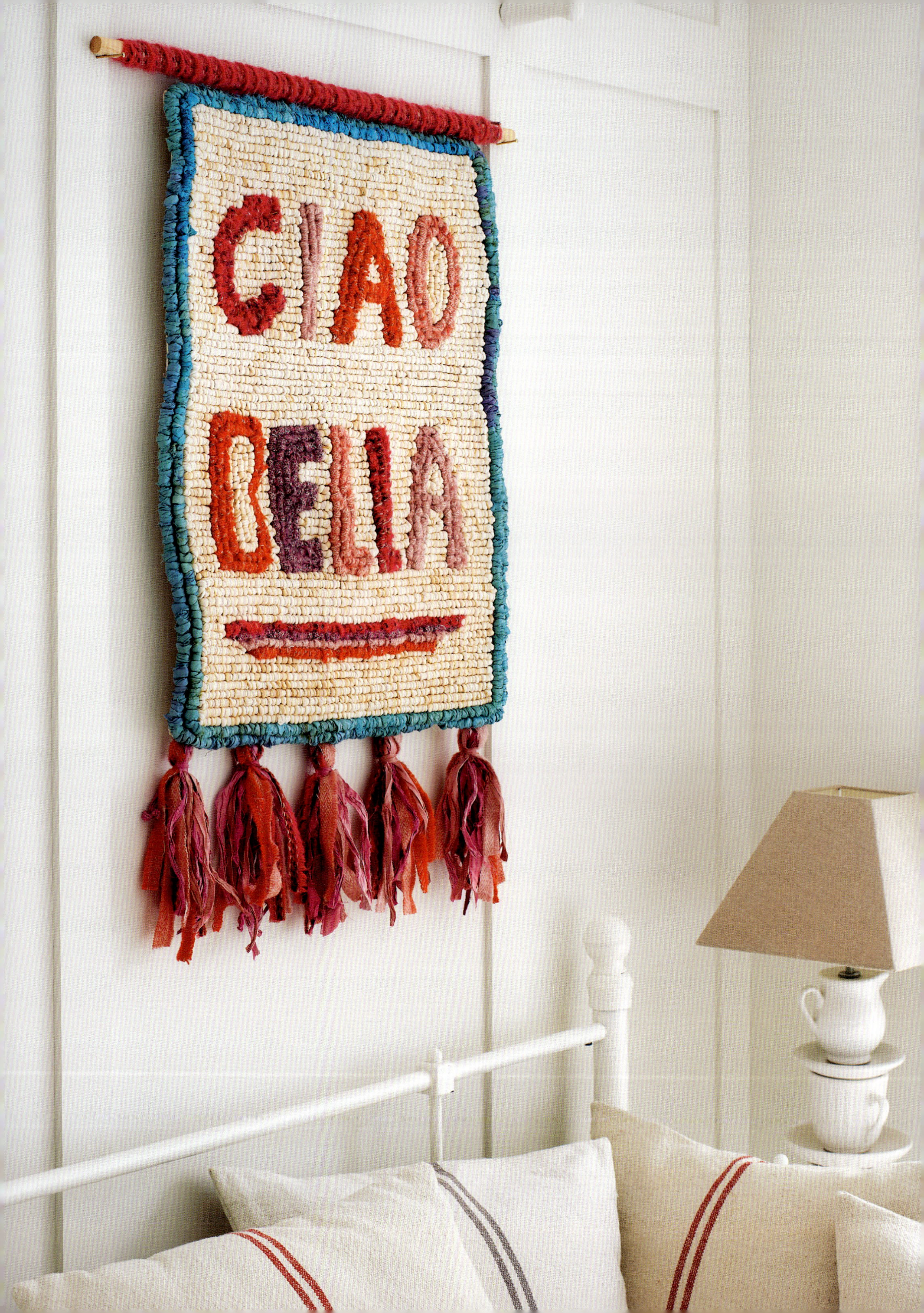
CIAO
BELLA

3 Cut your fabrics into long strips using any of the techniques on pages 11–12, then locker hook the border of the piece in turquoise fabrics, working from the outer edge inwards in concentric rectangles. Pull your locker hooked loops to approximately ⅝in (1.5cm) in height and try to keep them even.

4 Locker hook the colorful letters and lines in shades of orange, pink, and purple. You can locker hook diagonally across the canvas, so locker hook the outline of each letter before filling in from the outside inwards.

5 Fill in the background of the wall hanging with cream locker hooking. Fill the inner parts of the letters "A," "O," and "B" first before working from the bottom of the wall hanging to the top in rows. Pay extra care when turning on the edges near the border to ensure that none of the cord shows through. The background loops should be slightly shorter than the letters (approximately ½in/1cm in height) to make the design features stand out better.

6 Once the background is complete, sew in your fabric and locking medium ends (see page 108). Remove the masking tape from the edge of the rug canvas and follow the steps for a folded over edge border on page 106 to secure the edges of your wall hanging. Mitre the corners of the cotton tape and fold the raw edge of the cotton tape under to prevent fraying and give a cleaner appearance.

7 Make five fabric tassels for the bottom of the wall hanging. These look best when you mix together colors you've used for the letters in the wall hanging itself. To make five tassels, cut fifty ⅝in (1.5cm) wide strips of fabric of approximately 16in (40cm) in length.

8 Take a bundle of 10 strips to make your first tassel. Cut one of the strips in half, to measure approximately 8in (20cm). Use one of the 8in (20cm) length strips to tie together the remaining nine 16in (40cm) long strips in the center.

9 Fold one half of the strips back on themselves over the knotted center and tie the second 8in (20cm) length piece of fabric around the top of the bundle of strips to create a tassel effect. Trim the 8in (20cm) length to disguise it. Repeat steps 8 and 9 to create all five tassels.

10 Hand sew the tops of the tassels at regular intervals across the bottom of the wall hanging. I started 1½in (4cm) in from each edge and made sure that the middle tassel was properly centralized. Trim any rogue fabric pieces that aren't lying as you would want them to.

11 Wrap the wooden dowel in the fabric of your choice, using tips from coiled rag rugging on page 63 and either glue or stitch it to keep it in place. Start and finish 1¼in (3cm) from the edge of the dowel. Once the dowel is completely wrapped, hand stitch the fabric covered bottom edge of the dowel to the top of the wall hanging, making sure to centralize it properly.

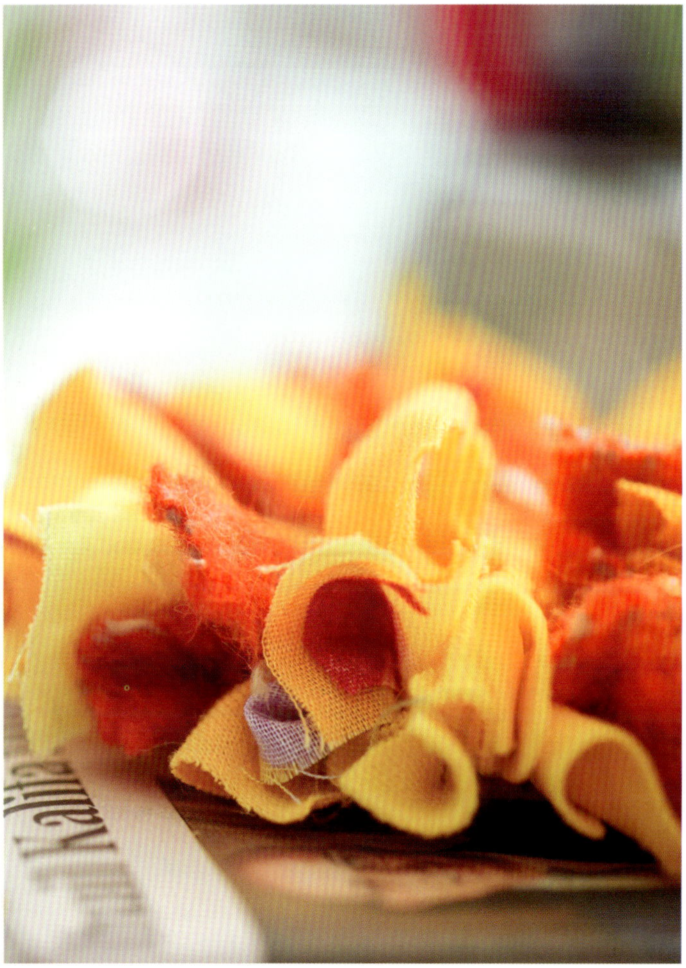
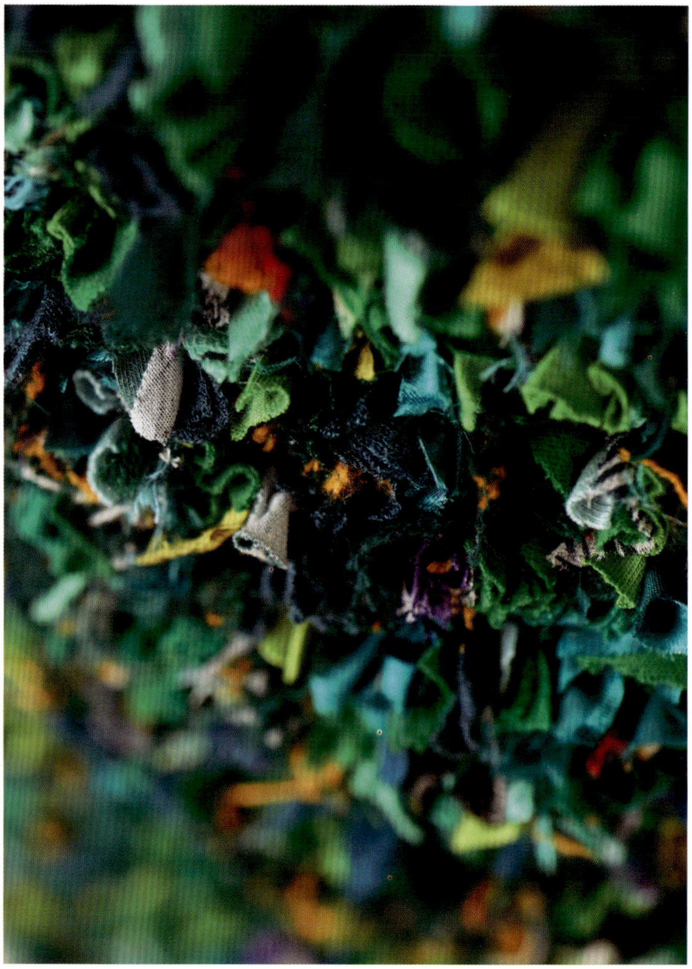
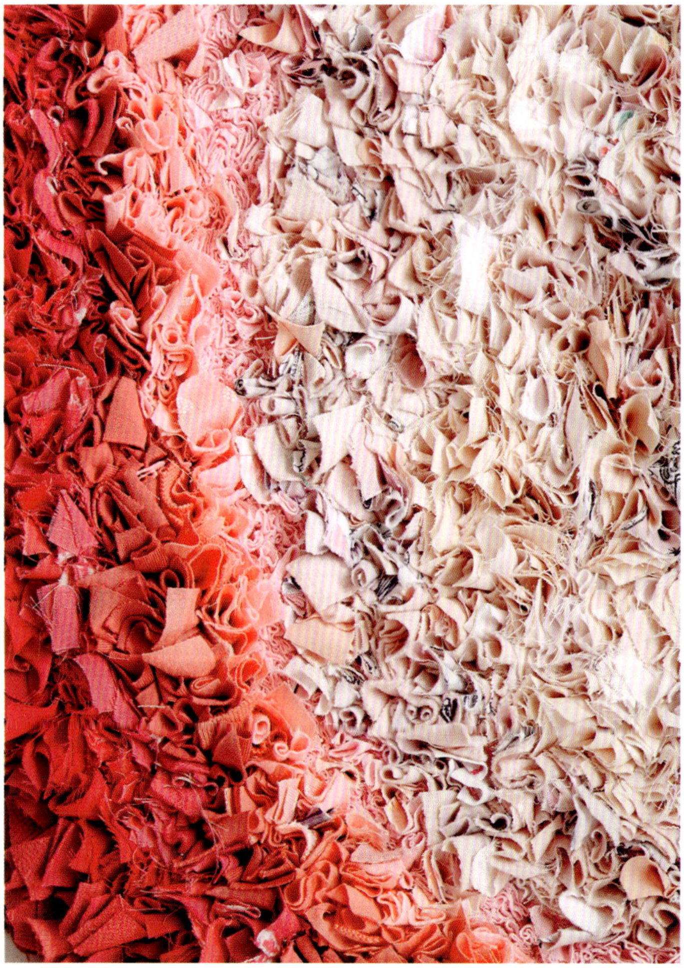
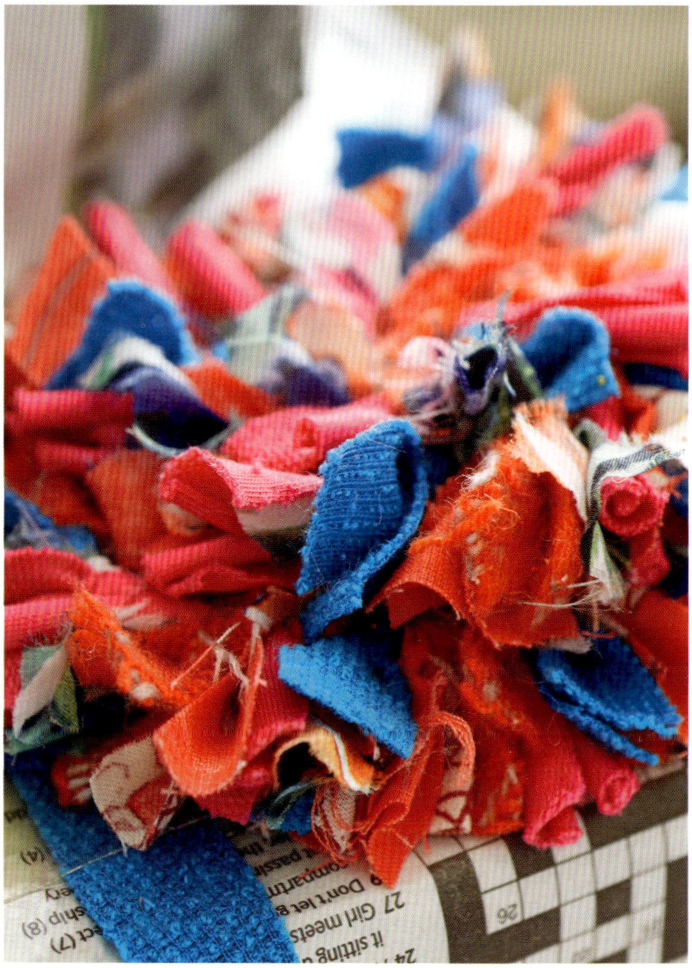

CHAPTER 6

TWO-STRING LOOM

The first and only time that I came across the Two-String Loom method of rug making, I was struck by how similar the finished rug looked to those made with the traditional shaggy method of rag rugging (pages 18–35). However, on closer inspection, the two methods couldn't be more different.

Two-String Loom rugs do not require any canvas or backing, just string and thread to hold them together. Fabric pieces are knotted one by one on to strings held in place on a basic wooden loom, then the resulting long strands are coiled and sewn together to create cushy rugs for the floor.

The Two-String Loom technique is probably one of the easiest methods of rag rug making out there. All you need to get going is a basic wooden loom, two balls of string, rags, and a needle and thread—that's it! Other than those very basic tools, you just need patience and plenty of fabric.

TOOLS AND MATERIALS

The clue's probably in the name, but to make a Two-String Loom rug, you need a two-string loom. However, the good news is that these basic wooden looms are easy to build or commission using the specs below or you can find details on where to buy one in the stockists list on page 174.

Two-string loom

A two-string loom is essentially made of two ¾in (2cm) thick planks of wood (one longer and one shorter) with wooden dowels and nails attached in specific locations. String is fed from the back of the loom and wound between nails, before being tied to the front dowel. This creates two lengths of taut string on which pieces of fabric can be knotted. You generally work with a two-string loom on your lap or on a table and the distance between the front wooden dowel and nails should be a maximum of an arm's length. If you would like to make your own loom, you can use my measurements below, but none of these have to be exact.

Other equipment you may need

Fabric scissors
Needle and thread
Glue gun

String

You will need two balls of cotton string (I use 1/16in/2mm thick) to thread up your loom. Preferably the balls of string should have a hole in the center so that they can be placed on the dowels at the back. If they do not, you can either perch them on top (see photo of my two-string loom, below) or re-wind the string around an empty toilet roll tube to fit onto the dowel. Whatever you use should be strong enough to take some tension and not be prone to breaking.

Fabric

You can use any fabric scraps on a two-string loom. However, as with many other rag rug techniques, fabrics that shed or fray when you cut into them will make more of a mess and thicker, stiffer fabrics are harder to knot around the string. The easiest fabrics to work with are soft, lightweight, and pliable. If your fabric has a right and wrong side to it, some of the wrong side of the fabric will almost always show.

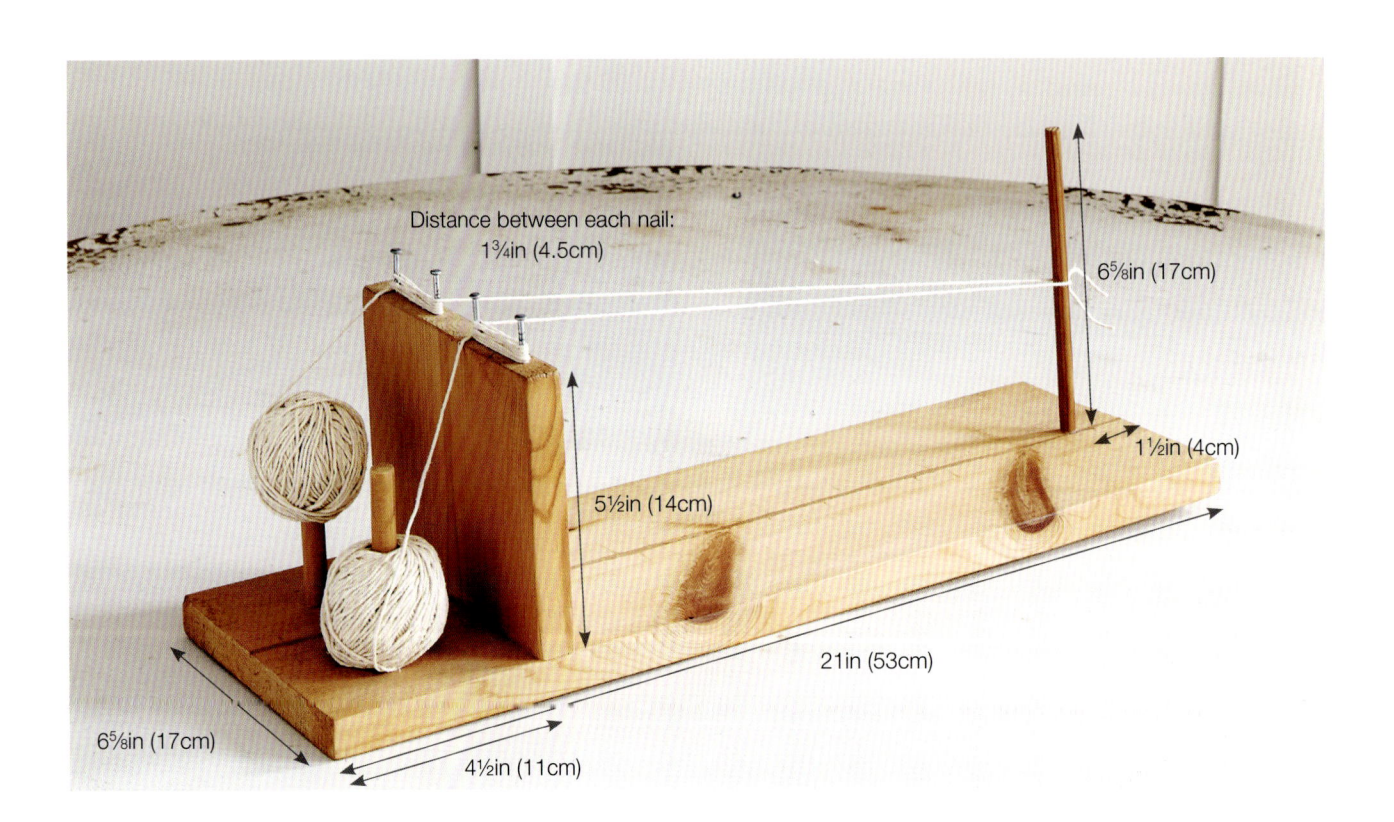

TECHNIQUES

SETTING UP THE LOOM

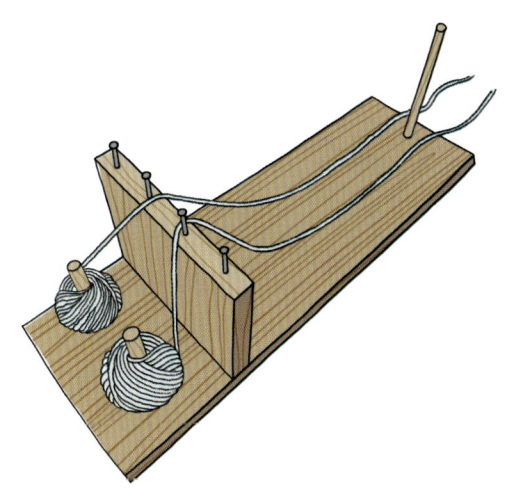

1 Place a ball of string onto each of the dowels at the back of the loom and unwind approximately 23½in (60cm) of string from each ball. This gives enough string to reach the front dowel, with about 8in (20cm) spare.

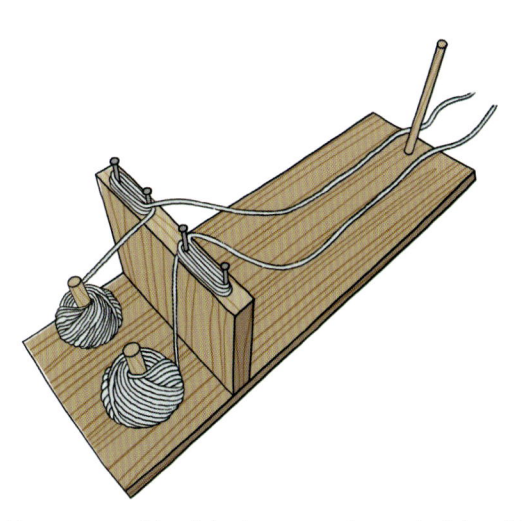

2 Working on one side of the loom at a time, wind the string around the outside of the two nails in front of the corresponding ball of string three times. The string should pass around the inner nail first and last.

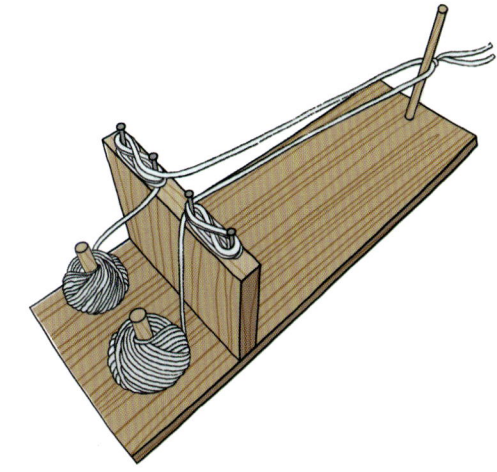

3 Wrap two figure-of-eights between each pair of nails to prevent the string from slipping. Push the wrapped string down the nails and bring the excess string to the dowel at the front of the loom. Tie the two pieces of string together in a double knot so that the string is held tightly in position. Do not trim these tail ends until the end of a project, as the extra string allows pieces of two-string loom rag rugging to be knotted together to create even longer pieces. If the string does not feel tight, pushing the knot down the dowel can make things tighter.

TECHNIQUES 123

RAG RUGGING ON A TWO-STRING LOOM

Rag rugging on a two-string loom creates a long strand of rag rugging that can be stitched or assembled in different ways. One side of the rag rugged strand will be flat, whilst the other will be shaggy in texture. Here's how it is done:

1 Cut your fabric into long, ½in (1cm) wide strips using any of the techniques on pages 11–12, then into short strips between 2–4in (5–10cm) in length. The length you cut the fabric pieces affects the shagginess of the final piece, so cut fabric strips longer for a thicker, cozier pile. You can save time cutting your pieces to a consistent length by using a rag rug gauge (see page 12).

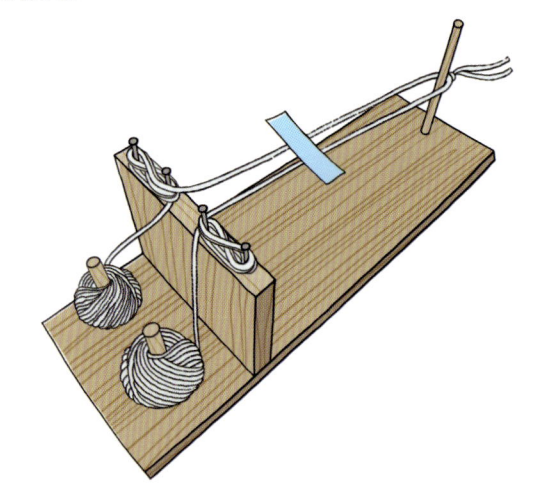

2 Place a fabric strip horizontally across both strings about halfway down the loom. If your fabric has a right and a wrong side, the wrong side should be face down, but remember, both sides will be visible in the end product.

3 Bring the two cut edges of the fabric strip up between the two-strings below the center of the strip (toward yourself and the wooden dowel).

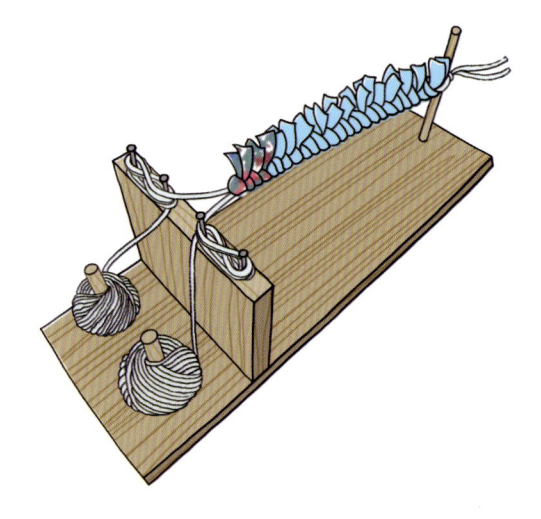

4 Pull the knotted fabric down the strings, so it is as close to the wooden dowel as possible. Once in position, pull the ends to tighten the knot.

5 Continue knotting fabric pieces up the strings until they are almost full. You can mix together different fabrics and change colors as you please.

124 TWO-STRING LOOM

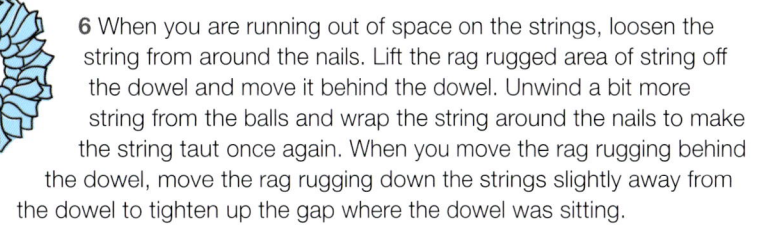

6 When you are running out of space on the strings, loosen the string from around the nails. Lift the rag rugged area of string off the dowel and move it behind the dowel. Unwind a bit more string from the balls and wrap the string around the nails to make the string taut once again. When you move the rag rugging behind the dowel, move the rag rugging down the strings slightly away from the dowel to tighten up the gap where the dowel was sitting.

7 Continue rag rugging in this way until you have created enough rag rugged string for your project or you have run out of string on one or both sides of the loom. To remove the rag rugging from the loom (to start a new section or replace a ball of string), cut the strings 4in (10cm) from your last knotted fabric piece. Take the rag rugging off the dowel and move the knotted fabric pieces down the strings to fill any gaps. Double knot the cut strings together at the end. Do not worry if your rag rugging curls a bit when you take it off the loom—this is normal.

JOINING

Joining lengths of two-string loom rag rugging together is easy. Knot together the tail ends where you began and finished your rag rugging. Trim the ends short to disguise them. The shagginess of the rag rugging will cover these joins. This allows you to rag rug larger projects in sections, rather than all one length.

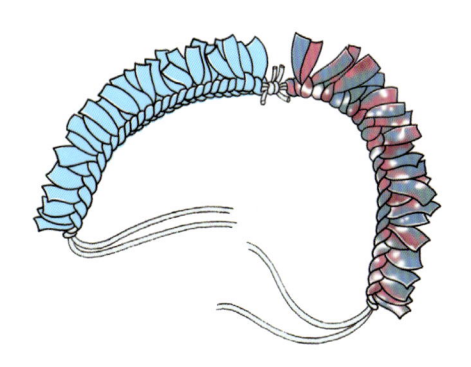

ASSEMBLING

Once you have created your rag rugged piece, you can assemble it in many ways to create a variety of different projects. Traditionally, lengths are hand sewn together to make rugs, but some projects may call for a glue gun, or maybe nothing at all (see the Christmas Tree on page 130). If you are hand sewing your project together, make sure to do so using a thick, robust thread and ensure you stitch loosely around curves to prevent your rug from curling. During assembly you will generally have to untangle the rag rugged strand so that the shaggy side all faces upwards and there are no twists. Hand sewing a rug together takes time, so make sure you do not need your table for a while before you start. Two-string loom rag rugging cannot be sewn together on a sewing machine because the stitching catches the shaggy pieces on the front. See the two-string loom projects on pages 126–131 for specific details on how to assemble various projects.

DESIGN TIPS

Two-string loom rag rugging is great for 3D projects as the strands of rag rugging can be easily wrapped around 3D objects. This technique is all about texture, which is why it works particularly well for thick, cozy rugs and for mimicking foliage.

As this technique is done using lots of small pieces of fabric, it is perfect for using up small scraps, which can be mixed together. Plain and pattered fabrics work equally well. Be careful when cutting elasticated fabrics as these will stretch when they are knotted on to the string. I prefer to cut elasticated fabrics shorter in length to account for a bit of stretch or you can cut these against the grain to reduce stretch. If in doubt, try a piece first before cutting up a whole garment. Feel free to incorporate other materials such as wool and ribbon into your two-string loom creations. Anything that can be knotted around the string can be used but do bear in mind whether you'll be walking on it or not. For a less uniform appearance, try knotting different lengths of fabric to the string.

Pink Ombré Rug

This two-string loom rag rug is the thickest and cushiest rug in the whole book. As it is sewn together by hand, it does require a bit of patience to assemble, but it is well worth the time as the resulting rug is a dream to walk on. I particularly love how the pinks gradate in color from light in the center to darker around the outside.

You will need
Two-string loom
Two balls of string
Pink fabric: I used about 25 garments
Fabric scissors
Rag rug gauge (optional)
Needle and strong thread (any color as it will not show)
Pins

1 Organize your pink fabrics in order from light to dark. Keeping each color separate, cut up your fabric into strips that are approximately ½in (1cm) in width and 3in (8cm) in length. This can be done quicker using a rag rug gauge (see page 12).

2 Set up your two-string loom as described on page 123.

3 Working from your lightest pink to your darkest pink, create approximately 65yd (60m) of rag rugging on the two-string loom (see pages 124–125). You can do this in shorter lengths that you tie together if the string is becoming too long and getting in the way (see page 125 for joining). Every time you run out of one color, change to the one shade darker.

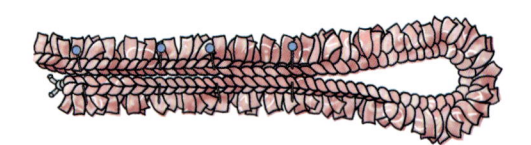

4 Once you have around 65 yards (60m) of rag rugging, you can begin assembling the rug. Measure 17¾in (45cm) from the light pink end of the rag rugging and bend the end back on itself to form a "U." Untwist the rag rugging so that the shaggy side is facing down and the flat side is facing up before pinning then stitching the edges together.

5 Continue coiling and sewing the shaggy rag rugging around this central "U," making sure to sew loosely around bends so that the rug will lie flat. Make sure to untwist the rag rugging as you go, so that the shaggy side is always facing down. Trim the tail ends of any joins in the string as you go to disguise them.

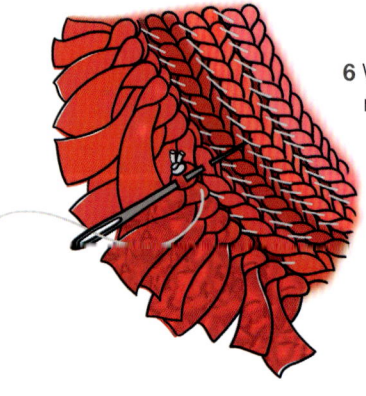

6 When you reach the end of your rag rugged string and are happy with the size of the rug, trim ends of the final knot and stitch it to the edge. The shagginess will disguise your stitching and handiwork.

Elspeth's tip
Don't be afraid to use scraps of fabric that aren't in your specific colorway. These will help to break up large blocks of one color.

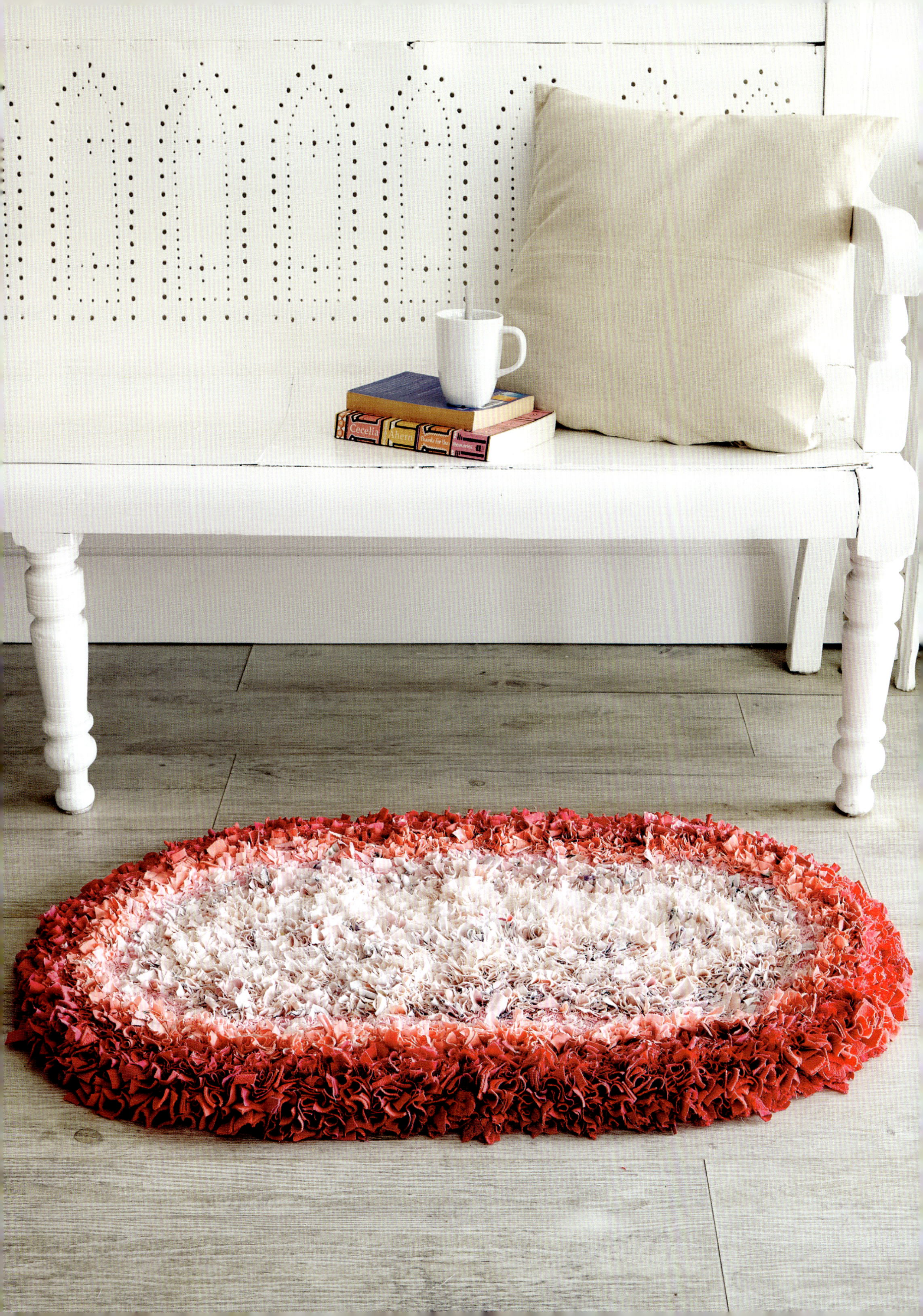
Cecelia Ahern

bride loses legal
to return to UK
Entrepreneurs
Jupiter silent on

Eco-Friendly Gift Wrap Spirals

These recycled fabric spirals are great for brightening up plain, recycled gift wrap. As well as looking great, they're so small and quick to make that you could easily rag rug a few in an evening ready to bring out when the occasion demands. What's more, the lucky recipient can re-purpose or re-use them.

You will need

Two-string loom

Two balls of string

Fabric scraps: approximately 12 x 12in (30 x 30cm) per spiral

Long strip of fabric to wrap around the gift

Fabric scissors

Glue/glue gun

1 Cut up your fabric into strips that are approximately ½in (1cm) in width and 2in (5cm) in length. As this is a small project, I like to use a variety of small scraps in each spiral.

2 Set up your two-string loom as described on page 123.

3 To make one spiral, create 13in (33cm) of rag rugging on the two-string loom (see pages 124–125) before cutting and tying it off. Trim the tail ends of string at both ends.

Elspeth's tip

Choose fabric colors that complement your gift wrap or colors that your recipient will like.

4 With the shaggy side facing outwards, coil and glue the length of rag rugging in a spiral. Do not use too much glue as this can show. If the final knot is showing, glue a piece of the rag rugging over the top to disguise the string.

5 Wrap a long strip of fabric around your gift and before tying it in place, safety pin or glue the spiral to the fabric strip. Safety pinning the spiral in position will allow the recipient to remove it and re-use it.

Christmas Tree

I've wanted to make a rag rugged Christmas tree for a long while now and the two-string loom technique gave me the perfect excuse to give it a go. I love the fact that you can re-use this tree year after year and its construction means that you can flat pack it down to store out of the way. What's more, you can use any old scraps of fabric, so don't feel like you have to go with a traditional green design—anything goes!

You will need

Two-string loom

Two balls of string

Green fabric: I used about 20 full garments

Wire Christmas tree form: these come in various sizes and are sometimes advertised for topiary

Chicken wire

Wire cutters

Elspeth's tip

Although this particular tree is 5ft (1.5m) tall, you can make smaller versions by using different sized forms or shaped chicken wire. This version took around fifty hours to make, so it is certainly not a "finish in an evening" project.

1 Cut up around five whole garments worth of fabric into strips that measure approximately 2½in (6cm) in length and ½in (1cm) in width. Try to include a variety of different greens and some odd pieces of other colors to break up the green (I used blues, whites, purples, and oranges). Mix the strips together in a bowl.

2 Set up your two-string loom as described on page 123.

3 Grabbing random pieces of fabric from the bowl indiscriminately, make approximately 11yd (10m) of rag rugging on the two-string loom (see pages 124–125). Cut and tie off the 11 yard (10m) length as described on page 125. Do not trim the tail ends of your knotted end as these will be used to attach the rag rugging to the tree.

4 Assemble your Christmas tree form if it came in pieces and carefully wrap the full length of it in chicken wire. This helps to smooth out the edges of the wire form to make the tree cylindrical, rather than squared off. If you are unable to buy a form then you can make one by shaping multiple layers of thick chicken wire. Do so carefully.

5 Tie one end of the rag rugged string to the top of the Christmas tree form and working from the top of your tree, begin to wrap the 11yd (10m) length of rag rugging around and down the form. When you reach the end of the rag rugged string, leave it hanging down to tie your next length of rag rugging to. This will give you a rough idea of how much more rag rugging you will need to make in order to fully cover the form.

Elspeth's tip

For a less uniform appearance, try knotting different lengths of fabric to the string. This would make the Christmas tree look more textured.

6 Repeat steps 1–5 until you have covered the entirety of the Christmas tree form. It helps to add new fabrics to the mixture in the bowl before you fully run out, so that you can gradually blend certain greens out and new ones in.

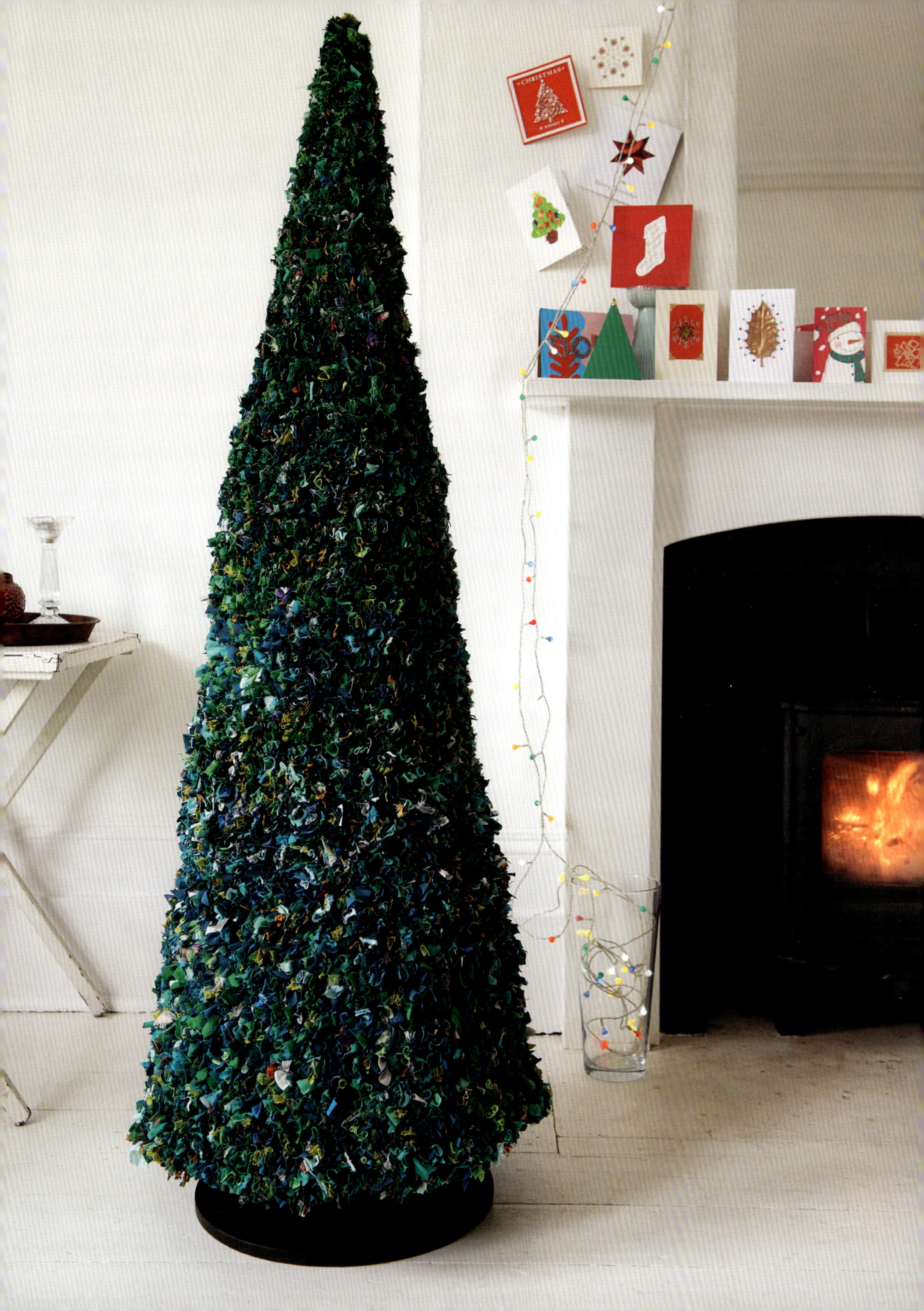
CHRISTMAS

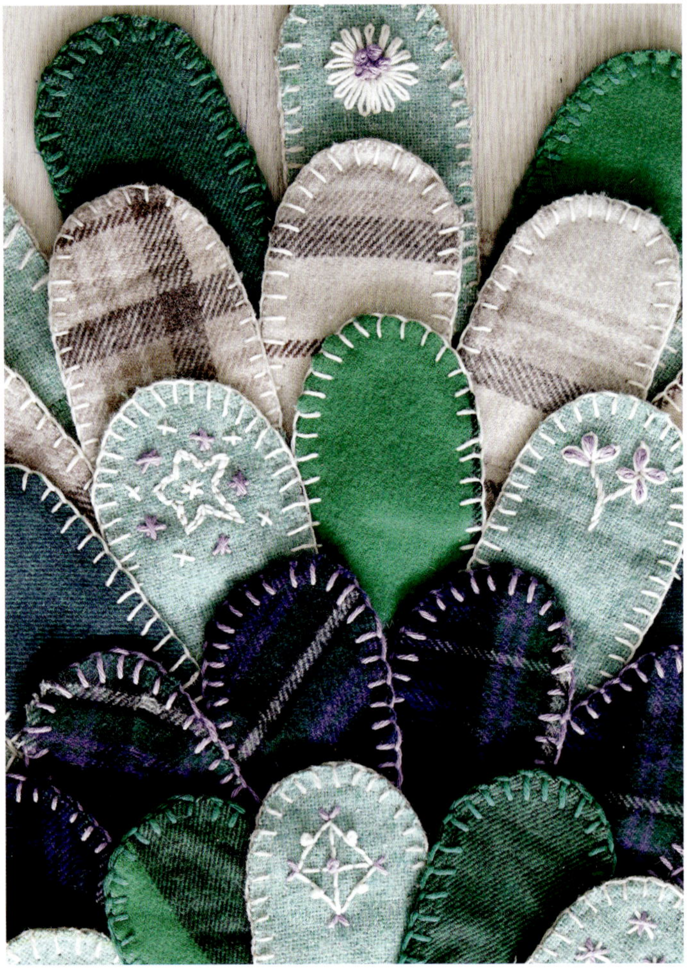
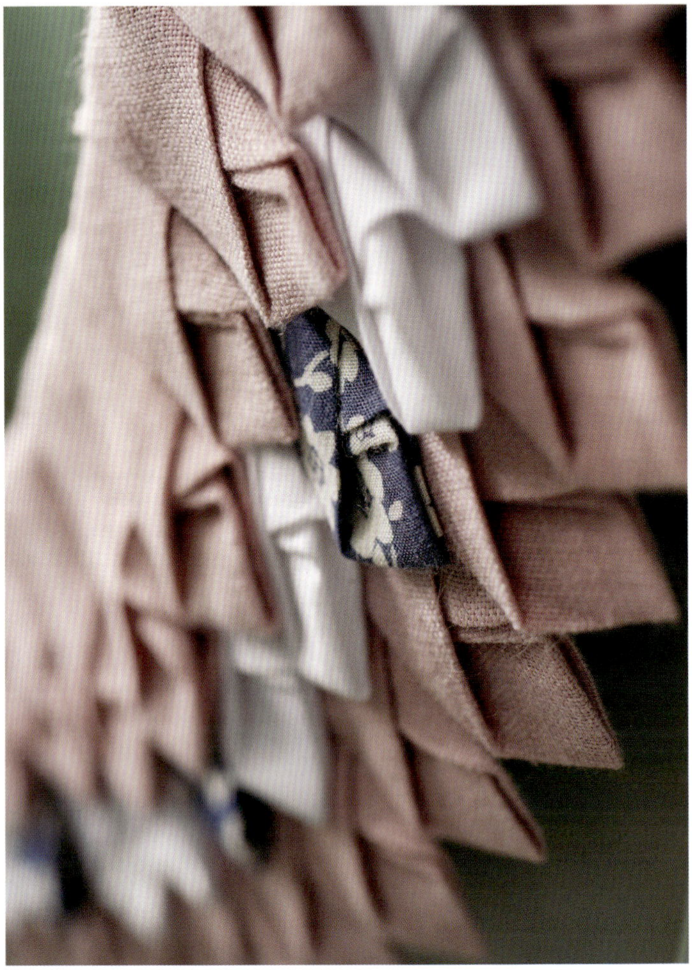
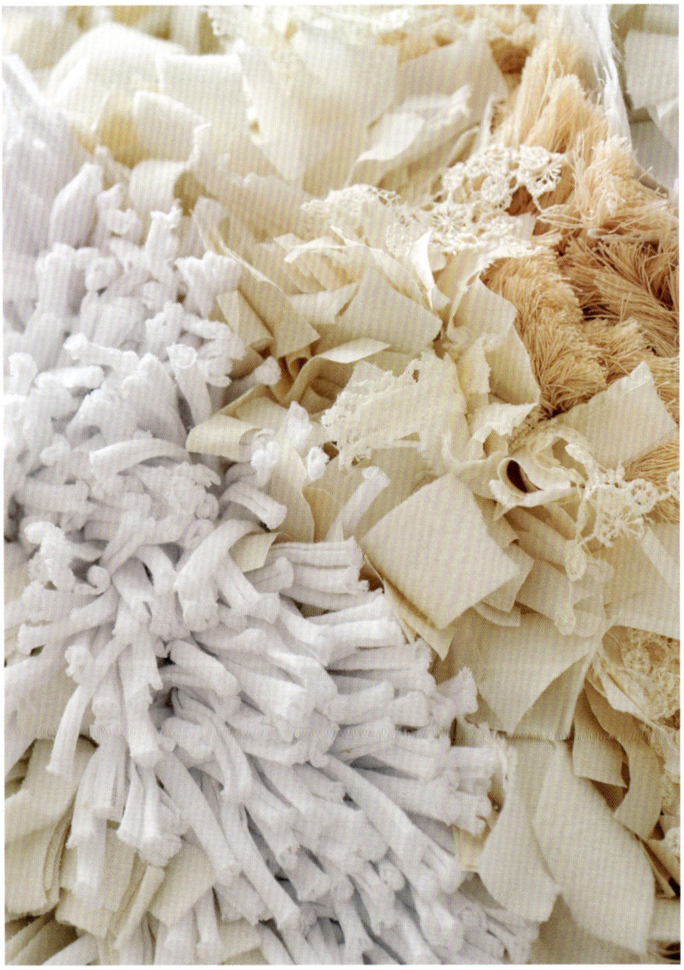
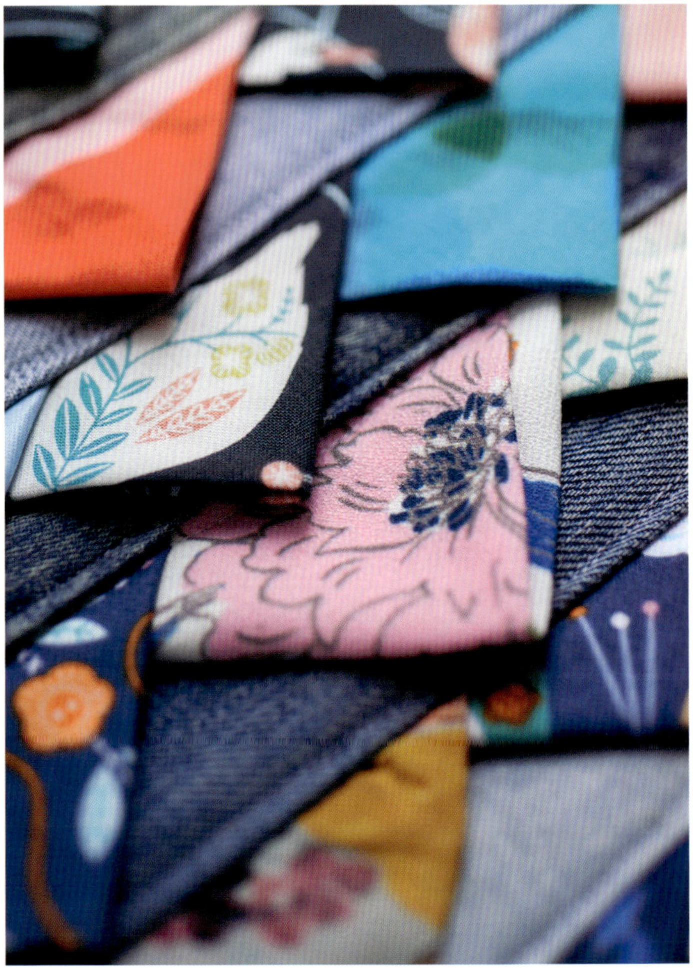

CHAPTER 7

STITCHED RAG RUGS

This chapter covers just a few of the ways in which you can stitch together old clothing and fabric offcuts to make beautiful and practical upcycled rag rugs and decorative homeware. Traditions of making recycled fabric stitched rugs exist in many cultures across the world—everywhere from Brazil and Scandinavia to Thailand and Tanzania—however each place does it differently. While there is some overlap between making stitched rag rugs and other sewing crafts, such as patchworking and appliqué, it is the cultural significance, traditions, and history associated with each method of rag rug making that sets them apart. The unique embroidery on Swedish Klackmattas (page 146), the specific folding of the fabric pieces in Brazillian Tapete de Retalhos (page 138), and the unique fabrics found in Sri Lankan mats make them instantly recognizable.

In general, sewing projects can be quite precise and unforgiving. This isn't really the case for the projects in this chapter. They are still rag rugs, where both imperfections and irregularity are a defining feature. Not a sewer? Not a problem. With a bit of patience and some care, anyone with a sewing machine (or even just a glue gun for our No-Sew Tulip Mirror project on page 142) can create something beautiful.

TOOLS AND MATERIALS

Sewing machine
The main bit of kit that you need to complete the projects in this chapter is a sewing machine. You don't need anything fancy. Just a machine that has the ability to do both a straight stitch and zig zag stitch. Where the stitching is visible, choose a matching thread color. Be careful when stitching through multiple layers of fabric at once as this can snap needles.

Other tools you may need
Needle and thread
Darning needle
Pins
Fabric scissors
Glue gun

Fabric
Each one of the projects in this chapter uses different fabrics. The only unifying feature is that they are all old clothing or textiles. Check out each individual project to see which fabric works best for it. Rugs often work best with thicker, cushier fabrics, such as woolen jumpers, old blankets, and scarves.

Statement Boho Pillow

At first glance, this cozy pillow looks a lot like it was made using the traditional shaggy technique of rag rugging covered on pages 21–23. However, the rags in this pillow are in fact stitched to a backing fabric. This makes the pillow clawing cat and grabby child-proof, and gives you complete freedom to play around with different weights and widths of fabric without worrying about how they will stay put in the burlap. I even managed to use up some old cotton rope, which would ordinarily be too fine to rag rug with. This project is all about texture, so the more unusual the fabric choices, the better the result.

You will need
24 x 24in (60 x 60cm) medium weight base fabric in a similar color palette to your rags

Iron

Marker pen/tailors' chalk

Ruler/tape measure

Fabrics: see Elspeth's tip, right

Fabric/rag rug scissors

Masking tape

Sewing machine (ideally use a zipper foot whilst assembling the pillow)

Cotton rope and hairbrush (optional)

Pins

Needle and thread

24 x 24in (60 x 60cm) medium weight backing fabric

20 x 20in (50 x 50cm) pillow pad

Elspeth's tip
I used the cream cotton lining of an old curtain for both the base and backing fabric of the pillow to save on buying new fabric. I then mixed together t-shirt yarn, twisted cotton rope, lace, fleece, cotton, and shiny polyester to create a contrast of textures in the pillow itself. Keep a similar color palette to emphasize the textural differences.

1 Iron your base fabric, then sketch a 20 x 20in (50 x 50cm) square onto your fabric, leaving at least a 3 1/8in (8cm) seam allowance around each edge.

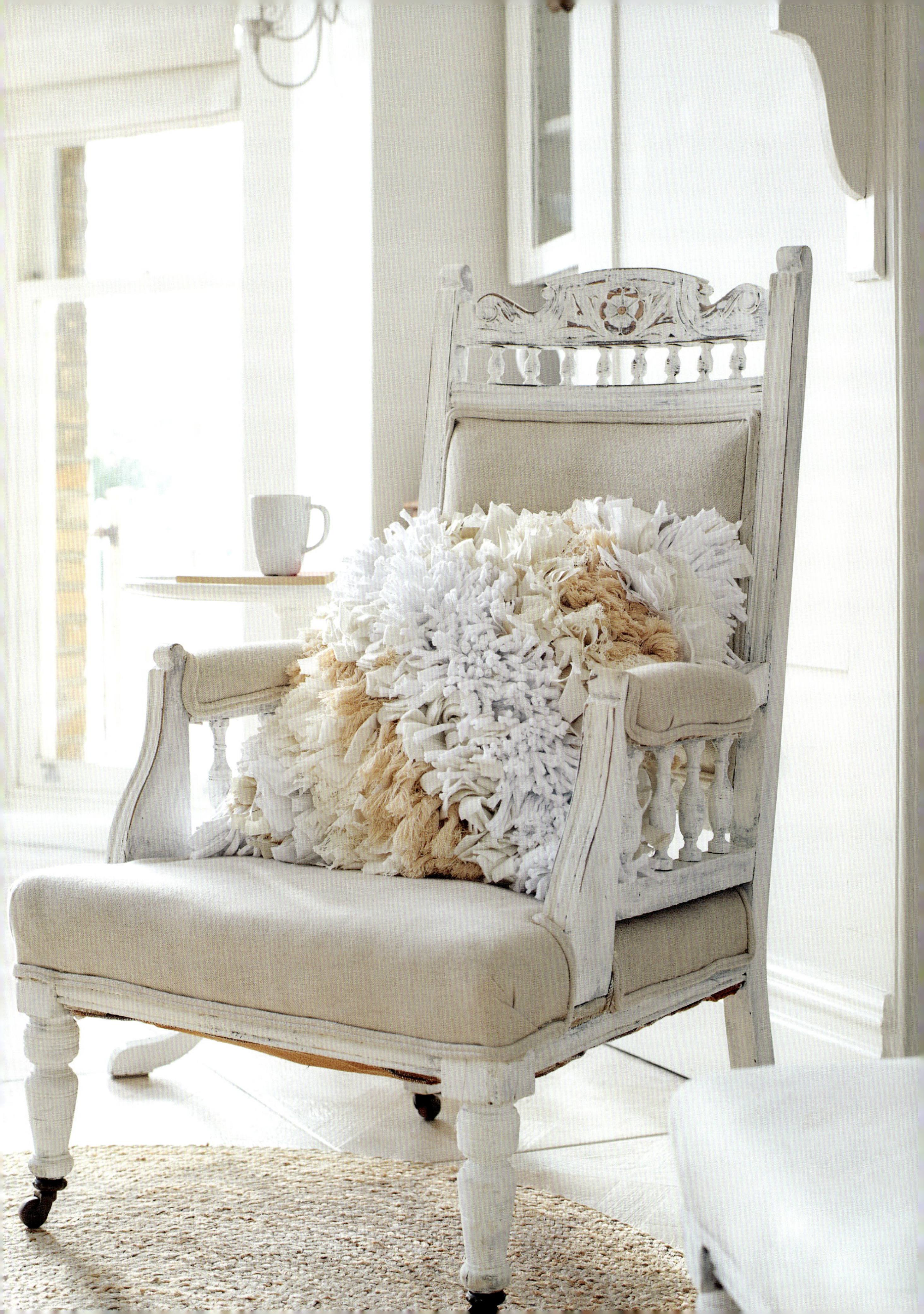

2 Draw a line diagonally from one corner of the pillow to the other, then draw lines at approximately 1¼in (3cm) intervals diagonally across the backing fabric.

3 Cut the t-shirt yarn into 6½in (16cm) lengths. Lay out a first row of t-shirt yarn strips side by side, with the midpoint of each strip lying over the central diagonal line. Tape down both ends of the strips using masking tape, so that they are held in position. Draw a line through the middle of all the strips, from one corner of the pillow to the other, as a stitching guide.

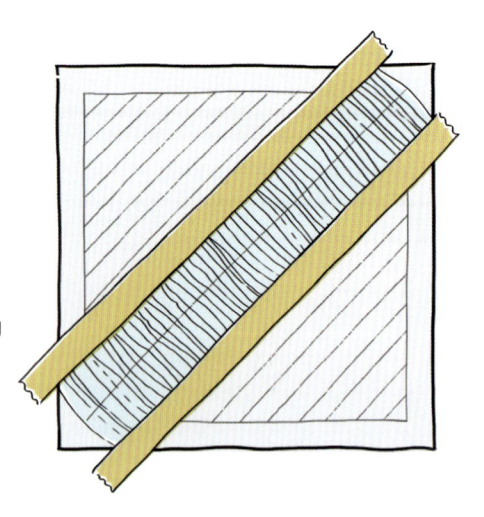

4 Adjust your stitch length to slightly shorter than default and zig zag stitch along the central drawn line to secure the first row of fabric strips in place. Backstitch at the beginning and end of each row and trim any loose threads.

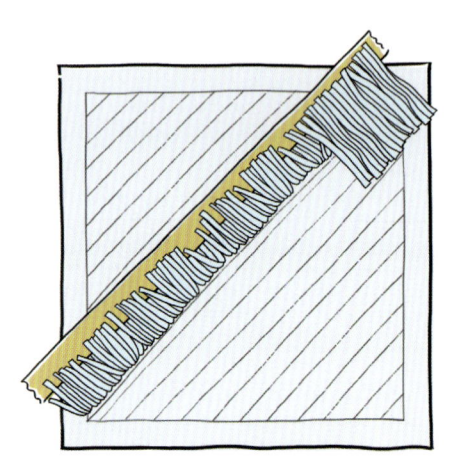

5 Remove the masking tape from one side of the fabric strips, then fold the row of fabric strips back on themselves. Lay out your second row of t-shirt yarn fabric pieces along the nearest diagonally drawn line, tape each side in place (you can reuse masking tape from previous rows) and draw a line along the center of the strips. Stitch in place as in step 4.

6 Following the method detailed in steps 3–5, continue stitching one row of fabric pieces in place one after another until you reach the corner of the square. Once you have filled one half of the pillow, start working in rows from the center in the opposite direction. To create this exact boho statement pillow, I built up the fabrics in the order below. For some fabrics, I laid out multiple strips of fabric on top of each other to make the row fuller; for some others I deliberately cut my strips wider or narrower to emphasize the texture.

Order of fabrics from corner to corner

4 rows white t-shirt yarn

1 row rope offcuts

1 double thickness layer of cream curtain backing—¾in (2cm) wide strips

2 rows double thickness white cotton—1½in (4cm) wide strips

3 rows of double thickness cream lace and shiny nightie—¾in (2cm) wide strips

1 row of tan rope offcuts

2 rows of cream fleece—1¼in (3cm) wide strips

4 rows of white t-shirt yarn

1 double thickness layer of cream curtain backing—¾in (2cm) wide strips

1 double thickness layer of cream curtain backing and fleece mixed—¾in (2cm) wide strips

2 rows of double thickness cream lace and shiny nightie—¾in (2cm) wide strips

2 rows rope offcuts

1 row double thickness white cotton—1½in (4cm) wide strips

1 row of cream fleece—1¼in (3cm) wide strips

2 rows of white t-shirt yarn

2 rows cream jersey

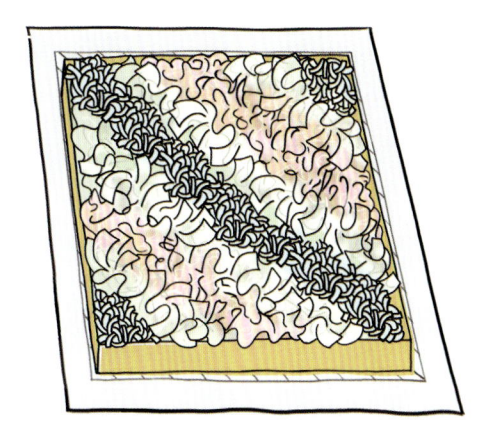

7 Once you have stitched fabric along each diagonal line, you are ready for assembly. Tape the fabric pieces along each edge of the pillow up and towards the center, so that you are able to get your sewing machine foot close to the drawn 20 x 20in (50 x 50cm) square. Trim any rogue pieces of fabric that fall outside of the 20 x 20in (50 x 50cm) square.

8 Place the 24 x 24in (60 x 60cm) piece of backing fabric on top of the rag rugged pillow face, right sides facing. Pin three of the edges of the backing fabric to the base fabric as close to the bottom of the masking tape as possible without catching it. Making sure to leave one side open, machine stitch a straight stitch along the three pinned edges of the pillow.

9 Trim away any excess fabric from around the edge of the stitched backing fabric to leave a 1¼in (3cm) border. Turn the pillow cover inside out. With the tape still on, insert the pillow pad, fold the remaining open edge of backing fabric inside the pillow cover, pin it to the rag rugged base fabric, and hand stitch the final opening closed. This does not need to look perfect as the long fabric pieces will cover your handiwork. If you would like the option to remove the pillow pad and wash your pillow cover then you can use an envelope back for your pillow instead (as described on pages 58–59).

Elspeth's tip

Cotton rope gives movement and softness to the design. To work with twisted rope, cut a piece to length, separate out the three twisted strands, then carefully brush the strands to flatten them out. Treat these groups of flattened strands as if they are an individual fabric strip.

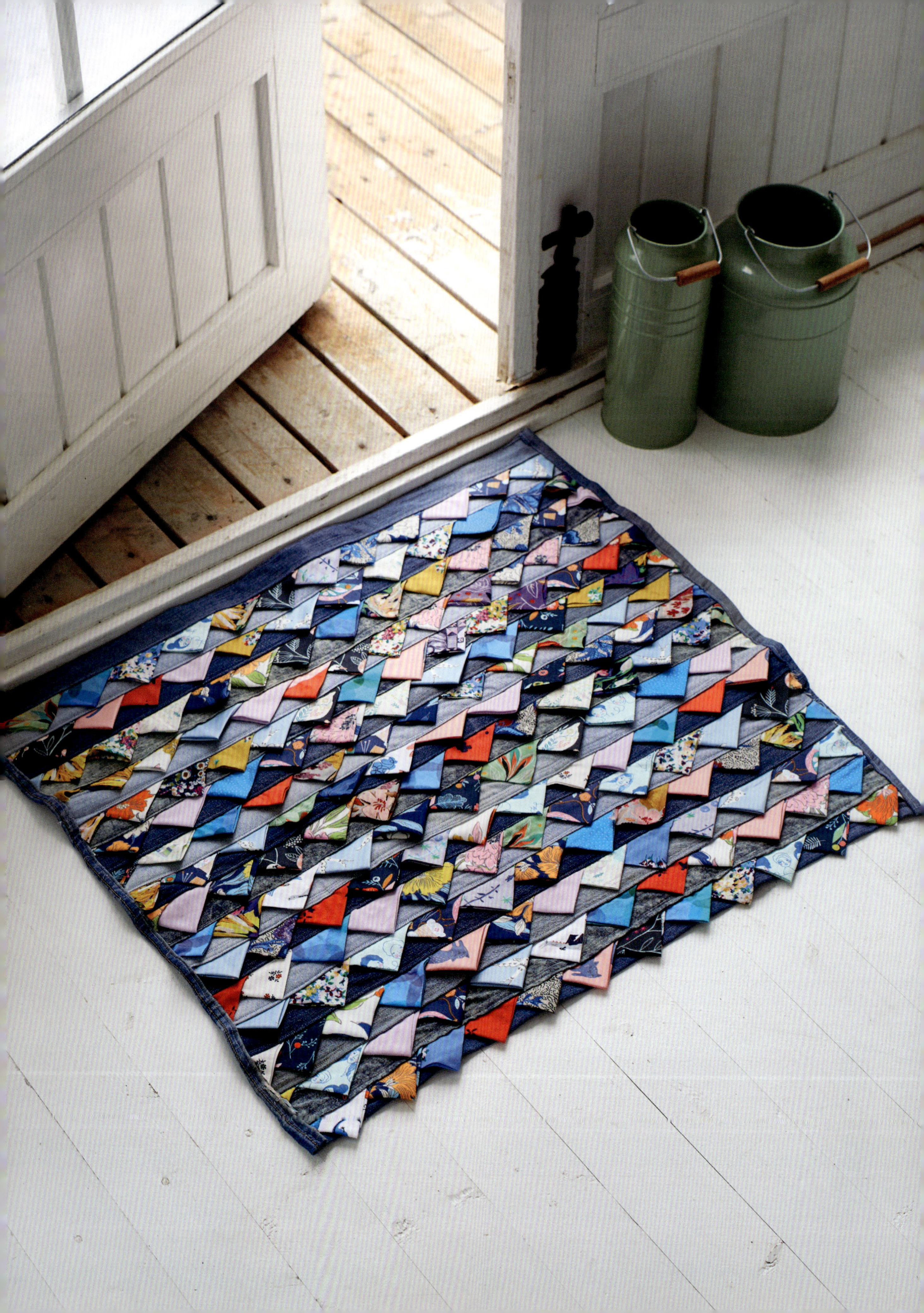

Stitched "Tapete de Retalhos" Rug

I'd never come across this style of rag rug before, but apparently they're quite commonplace in Brazil, where they're called "Tapete de Retalhos." It was fun mixing and matching the different fabric scraps to create this patchwork effect. I can see how it could become addictive. Particularly as it's so good for using up smallish scraps.

You will need

Mixed fabrics: Approximately 67 x 55in (170 x 140cm) of relatively similar weight fabrics (I used mainly viscose, cotton, jersey, and polyester)

Fabric scissors or cutting mat and rotary cutter

Card

Tape measure or ruler

Iron

Ironing board

4 pairs of non-stretchy denim jeans, minimum leg length 34in (86cm)

Clothes pins

1 Cut out 208 4 x 4in (10 x 10cm) squares of fabric. As this is still a rag rug (so a bit characterful) the squares do not have to be perfect. It is best to cut the squares with either a rotary cutter and cutting mat or make a basic card template to roughly cut the squares to size with a pair of fabric scissors.

Elspeth's tip

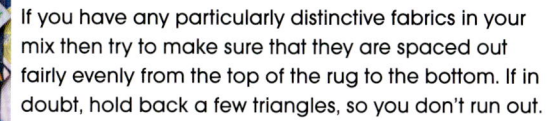

If you have any particularly distinctive fabrics in your mix then try to make sure that they are spaced out fairly evenly from the top of the rug to the bottom. If in doubt, hold back a few triangles, so you don't run out.

2 Fold each square in half diagonally twice then press with an iron to create 208 triangles. The right side of the fabric should be visible.

STITCHED "TAPETE DE RETALHOS" RUG 139

3 Take your first pair of jeans, cut off all the seams and iron the denim flat. Depending on the size of jeans you are working with, cut out as many 4 x 32in (10 x 81cm) rectangles from the denim as possible. A medium to large pair of jeans should have enough fabric for 8 rectangles. Deconstruct as many jeans as needed to create sixteen 4 x 32in (10 x 81cm) rectangles of denim.

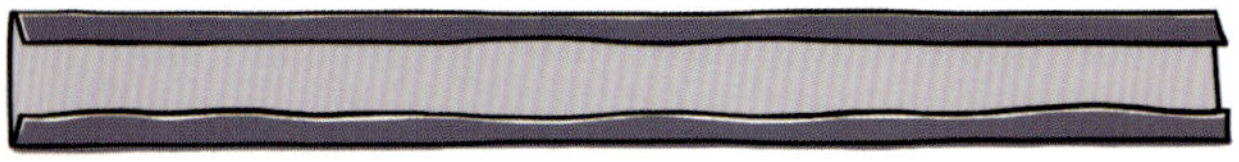

4 Fold each 32in (81cm) edge of the denim rectangles over ½in (1cm) and press with an iron. To create more variation in the denim, press half the rectangles with the right side up and half with the wrong side up. This will give you two shades of denim for the price of one.

5 Lay out 13 triangles along the first denim strip, overlapping the bases of the triangles about ¾in (2cm). Once you are happy with the order, sew the bases of the triangles to one of the pressed seams of the denim rectangle using a straight stitch. Either pin the triangles in position before sewing or slide triangles of fabric under the sewing machine foot as you work. The triangles may overhang the beginning and end of the rectangle slightly—this is normal.

6 Fold the denim strip in half to sandwich the bottoms of the triangles between the pressed denim edges. Stitch along the folded edge of denim to secure it to the bottom of the fabric triangles. Press the finished strip of triangles so it lies flat.

7 Repeat steps 5 and 6 with all 16 strips of denim. To understand how your rug is looking, lay the strips you've stitched one on top of the other as you work to see how the pattern is building.

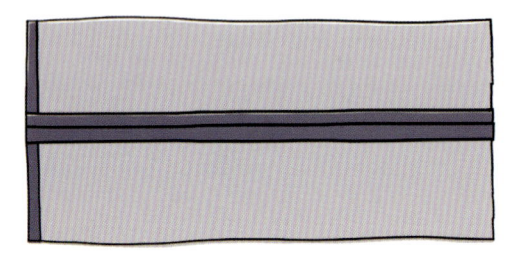

8 Cut the legs off a pair of jeans then cut down the inner leg seam of each leg to open them up flat. Cut the inner leg seam off, but leave the bottom hem attached. Square off each leg, so they are 33in (84cm) long and as wide as possible. A seam should run down the middle of the two denim rectangles.

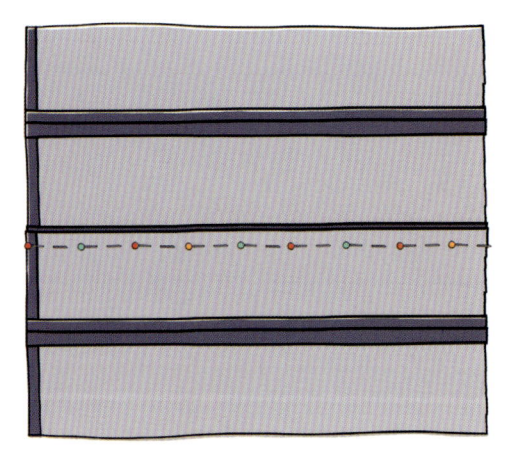

9 With the right side of the denim pieces face down, fold one long edge of each rectangle of denim over ½in (1cm) and press. Pin the ½in (1cm) folded edges of each denim rectangle together, right sides facing, and join them together with a straight stitch. Open the seam and press each side flat to the denim with the iron.

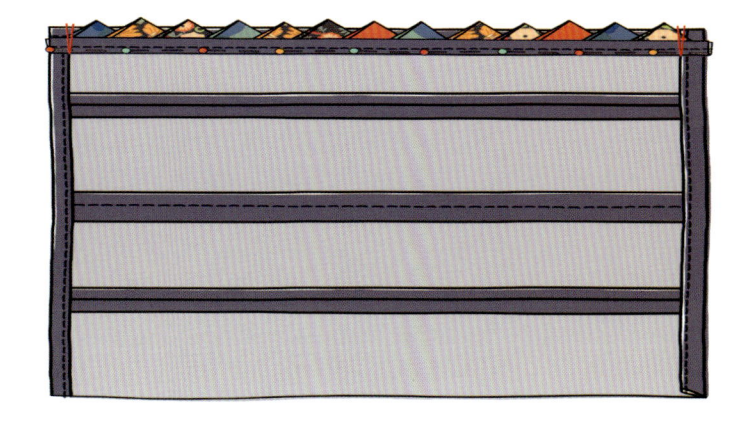

10 Hem one long edge and one short edge of the denim rectangle by folding the raw edge of the denim over twice about ¾in (2cm) and stitching it in place with a running stitch. Leave one edge of the rectangle unhemmed.

11 With the wrong side of the denim rectangle face-up and starting on the edge of the denim rectangle opposite the unhemmed edge, pin your first strip of fabric triangles to the denim base. It is up to you how much you would like the tips of the triangles to overlap the outer denim edge, if at all. Cut the edges of the denim strip and triangles along our marked red lines, so that the strips finish just on the inside of the denim hem at each side of the rectangle.

12 Stitch the top and bottom edge of the denim strip to the base, stopping and starting just on the inside of the hem on each edge of the base.

13 Pin the next strip of triangles in place below the first, overlapping them slightly so none of the denim base shows through. Repeat steps 11 and 12 to stitch the row in place and continue to add one row after another to the rug. Continue from one end of the rug to the other, continuing over the seams in the center of the denim base as normal.

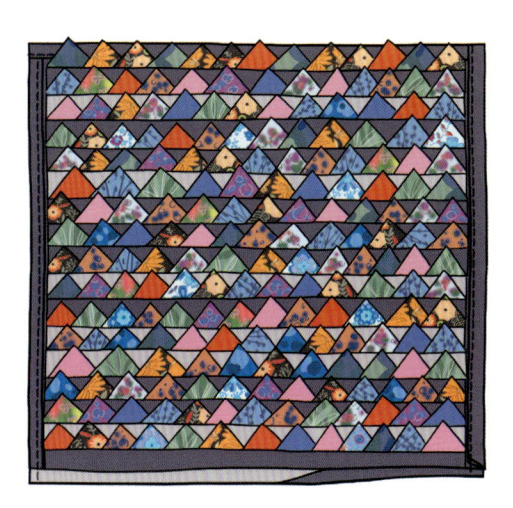

14 Once you have stitched 15 strips of fabric to the base, place your last strip in position. Cut the remaining base fabric as short as necessary and fold the raw edge to the front of the rug so it will be covered by the final strip of triangles. Pin the last denim strip in position and stitch it in place as you have done with the previous rows.

15 To finish the edges of the rug, fold the hems on the edge of the rug over to the front and pin them in position. Sew a straight stitch along each edge to secure the hem in place and cover the raw edges of the fabric triangles and denim strips. Be careful when stitching through multiple layers of denim as this can snap needles. Take it slow.

No-Sew Tulip Mirror

The shape of folded fabric used in this project is often used in Tapete de Retalhos in Brazil. We've put this tulip shape to good use in a no-sew project to upgrade old forgotten mirrors and frames, but the shape could easily be used instead of the triangles in the Tapete de Retalhos Rug on page 138, for a different look.

You will need

Fabric: I used 39½ x 35½in (100 x 90cm) pink fabric, 25½ x 11¾in (65 x 30cm) blue floral fabric, and 35½ x 15¾in (90 x 40cm) white fabric. I used part of an old shirt, a girl's floral dress, and two pillow cases

Iron and ironing board

Ruler

Fabric scissors

Circular mirror or frame: I used an old IKEA Tranby mirror, which was 19¾in (50cm) in diameter with a 3in (8cm) frame.

Glue gun

1 Iron your fabrics and cut them into 3½ x 3½in (9 x 9cm) squares. For this 19¾in (50cm) diameter mirror, I used 50 pink squares for the inner row, 59 pink squares for the outer row, and 38 white squares and 19 blue squares for the middle row. The squares don't have to be exactly perfect so eyeballing them with a ruler on hand is fine.

2 Fold the squares into little "tulips" using the method on page 144. When you are happy with the positioning of each fold, press the folded fabric with an iron to help it keep its shape. There will inevitably be some slight variation between your "tulips."

Elspeth's tip
If you do not have enough of a certain color to complete this project, you can change the pattern or mix two colors together.

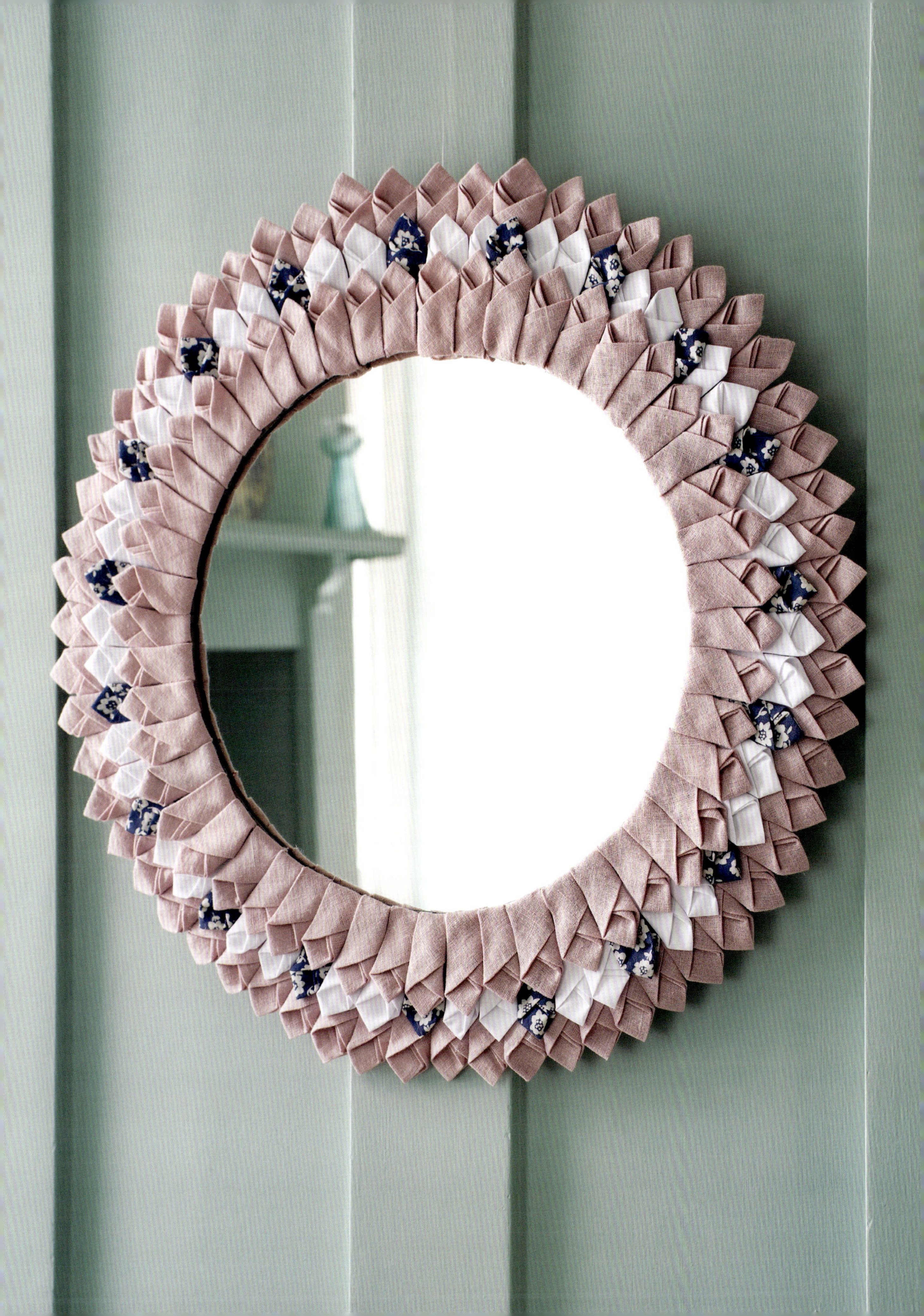

How to fold the tulips

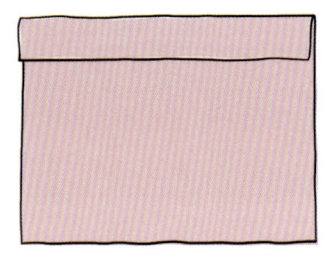

1 Fold the top edge of the 3½in (9cm) square over approximately ¾in (2cm).

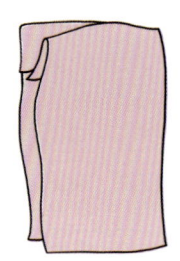

2 Fold the square in half widthways to enclose the folded edge from step 1.

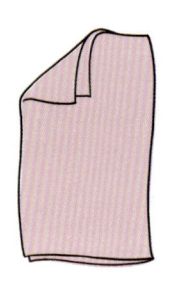

3 Fold the top left corner diagonally towards the center.

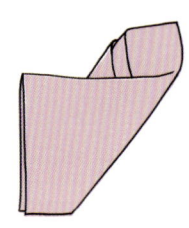

4 Fold the bottom right corner diagonally across the fold. Press with an iron.

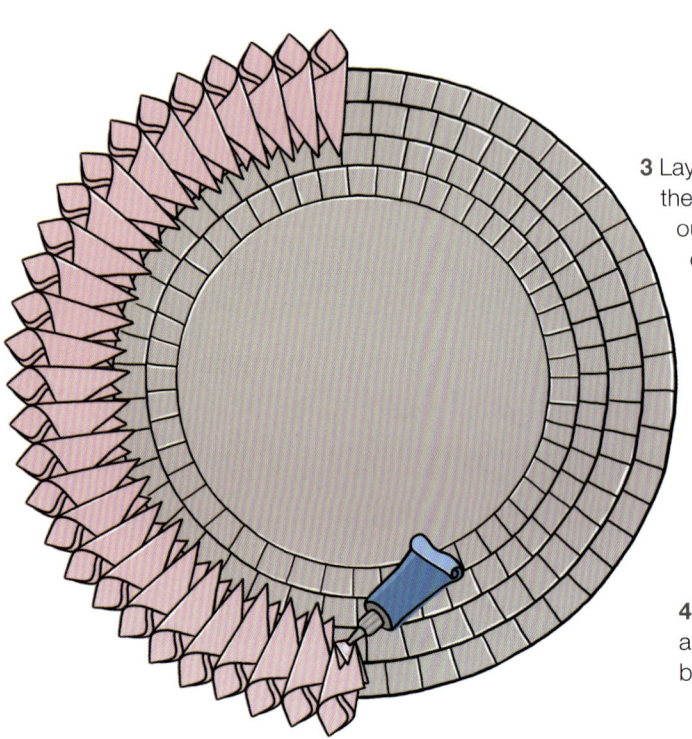

3 Lay out the first row of pink tulips counterclockwise around the outside of the mirror. The tips of the tulips should protrude out slightly further than the edge of the mirror. Glue the row of tulips to the mirror. Use small spots of glue underneath the front flap of fabric to secure it from opening up before placing the next tulip down. The last tulip in the circle will need its front flap of fabric folded round and glued to its underside before it is glued to the mirror. This will give it a clean edge.

4 Trim the jagged bottom edges off the white and blue "tulips". This will be prevent them from being visible at the end of the project.

Elspeth's tip

Do not use too much glue as you do not want it to ooze out from under the edge of the fabric piece. You can always add more later.

5 Glue the second row of blue and white tulips just inside the first row, alternating two white and one blue. The pointed tips of the tulips should sit roughly between those of the row above. As you are creating a pattern in this row, when you are approximately ten pieces away from completing the circle, lay out the rest of the folded fabric to gauge whether you will need to space them closer together or further apart to ensure you don't mess up the pattern. Once again glue the front flap of fabric to the underside of the last tulip in the row before it is glued to the mirror.

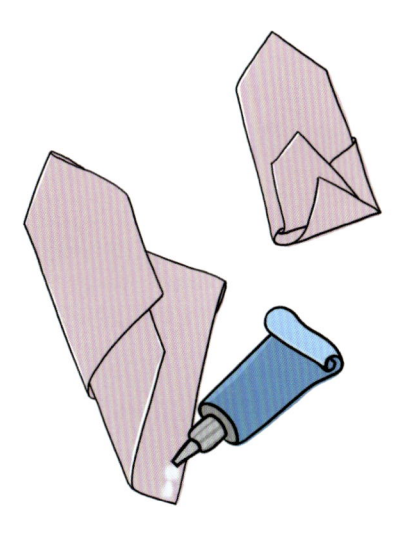

6 For the innermost row, fold and glue the bottom edge and flap of each tulip behind to create a clean edge before laying them out and gluing the pieces in place.

NO SEW TULIP MIRROR 145

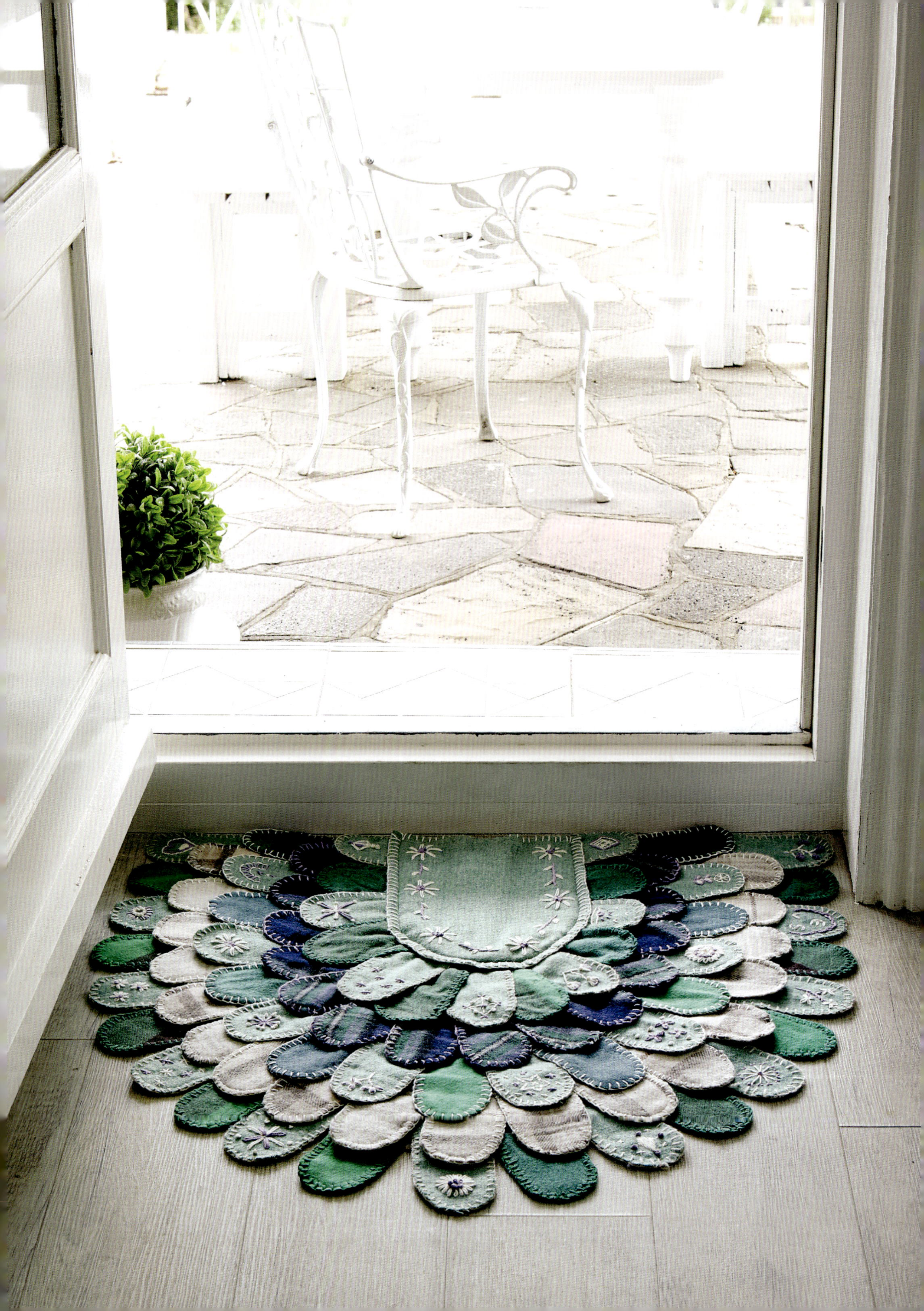

Swedish "Klackmatta"

A "klackmatta" is a traditional style of rag rug from Sweden. Old woolen garments, blankets, and coats are cut into pieces and sewn onto a burlap base to become practical rugs, doormats, and even tablecloths. Often, the pieces of woolen fabric are edged with a blanket stitch and embroidered with simple designs, such as stars, hearts, and flowers, to add pizzazz to the design. The "klackmatta" gets its name from the shape of the overlapping pieces of fabric, which are shaped like a heel or "klack."

You will need

Template on page 173

Marker pen

Fabrics: I used approximately 51¼ x 23½in (130 x 60cm) light green fabric, 39½ x 23½in (100 x 60cm) dark green fabric, 19¾ x 15¾in (50 x 40cm) dark tartan, and 19¾ x 19¾in (50 x 50cm) light tartan

Iron

Pins (optional)

Burlap (hessian): Approximately 27½ x 27½in (70 x 70cm)

Wool: I used 71in (180cm) length per heel, plus extra for the hand embroidery in shades of green, cream, and lilac

Darning needle

Sewing machine and thread

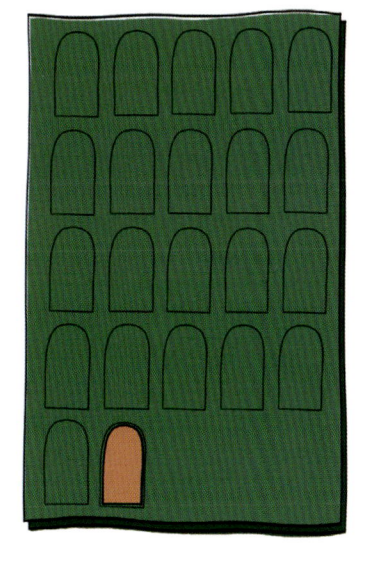

Elspeth's tip

Klackmattas are all about warmth and comfort, so make sure to choose thicker fabrics for this project, such as old jumpers, blankets and thick upholstery materials.

1 Print and cut out the "heel" template on page 173. Fold your fabrics in half to double them up and draw around the template, creating 26 pairs of light green heels, 25 pairs of dark green heels, 18 pairs of light tartan heels and 14 pairs of dark tartan heels. Cut out the pairs of heels. When placing your template on the light green fabric, make sure to leave enough space to fit the large central heel later (see step 9) if you'd like to use the same fabric.

2 Press each pair of heels with an iron. Stack each pair of heels wrong side together, and starting at the straight bottom edge as it will be less visible, blanket stitch around each pair to join them together using wool or twine. This protects their edges, lessens fraying, and gives the klackmatta its distinctive look.

3 Once all the heels have blanket stitch all around, embroider some of them with designs. I embroidered designs on to all 26 light green heels using a mixture of French knots, lazy daisy stitch, stem stitch, and running stitch. When it comes to this basic embroidery, there is no right or wrong, but traditional klackmattas often feature stars, hearts, and flowers. I thought of it as doodling with wool. Remember, only the top half of the heel will be visible, so the design does not need to stretch all the way down.

4 At this stage, I like to lay out the heels on the burlap base to see how they are looking and whether I'd like to make more to increase the size of the rug. Fold the bottom edge of the burlap over approximately 1½in (4cm), press and pin in place to create a hem. Starting with light green at the bottom, lay out 21 green heels in an arc, alternating light then dark green, overlapping them slightly on the curve.

5 Once you are happy with how that row is looking, lay out 18 cream heels, starting slightly in from the bottom edge, between the first and second green heels, and overlapping them slightly on the curve. The third row consists of 17 heels, alternating dark then light green, the fourth row is made up of 14 dark tartan heels, and the fifth row consists of 13 heels, alternating light then dark green. If you are happy with the size, draw around the outside arc of heels, and then cut the burlap along the line to create a semi-circle base for the rug. You will still see some of the burlap between the outer heels at this point.

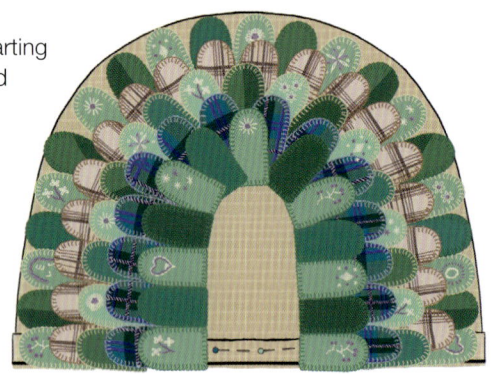

6 Fold the unhemmed semi-circular edge of the burlap over approximately 1½in (4cm) to the front and press with an iron to create a clean edge. You will need to lift up and replace the heels in order to do this. Fold enough over so that when you pin the first row of heels in position on top, the hem is secured and none of the burlap is visible between the heels.

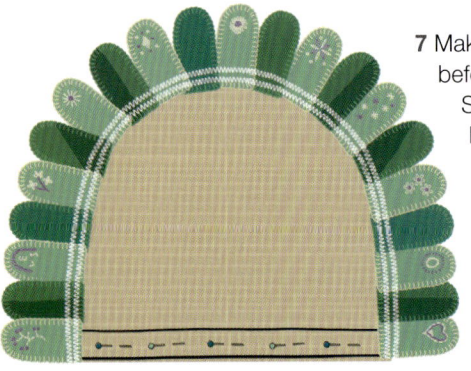

7 Make sure that you are happy with the positioning of the heels before pinning and stitching the first (outer) row in position. Stitch two rows of zig zag stitch to secure the heels to the base. One row of stitching should be approximately ½in (1.5cm) up from the straight bottom edge and the other should be 1¼in (3cm) up from the straight bottom edge. Any higher and the stitching may not be covered by the next row of heels.

148 STITCHED RAG RUGS

8 Stitch each row of heels to the base one row at a time until you have covered all but the central panel. Depending on how you have laid out your heels, this gap will vary in size. Cut a piece of fabric to level out the gap between the heels. This fabric will not be visible, but it should be two layers thick. Pin this panel in position before stitching it to the burlap backing with a straight stitch. This creates a level area in the center of the klackmatta.

9 Take a large piece of paper or card and create a template to make a large heel to finish the center of the rug. The heel should fully cover the zig zag stitching from the innermost row. Double up your light green fabric, press with an iron, draw around the template and cut out the large heel. Blanket stitch around the two layers of fabric to join them together and embroider the center with a design of your choice. Pin the large heel in place in the center of the rug and stitch it in position with a straight stitch just inside the blanket stitch. Try to line up the bottom of the large heel with the bottom of the mat.

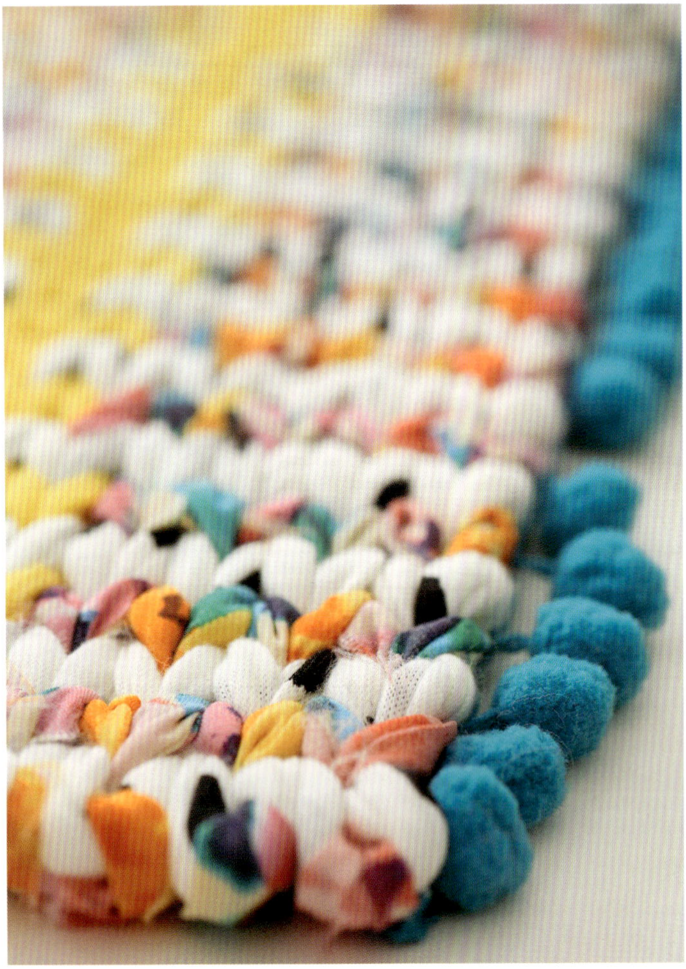
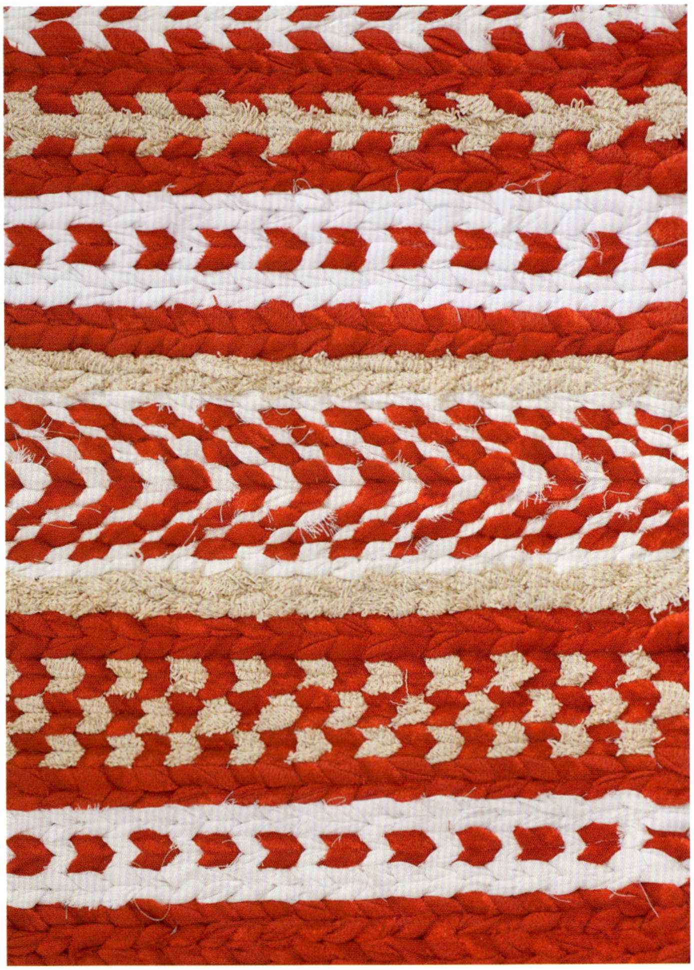
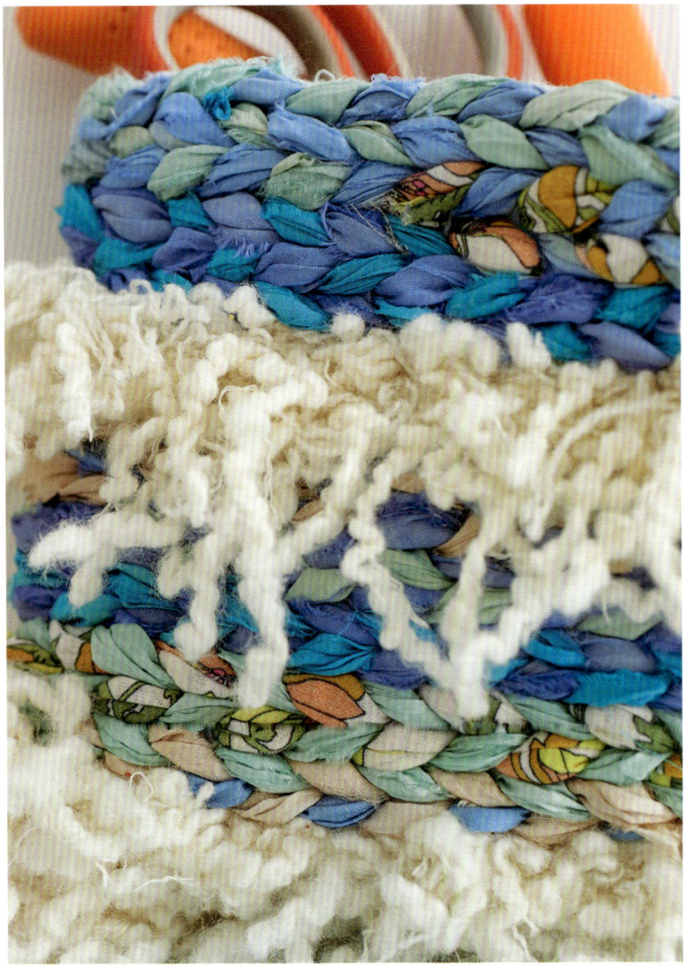
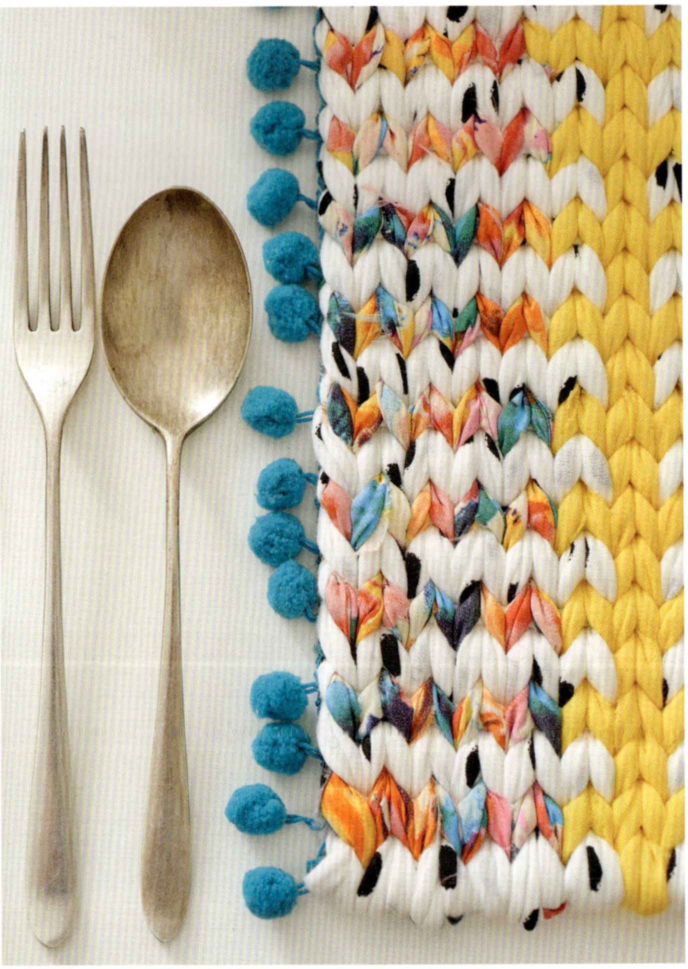

CHAPTER 8

TWINING

Twining is a form of rag-rug making that has become increasingly popular in the USA in particular. Twining is regularly confused with weaving, but while the two techniques share many similarities, twining is actually considered its own unique textile technique by those in the know. The main difference between twining and weaving is that in twining, you always work with two horizontal strands (called wefts) at once, which is not always the case in weaving. Also, in twining the vertical strands (collectively called "the warp") are covered and enclosed at the end of a project, whereas in weaving they are often visible. Twined rugs have a beautiful, compact appearance that looks almost woven or knitted. It's this compactness that makes them extremely practical as rugs for the home.

Before we get going, here is some basic twining terminology.

Warp: the warp is the name that we give the vertical strands that wrap around the pegs or nails at the top and bottom of your loom and act as a framework on which to build up your twining.

Weft: the weft is the name we give the horizontal strands that weave in and out of "the warp" (see above) to form a twisted pattern. Twining is unique in that it always uses at least two weft strands, both of which travel in the same direction at the same time.

TOOLS AND MATERIALS

Twining loom
At its most basic level, you can make a small, sample-size twining loom by hammering nails at 1in (2.5cm) intervals across the top and bottom edges of an old wooden photo frame. However, if you scaled this basic loom up large enough to make a twined rug, the sides of the rug would be likely to bend inward, and not stay straight. Specialist twining looms feature metal rods at each edge, which are positioned as close as possible to the first and last pegs to prevent this.

Fabric or cord for the warp
The material you use for your warp should be strong and not too stretchy. Before you begin a project, you have to pull the warp taut, so overly stretchy fabric can be problematic and cause your rug to lie unevenly when you take it off the loom. I recommend long strips of cut-up cotton bedding, ¼in (6mm) diameter macramé cord, or mildew resistant clothesline cord for the warp. Whatever you choose, it will need to be stitched into one long strip for the continuous warping method on page 153. Traditionally, the warp is slightly thinner than the weft. If using cotton bedding, cut strips approximately 1in (2.5cm) wide for the warp. I prefer to cut, not tear, the cotton sheets into strips, as tearing creates loose threads which can interfere with your twining and even rip the warp. When choosing a warp material, it's worth noting that it will only be visible on the very top and bottom edges of the finished piece.

Fabric for the weft
Choosing material for the weft is the fun part of twining; these are the fabrics and colors that will make up your design. Twined rugs are often made using old bedding, as they take a lot of fabric and long strips work best. However, the good news is that pretty much any fabric goes. Just bear in mind that generally the more a fabric ravels (comes apart), the harder it is to twine with and join.

When mixing fabrics in a piece, it is important to balance the different weights of fabric by cutting them to different widths. The general rule of thumb is that whatever fabric you use, the strips should roll up to at least the diameter of a pencil in thickness.

Some twiners prefer to press the edges of their weft strips under or fold the edges in as they twine, similar to bias binding, to create a neater, less thready appearance in their twining, but a frayed texture doesn't bother me.

Aside from fabric type, you can also experiment with color. Plain fabrics show the natural pattern of twining more clearly, so look very effective when you have a complicated design. Patterned fabrics look less crisp and become a blur of the various colors in the pattern.

You don't want your weft strands to be too long before you start twining, as it makes them cumbersome to pull through the warp. I like to cut my strips so they are a maximum of 2yd (2m) in length, but to reach from one side of the loom to the other with one weft strand, it must be at least 1.5 times the width of the loom in length.

As with all rag-rugging techniques, it can be tricky to calculate how much fabric you will need to complete your project. Some twiners prefer to cut their fabric into strips then divide the strips in two to ensure they use the same quantity of that color on both ends of the rug to keep things symmetrical. Twining uses more fabric than you think it will, so try to save some of the first colors you worked with for near the center of the rug to bring the design together.

Latch hook/large darning needle/crochet hook
You will need one or other of these tools to sew your ends in at the end of the project.

Other tools you may need
Fabric scissors/rotary cutter and cutting mat
Pins/safety pins/food storage bag sealing clips
Needle and thread/sewing machine
Hemostatic forceps (great for twining the last few tight rows)

TECHNIQUES

SETTING UP YOUR LOOM

Before starting any twined project, set up your loom so that the metal rods and cross beams are in the correct position. The distance between the metal rods dictates how wide your twined piece will be, and the position of the middle or bottom cross beam dictates the length of your twined piece. If you are planning to twine the full length of the loom, then remove the middle cross beam. If you are only twining to the middle cross beam, leave the bottom cross beam in to keep your loom sturdy.

Most twining looms are designed to lean against a wall or stand on a frame, so get comfortable. The loom below is an example of an adjustable twining loom, which allows you to twine rugs of different widths and lengths.

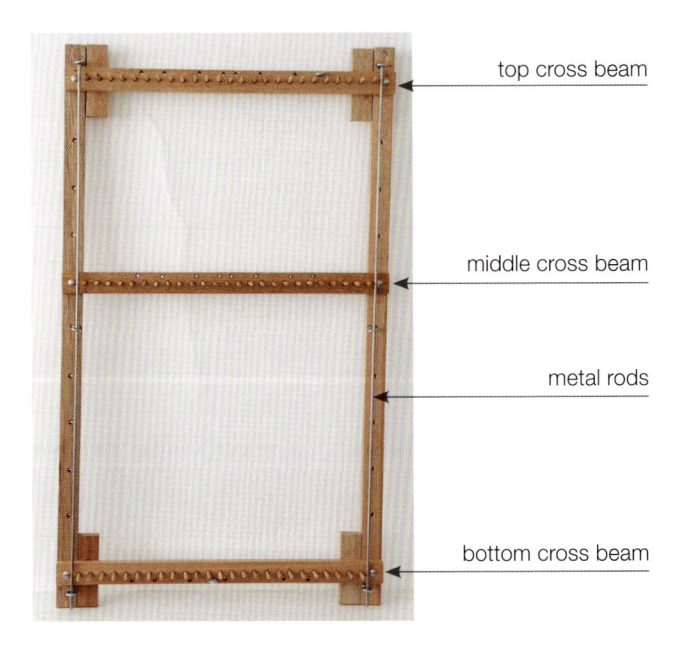

WARPING THE LOOM

"Warping the loom" is the process of constructing your warp on the loom. First, it's important to remember that the only part of the warp that will show at the end of your project will be at the very top and very bottom of your rug. If you want your warp to completely blend in with the finished rug, then warp the loom using one of the colors that you will use for your first and last row of twining. If you are twining a very pale rug, avoid a dark warp, as it can show through the fabric.

There are generally two types of warping—continuous warping and looped warping. The projects in this book all use the continuous warping method, which will always create an odd number of warp strands to work with. The difference between an odd and even number of warp strands doesn't come into play until you start to twine complicated patterns, like diamonds, which involves counting warp strands. The twined projects in this book are beginner ones to get you started.

Continuous warping is done by threading one long fabric strip or cord between one peg and the next from the top left corner to the bottom right. To do this you will need one long continuous length of warp material, so if you're working with fabric this will require some joining of strips (see methods on pages 13–14).

Calculating the length of warp required

To calculate the approximate length of fabric or cord you will need for the warp, decide how wide and long you want your twined project to be and set up your loom. Count how many pegs you'll need to fill the top cross beam of the loom. Double that number then multiply it by the length that you would like your twined piece to be. This figure will give you the approximate length of strip or cord you'll need, including a little bit extra to start and finish your warp.

For example, if my twining project uses 13 pegs in between the metal rods, and the gap between the pegs on the top and bottom cross beams is 15in (38cm):

> Number of pegs across top = 13, 13 x 2 = 26
> Gap between top and bottom pegs = 15in (38cm)
> 26 x 15in (38cm) = 390in or 10yd 2ft 6in (9.88m)

So in this example, the approximate total length of warp needed is 10yd 2ft 6in (9.9m).

Continuous warping

Once you've joined together your continuous fabric strip for the warp, here's how to do continuous warping.

1 Starting in the top left corner of the loom, loop the end of the warp over the first peg by approximately 3in (7.5cm) and safety-pin it temporarily to form a loop around the first peg. The loose/free end of the warp should be in between the first and second pegs.

2 Serpentine the warp between the top and bottom rows of pegs, making sure to keep the warp taut and straight.

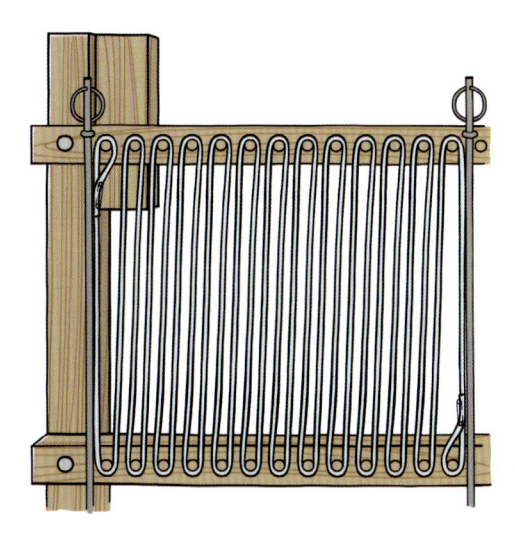

3 End in the bottom right corner of the loom and loop the warp around the last peg towards the center of the loom and temporarily safety-pin it in place as you did in step 1. Do not cut it to length at this stage.

4 Starting in the top left corner of the warp and working from left to right, tighten up the warp by gently tugging the warp strands one by one. The aim is for the warp to have a little bit of give in it when you push your palm flat against it, but very little. Gather any excess warp in the bottom right corner of the loom and re-pin the bottom right end, so that the warp remains tight.

5 In the top left corner of the loom, sew the loose end of the warp to the **second** warp strand. In the bottom right corner, trim the loose end to approximately 3in (7.5cm) and sew the end of the warp to the **penultimate** warp strand. Ensure your warp tails are securely stitched or your project could fall apart when you take it off the loom

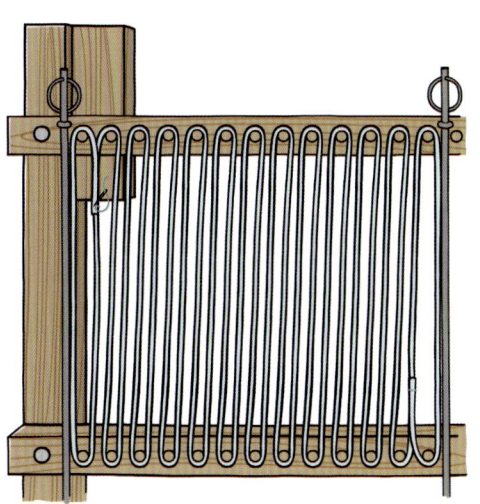

TECHNIQUES 153

TWINING METHODS

There are two main ways of twining. The first is called the "over method" and the second is the "under method." These methods affect whether your "stitches" (sometimes called weft segments) lean in the direction that you are traveling or in the opposite direction. In the following illustrations, we've used different colors to differentiate between the two weft strips, which would be joined together using one of the methods on pages 13–14. However, you can also twine with just the one fabric strip, folded in half lengthwise, without the need to join. This will create a row of twining in one solid color.

Elspeth's tip
The over and under methods can be mixed to create patterns in your twining.

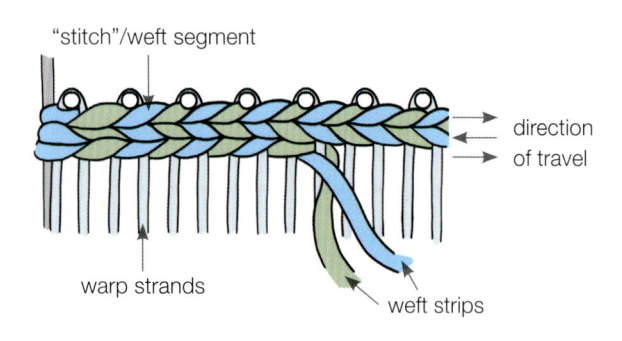

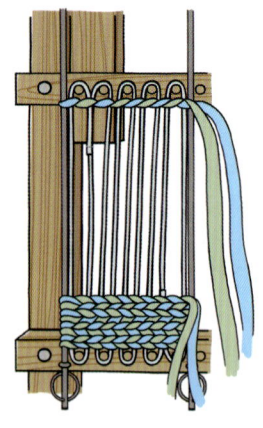

Getting Started

Generally, you begin twining in the top left-hand corner of the loom (although this is personal preference), traveling from left to right, turn when you meet the metal rod, work from right to left below the first row, turn at the metal rod, twine from left to right again, and so on.

After you have twined a number of rows at the top, switch to working from the bottom of the warp. If you are making a rug, this generally involves turning the loom round so the bottom is now at the top. Working from the top and bottom of the loom alternately helps to secure the warp on the pegs, helps to keep the twining tension even across the rug, and means you won't have to finish your last rows close to the pegs, which can be a bit tricky. It's personal preference how many rows you twine before switching to the other end, but often the design dictates when to do this. Twining from the top and the bottom of the loom also helps to keep designs symmetrical, and helps you calculate how far your fabric will go.

Over method

Twining using the over method makes the weft segments lean in the same direction as you are traveling.

IMPORTANT: Twining is always explained in relation to the leading and trailing weft strands. The leading weft strand is the fabric piece that has just passed behind the previous warp strand. The trailing weft strand is still the other side of that warp strand. So in steps 1 and 2, the blue weft is the leading strand, and the green is the trailing, but in steps 3 and 4 green is leading, and blue is trailing.

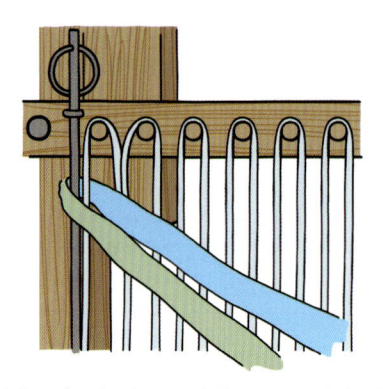

1 Starting in the top left corner of the loom, pull one end of your weft fabric strip behind the metal rod and the first warp strand and bring it forward between the first and second warps. If you have joined two strips together, adjust the join so that it sits behind the metal rod. In this illustration, the green weft strand will be the color that shows at the edge of the rug.

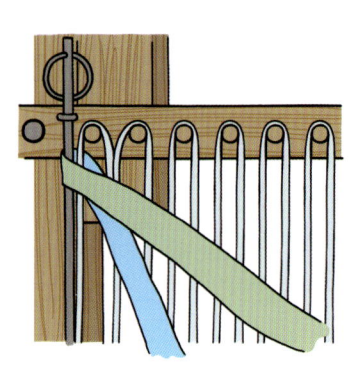

2 Take the trailing weft strand (green) and cross it over the top of the leading weft strand (blue).

154 TWINING

3 Pass the trailing weft strand (green) behind the next empty warp strand and to the front. So, in this case, the weft strand comes back to the front of the loom between the second and third warp strands. You can tell the next empty warp strand as it doesn't have any weft fabric passing behind it. The trailing weft strand has now become the leading weft strand.

NOTE: Because of the way that we have warped up the loom, the second warp strand will be a bit chunkier as it has the loose end of the warp stitched to it. Ignore this bulk and treat the stitched tail and second warp as one.

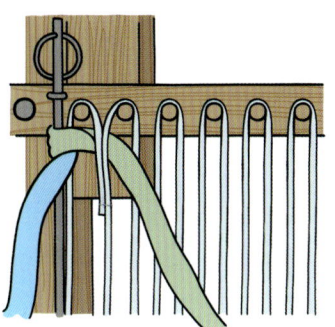

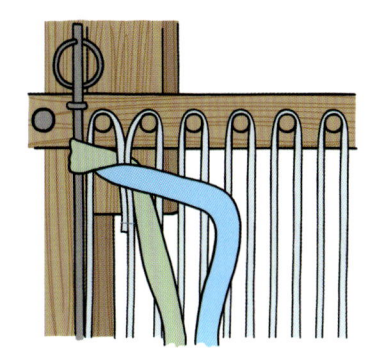

4 Repeat steps 2 and 3 until you reach the far side of the loom where you've positioned the other metal rod. Push your rows of twining up so that the "stitches" sit close to the pegs. This can be done using your fingers or a wide toothed comb. Try to keep your weft segments even in size by keeping your tension even as you twine.

Under method

Twining using the under method makes the weft segments lean in the opposite direction to the one that you are traveling in.

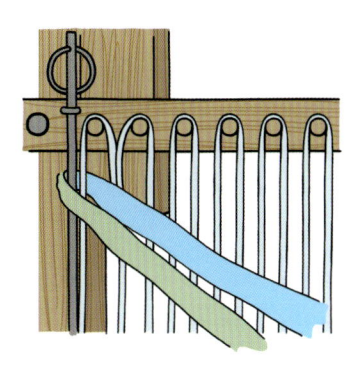

1 Starting in the top left corner of the loom, follow the same instructions for the Over Method step 1. In this illustration, the green weft strand will be the color that shows at the edge of the rug.

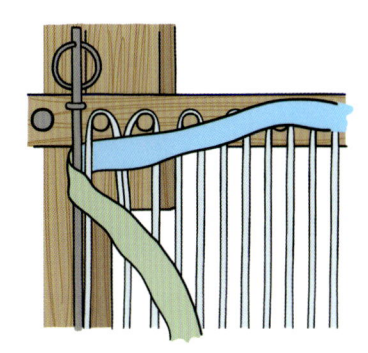

2 Hold the leading weft strand (blue) up and out of the way to enable you to position the trailing weft strand (green) below the leading weft strand.

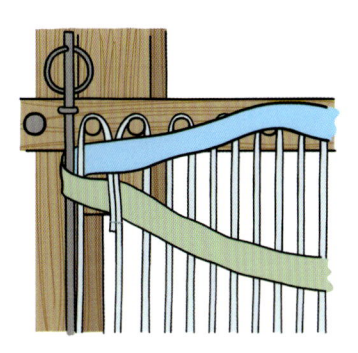

3 Pass the trailing weft strand (green) behind the next empty warp strand and to the front. So, in this case, the weft strand comes to the front of the loom between the second and third warp strands. You can tell the next empty warp strand as it doesn't have any weft fabric passing behind it. The trailing weft strand has now become the leading weft strand.

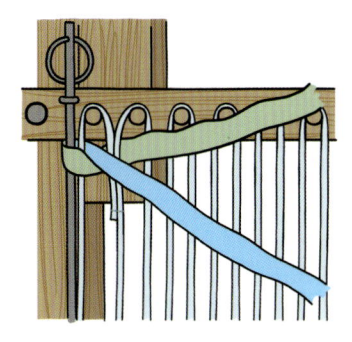

4 Now repeat step 2, so hold the new leading weft strand (green) up and out of the way to enable you to position the new trailing weft strand (blue) below the leading weft strand.

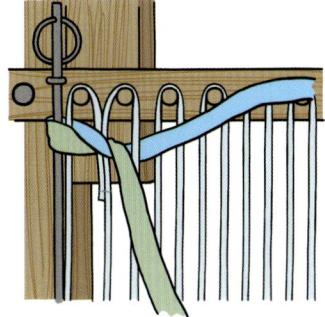

5 Pass the trailing weft strand (blue) behind the next empty warp strand and to the front, and repeat steps 2 and 3 until you reach the far side of the loom and the other metal rod. Push your rows of twining up so that the "stitches" sit close to the pegs. Try to keep your weft segments roughly even in size by keeping your tension even as you twine.

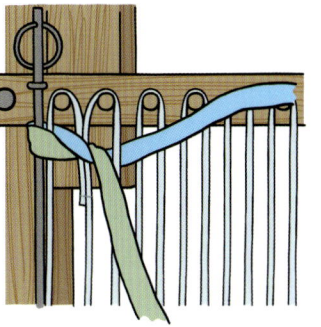

Elspeth's tip

As you play around with the two twining methods, you can control whether the weft segments from one row to the next lean in opposite directions (almost forming a chevron)—this is called "countered twining"—or whether they lean in the same direction, called "same-pitch twining." Using the same method in both directions produces countered twining, and using alternate methods from one row to the next produces same-pitch twining.

TECHNIQUES 155

TURNS

Regardless of which direction you are traveling (left to right or right to left), when you reach the last warp strand and metal rod, you will need to change direction. This is done using turns. There are two main turns in twining: a regular turn and an alternate turn. Different turns are used to create different patterns in your twining.

It is best explained using two different color weft strands. When using regular turns, the same colored weft segments will sit diagonally from each other from one row to the next, regardless of which twining technique you use (the over or under method).

Alternate turns allow you to stack colors on top of each other, by swapping the leading and trailing weft strands on the edge. Look at the diagrams on the right to understand how turns create patterns in twining.

When making turns, you always treat the final warp strand and the metal rod as one and the same.

Elspeth's tip
Before starting a turn, check your row of twining to make sure that you've made no mistakes (missed warp strands, uneven tension, etc.)

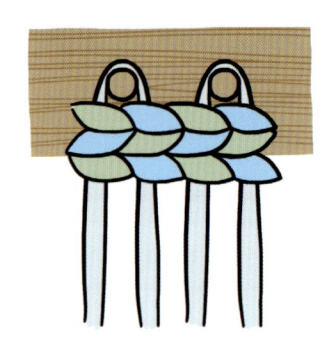

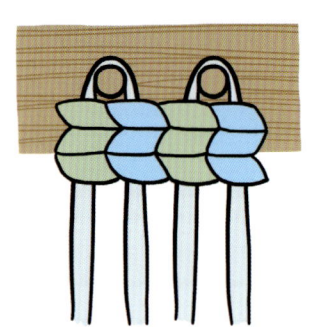

Regular turns   Alternate turns

Regular turns

Regular turns are the easiest and most common form of turn. Regardless of how many rows of twining you've completed or whether you're on the right or left of the loom, these instructions remain the same. Regular turns cause the same colors to zig zag down the twining from one row to the next.

Elspeth's tip
To make a successful turn, both weft strands should come around the metal rod and final warp strand. If only one weft has gone around then you've done something wrong, so best to unpick.

Regular turns finishing a row twined in the over method

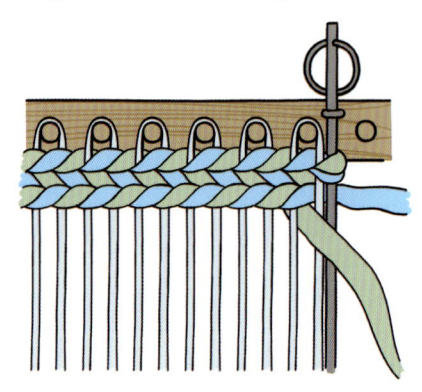

1 Continue twining until you reach the final warp strand and metal rod. The leading weft strand should have passed behind both the final warp strand and the metal rod.

2 Pass the trailing weft strand (green) over the leading weft strand (blue) as if you were continuing to twine.

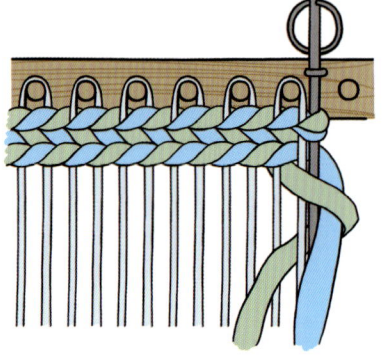

3 Bring the trailing weft strand (green) around behind the metal pole and final warp strand and through to the front of the loom between the final and penultimate warp strands. The final warp strand has now become the first warp strand and the penultimate one has become the second. This begins a new row below the one you just completed.

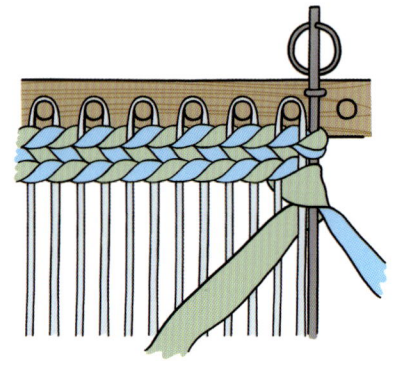

4 Make sure the turn is nice and tight then continue twining using either the over or under methods explained on pages 154–155. In this illustration the green strand has now become the leading weft, and the blue is the trailing.

Regular turns finishing a row twined in the under method

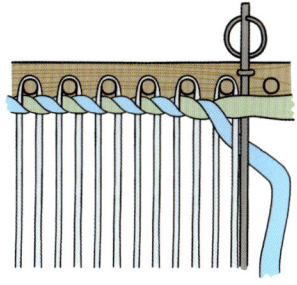

1 Continue twining until you reach the final warp strand and metal rod. The leading weft strand (blue) should have passed behind both the final warp strand and the metal rod. Remember that you always treat these as one and the same.

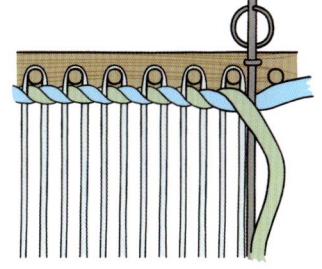

2 Hold the leading weft strand (blue) up and out of the way to enable you to pass the trailing (green) weft strand below the leading weft strand (green).

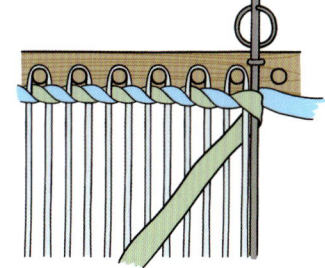

3 Bring the trailing weft strand (green) around behind the metal pole and final warp strand and through to the front of the twining between the final and penultimate warp strands. The final warp strand has now become the first warp strand and the penultimate one has become the second. This begins a new row below the one you just completed.

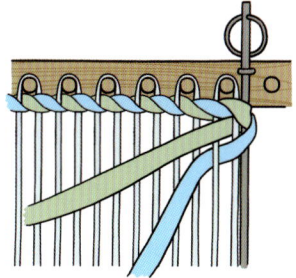

4 Make sure the turn is nice and tight then continue twining using either the over or under methods explained on pages 154–155.

Alternate turns

Alternate turns are used to create columns of the same color in your twined pieces. They are done the same way regardless of which twining method you are using. The Sunny Side Up Placemat on page 164 is a great project for practicing this technique.

Alternate turns finishing a row twined in either method

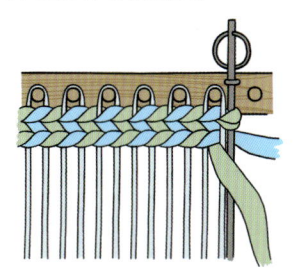

1 Continue twining until you reach the final warp strand and metal rod. The leading weft strand (blue) should have passed behind both the final warp strand and the metal rod. Remember that you always treat these as one and the same.

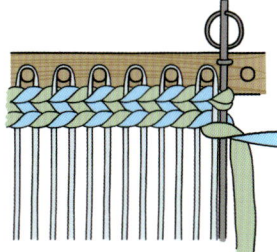

2 Pass the trailing weft strand (green) over the leading weft strand (blue) to form a right-angle.

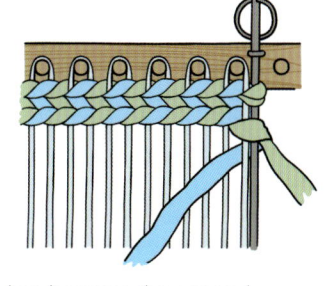

Elspeth's tip

After each row, push the twining up to tighten it against the pegs or previous row, and compact the rows together. Occasionally, run your fingers through the warp strands to make sure that none have crossed over. Your rows should be as tightly compacted together as possible so that when you take the twining off the loom, the warp loops around the pegs disappear completely.

3 Pass the leading weft strand (blue) behind the metal rod and final weft strand and through to the front of the twining between the final and penultimate warp strands. The final warp strand has now become the first warp strand and the penultimate one has become the second. This begins a new row below the one you just completed.

4 Make sure the turn is nice and tight then continue twining using either the over or under methods explained on pages 154–155. To ensure that the alternate turn doesn't create a bulky knot on the edge, pull the blue weft strand tight.

Elspeth's tip

You've successfully completed the turn when both wefts have passed around the metal rod and final warp strand, and the color at the beginning of the new row is the same as the one that finished the previous row.

TECHNIQUES 157

JOINING FABRIC STRIPS

Your weft fabric strips may not be long enough to get you to the end of the row, or you may want to change color, in which case you will have to join another fabric strip to the weft. You can do this using any of the methods on pages 13–14. As you twine, these joins can be a bit bulky, so adjust the twining by tugging the weft segments tighter or looser to ensure any lumpy joins are on the back on the twining. Joins tend to be fatter when working with thicker materials such as denim, fleece, and blankets.

If both your weft strands are roughly the same length, it is generally advised to cut one of them slightly shorter so that you can stagger the joins. This will make the joins easier to disguise. It is easier and neater to join fabric strips part way through a row, as opposed to on the edge. However, this is not always possible if you are doing a striped design as in our English Cottage Rug (page 168).

It's necessary to join strips together as you twine, as opposed to all at the beginning, as otherwise the weft strands become too long and cumbersome to pull through the warp. I like my weft strands to be a maximum of 2yd (2m) long, but it's down to personal preference.

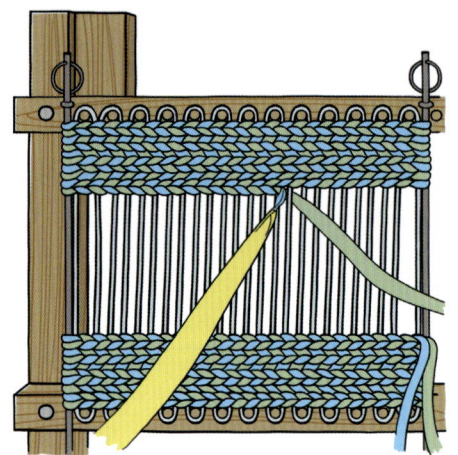

JOINING ON THE EDGE

To create stripes in your twined piece, you need to join new colors at the edge of the twining. To get a clean color change on the edge, twine around the turn then cut the weft strip you are changing where it passes behind the metal rod. Undo the twining slightly before joining your new strip using any of the methods on pages 13–14.

When you only have to join one new color at the edge, these joins aren't too hard to disguise, but joining two new fabrics in the same area can be bulky and lead to a lumpy edge (particularly when working with thicker fabrics). That's why, whenever I have to change both the weft colors for a new row, I clip the weft strands at the end of the row I have just finished using food storage bag clips (to sew in those ends at the end of the project) and begin the new row as I would when starting a new rug in the top left or right corner of the loom. This creates more ends to be sewn in at the end (see page 159), but can give a more even edge to your rug.

FINISHING YOUR TWINED RUG

The last twined rows

In any twined piece, the last few rows are by far the hardest to do. As the space left to fill gets smaller, it becomes harder to see the warp strands and to pass the fabric strips in between them. It's important to pack in as many rows as possible as this will help to disguise the warp loops at the top and bottom of the rug, as well as the warp itself. This is why we push our rows together to compact them as we work.

It's even harder to twine the last few rows near pegs or nails, which is another reason why twiners generally work from both the bottom and top of the twining loom at once to end somewhere near the center.

I like to work with a toothbrush rug needle (similar to a tapestry weaving needle) for the last two rows of twining. I thread the ends of each weft strand on to a needle and use the pointed end to weave across the front of the twining.

Other twiners use hemostatic forceps (curved medical forceps), large darning needles, crochet hooks, or other implements to work into the last couple of rows. You can use your fingers, but it can be a little tricky. If using a crochet hook, some twiners like to cut a small hole in the end of the strip to hook onto.

When you reach the end of your project, your weft strands should be pushed through to the back of the piece. Make sure that you have completed your last stitches, so that the design looks even. If you are ending at the edge of the rug, sandwich clip or pin your weft strands together so that they do not come unravelled as you take it off the loom.

Taking twining off the loom

Once you have packed as many rows as possible into your twined piece, it's time to take it off the loom.

1 Carefully pull out the metal rods from each side of the loom. Watch your ceiling!

2 Peel the twined piece off the pegs on the top and bottom of the loom, one peg at a time.

3 Lie the twined piece right side up on the ground and push any lumps and bumps you're not happy with to the back of the twining. Turn the twined piece wrong side up to sew the loose ends in.

Sewing in your ends

1 Cut any weft strands to approximately 2¾in (7cm) in length and taper them to a point. This will help to make them less bulky as you sew them in.

2 With the latch open, insert your latch hook underneath 2–4 weft segments nearby. You are aiming to pull the weft tails into the space where the warp is (between the two layers of twining), so it helps to insert the latch hook vertically up the twining unless you're on the very edge.

3 Place the pointed tail of the cut weft strand into the hook. Pull the handle of the latch hook, so that the latch closes over the fabric strip (it does so when it hits the weft segments). Carefully pull the weft strand end under the weft segments and through to the other side.

4 Repeat steps 2 and 3 until the weft end has passed under a minimum of 8 weft segments, then trim to disguise.

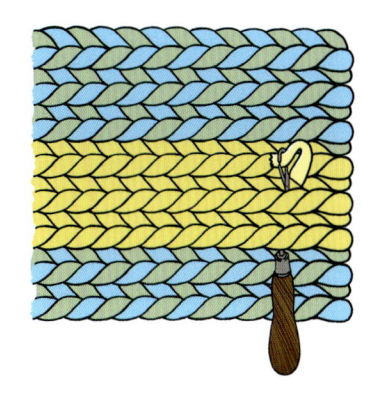

Generally, the edges of the twined rug are the weakest spots, so try to bring any loose weft strands that are near the edge in towards the center of the rug, by passing the latch hook diagonally across weft strands before moving vertically. It won't look as neat, but will create a longer lasting rug.

If you have sandwich clipped the ends of multiple rows to sew in later to create a cleaner edge (as in the English Cottage Rug on page 168), it helps to knot the two weft strands on the edge first before sewing them in. Before tightening the knot on the back, check how the weft segments are looking from the front. Leave a decent tail to sew in so that there is no chance of them coming loose.

TROUBLESHOOTING

Here are some of the most common mistakes beginners need to watch out for when twining.

1 Forgetting to twine around both the metal rod and last warp strand as one. This is one of the most common mistakes beginners make. If you treat the rod as a separate warp, this creates large loops on the side of the rug, which are tricky to disguise when it is taken off the loom.

2 Crossed warp strands. Every now and then, run your fingers through your warp to make sure that they remain straight and uncrossed. Crossed warp strands cause problems further down the project.

3 Unbalanced twining. Leave weft segments a little bit looser if they are sinking in behind the other weft color. Or better yet, cut those strips wider. It's slightly harder to do, but you can also twine with multiple strands at once to balance things up if you have cut your strips too narrow.

4 Visible warp strands. If you miss out warp strands, you will see some of the warp in your twining or one of the weft segments may be longer than all the others. You know you've gone wrong when both weft strands come forward between the same warp strands. If you swap from one technique of twining to the other part way through a row (from over to under or vice versa) then one weft segment will lie horizontal, not diagonal and some of the warp may show.

5 Forgetting to secure the ends of the warp properly. If you do not secure your warp properly at the beginning and end (as described on page 153), the twining will come unraveled when you pull it off the loom.

6 Not compacting your rows as you work. This can lead to visible warp strands and loops at the end of the rug which won't disappear into the rug. You can compact rows with your fingers, a wide toothed comb, chopstick or other tools.

7 Incorrect turns. You've gone wrong with your turn, when only one of the weft strands has passed around the metal rod and final warp strand (which are treated as one).

8 Accidentally pulling the tail of the leading weft strand through when you're working with the trailing strand. This means you are more likely to end up with the two weft strands between the same warps. If in doubt, undo the twining a few stitches.

9 Working too many rows in succession in "same-pitch" twining. This can make your rug unbalanced.

Crafty Toolbag

I use this style of twined tool bag to keep rag rug tools organized in my work area. Leaving the bag without a zip or fastening means that tools can stand up straight next to one another, making them easy to see and grab quickly mid-project. The lining prevents hooks and sharper tools from getting snagged, plus, who doesn't love a bit of color and texture on their desk!

Elspeth's tip:
This particular tool bag features stripes of shaggy woollen fringe, but for a beginner, you could swap out this slightly tricky material for easier textured fabrics such as fleece, mohair, or just plain cotton.

You will need

Fabric scissors

Adjustable twining loom

Warp fabric: approx. 9½yd (8.6m) of blue t-shirt yarn

Weft fabrics:

29½ x 74¾in (75 x 190cm) of mixed blue fabrics

Approximately 29½ x 12in (75 x 30cm) of floral-patterned fabric

Approximately 29½ x 59in (75 x 150cm) of cream fabric

I also used a small amount of shaggy woolen fringe, but this can be swapped out.

Needle and thread (blue or white, plus color matched to the lining)

Pins

Latch hook/crochet hook (for sewing in ends at the end)

Sandwich clips (optional)

15¾ x 15¾in (40 x 40cm) piece of lining fabric (this can be cut from a garment)

Amish toothbrush needle/hemostatic forceps (optional)

Sewing machine (optional)

Popper fastener (optional)

1 Set up your twining loom to the desired size. For this exact tool bag, which is relatively wide but shallower (to fit more tools in) the metal side rods were spaced 13in (33cm) apart (13 pegs) and the top and middle cross beams were spaced 13in (33cm) apart.

2 Starting in the top left corner, warp up the loom using the continuous method of warping on page 153. Use blue fabric so that the warp will disappear into the final bag. I used t-shirt yarn, but if you are working with fabric, cut strips approximately 2in (5cm) in width and join them using either method on pages 13–14. You will need a strip that is approximately 9½yd (8.6m) in length for a bag this size.

3 Cut your weft fabrics into strips using any of the methods on page 11. Make sure to balance the weights of your fabrics by cutting strips different widths based on how thick or thin they are (see page 152). This design works best with multiple changes of color, so my strips were all 29½in (75cm) in length or less.

4 Stitch together two different blue fabric strips using the onelooped join method on page 14. These two colors will make up the alternating colors in your first row, so try to choose blues that contrast.

5 Starting in the top left corner of the loom, working from left to right to start with, using chart 1, twine the first section of the bag, rows 1–8. Whenever you need to join strips (see techniques on pages 13–14), do so part way through a row and stagger joins so that two wefts aren't joined in the same spot. Include some floral/patterned fabric after a few rows to add interest to the block.

Note: Twine around the metal rod and neighboring warp strand as if they are one and the same. Do not twine around solely the metal rod as this will create an extra loop on the edge of your twining. This is a very common mistake that beginners make.

6 After eight rows of twining with mixed blue and patterned fabrics, twine rows 9–12 using a contrast-colored fabric (like cream) or a fabric with unusual texture like shaggy woollen fringe, mohair, or fleece. See page 158 for how to join two new wefts on the edge at the same time to create a contrast stripe.

7 After the contrast stripe, twine rows 13–20 using mixed blue and patterned fabric as in step 5. You will need to start this block using one of the joining on the edge techniques from page 158.

160 TWINING

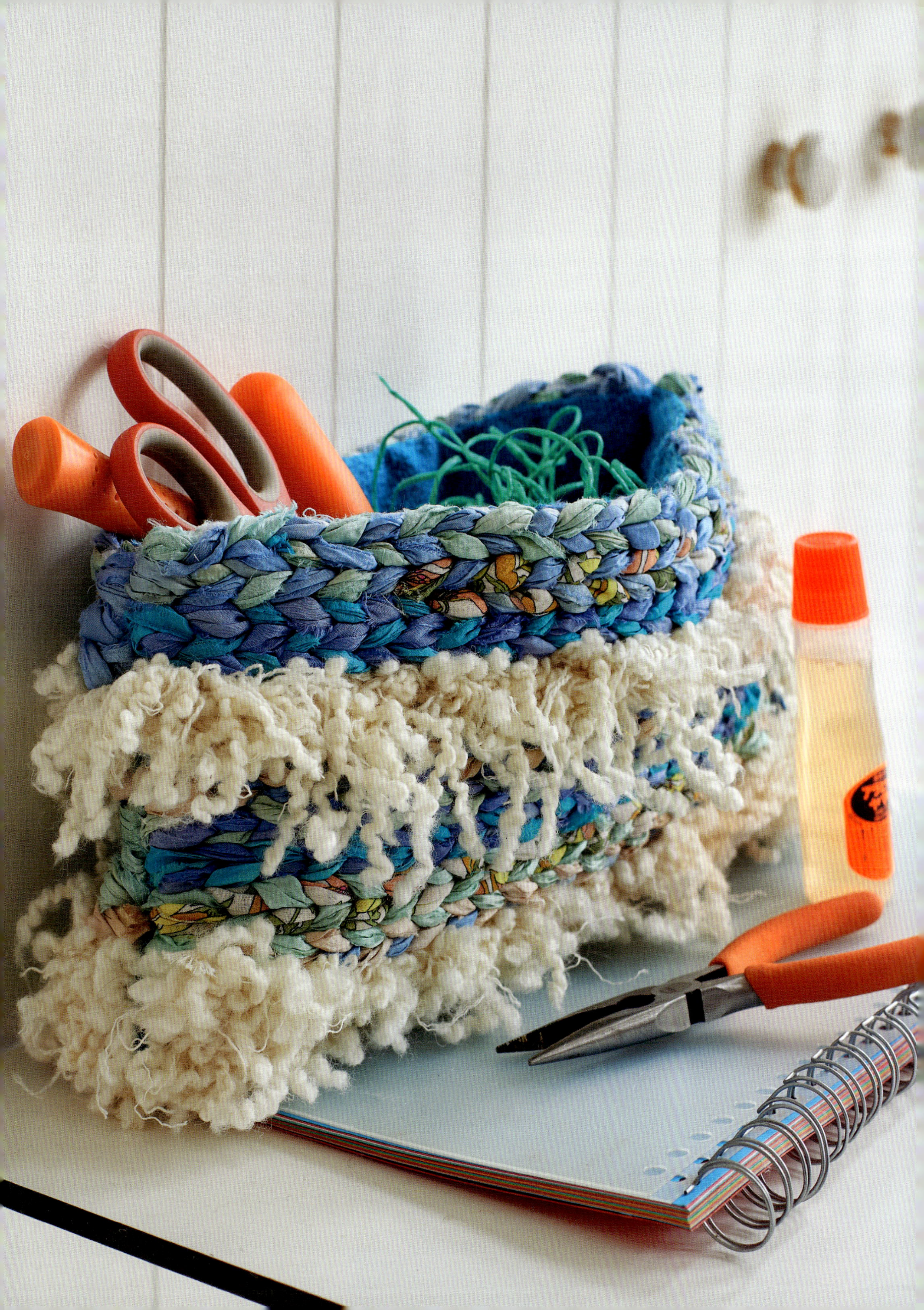

CRAFTY TOOLBAG Chart 1

key to chart — Dark blue fabric — Light blue fabric — Floral patterned fabric — Cream contrast fabric

O Over method
R Regular turns
→ Direction of travel

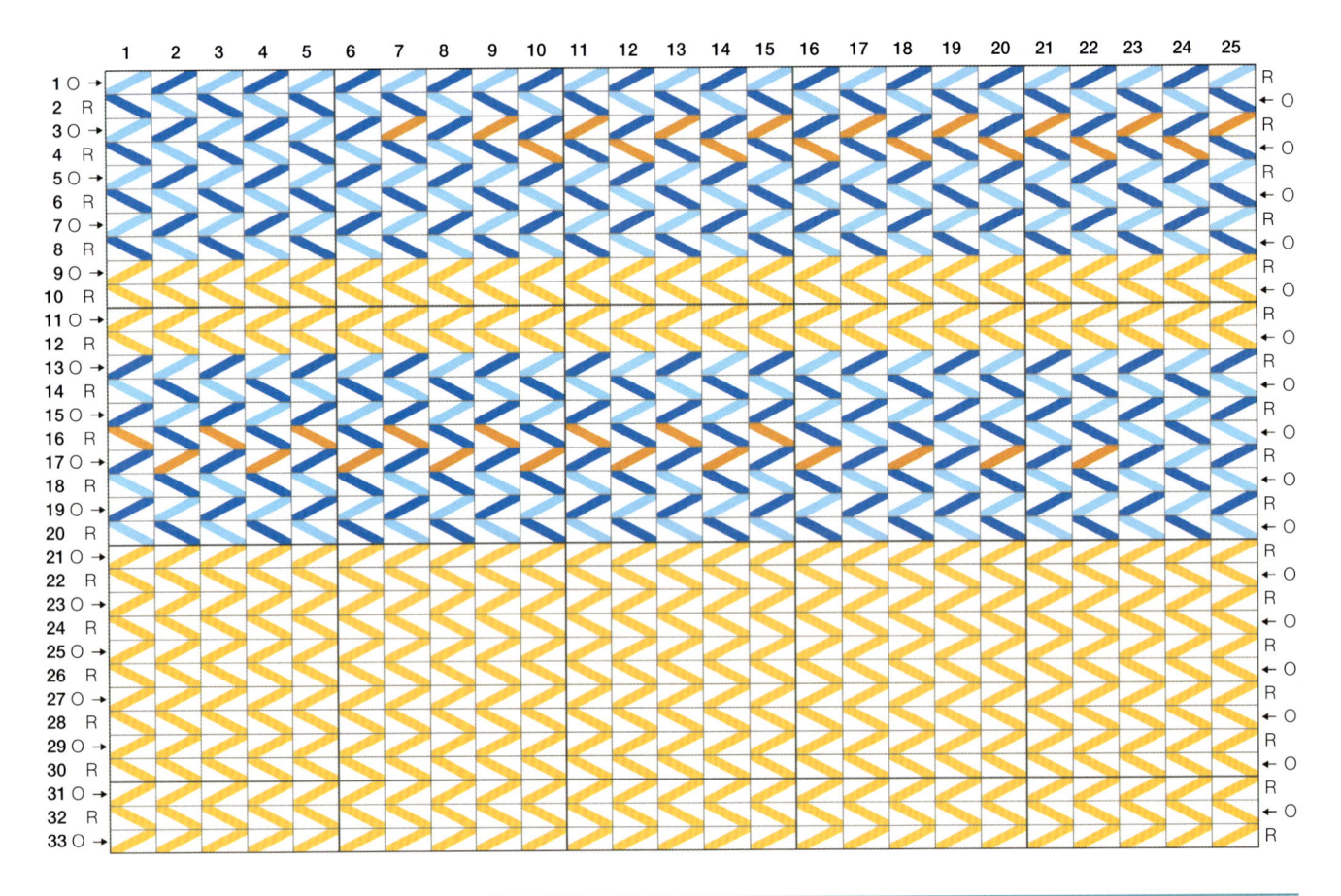

Elspeth's tip:
Some twiners believe that ending your twining on the edge of a project makes it less secure and hardwearing. This could be argued in the case of rugs, but for this tool bag project it is fine, as the edges will be stitched together and will be less exposed to wear and tear than rugs.

8 Flip the loom upside down and, working from chart 2, follow steps 4–7 to create a similar block of 20 rows of twining at the other end of the warp. The changes in color do not have to be exactly the same as before, so use whichever blues you have to hand. You are still using the over technique and regular turns on each edge.

9 Flip the loom again and join two wefts of your contrast fabric on the left of the loom (see page 158 for how to join fabrics on the edge). Working from chart 1, twine approximately 13 rows until you reach the blue twined section below and have crammed in as many rows as possible. If you twine an odd number of rows for this section, then your weft segments will form chevrons throughout the entire project (called "countered twining", see page 156). The number of rows needed to fill this section is impacted by how thick your fabrics are and how tight you twine. Finish the twining on the edge. Sandwich clip the weft strands together on the edge to weave in later. Often when I think that I'm finished, I use a wide-toothed comb to push the rows up, exposing more of the warp so that I can fit one more row of twining in.

10 When you are happy with how the twining is looking, pull out the metal rods, and pull the twined square off the loom one peg at a time using tips from page 158. Be careful that your sandwich clips don't come unclipped.

11 Trim the weft strands to approximately 2¾in (7cm) in length each and taper them each to a point. Weave in your weft strands using the technique described on page 159. Remember, to knot weft strands that were finished on the edge once, before weaving them in towards the center of the twining.

162 TWINING

CRAFTY TOOLBAG Chart 2

key to chart

- Dark blue fabric
- Light blue fabric
- Floral patterned fabric
- Cream contrast fabric

O Over method
R Regular turns
→ Direction of travel

12 Cut out a rectangle of lining fabric that is approximately 2½in (6cm) wider and 2½in (6cm) longer than the final twined piece. It should be approximately 15½ x 15½in (39 x 39cm).

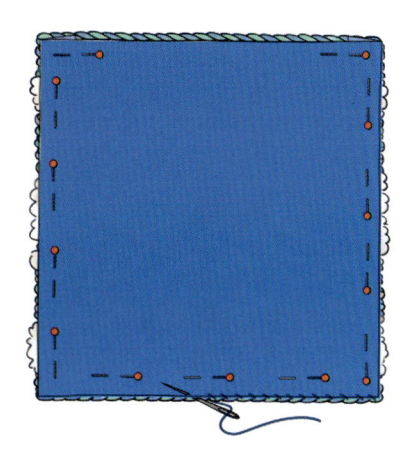

13 Fold each edge of the lining fabric under 1¼in (3cm) and pin the fabric to the wrong side of the twining (wrong sides facing if your lining fabric has a right and wrong side) with the folded hem trapped underneath. Hand stitch the lining fabric to the back of the twining, ideally using color-matched thread. Make sure that the lining fabric does not peek out further than the twining, so fold more of the lining under if necessary.

14 With the lining inside, fold the twined square in half so that the twined stripes run horizontally. Loosely pin the twined edges together and hand stitch them to join. Your sewing doesn't have to be perfect, as the twining will hide imperfections.

15 (Optional) Hand sew each side of a popper fastener to the inside edges of the bag opening, near the middle at the top. This will create two loose "pockets" on each side of the fastening, which can help to keep tools even more organized.

CRAFTY TOOLBAG 163

Sunny Side Up Placemat

Twined placemats are a fun and easy project to start out with when you're first learning how to twine, and this particular project is ideal for practicing both techniques of twining (the over and under techniques) as well as alternate turns. When choosing the colors for this project, start with one patterned fabric (I used a tropical print), look at what colors are featured in the pattern, then choose one or two for the plain blocks in this design.

What you will need:

Fabric scissors

Adjustable twining loom

Warp fabric: 31½ x 19¾in (80 x 50cm) of white spotty fabric to make a strip measuring 2in x 8¾yd (5cm x 7.92m)

Weft fabrics:

55 x 35½in (140 x 90cm) tropical patterned fabric

55 x 39½in (140 x 100cm) white spotty fabric

19¾ x 11¾in (50 x 30cm) blue fabric

23½ x 19¾in (60 x 50cm) yellow fabric

Dinner plate (to estimate size of placemat)

Safety pins/pins

Needle and thread (color matched to fabrics and pom pom trim)

Latch hook/crochet hook (for sewing in ends at the end)

½in (15mm) pom pom trim (I used two 12in/30cm lengths)

Amish toothbrush needles/hemostatic forceps (optional)

Sandwich clips (optional)

Sewing machine (optional)

1 Set up your twining loom to the desired size. We are twining the placemat so that the row closest to the crossbeam will be one side of the placemat (not the top or bottom). So, the position of the middle crossbeam will dictate the width of your placemat and the position of the right metal rod will dictate how deep your placemat will be. Hold up a plate to gauge where these should be positioned. For this exact placemat, the metal side rods were spaced 11¾in (30cm) apart (12 pegs) and the top and middle crossbeams were spaced 13in (33cm) apart.

2 Starting in the top left corner, warp up the loom using the continuous warping method on page 153. Use the white spotty fabric so that the warp will disappear into the final design. I cut my white spotty t-shirt fabric into strips 2in (5cm) wide and joined them using the diagonal seam join method on page 13 to create a strip that was approximately 8¾yd (7.92m) in length.

3 Cut your weft fabrics into long strips using any of the methods on page 11. Make sure to balance the weights of your fabrics by cutting strips of different widths based on how thick or thin they are (see page 38). The average width of strip is about 2–2½in (5–6cm) wide, but this project was made using slightly narrower strips.

4 Starting in the top left corner of the loom, twine the first section of the rug, rows 1–8, using chart 1 on page 166. The white weft should be visible on the edge, so is the trailing weft to begin with. Whenever you need to join strips (see techniques on pages 13–14), do so part way through a row and stagger the joins so that the two wefts aren't joined in the same spot.

Note: Twine around the metal rod and neighboring warp strand as if they are one and the same. Do not twine around solely the metal rod as this will create an extra loop on the edge of your twining. This is a very common mistake that beginners make.

5 Flip the loom upside down (you may need to prop it up on a table so that the twining is the correct height to work at) and working from chart 2 (on page 167), repeat this block of eight rows at the other end of the warp, but make sure to use the under technique (see page 155). This mirrors the other block, making the design symmetrical.

6 Continuing on the same side of the loom, using the under technique and weft colors, twine roughly two thirds of the way along the ninth row. When you reach roughly the 16th weft segment in row 9, cut the tropical fabric and join a yellow strip.

> **Elspeth's tip:**
> This avoids having to join weft strands on the edge (see technique on page 158) but if you'd prefer a crisper color change then wait until the end of the ninth row to join your yellow fabric.

> **Elspeth's tip:**
> If you're looking to make a full set of matching placemats then make sure that you have enough of the same fabric. Twining uses more fabric than you think.

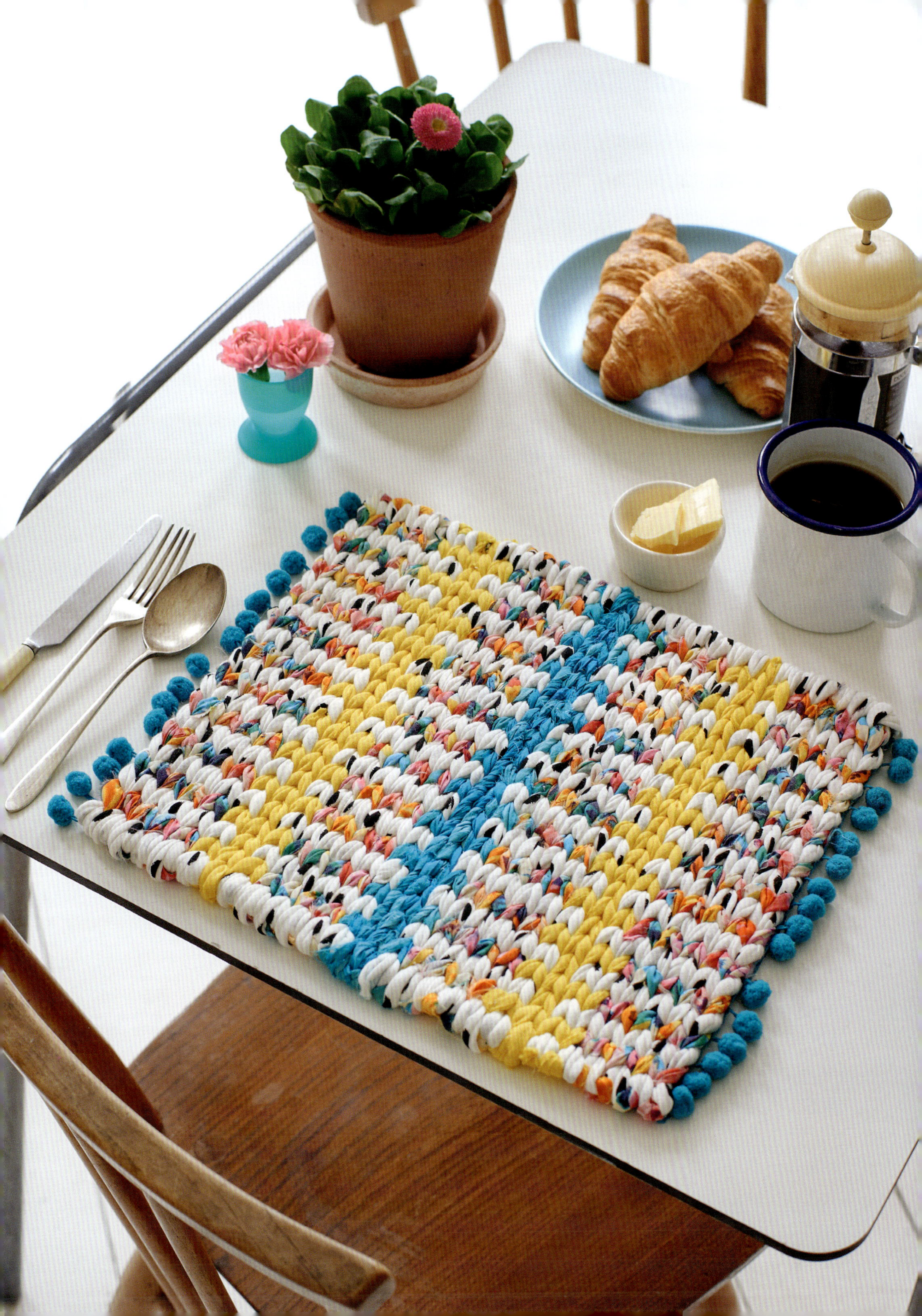

SUNNY SIDE UP PLACEMAT Chart 1

key to chart — White spotty fabric | Tropical fabric | Yellow fabric | Blue fabric

U Under method O Over method A Alternative turns → Direction of travel

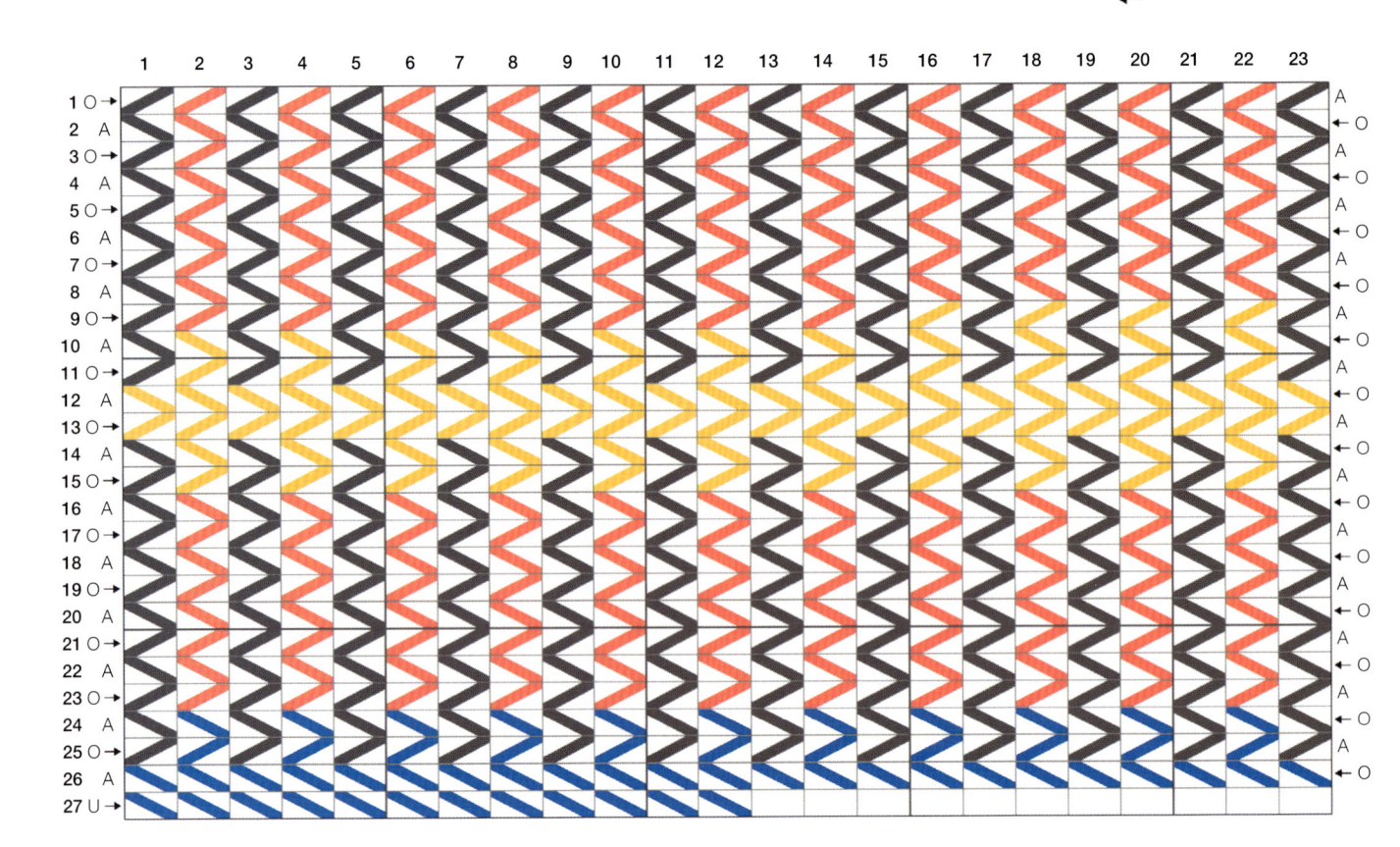

7 Continue twining to the end of row 9, and then two full rows, 10 and 11, with the white and yellow weft strands. At the end of row 11, cut the white weft on the edge and join a yellow weft, so you are now working with two yellow wefts (see page 158 for how to join fabrics on the edge). Twine rows 12 and 13 using the two yellow wefts to create a strip of block color.

8 At the end of row 13 (you should be on the right of the loom), twine around the last warp strand and metal rod as usual, identify which of the yellow wefts would begin on the edge of the placemat in the new row and cut that yellow weft where it passes behind the metal rod. Untwine the previous row slightly and join the spotty white weft, so that this is the color you see on the edge.

Alternatively, sandwich clip off both of the yellow wefts to trim and sew in at the end of the project. Sew together a yellow and white weft and begin twining row 14 from right to left with the white spotty weft visible on the edge (see joining techniques on pages 13–14).

9 Twine rows 14 and 15 using the white and yellow wefts, then cut the yellow weft on the edge and join the tropical weft. Continue twining eight full rows (rows 16–23) with the tropical and white wefts.

10 Flip the loom upside down once again and, using chart 1 and steps 6–9, complete the same section at the other end of the warp, making sure to use the over technique, so that the design is mirrored.

Elspeth's tip:

To create roughly the same amount of blue twining in the center of the placemat as you did with the yellow sections, you may need to twine more rows on both ends of the loom using the white and patterned fabrics. Twine as many rows as needed, so that the gap between your blocks for the blue section will fit roughly seven rows of twining. Use a ruler to measure one of the yellow sections as a guide.

166 TWINING

SUNNY SIDE UP PLACEMAT Chart 2

key to chart: White spotty fabric | Tropical fabric | Yellow fabric | Blue fabric

U Under method
A Alternative turns
→ Direction of travel
←

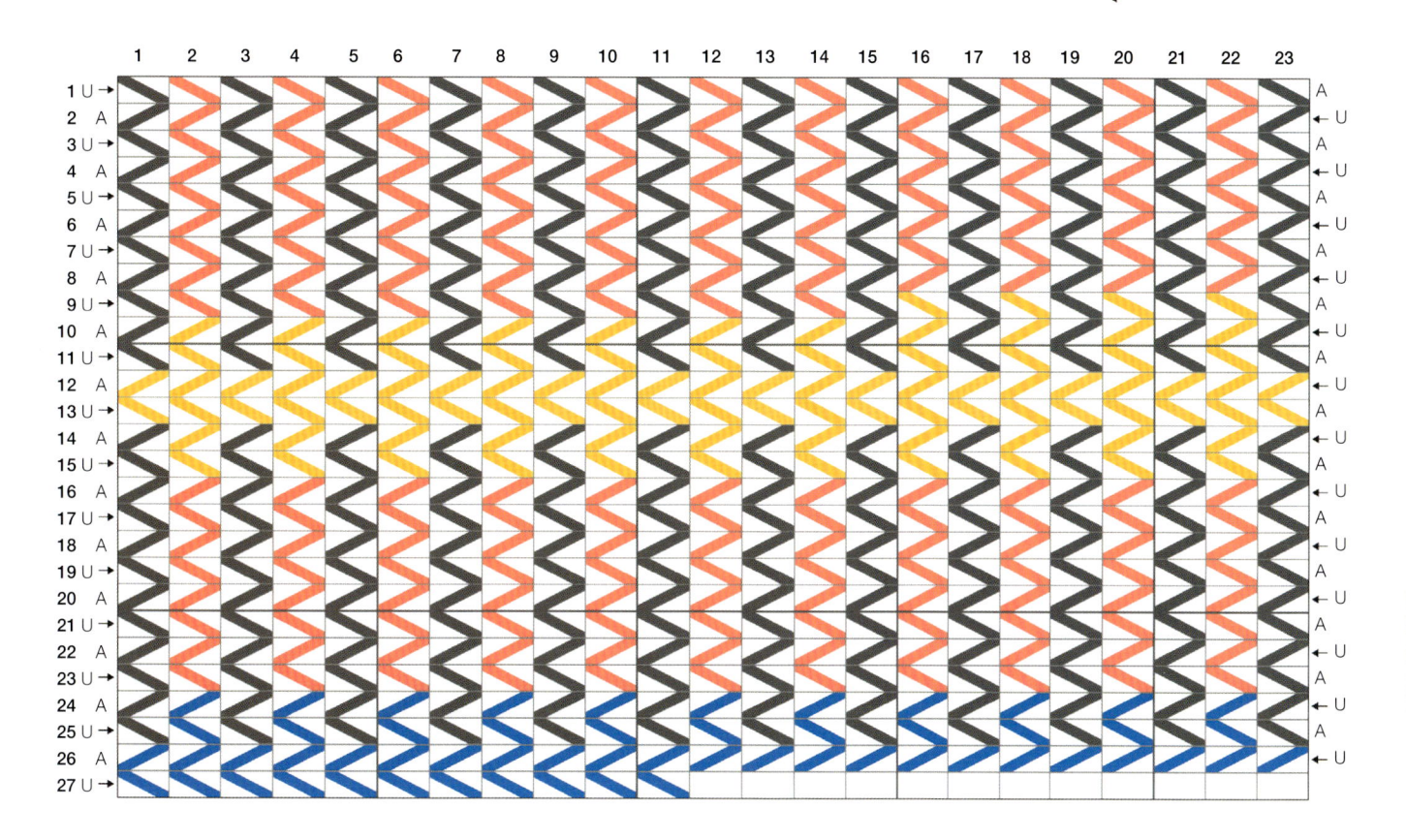

11 Flip the loom, cut the tropical fabric on the edge and join a blue weft strand. Using chart 2, twine rows 24 and 25 using the blue and white wefts.

12 Flip the loom, and starting from the right to left, using chart 1, twine rows 24 and 25 using the blue and white wefts. At the end of row 25, cut the white weft behind the metal rod and join a blue weft. Twine one blue row using the over technique then after the alternate turn on the edge, switch to the under technique and twine part of the next row. This switch in technique means that your weft segments will slant the same direction from one row to the next. The gap in the center of the placemat will be getting quite tight now, so take a look at page 158 for tips on how to twine the last few rows of your piece.

13 Flip the loom upside down, cut the white weft and join a blue weft. Twine one full row and part of the next using the under technique. The switch in technique in step 12 means that your weft segments will slant the same direction as the partially twined row you are working towards.

14 Continue twining along the row until the 4 wefts meet. Carefully poke the wefts through to the back of the twining, ensuring that the last few "stitches" are completed as usual. It doesn't matter if two wefts pass through the same hole to the back and if the meeting in the middle looks odd, you can always poke the ends back through to the front and try again.

15 Remove the metal rods and pull the twined placemat off the loom.

16 Trim the weft strands to approximately 2¾in (7cm) in length and taper them to a point. Weave in your weft strands using the technique described on page 159.

17 Hand stitch the pom pom trim to the wrong side of the placemat, along each short edge. Trim and fold the end of the trim under before stitching to secure it better. Pin beforehand if necessary.

SUNNY SIDE UP PLACEMAT 167

English Cottage Rug

The color scheme for this twined rag rug was inspired by classic red and white gingham often found in country cottages. The subtle ivory color was added to make the design a little bit more sophisticated. The chopping and changing in this rug involves a slightly more advanced form of twining, so I recommend that you start with one of the smaller projects first before taking on this design.

You will need

Fabric scissors/rotary cutter and mat

Adjustable twining loom

Warp fabric:

Approximately 101½ x 39½in (258 x 100cm) of red fabric to create a strip measuring 2in x 56⅜yd (5cm x 51.5m)

Weft fabrics:

Approximately 78¾ x 59in (200 x 150cm) of red and white fabrics

Approximately 59 x 39½in (150 x 100cm) of ivory fabrics

(I used old net curtains and part of a sheet for the white, crochet curtains for the ivory, and an old red fleece blanket mixed with sports tops for the red)

Safety pins/pins

Needle and thread (color matched to fabrics) (optional)

Sandwich clips (optional)

Latch hook/crochet hook

Amish toothbrush needles/hemostatic forceps (optional)

Sewing machine (optional)

Joining on the edge

In this rug, there are many places where the pattern changes from one distinct pattern to another on the edge (e.g. two red wefts become one red and one white weft in the next row). To do this requires joining a new weft strand on the edge of your rug. If you are changing both the weft strands in the same place on the edge, this can be difficult to hide effectively and can create a lumpy edge. See page 153 for how to join fabrics on the edge, changing either one weft strand or both. This rug was done using a combination of both techniques, so it really is personal preference which methods you use, where.

1 Set up your twining loom to the desired size. I used the full length and width of my loom. This pattern works at any width and pattern sections can be removed or repeated for a shorter or longer rug. For this exact rug, the metal side rods were spaced 24¾in (63cm) apart (25 pegs) and the top and bottom cross beams were spaced 40½in (103cm) apart. Remove the middle cross beam before you start.

2 Starting in the top left corner, warp up the loom using the continuous method of warping on page 153. Use red fabric so that the warp will disappear into the final design. I cut my red fabric into strips 2in (5cm) in width and joined them using the diagonal seam join method on page 13 to create a strip that was approximately 56⅜yd (51.5m) in length.

3 Cut your weft fabrics into long strips using any of the methods on page 11. Make sure to balance the weights of your fabrics by cutting the strips into different widths based on how thick or thin they are. The average strip width is about 2–2½in (5–6cm).

4 Starting in the top left corner of the loom, twine the first section of the rug using chart 1 on page 170 (rows 1–18). Whenever there are rows of block red, I worked with two different reds (one for each weft). When you change from one block color to another, use either of the two joining methods on pages 13–14.

5 Flip the loom upside down and, using chart 2 on page 171, twine the same design as described in step 4 at the other end of the warp (rows 1–18). To mirror the pattern exactly and ensure that the chevrons point the same direction at both ends of the rug, follow the chart exactly for which technique to use for each row.

6 Without flipping the loom, continue on. Twine the second design block using rows 19–32 of chart 2.

7 Flip the loom upside down and twine rows 19–32 of chart 1 at the other end of the warp. To mirror the pattern exactly and ensure that the chevrons point the same direction at both ends of the rug, follow the chart exactly for which technique to use for each row.

8 Without flipping the loom, continue on. Twine the third design block using rows 33–49 of chart 1.

9 Flip the loom upside down and twine rows 33–49 of chart 2 at the other end of the warp.

Elspeth's design tip

You could do this rug in any colorway of your choosing. All it requires is three colors.

Some twiners prefer to cut and prepare all their fabric strips before they start twining, by rolling them into neat balls.

10 Without flipping the loom, continue on. Twine the fourth design block using rows 50–59 of chart 2.

11 Flip the loom upside down and twine rows 50–59 of chart 1 at the other end of the warp.

12 Without flipping the loom, continue on. Twine the fifth design block using rows 60–63 of chart 1.

13 Flip the loom upside down and twine rows 60–63 of chart 2 at the other end of the warp.

14 Measure the distance between the blocks of twining to roughly estimate how many rows you have left to fill. This will dictate your design. The space left to fill at this point will come down to the thickness of fabric used, tightness of your twining, and other factors. I estimated that I had the space for about 12 rows.

Elspeth's design tip:

When you take the rug off the loom at the end of the project, it will relax and compress up slightly. Areas of same pitch twining can cause the edges of the rug to bow in slightly, so take care to keep your tension even as you work these sections.

ENGLISH COTTAGE RUG Chart 1

key to chart

- Red fabric
- Ivory fabric
- White fabric

O - Over method
U - Under method
R - Regular turn
A - Alternate turn

→ Direction of travel
←

15 Without flipping the loom, continue on. Twine the next design block using rows 64–75 of chart 2, but add or subtract rows using just red twining (rows 64–65 and 74–75 in chart 2) to account for how many rows you have left to fill. The gap in the center of the rug will be getting quite tight now, so take a look at page 158 for tips on how to twine the last few rows of your piece.

16 Sandwich clip the final wefts on the edge to sew in. When you are happy with how the twining is looking, pull out the metal rods and pull the twined rug off the loom one peg at a time using tips from page 158. Be careful that your sandwich clips don't come unclipped.

17 Trim the weft strands to approximately 2¾in (7cm) in length each and taper them each to a point. Weave in your weft strands using the technique described on page 159. Remember to knot weft strands that were finished on the edge once, before weaving them in toward the center of the twining.

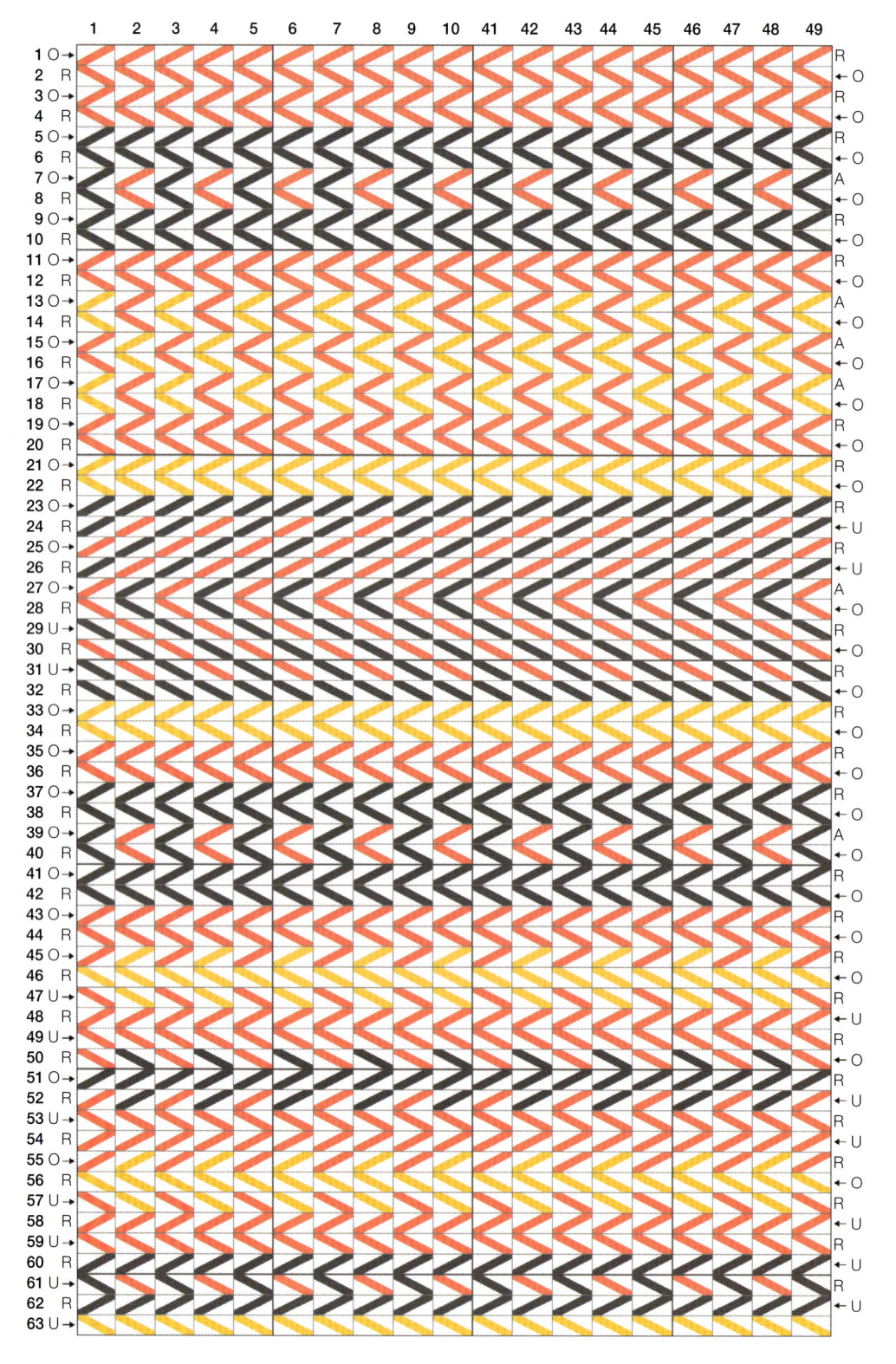

Elspeth's tip:

After each row, push the twining up against the previous row to compact the rows together. Occasionally, run your fingers through the warp strands to make sure that none have crossed over.

170 TWINING

ENGLISH COTTAGE RUG Chart 2

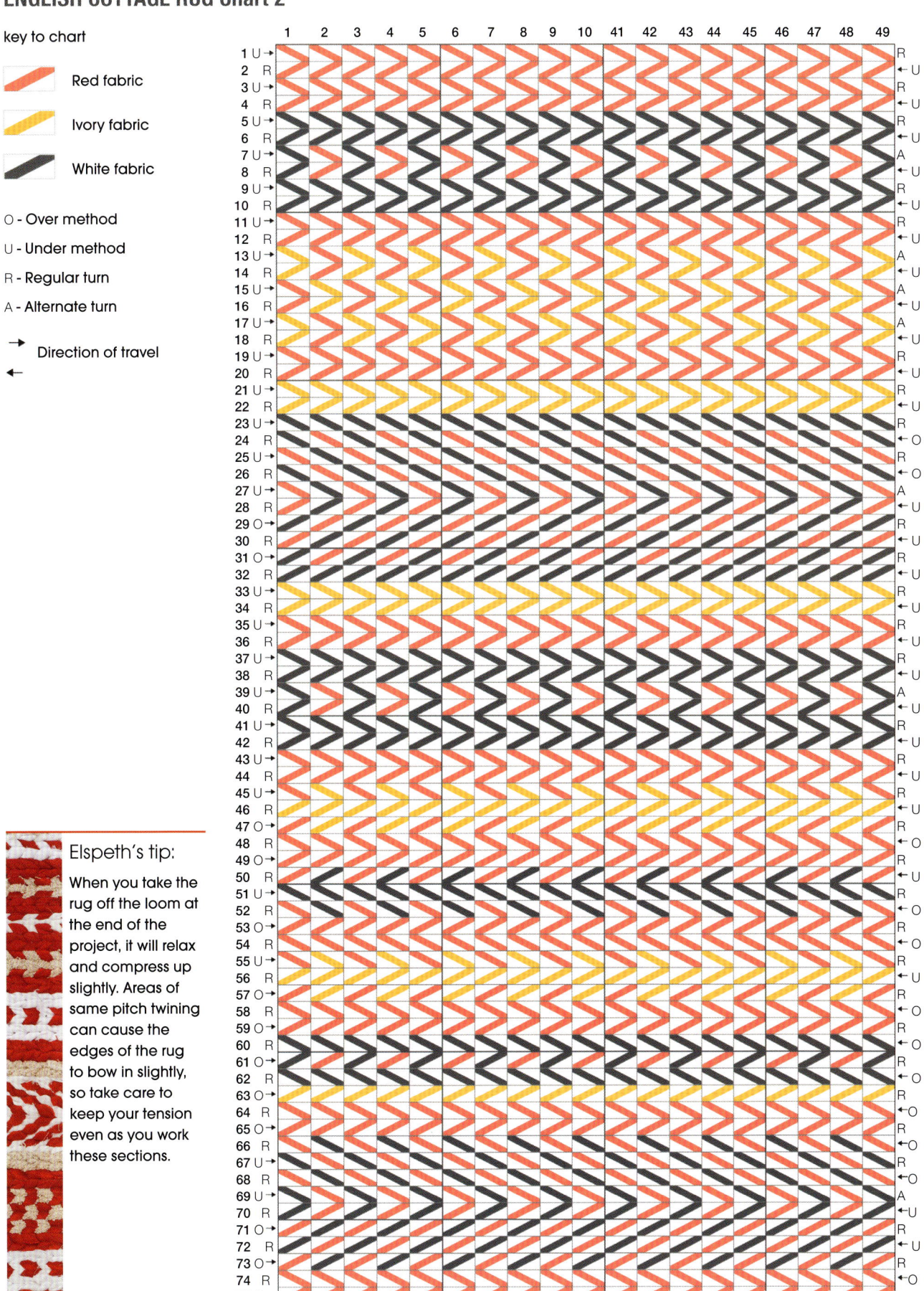

key to chart

- Red fabric
- Ivory fabric
- White fabric

O - Over method
U - Under method
R - Regular turn
A - Alternate turn

→ Direction of travel
←

Elspeth's tip:
When you take the rug off the loom at the end of the project, it will relax and compress up slightly. Areas of same pitch twining can cause the edges of the rug to bow in slightly, so take care to keep your tension even as you work these sections.

ENGLISH COTTAGE RUG 171

Templates

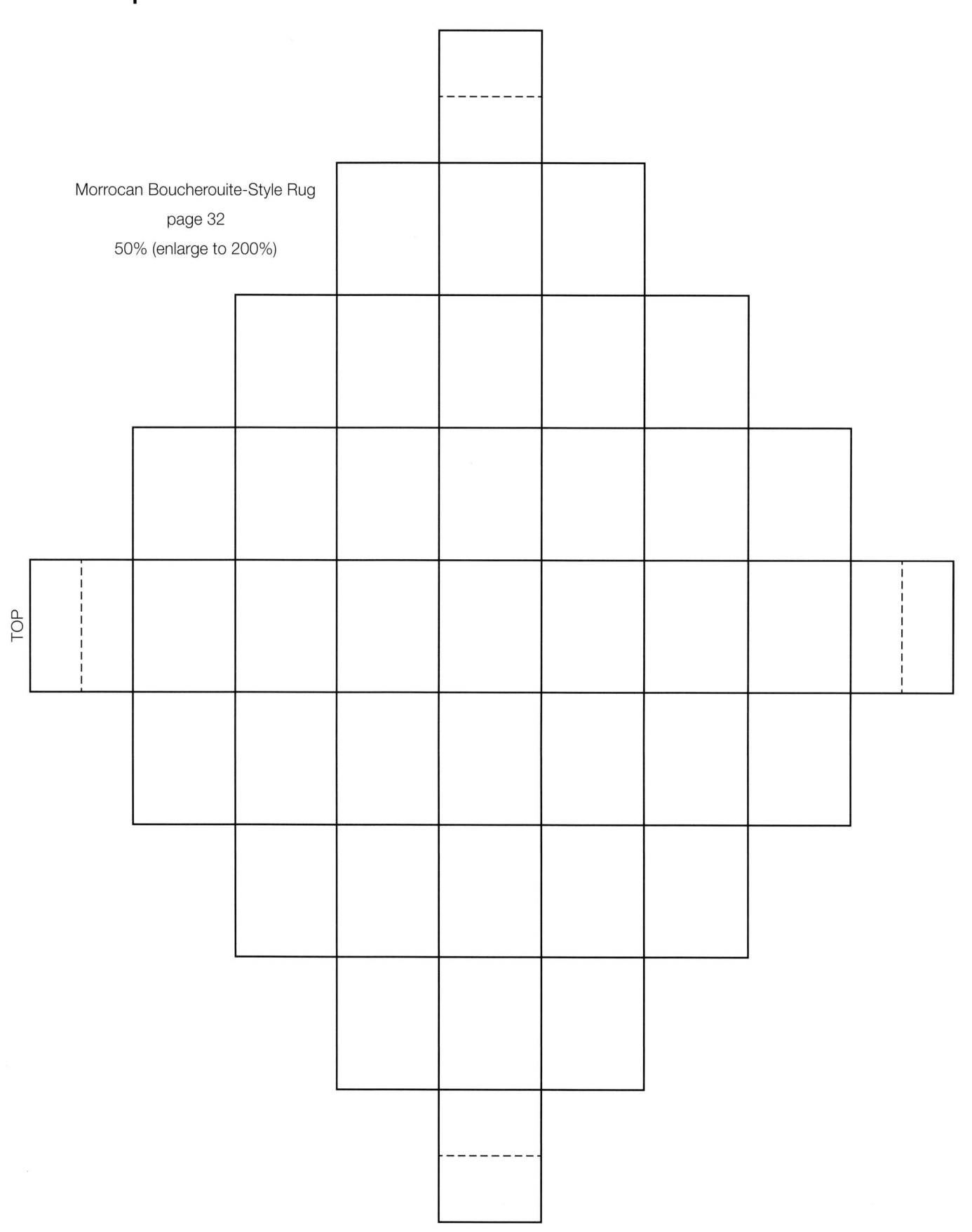

Morrocan Boucherouite-Style Rug
page 32
50% (enlarge to 200%)

TOP

172 TEMPLATES

heel

Swedish "Klackmatta" Rug
page 146
full size

Classic Christmas Stockings
page 52
50% (enlarge to 200%)

TEMPLATES 173

Stockists

ONLINE

Ragged Life

On Elspeth's Ragged Life website you can buy all the rag rug tools and looms used in the projects in this book or book yourself on to a rag rug workshop. Ragged Life ships globally.

Rag Rug Textile Studio
The Stables,
Delamere House,
Great Wymondley
Hitchin
Hertfordshire SG4 7ER
+44 (0)7815 796285
www.raggedlife.com

eBay

A useful place to buy vintage rag rug tools. You can sometimes find rag rug spring tools under the name "Brown's patent rag rug tool."

www.ebay.com
www.ebay.co.uk

Etsy

A great place to see other crafters' rag rug designs and track down hard-to-find equipment.

www.etsy.com
www.etsy.com/uk

US

The Woolery

Stocks an extensive range of rug making equipment, including Ragged Life rag rug kits, peg looms, locker hooking materials, woollen selvedges, and much more.

info@woolery.com
www.woolery.com

Hobby Lobby

Stores nationwide. Stocks the basic rag rug tools.

www.hobbylobby.com

Jo-Ann Fabric and Craft Stores

Stores nationwide. Pick up latch hooks and rug canvas here.

www.joann.com

Michaels

Stores nationwide. Lots of burlap options.

www.michaels.com

Halcyon Yarn

Nice for rug making inspiration.

12 School Street
Bath, ME 04530
800-341-0282
www.halcyonyarn.com

Libbylula Looms

Great for quality, handmade twining and peg looms.

www.etsy.com/uk/shop/LibbyLuLa

UK

Cornish Stitch Designs

Rag rug and other craft equipment.

Singer Sewing Centre
2 Queen Street
Penzance
Cornwall TR18 4BJ
01736 363457
www.pensans.co.uk

Rag Art Studios

Great for tools and workshops.

Trefenter
Llanddewi-Brefi
Tregaron
Ceredigion SY25 6SB
01974 298100
www.ragartstudios.com

Hobbycraft

Stores nationwide.
0330 026 1400
www.hobbycraft.co.uk

Cool Crafting

For rag rug kits and tools.

40 Market Place
Kendal LA9 4TN
01539 724099
www.coolcrafting.co.uk

The Craft Store

A TV channel dedicated to bringing you live demonstrations that inspire all your craft, hobbies, and art needs.

www.thecraftstore.com

Dales Looms

For handmade, adjustable peg looms.

www.daleslooms.co.uk

Fred Aldous

Lovely independent shop with everything crafty, including rag rug equipment. Also sells online.

37 Lever Street
Manchester M1 1LW
0161 236 4224

34 Kirkgate
Leeds LS2 7DR
0113 243 3531

9 Fitzalan Square
Sheffield S1 2AY
0114 349 8142

www.fredaldous.co.uk

Index

A
All the Blues Blanket Box 48–51

B
burlap (hessian) 9
   hemming 16–17
   weave 9
   working in straight lines 15

C
Checked Sari Rug 24–25
Christmas
   Christmas Tree 130–131
   Classic Christmas Stockings 52–55, 173
   Joyful Mini Wreaths 26–29
"Ciao Bella" Wall Hanging 117–119
coiled rope 8, 60–79
   fabrics 62
   Gold Coast Rug 66–69
   Let's Go to the Beach Basket 70–73
   No-Sew Plant Pot Cover 74–75
   Rag and Rope Rainbow Hanging 76–79
   techniques 63–65
   tools and materials 62
Crafty Toolbag 160–163

D
design tips
   locker hooking 108
   loopy rag rugging 41
   peg loom weaving 87
   shaggy rag rugging 23
   two-string loom 125
Domino Thread Catcher 112–116

E
Eco-Friendly Gift Wrap Spirals 128–129
English Cottage Rug 168–171
equipment, general 9

F
fabrics 9
   deconstructing clothing 10
   quantity, calculating 17
   raveling (fraying) 9
   scraps 9, 20
   weights 9
   see also strips
frames 38

G
gauge 12–13, 20
glue gun 9
Gold Coast Rug 66–69

H
hemming burlap 16–17
   edge hemming 16–17
   placeholder hemming 17
Highlands Rug 88–90

J
joining strips 13–14
   buttonhole join 14
   diagonal seam join 13
   enclosed end join 14
Joyful Mini Wreaths 26–29

K
Knick-Knack Storage Bag 94–97

L
Let's Go to the Beach Basket 70–73
locker hook 104
locker hooking 8, 102–119
   "Ciao Bella" Wall Hanging 117–119
   Domino Thread Catcher 112–116
   fabrics 104
   Patchwork Rug 109–111
   techniques 105–108
   tools and materials 104
loopy rag rugging 8, 36–59
   All the Blues Blanket Box 48–51
   Classic Christmas Stockings 52–55, 173
   common mistakes 42
   fabrics 38
   Ocean Waves Pillow 54–59
   techniques 40–41
   tools and materials 38
   Tranquil Triangles Rug 42–44
   "You Are My Sunshine" Rug 45–47

M
marker pen 9
Moroccan Boucherouite-Style Rag Rug 32–35, 172

N
No-Sew Plant Pot Cover 74–75
No-Sew Tulip Mirror 142–145

O
Ocean Waves Pillow 54–59

P
Pastel Paint Drip Pillow 98–101
Patchwork Rug 109–111
peg loom 82
peg loom weaving 8, 80–101
   fabrics 82–83
   Highlands Rug 88–90
   Knick-Knack Storage Bag 94–97
   Pastel Paint Drip Pillow 98–101
   techniques 83–87
   Toasty Fall Leaves Scarf 91–93
   tools and materials 82–83
pillows
   Ocean Waves Pillow 54–59
   Pastel Paint Drip Pillow 98–101
   Statement Boho Pillow 134–137
Pink Ombré Rug 126–127

R
Rag and Rope Rainbow Hanging 76–79
rag rug spring tool 20, 22
Ragged Flower Bouquet 29–31
rotary cutter, mat, and ruler 9, 11
rug canvas 104
rug (latch) hook 38
rugs
   Checked Sari Rug 24–25
   English Cottage Rug 168–171
   Gold Coast Rug 66–69
   Highlands Rug 88–90
   Moroccan Boucherouite-Style Rag Rug 32–35, 172
   Patchwork Rug 109–111
   Pink Ombré Rug 126–127
   Stitched "Tapete de Retalhos" Rug 138–141
   Swedish "Klackmatta" 146–149, 173
   Tranquil Triangles Rug 42–44
   "You Are My Sunshine" Rug 45–47

S
scissors 9, 11
sewing machine 9
shaggy rag rugging 8, 18–35
   Checked Sari Rug 24–25
   common mistakes 23
   fabrics 20
   Joyful Mini Wreaths 26–29
   Moroccan Boucherouite-Style Rag Rug 32–35, 172
   Ragged Flower Bouquet 29–31
   techniques 21–23
   tools and materials 20
Statement Boho Pillow 134–137
stitched rag rugs 8, 132–149
   No-Sew Tulip Mirror 142–145
   Statement Boho Pillow 134–137
   Stitched "Tapete de Retalhos" Rug 138–141
   Swedish "Klackmatta" 146–149, 173
   tools and materials 134

stockists 173
storage
   All the Blues Blanket Box 48–51
   Crafty Toolbag 160–163
   Domino Thread Catcher 112–116
   Knick-Knack Storage Bag 94–97
   Let's Go to the Beach Basket 70–73
strips
   cutting 11, 12
   joining 13–14
   tearing 12
   winding and cutting on a gauge 12–13
Sunny Side Up Placemat 164–167
Swedish "Klackmatta" 146–149, 173

T
techniques, general 10–17
Toasty Fall Leaves Scarf 91–93
Tranquil Triangles Rug 42–44
twining 8, 150–171
   common mistakes 159
   Crafty Toolbag 160–163
   English Cottage Rug 168–171
   fabrics 152
   Sunny Side Up Placemat 164–167
   techniques 152–159
   tools and materials 152
   warp and weft 151
twining loom 152

two-string loom 8, 120–131
   Christmas Tree 130–131
   Eco-Friendly Gift Wrap Spirals 128–129
   fabrics 122
   Pink Ombré Rug 126–127
   techniques 123–125
   tools and materials 122

W
wall hangings
   "Ciao Bella" Wall Hanging 117–119
   Rag and Rope Rainbow Hanging 76–79

Y
"You Are My Sunshine" Rug 45–47

Acknowledgments

Writing a book is never as simple as it seems and without the unwavering support of the incredible people below, this riot of color and texture wouldn't have been possible.

First, a hug and a kiss to my partner in crime, Christian. You kept me fed, watered, and showered with love. There's no one I'd rather have been locked down with. Thanks to my darling mum, Victoria, whose eye for color and design is beyond compare. Lots of love to my dad, David, for the business nous and creative flair. To my big brother, Ross—you're my number one fan and I'm yours. And thank you, Kellie, for the objective eye—I promise I won't mix up "less" and "fewer."

To my Ragged Life team—in particular Lizzie, Sany, Nicole, Nigel, and Anil—thank you for taking up the reins and spurring me on while I was immersed in these rag rug projects. I am enormously thankful to work with such kind and switched-on people.

Thanks to everyone at CICO Books for keeping the momentum going on this beast of a book. As my publisher, Cindy, put it, "this book has been more complex than any of us had thought it would be,"—but it was all worth it in the end. Thank you in particular to my editor, Martha, for putting in the extra work editing rag rug techniques that she'd never even heard of before with a careful and diligent eye. Thanks to Sally and Geoff for their beautiful designs and layouts; Cathy for her carefully crafted illustrations; Nel for the gorgeous styling; and James and Penny for their stunning photography. To Cindy and Penny—my sincerest thanks for your professionalism, exceptional patience, and support.

Finally, a big thank you to all the wonderful creatives and crafters reading this book. You never fail to astound me with your passion for all things handmade. I hope this book inspires you as much as you all inspire me.

ASSAULT
AREA.
92X
1354X
C DE LA HE
LE HAVRE
1215X
FORCE "D"
D
S5
SCYLL
LARGS
S
SWORD
BAND
S
HONFL
VILLERS
HOULGATE
LION-S-MER
CABOURG
QUISTREHAM

Published by the Portsmouth D-Day Museum Trust to commemorate the 80th anniversary of D-Day, 6 June 2024.

Concept and Editor, Cathy Hakes

Written by Steve Humphrey

Designed by Janice Kalsi, StudioMoö Design

Copyright © Portsmouth D-Day Museum Trust.

All images remain the copyright of the credited owners.

All rights reserved. No part of this publication may be transmitted in any form or by any means, electronic or mechanical, including photocopy, recording or any storage or retrieval system without the prior permission in writing of the copyright holder and publisher.

A catalogue record for this book is available from the British Library.

ISBN: 978-1-3999-8420-1

Printed and bound in the UK by L&S Printing Company

Front and back covers *Betty White's Coat*.
Photography by Pete Langdown.

The publication of this book has been supported by the generous sponsorship of Wates and Sir Robert McAlpine. Further information about the involvement of these companies in D-Day can be found on pages 110-111.

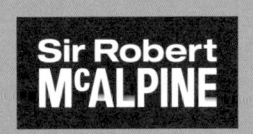

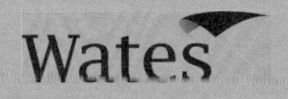

D-DAY IN 80 OBJECTS

THE D-DAY STORY PORTSMOUTH

THE NATIONAL MUSEUM ROYAL NAVY

IWM IMPERIAL WAR MUSEUMS

NATIONAL ARMY MUSEUM

ROYAL AIR FORCE museum

This photograph of the Supreme Command, Allied Expeditionary Force, was taken in London in February 1944. From left to right:

Lieutenant General Omar Bradley, Commander in Chief, First US Army
Admiral Sir Bertram Ramsay, Allied Naval Commander in Chief, Expeditionary Force
Air Chief Marshal Sir Arthur Tedder, Deputy Supreme Commander, Expeditionary Force
General Dwight D. Eisenhower, Supreme Commander, Expeditionary Force
General Sir Bernard Montgomery, Commander in Chief 21st Army Group
Air Chief Marshal Sir Trafford Leigh-Mallory, Allied Air Commander, Expeditionary Force
Lieutenant General Walter Bedell-Smith, Chief of Staff to General Eisenhower.

Photograph: Courtesy of Imperial War Museums

FOREWORD

Operation Overlord was extraordinary, and it changed the course of world history.

It was an amalgamation of bravery and ingenuity, underpinned by colossal logistics to make sure those on the front line had the weapons and supplies they needed for victory on the battlefield.

The operation involved the cooperation of land, sea and air forces from 12 countries.

It was the largest seaborne military operation in history and it paved the way for Allied forces to free occupied Europe from Nazi oppression.

My grandfather, General Montgomery, was in command of all Allied ground forces during Operation Overlord.

Writing on the 10th anniversary of D-Day he said:

"We knew the invasion would be difficult. But I had complete confidence we would succeed. We had on our side the great asset of surprise."

"We also had the benefit of meticulous planning and rehearsing, great concentration of strength and a big advantage in morale."

The statistics behind D-Day speak volumes about the multi-national effort by both military personnel and civilians.

This collection of D-Day in 80 Objects illustrates both the complexity of the planning process and the heroism of those who took part, giving us a glimpse of some of the human stories behind the headlines.

Above all else, they show that D-Day and the battles that followed were the result of a collective effort by millions of people bound together by a common determination to free Europe from the grip of a tyrannical power.

As we commemorate the 80th anniversary of D-Day we must also remember my grandfather's words that have echoed down the decades:

"Do not let us forget that many brave men gave their lives so that we who remain might have freedom and a better world."

Henry, 3rd Viscount Montgomery of Alamein
May 2024

INTRODUCTION

This book is dedicated to all of those who took part in the D-Day landings and the people who made it possible.

Over many decades I have had the privilege and the honour of interviewing over 100 D-Day veterans. The people who put their own lives at risk in the quest to rid occupied Western Europe of Nazi oppression.

All the veterans have been humble and self-effacing about their own part in the biggest amphibious military operation in history. They always say the real heroes were their mates who didn't come home; whose names are now etched in their thousands on memorials across the Normandy countryside.

In the countdown to the 80th Anniversary of D-Day, I have had more precious moments interviewing surviving veterans for the BBC's 'We Were There' project and the South Today programme.

Amongst them Stan Ford and John Roberts, who both served in the Royal Navy.

In February 2024, their names were added to the Normandy Memorial Wall at the D-Day Story Museum in Portsmouth.

John, who was 99 at the time of the ceremony, hopes the veterans' personal stories will help keep the story of D-Day alive for generations to come.

John said, *"I hope they will not only remember me but remember World War Two and all who gave their lives."*

"It's more important every year because there will be less and less veterans alive. In ten years', time there will be no veterans left."

Stan Ford's ship HMS Fratton was sunk on D-Day. 31 of his shipmates were killed and Stan was badly wounded.

Mr Ford, who was 98 when I met him at the D-Day Story Museum, said

"I survived and there are 31 reasons why I keep going back to Normandy to pay my respects, that's the 31 guys that never made it."

"I hope the young people will hear of the exploits, take it on board and see that it doesn't happen again."

"I wouldn't say it was a pleasure, but it was a necessary evil that it was done."

This book is dedicated to Stan and John and all the people who played a part in making sure D-Day was a success. Those who came home and those that made the ultimate sacrifice to set Europe free.

The 80 objects in this book help tell the story of D-Day. The personal stories of those who planned and gathered intelligence, the people who made the equipment, the civilians who invited troops into their homes and those who served in the army, the navy and the air force.

The objects not only tell a story. They give us a direct link to the events of 80 years ago. A time when the future of Europe still hung in the balance. Stan and John, and hundreds of thousands of people like them, changed the course of history.

Steve Humphrey
May 2024

Stan Ford and John Roberts at the D-Day Story Museum in Portsmouth in February 2024.

Photograph courtesy of Sarah Standing, The News, Portsmouth

Stan Ford

John Roberts

01

DEAR MUM & DAD

The letter Jack Gollin wrote to his Mum and Dad and younger brother in the summer of 1943 shows that he found joining the British Army was something of a culture shock.

Courtesy of The D-Day Story.

In this letter 18 year old Jack Gollin complains about life in the army and the lack of leave. He tells his family about the inoculations he and his friends have been having and asks for several things to be sent to him, including his shaving brush and nose cream. He also apologises for writing his army number incorrectly saying "… it's all blasted numbers in the army."

Private Gollin served in the York and Lancaster Regiment. He was killed during fighting to the west of Caen on 23 July 1944. He was buried at Tilly-sur-Seulles cemetery in Normandy.

There were an estimated half a million troops in the Free French Forces by the time of the D-Day landings. Several French units landed on the Normandy beaches and eventually led the drive by the Allies towards Paris. Amongst them were the famous 2nd Armoured Division under General Leclerc. The Free French Navy also served alongside the Allies and there were Free French units in the Royal Air Force. Inside France, secret agents and resistance groups gathered intelligence and carried out acts of sabotage.

FREE FRENCH RECRUITING POSTER

This poster is a direct appeal to French people in Allied countries to join the Free French Forces and help liberate their homeland.

Courtesy of Imperial War Museums.

03

ARIZONA METAL

A fragment of metal from the battleship USS Arizona highlights the link between the Japanese attack on Pearl Harbour and D-Day.

Courtesy of The National WWII Museum.

The USS Arizona was hit by several bombs and sank when the Japanese attacked the naval base at Pearl Harbour in Hawaii in December 1941.

When the smoke cleared, 2,333 Americans had been killed and over 1,000 were wounded. President Roosevelt described 7 December 1944 as "... a date which will live in infamy." Within days, the US was at war with Japan, Germany and Italy.

The attack on Pearl Harbour was carried out by Japan, but it meant that a slumbering giant was spurred into action and American forces would play a decisive part in D-Day and the liberation of Nazi occupied Europe.

04

Biscuit tin radios dropped by parachute were vital as the Germans had confiscated the vast majority of civilian radios. During BBC broadcasts, special messages were read out, which had a secret meaning.

Just before the D-Day landings, the BBC's 'Radio Londres' broadcast the first part of Paul Verlaine's poem 'Chanson d'automne' to tell resistance groups the invasion was about to take place. The radios were made by Philco and were contained in a water-tight steel tin, which is why they got the nickname 'Biscuit Tin Radios'. By the end of the war 30,000 had been made.

BISCUIT TIN RADIO

Miniature 'biscuit tin radios' were supplied to resistance groups in Nazi occupied Europe so they could receive secret messages broadcast by the BBC, before and after D-Day.

Courtesy of Imperial War Museums.

05

RECONNAISSANCE SUIT

These suits were worn by the heroic men who carried out secret reconnaissance work on the Normandy beaches in the countdown to D-Day.

Courtesy of Imperial War Museums.

Some of the greatest stories of bravery connected with D-Day happened months before the first troops waded ashore on the 6 June 1944. Dressed in these suits, men from a top-secret unit swam ashore from boats or on one occasion, from a midget submarine.

Their job was to check to see if tanks could drive across the beaches without sinking and to gather information on German defences. The men who carried out the work were members of the Combined Operations Pilotage Parties. On D-Day they used their navigation skills to try to ensure the Allied forces landed in the right places.

06

This postcard of holidaymakers on the beach at Villers-sur-Mer was a crucial part of the information gathering that took place before D-Day.

People across the UK had enthusiastically responded to a BBC radio appeal in 1942 to send in postcards and photos from pre-war holidays to Europe.

By 1944, around 10 million had arrived by post. Information gathered from the pictures was incorporated into maps and the special models of the Normandy coast that were made to brief troops. Intelligence gathered by the French resistance and air reconnaissance was also crucial to the success of D-Day.

BEACH POSTCARDS

An appeal was made on BBC radio for people to send in holiday postcards and photographs to help in planning D-Day.

Courtesy of Imperial War Museums.

07

3-D BEACH MODEL

3-D models of the French coast were made to brief troops in the countdown to D-Day to make sure they knew the location of German strongpoints that had to be knocked-out.

Courtesy of Imperial War Museums.

Troops taking part in the D-Day landings went through an intensive period of briefings. Along with maps, 3-D models were made so they could absorb the lie of the land in the areas where they would be fighting. Information for the models came from aerial reconnaissance missions, covert surveys of the landing beaches, and information from the French resistance, which provided crucial information on defences and troop movements. Details were also gleaned from holiday postcards and photographs sent in by members of the public. The models aimed to show every German pillbox and gun emplacement.

08

Buck Grabert used this hand-held welder's shield to protect his eyes when he worked at Higgins Industries in the United States. The company, which had factories in the New Orleans area, produced just over 23 thousand landing craft during World War Two. They were known as Higgins Boats. The demand was so great the company expanded from 75 staff at the start of the war to around 25 thousand by the end of the conflict.

WELDING FOR VICTORY

Welders were critical to the war effort. Their skills helped make everything from ships and tanks to aircraft.

Courtesy of The National WWII Museum.

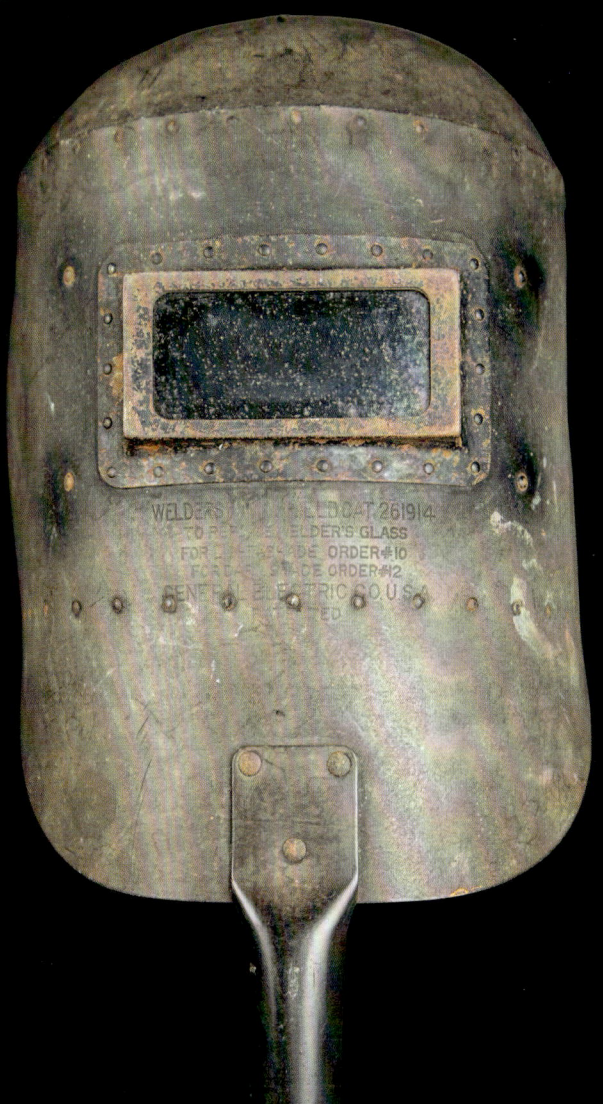

convey the message that with a final effort, the end of the war would be in sight. By the summer of 1944, it was common knowledge that D-Day was approaching but the location and the date were closely guarded secrets.

10

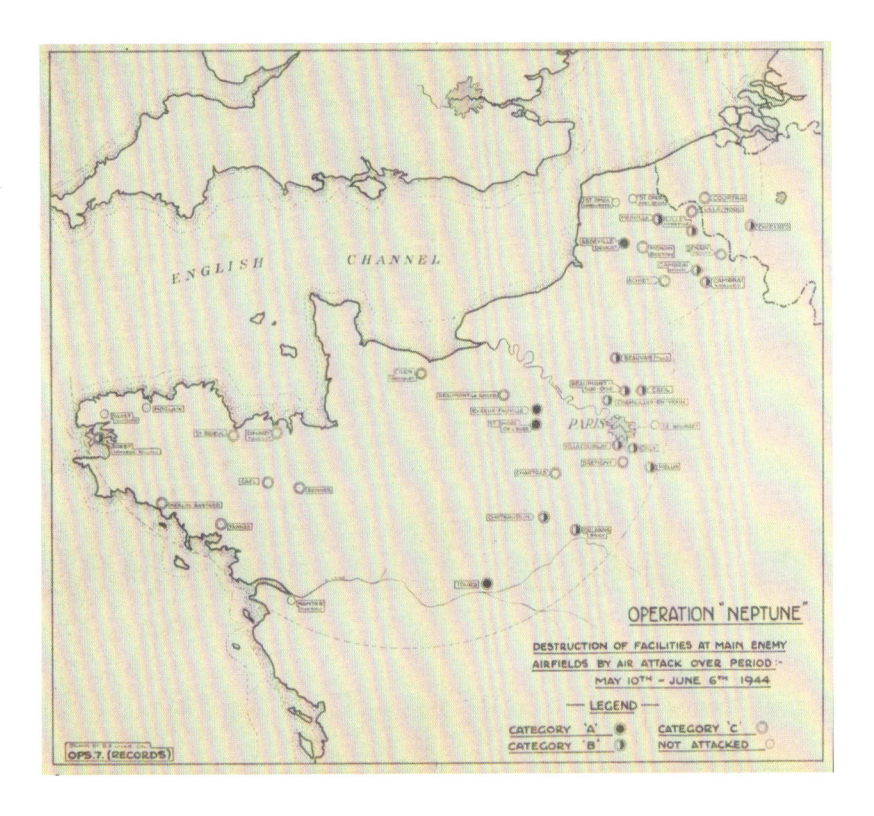

AIR ATTACKS MAP

Relentless attacks on German military forces, coastal defences and the railway system by Allied aircraft were crucial to the success of D-Day.

Courtesy of Royal Air Force Museum.

By the spring of 1944, the Allied air forces had achieved aerial superiority over the Germans. The German fighter force had been decimated by the Allies – a key factor in the Luftwaffe's poor performance in Normandy.

Along with naval firepower, aerial bombing was used to soften up the defences around the Normandy beaches.

This map shows the role played by Allied aircraft in the countdown to the landings. Air attacks were not just made on Normandy. To maintain the big secret about where exactly the Allies would land, targets were attacked across France and the low countries. Just over 11,500 Allied aircraft were available to support the D-Day landings. Opposing them were just over 800 German aircraft.

11

MONTY'S NOTE

This is Field Marshal Montgomery's handwritten "plan on a page" in which he outlines the military forces that will need to work together to achieve victory on D-Day and he stresses the need for simplicity.

Courtesy of Imperial War Museums.

In this document labelled "most secret" Monty lists the special tanks that will be used. They include the "Duplex Drive" tanks that swam ashore from landing craft and a tank with a huge mortar for attacking German fortifications. Other tanks had flame-throwers, and some were fitted with rotating chains for clearing explosive mines.

In his note, Montgomery also notes the importance of using "heavy air bombing" to attack enemy defences before the Allied forces land on the beaches.

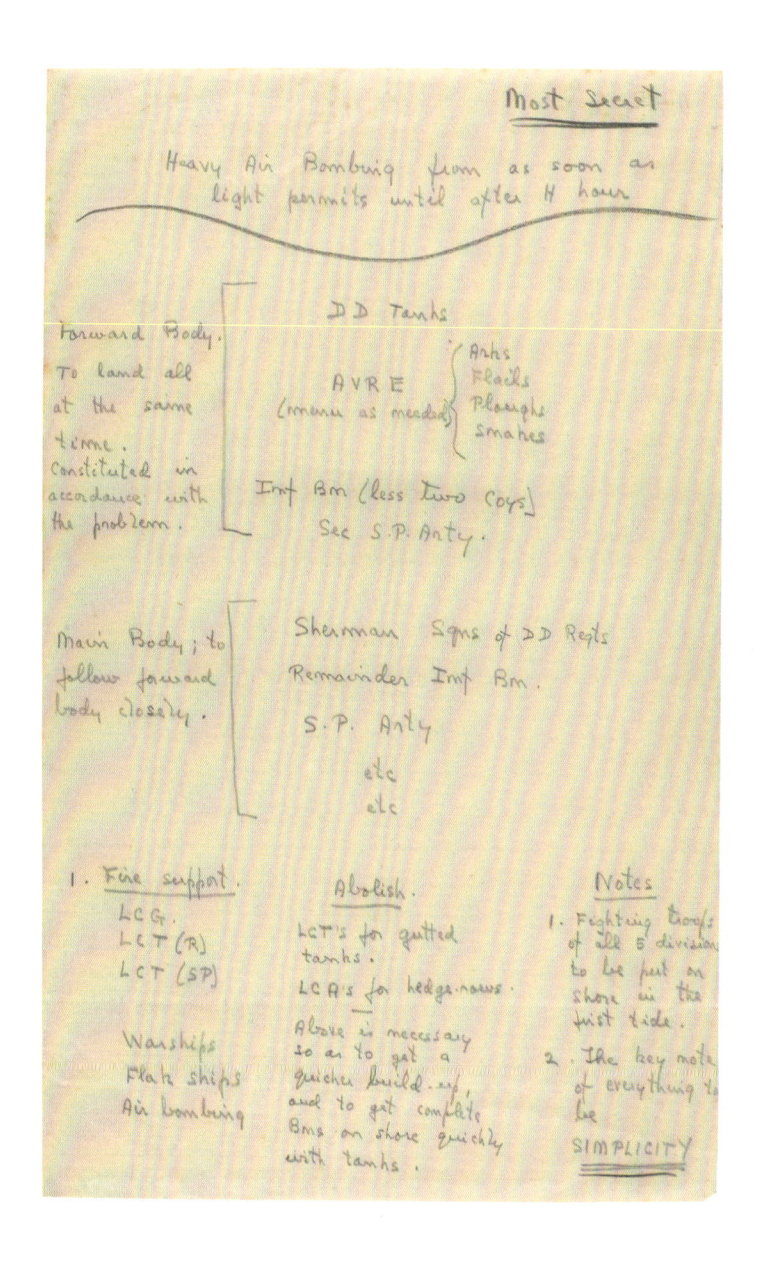

12

GUNNING FOR VICTORY

The Sexton was a self-propelled artillery gun manufactured in Canada that played an important role during the D-Day landings.

Courtesy of Royal Armouries, Fort Nelson.

The Sexton was a tracked vehicle that had a 25-pound gun firing either high-explosive shells or armour-piercing shells. During the D-Day landings, some Sexton crews were ordered to open fire from their landing craft as they approached the beaches.

The Montreal Locomotive Works made just over 2,000 Sextons for use by British and Canadian forces. It was generally regarded as a good and reliable design and Sextons remained in use in the British Army until 1956.

13

GERMAN BEACH ART

This carefully drawn diagram was produced by a German soldier to help the troops in a coastal bunker shoot accurately at Allied troops landing on the coast.

Courtesy of The D-Day Story.

The diagram has the title "Zielpunktplan" which means "aiming point plan". It was found in a bunker just to the east of Asnelles on Gold Beach. It shows landmarks and the distances between them. This strongpoint had an anti-tank gun and two machine guns. There were about 50,000 German troops defending Normandy.

On D-Day 18,000 Allied paratroopers were dropped into the invasion area and 132,000 troops landed on the beaches. The quality of German formations varied greatly. While some, like the Waffen-SS, were highly effective, a number of defensive positions were manned by older and medically unfit troops, along with conscripts and volunteers from the Soviet Union and other occupied countries.

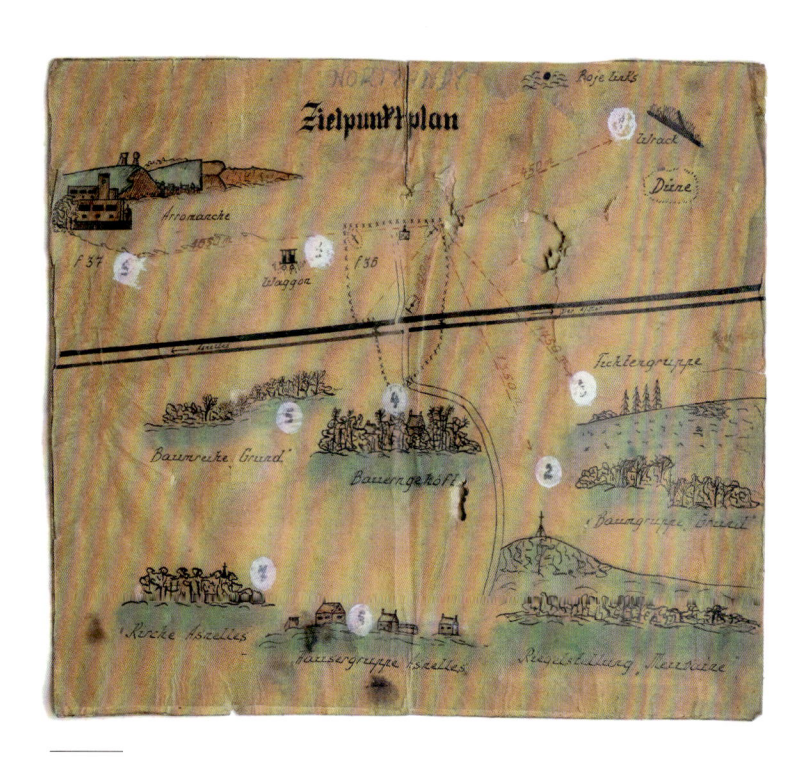

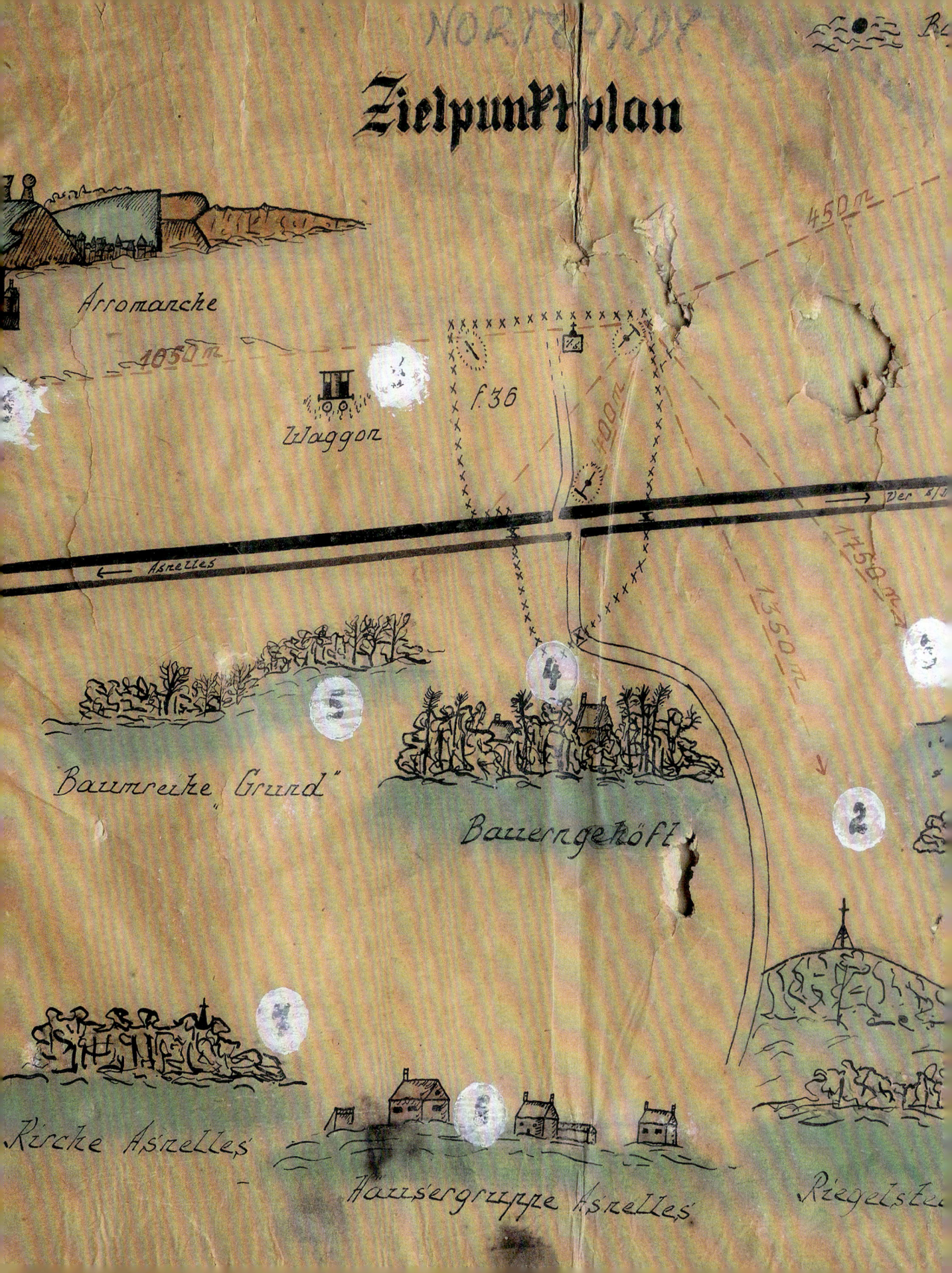

Zielpunktplan

NORMANDY

Arromanche
1650 m

Waggon
f.36

450 m
400 m
Der S/J
1750 m
1350 m

← Asnelles

Baumreihe "Grund"
5
4
Bauerngehöft
2

Kirche Asnelles
1
3
Häusergruppe Asnelles
Riegelst...

14

'VERA' ARMOURED RECOVERY VEHICLE

'Vera' was one of the strange looking armoured recovery vehicles used on the Normandy beaches to drag away damaged or broken down tanks.

Courtesy of The D-Day Story.

Keeping things moving on the Normandy beaches was a top priority on D-Day.

To stop the landing areas being clogged up by immobile tanks, special Beach Armoured Recovery Vehicles were built, based on a Sherman tank. The design allowed them to operate in fairly deep water and they could also be used to nudge stranded landing craft back into the sea.

Whenever possible, mechanics repaired broken down tanks, lorries and jeeps. Mobile vehicle workshops operated near the front line to keep the army on the move.

15

During World War Two, the Ford Motor Company manufactured 280,000 Jeeps. Another American company, Willys Overland Motors, produced 360,000. Jeeps were amongst the first vehicles to be off-loaded from landing craft on D-Day and some also landed inside gliders. They were simple to drive and were reliable and easy to fix if they went wrong. They were used for a wide variety of tasks, including hit and run missions, carrying supplies and evacuating wounded troops. Over 100,000 Jeeps were used by British, Australian and Indian forces.

THE WORKHORSE JEEP

The Jeep was the workhorse of the Allies during World War Two and was used extensively during the Normandy campaign.

Courtesy of Imperial War Museums.

16

EMBARKATION MAP

To make sure troops got to the right place to board landing craft and ships, detailed maps were produced showing the routes from their camps to ports on the south coast of England.

Courtesy of The D-Day Story.

This map shows what was known as 'Area A' around Portsmouth and Gosport where about 27,000 of the troops involved in the D-Day landings moved from their camps to embarkation points. It was a massive logistical challenge, and the map shows the level of detail involved in making sure troops and equipment got to the right place at the right time. The movement of troops across the English Channel continued non-stop after D-Day. By the end of August 1944, there were two million Allied troops in France.

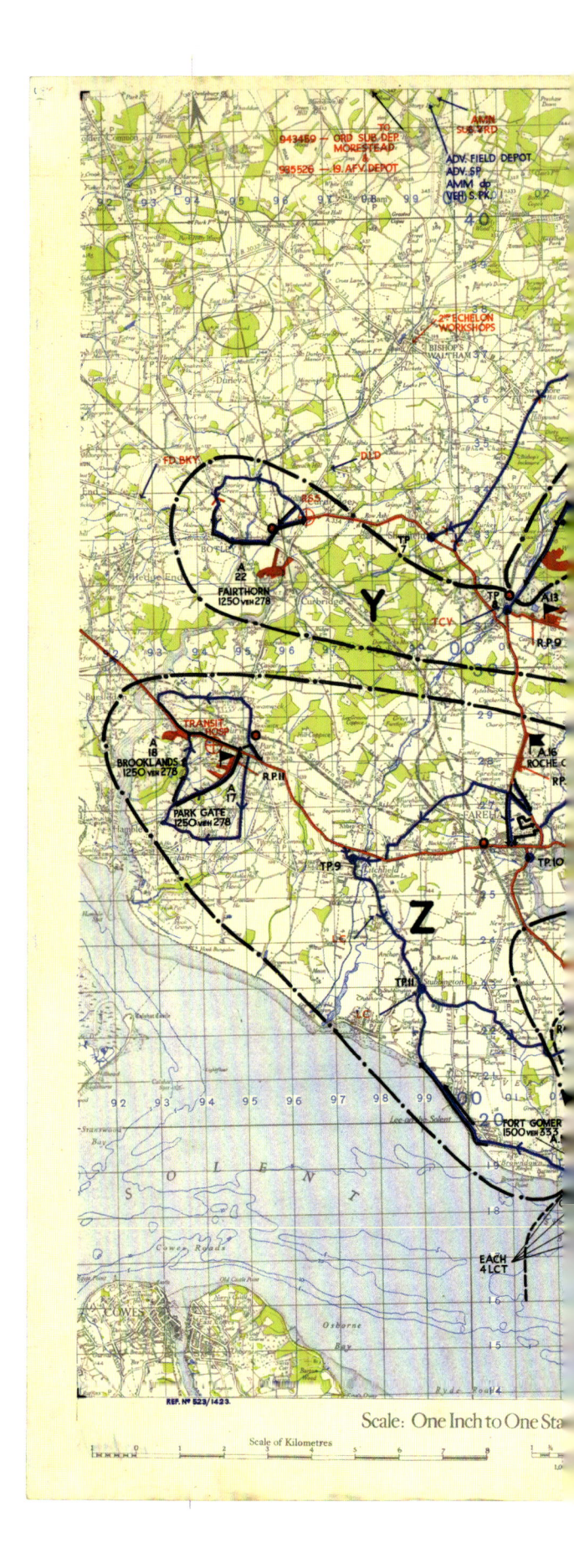

NOT TO BE REPRODUCED
Copy No. 251
TOP SECRET

AREA 'A'
OVERLORD
ADMINISTRATIVE MAP
1. MAY 1944.

SHEET ONE OF FIVE

LEGEND

	MARSHALLING AREA H.Q.
	SUB-AREA H.Q.
	CAMPS (No Shown - e.g. A.I.)
RCRP	ROAD CONVOY REGULATING POINT
TP	TRAFFIC POST
	VEHICLE PARK or STANDINGS
	ONE-WAY ROUTE
	ONE-WAY OPERATIONAL - TWO-WAY ADM. & CIVILIAN
	TWO-WAY ROUTE
	SUB-AREA BOUNDARY
	EMBARKATION AREA BOUNDARY
PETROL	PETROL OIL & LUBRICANT DUMP
RP	RECOVERY POST (VEHICLE)
P. WKSP	PORT WORKSHOP
	DETRAINING STATION
PW	PRISONERS of WAR CAGE
+	HARDS (No Shown - e.g. S.I.) } Capacities
⊕	EMBARKATION POINTS } given
ENGR DEPOT	ENGINEER DEPOT

EQUIVALENT INSTALLATIONS

BRITISH		U.S.
ADV. SP.		
ADV. FIELD DEPOT		
ORD DEPOT	ORDNANCE DEPOT	ADVANCE FIELD DEPOT & ADVANCE SHOP
VEH. S. PK.	SUB VEHICLE RESERVE DEPOT	VEHICLE SUPPLY PARK
AMN dp	AMMUNITION SUPPLY DEPOT	AMMUNITION DISTRIBUTING POINT
L.R.S.	LIGHT REPAIR SECTION	
ENGR. d.p.		ENGINEER DUMP
QMdp	DETAIL ISSUE DEPOT	QUARTER-MASTER DISTRIBUTING POINT
D.I.D.		
QM BKY / FD BKY	FIELD BAKERY	QUARTER-MASTER BAKERY
C S D	COMMAND SUPPLY DEPOT	
E S D	EMBARKATION SUPPLY DEPOT	
PX dp		POST EXCHANGE DUMP
R.S.	RECEPTION STATION	
TRANSIT HOSP. / FIELD HOSP.	EMS TRANSIT HOSPITAL	FIELD HOSPITAL
PORT HOSP. / STA. HOSP.	EMS PORT HOSPITAL	STATION HOSPITAL
MIL HOSP / GEN HOSP	MILITARY HOSPITAL	GENERAL HOSPITAL
d.p.		MEDICAL DISTRIBUTING POINT
F A P		FIRST AID POST
AMB P		AMBULANCE POST
SIG. S dp		SIGNAL SUPPLY DUMP
SIG. RE. SR		SIGNAL REPAIR SHOP
CWS dp		CHEMICAL WARFARE DUMP
TCV or LC	TROOP CARRYING VEHICLES / LOAD CARRIERS	
ENGR. BR dp		ENGINEER BRIDGING DEPOT

APPROVED BY CENTRE
ZONE SUB COMMITTEE
18 APRIL 1944

(SIGNED) P.W. KEMP WELCH
LT. COL. AQMG (OPS)

(SIGNED) G.M. BOSTOCK COL FA
PLANNING DIVISION SBS

PT. OF 1" SHEET 132 OF G.S.G.S. SERIES No 3907.

69/1995/1

17

D-DAY WOMEN

The two female figures on this unofficial coat of arms represent the women who worked in a D-Day operations room and in coastal radar stations.

Courtesy of The D-Day Story.

By June 1944, the Women's Royal Naval Service and the Women's Auxiliary Air Force had 75,000 personnel. They carried out vital roles before and during the D-Day landings. Their roles included working as wireless and radar operators, codebreakers and as plotters – who updated the maps showing the position of ships, planes and army units taking part in Operation Overlord. The figure on the left represents a plotter working in the Combined Operations Underground headquarters under Fort Southwick north of Portsmouth. On the right is a radar operator.

18

GIRL GUIDE'S SKIPPING ROPE

This skipping rope was made for 12 year old Hazel Perkin by some soldiers who were camped out near her home on the Isle of Wight before they took part in D-Day.

Courtesy of Imperial War Museums.

Just before D-Day, Hazel Perkin told a group of soldiers she had lost her beloved skipping rope on the beach at Seaview on the Isle of Wight. After failing to find the skipping rope when they searched for it, the soldiers decided to make a replacement.

The handles were made from wood taken from the side of a landing craft. Hazel said that as the boats left to sail to France, she hoped the soldiers would survive the D-Day landings. She said "I never did learn their names but I would have liked them to know how grateful that young Girl Guide was."

19

THE LUCKY FLAG

This flag was given to a tank crew who made friends with the Whittle family in Bedhampton while they were parked outside their house just before D-Day.

Courtesy of The D-Day Story.

In the days before they embarked on landing craft and ships, many tanks and trucks were parked in residential areas near south coast ports. One tank crew from the 2nd Battalion of the Grenadier Guards struck up a friendship with the Whittle family who invited the soldiers into their home for meals and baths. Four-year-old Shirley Whittle gave them a flag, which they flew from their tank during the advance across France and into Germany. When the original flag was lost the family sent the tank crew a replacement.

27

20

SEASICK SOLDIERS

Over 130,000 troops taking part in D-Day travelled to Normandy on ships and landing craft and with far from perfect weather, sea sickness was widespread.

Courtesy of Imperial War Museums.

This is one of the sea sickness bags issued to the troops, or as it says on this one "This is the famous Army vomit bag." Cecil Newton of the 4th/7th Royal Dragoon Guards described it like this: "I slung my hammock from the side of the LCT to the tank, but the weather became so bad that the thought of sleep had to be abandoned. On 5th June the flotilla sailed out of the Solent for France. Everyone, except the Sergeant, was very seasick and no one slept."

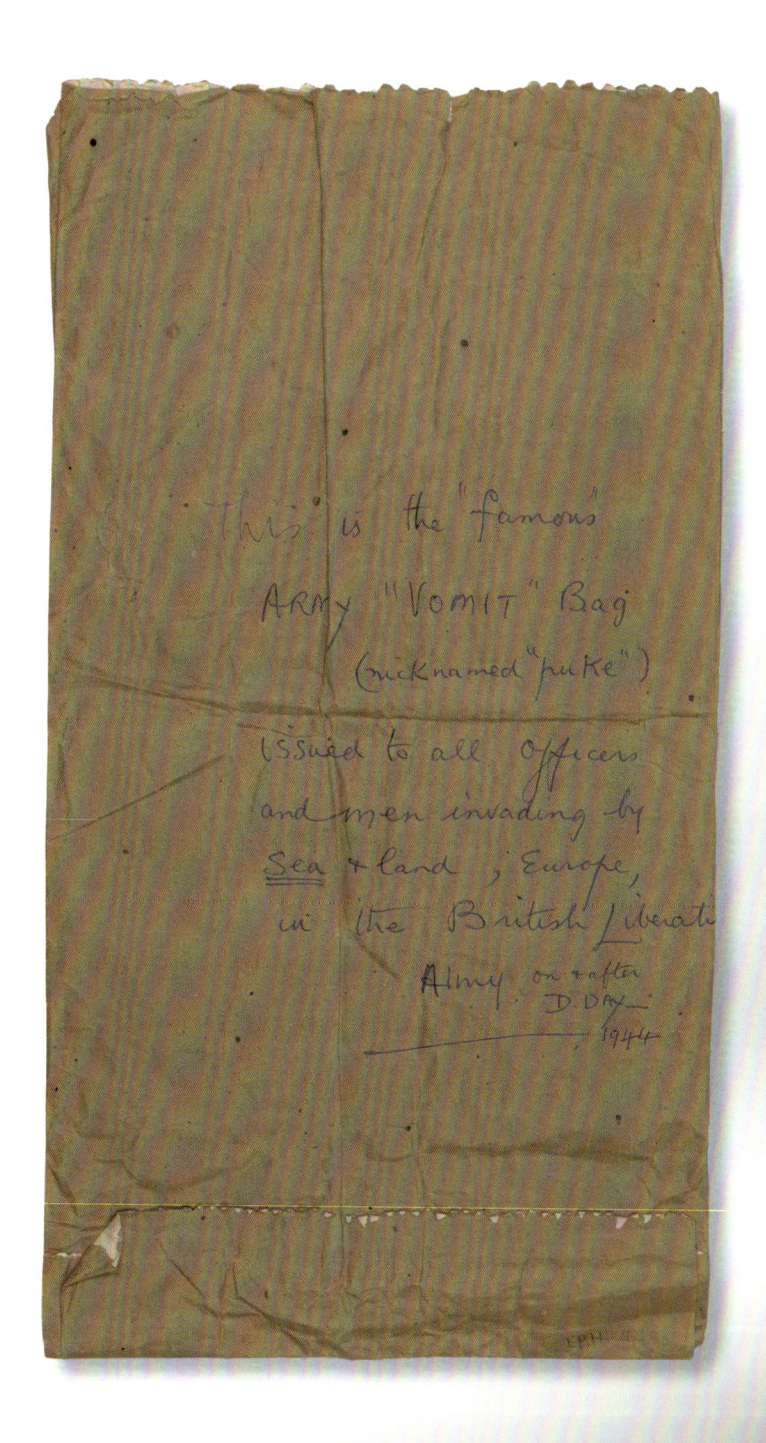

21

The weather was so crucial that Allied commanders met the Meteorological Committee twice a day. The forecasting team was led by Group Captain J.M.Stagg, described by Supreme Allied Commander Dwight D Eisenhower as a "dour but canny Scot".

The information contained in these reports led to the decision to postpone the landings. But, the next day, the forecasters revealed there would be a period of relatively good weather which would enable the invasion to go ahead on 6 June.

STORM DELAYS

These weather reports underline the fact that the decision to proceed with the D-Day landings was balanced on a knife edge in the first few days of June 1944 because of high winds and low cloud across the invasion area.

Courtesy of Royal Air Force Museum.

30

22

BETTY'S BADGES JACKET

A little girl's jacket provides a unique snapshot of the number and variety of military units passing her house and the rapport that quickly developed between troops and civilians on the south coast of England.

Betty White was given 90 metal and cloth badges by personnel from British, Canadian and United States units and her mother sewed them onto her jacket.

The troops were passing her family's home in Gosport as they made their way to an embarkation point known as the Hardway. The family were living in Gosport because they had been bombed out of their home in Portsmouth.

Betty White was five years old at the time of D-Day and collected badges from the troops who passed her family's home in Gosport on their way to get on landing craft and ships.

Courtesy of The D-Day Story.

23

OVERLORD OVERVIEW

The large map covering an entire wall at Southwick House near Portsmouth gave Allied commanders an overview of the naval operation to transport troops across the English Channel and land them on five beaches in Normandy.

Courtesy of The National Museum of The Royal Navy.

It was in the library at Southwick House that General Dwight D. Eisenhower, the Allied Supreme Commander, made the historic decision to launch the invasion. When D-Day took place, his headquarters were in a tented encampment hidden in a wood near Southwick House. It was the ultimate control centre for the Normandy landings.

The wall map inside Southwick House charted the progress of Operation Neptune, the naval element of D-Day. A small ladder was used by members of the Women's Royal Naval Service to mark the positions of naval ships every hour.

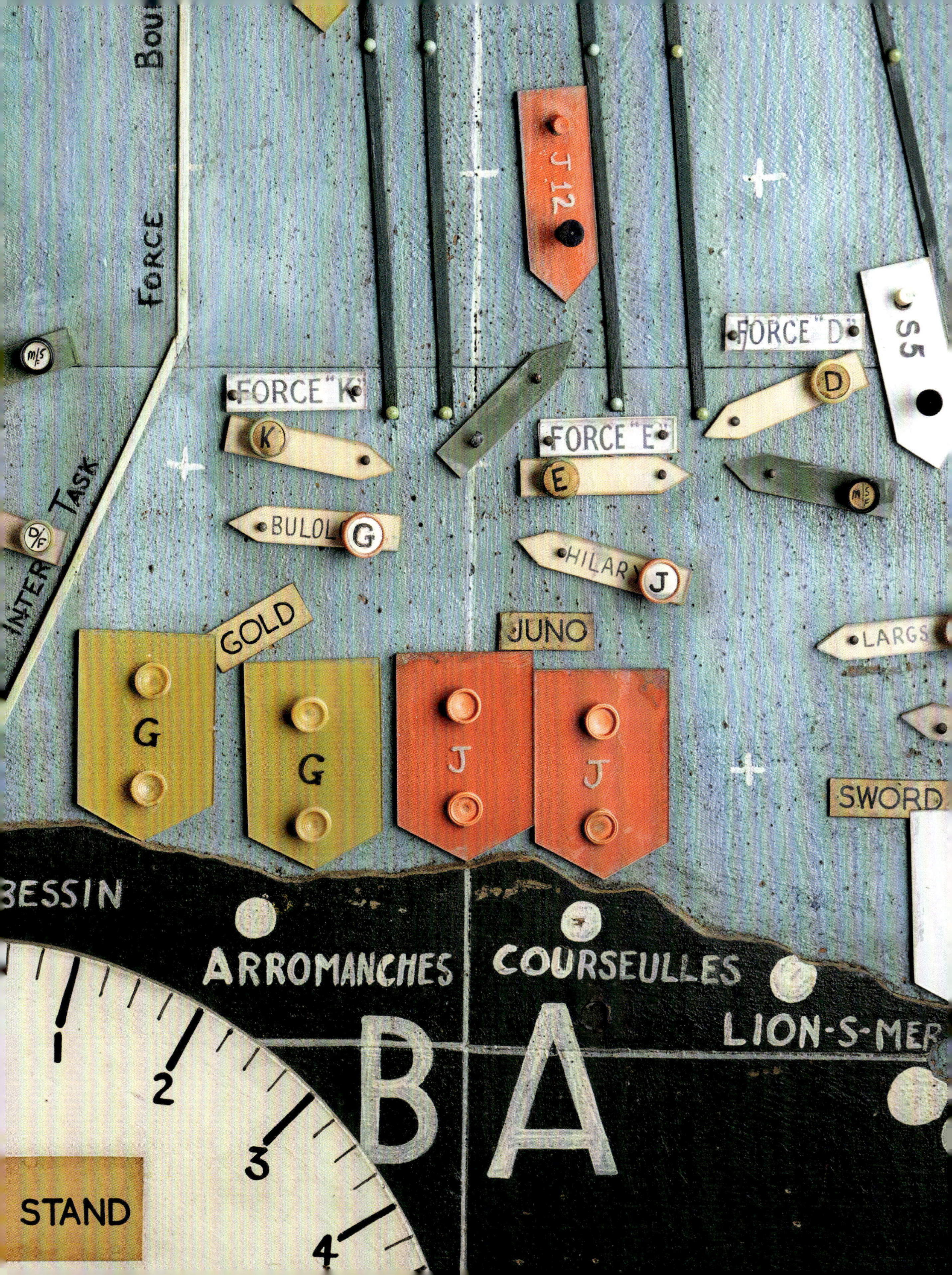

FORCE
INTER TASK
M/S
D/F
FORCE "K"
K
BULOL
G
FORCE "E"
E
HILAR
J
J 12
FORCE "D"
D
S5
M/S
LARGS
GOLD
G
G
JUNO
J
J
SWORD
BESSIN
ARROMANCHES
COURSEULLES
LION-S-MER
B
A
1
2
3
4
STAND

24

SWEEPING FOR KILLER MINES

This map was drawn by Royal Navy sailor Joseph Newbold who was involved in the highly dangerous job of searching for explosive mines along the Normandy coast on D-Day.

Courtesy of The D-Day Story.

Clearing mines was so important in the hours before the invasion that around 350 boats were involved in clearing safe routes through the German minefields.

Joseph Newbold was on board a minesweeper operating off Utah Beach, where United States forces landed on D-Day. His map shows the areas where his minesweeper was operating. The operation was a success. Very few Allied ships or landing craft were damaged or lost after coming into contact with mines.

25

Getting troops to the right place on D-Day was the job of 4,126 landing ships and landing craft. Some of the landing craft were quite small and could carry 36 troops. Larger landing ships carried up to 20 tanks and 200 soldiers.

Landing Craft Support (Medium) 79 supported operations on Gold Beach, possibly in the Asnelles area. The white ensign it displayed was signed by several members of the crew. By the end of D-Day LCS(M) 79 had been damaged and was returned to the UK.

FLYING THE FLAG

This flag was flown by one of the landing craft that delivered troops onto the Normandy beaches.

Courtesy of The D-Day Story.

26

A SYMBOL OF FRIENDSHIP

This reserve parachute belonged to Private Oscar Prasse of the United States 82nd Airborne Division and symbolises his efforts to rescue an injured friend.

Courtesy of Imperial War Museums.

Private Oscar Prasse parachuted into Normandy near the commune of Picauville, along with his good friend Private Joe Bressler, who broke his ankle when he hit the ground. Determined not to leave his friend behind, Prasse carried Bressler on his back. They were separated during a battle with German troops, but Prasse returned to carry his friend to a farmhouse. They hid for five days before being found by an American patrol. The parachute pack was left behind, along with a 100 franc note as a thank you to the owners of the house. Both men survived the war.

27

This is the cockpit from Dakota KG437 that was used by the RAF's 233 Squadron. On 5 June 1944 it was amongst a fleet of 108 aircraft that took off late in the evening to drop the British 3rd Parachute Brigade into Normandy in advance of the beach landings. The Brigade had the challenge of securing canal and river bridges and knocking out German coastal gun batteries. Dakota KG437 then carried out missions on 6 June to drop supplies to the British 6th Airborne Division. After the war the aircraft was used by several civilian companies, including British European Airways.

DOUGLAS DAKOTA COCKPIT

The Douglas C-47 Dakota was the workhorse of the skies in World War Two, delivering troops and supplies, and this type of aircraft played a key role on D-Day.

Courtesy of Royal Air Force Museum.

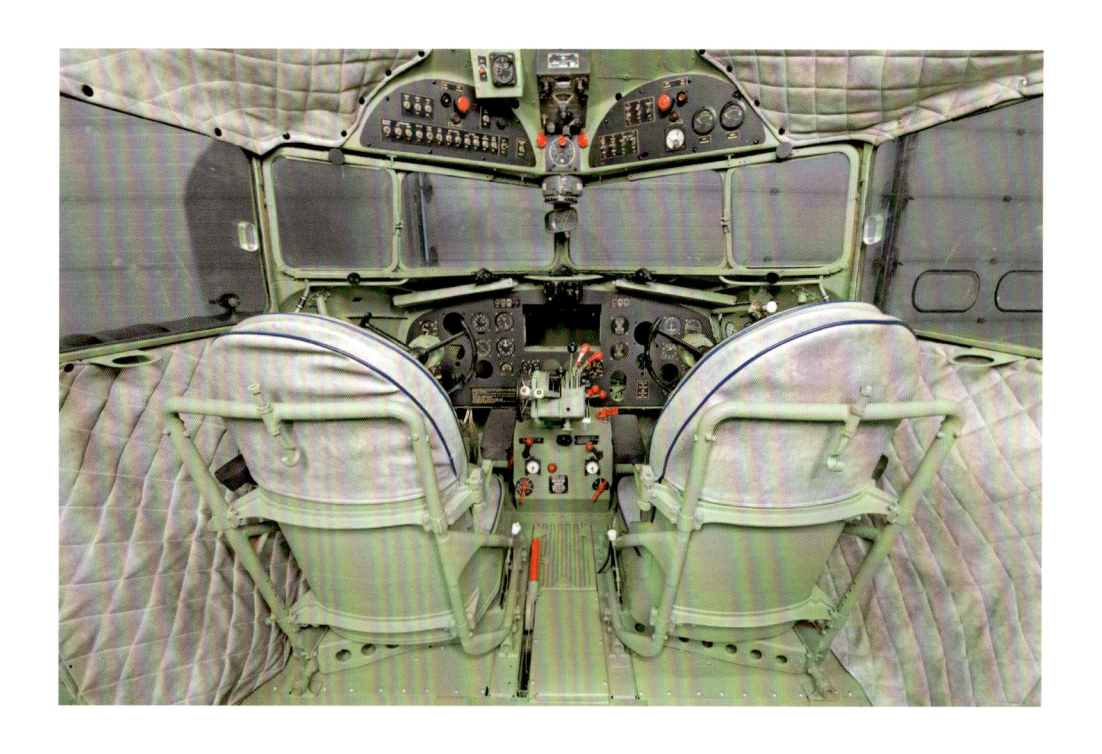

28

DECOY DUMMY

Dummies were dropped by parachute on D-Day to confuse the Germans and divert their troops from areas where the real landings were being made.

Courtesy of Imperial War Museums.

The parachute dummies were nicknamed 'Ruperts' by British troops and 'Oscars' by the Americans. They were made from sackcloth stuffed with sand and straw. The dummies were a crucial part of the Allies' deception plan for the Normandy landings, designed to give the invasion force the crucial element of surprise.

About 500 dummies were dropped and despite being only three feet tall they looked very realistic in the sky. Some of them were fitted with a timed detonator so they exploded on landing. The use of 'paradummies' was featured in the film 'The Longest Day'.

29

A special short range radar navigation system that was used during the Normandy campaign came in two parts. The Eureka beacons were placed on the ground where airborne forces and their supplies were supposed to land. The Rebecca transceiver and aerials were fitted to the aircraft carrying out the mission.

It indicated the position of the Eureka beacon. Before D-Day, the system had been used across occupied Europe to drop supplies to resistance groups. The system was developed in the UK at the Telecommunications Research Establishment. It was also used to indicate bombing targets, and to help aircraft land at their home bases.

THE EUREKA MOMENT

Ultra-lightweight Eureka Beacons were used on D-Day to try to make sure paratroopers were dropped in the right place in Normandy.

Courtesy of Royal Air Force Museum.

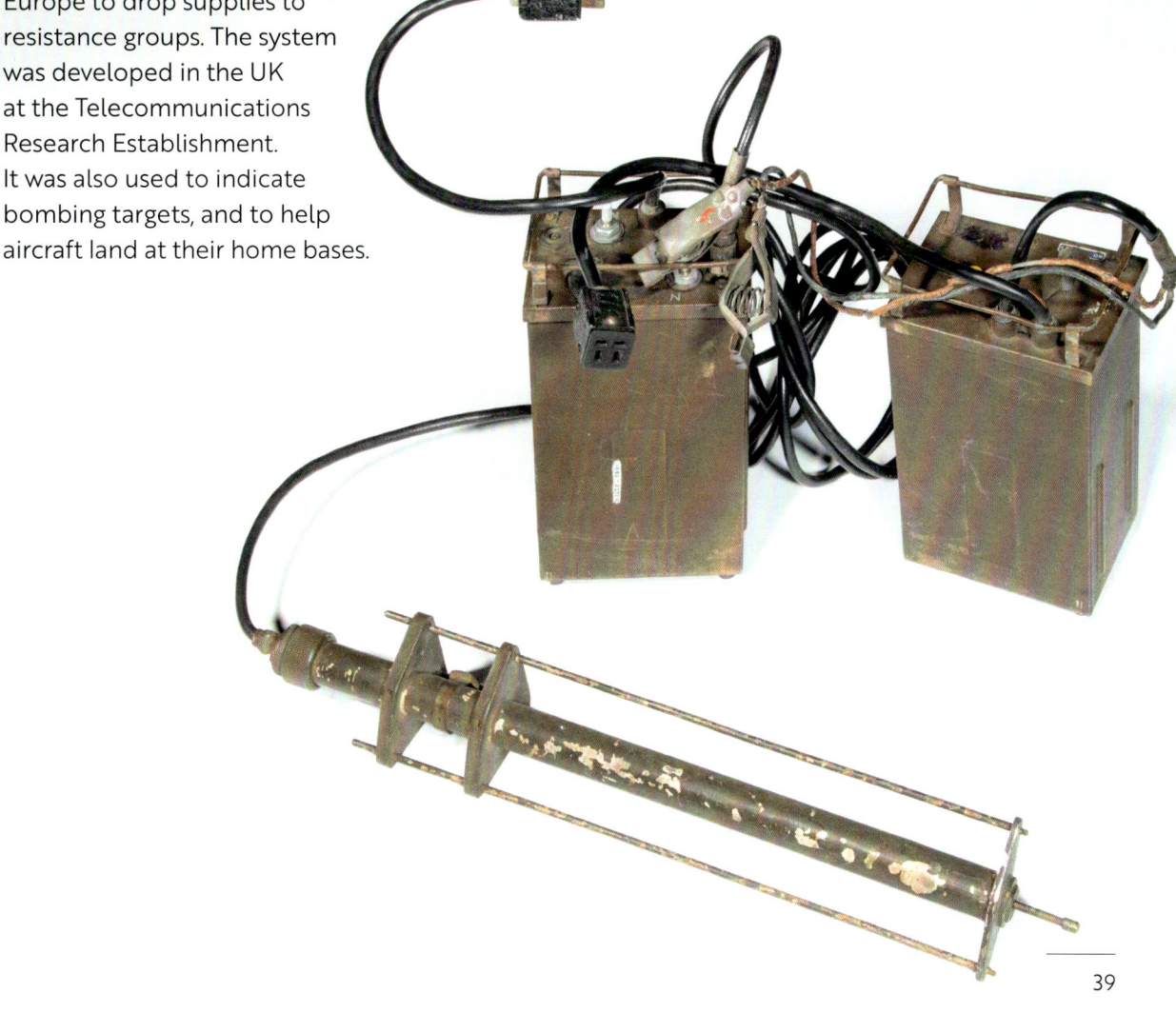

30

SEABORNE SPOTTERS

Volunteers from the Royal Observer Corps were experts in identifying aircraft and they joined ships taking part in the D-Day landings to help spot enemy planes and to prevent gunners firing on friendly aircraft.

Courtesy of Royal Air Force Museum.

In total, 796 civilian volunteers from the Royal Observer Corps took part in Operation Overlord, after being temporarily enlisted into the Royal Navy. Originally set up in the 1920's, the Observer Corps eventually covered the entire UK with 27,000 people.

They played a crucial role in the Battle of Britain in 1940. During the D-Day landings, the observers wore their own uniforms along with a shoulder badge bearing the word 'Seaborne'.

31

This 'bogus' map of Sword Beach had all the place names changed to maintain secrecy.

Even though the place names are not real, the map shows genuine roads, buildings and defences. It also provides information about the future location of refugee camps, burial sites, and the facilities that would be used to provide supplies to the troops as they advanced inland.

KEEP IT HUSH HUSH

Special maps of Normandy were created with dummy place names, so troops could be briefed about their objectives – without revealing where the invasion was going to take place.

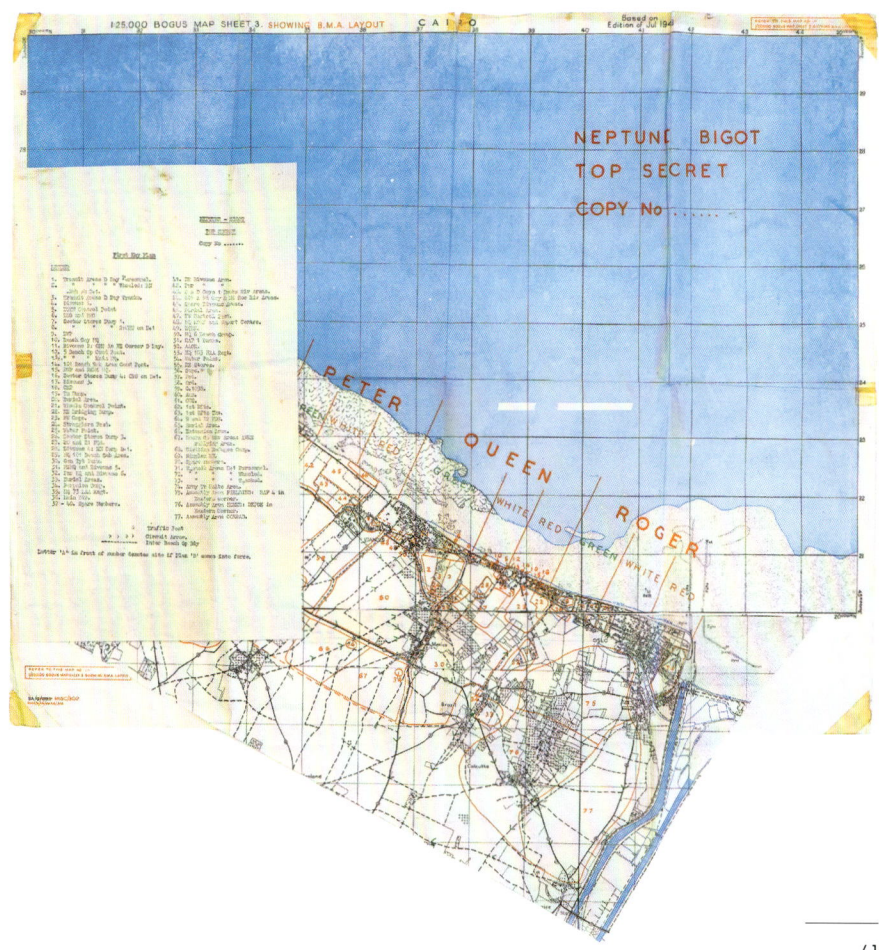

Courtesy of The D-Day Story.

32

HERO PIGEON

The first news of the landings on D-Day was brought back to the UK by a pigeon, as the invasion fleet was operating under conditions of 'radio silence' as they did not want to alert the Germans.

Courtesy of The D-Day Story and the family of Frederick Jackson.

The first message to reach the UK, confirming the invasion had started, was carried by a pigeon called Gustav, which was bred by Frederick Jackson in Cosham in Portsmouth. It was one of six birds given to Reuters' correspondent Montague Taylor so he could send messages back from the landing craft, where he was observing the landings. When the invasion began he sent a message saying "We are just 20 miles or so off the beaches. First assault troops landed 0750. Signal says no interference from enemy gunfire on beach… Steaming steadily in formation." Gustav was awarded the Dickin Medal for bravery.

Courtesy of the PDSA

43

These boots were worn by Sergeant Tom Ruggiero of the US 2nd Ranger Battalion which had the objective of scaling the 100 foot high cliffs at Pointe du Hoc on D-Day to capture a German stronghold.

Courtesy of The National D-Day Memorial Foundation, Bedford, Virginia.

was too small, but he was accepted by the Army Rangers. On the way to the beach, an enemy shell capsized his landing craft. Tom was in the sea for two hours before being rescued. He was awarded two Purple Hearts and two Bronze Stars for his service in France and Germany. He returned home after being seriously wounded. Tom was 95 when he died in 2016.

34

Captain F. H. Wilson says it was "... just a big mad scramble. Off the boats and run like hell, right across an open beach. It was maybe a couple of hundred yards to the wall, but it seemed like a couple of hundred miles. Jerry sure threw plenty of stuff at us."

Captain Wilson served in the Queen's Own Rifles of Canada. Later in the war he wrote letters about battles in the Netherlands and one describing the scenes in Belgium on VE Day.

RUN LIKE HELL

In a letter home, a Canadian soldier gives a vivid description of what it was like to land on the beaches on D-Day.

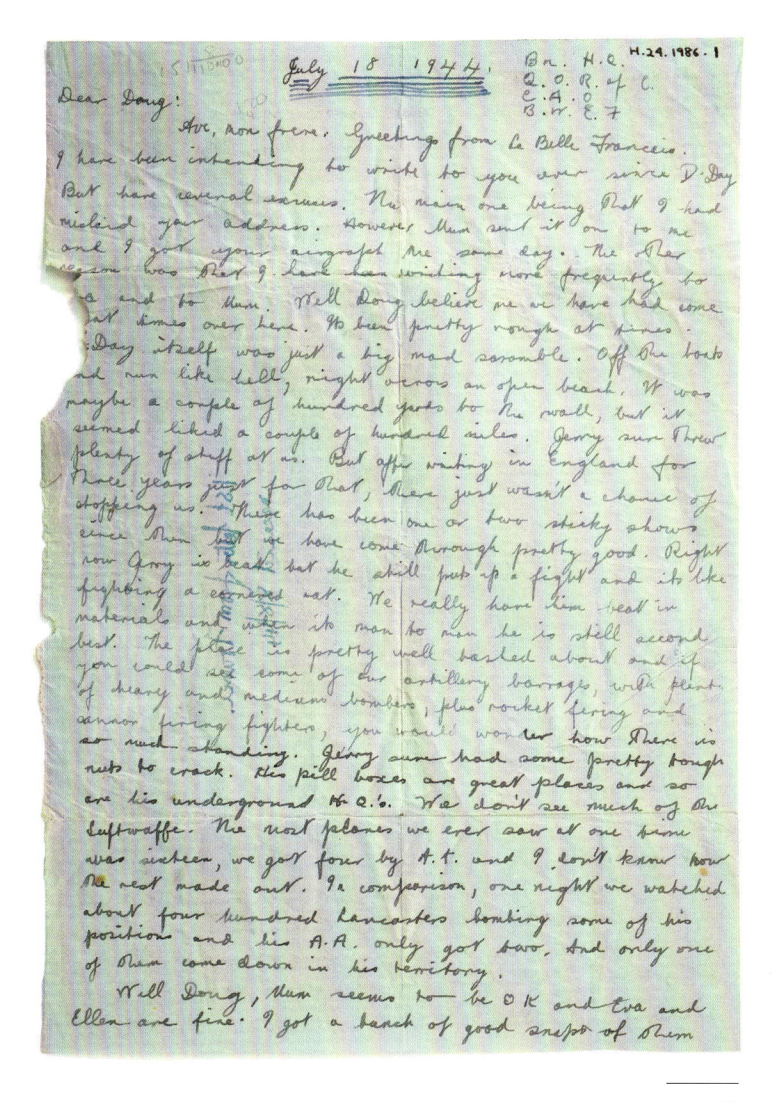

Courtesy of The D-Day Story.

35

RARELY SIGHTED FOE

The Focke Wulf 190 was one of the types of German fighter aircraft operating in Normandy during the D-Day landings, but they were rarely seen because of the Allies' aerial superiority.

Courtesy of Royal Air Force Museum.

Months before the landings, Allied commanders made the destruction of the Luftwaffe's air combat strength a top priority. In fact, it was already being achieved, as many Luftwaffe aircraft were being shot down by American fighters escorting bombers carrying out raids on targets in Germany.

As a result, aircraft from squadrons in France were moved to Germany, to shore up the defences. It meant the Luftwaffe could offer little resistance to the large numbers of Allied aircraft supporting the Normandy landings.

36

NAVY'S BIG GUNS

The big guns on Allied warships just off the Normandy coast fired large shells that destroyed German defences on D-Day.

Courtesy of Imperial War Museums.

HMS Belfast, now a floating museum in London, was one of the biggest ships that took part in the bombardment. Her guns supported troops landing on Gold and Juno beaches. In total, HMS Belfast supported the landings for 33 days, firing over 4,000 six inch shells and 1,000 four inch shells. Her guns could hit targets up to 14 miles inland. The ship's sickbay was used to treat some of the troops wounded during the invasion.

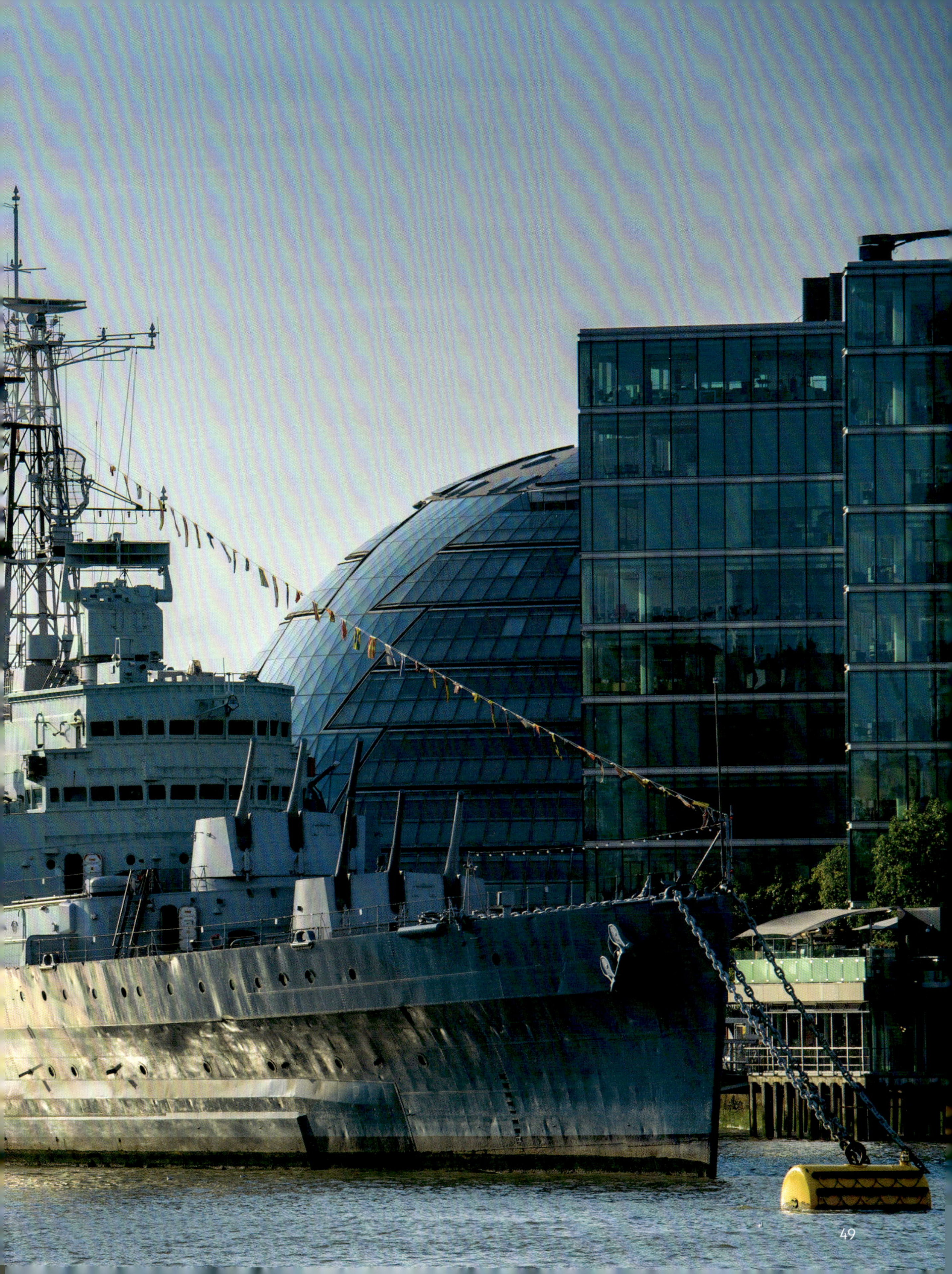

37

DEVASTATING SHELLS

The almost silent approach of the Allied invasion fleet was shattered when the big guns of the warships opened up, firing salvo after salvo at the German defences.

Courtesy of The National Museum of The Royal Navy.

This 15 inch semi armour piercing shell gives an idea of the size of some of the munitions that were used on D-Day. While the big warships remained slightly offshore to fire thousands of shells at enemy positions, smaller destroyers swept close to the beaches to attack whatever targets presented themselves. The Allied ships bombarded the German coastal defences before and after troops landed. They continued to provide gunfire support after D-Day, as troops moved inland.

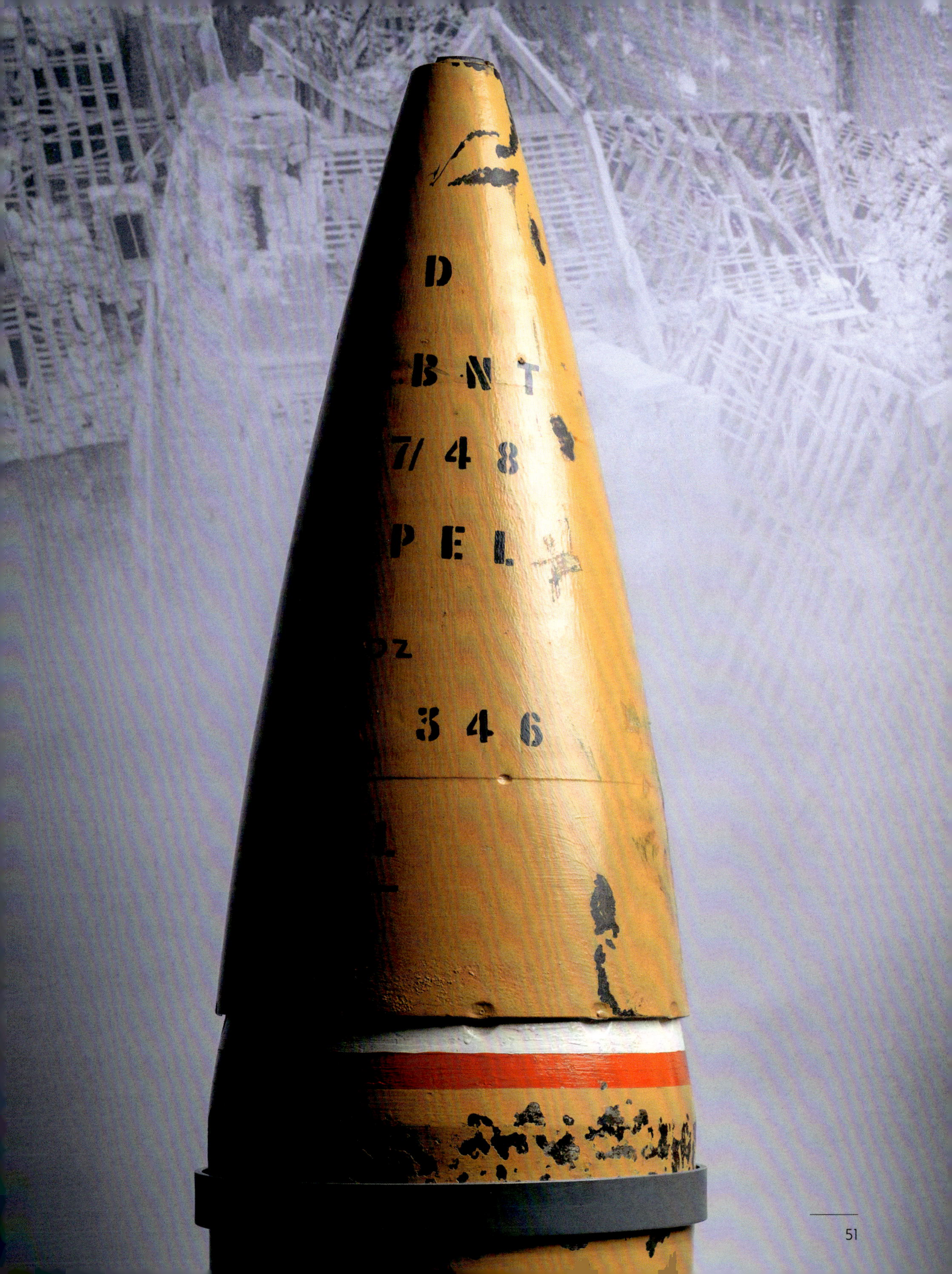
D
BNT
7/ 4 8
PEL
3 4 6

38

GOLD BEACH

On D-Day nearly 25,000 men of the British 50th Division landed at Gold Beach, which was the centre beach of the five landing areas on the Normandy coast.

Courtesy of National Army Museum.

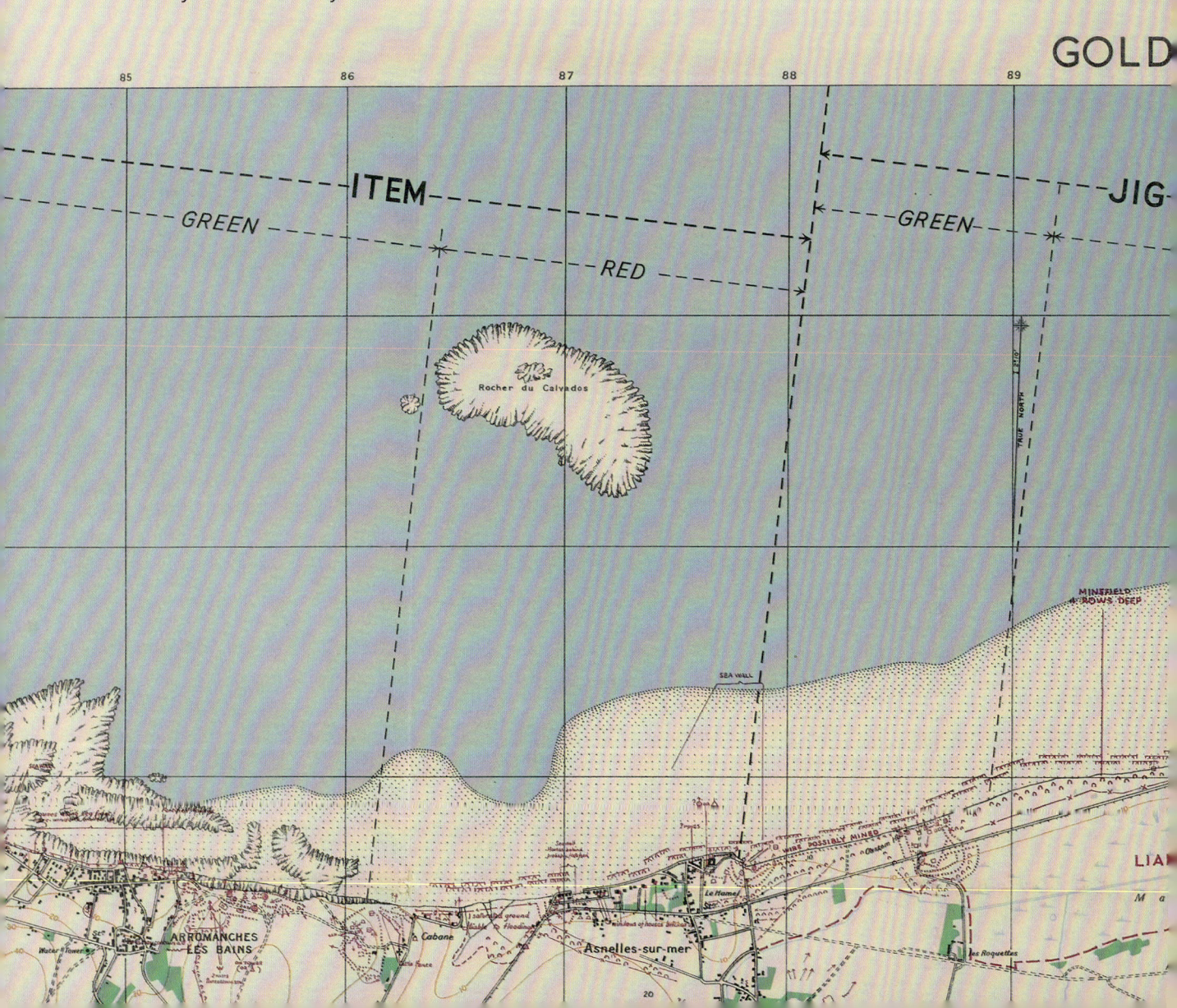

Maps were essential as the troops had to find their way to specific objectives and be aware of the position of German defences.

The objectives for the 50th Division were to capture the town of Bayeux, take control of the Caen to Bayeux Road and link up with the Americans landing at Omaha Beach. At the end of D-Day, not all the objectives had been reached but the British troops had advanced six miles inland and joined-up with soldiers from the Canadian 3rd Division, who landed at Juno Beach.

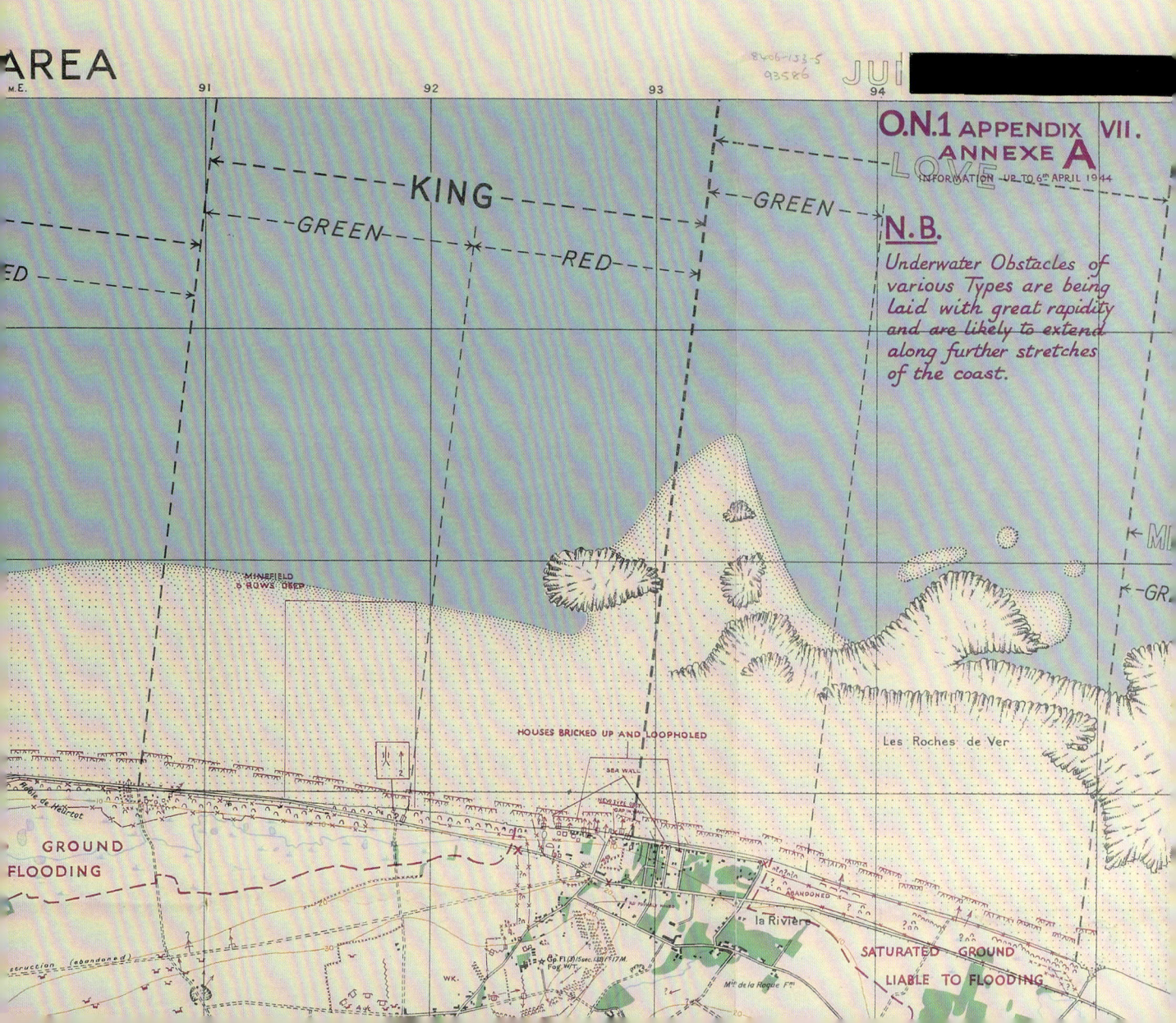

O.N.1 APPENDIX VII.
ANNEXE A
INFORMATION UP TO 6th APRIL 1944

N.B.
Underwater Obstacles of various Types are being laid with great rapidity and are likely to extend along further stretches of the coast.

39

RACE AGAINST TIME

This photograph captures the dramatic moment when Lord Lovat, commander of the British 1st Special Service Brigade and his piper Bill Millin were moments away from landing on Sword Beach.

Courtesy of The National Museum of The Royal Navy.

Lord Lovat and his commandos were involved in a race against time, because they had the job of swiftly marching inland to Pegasus Bridge. The strategically important canal bridge and another over the Orne River, had been captured in the early hours of D-Day by airborne troops of the Oxfordshire & Buckinghamshire Light Infantry. They had landed in gliders. Bill Millin played the bagpipes as the commandos went ashore. They arrived at Pegasus Bridge at 1pm on D-Day.

40

Large numbers of American troops were taken ashore in landing craft crewed by British Royal Navy sailors and Royal Marines.

These flags were used by Sub Lieutenant Wilf Thomas of the Royal Navy Volunteer Reserve. He was a signals officer working on Utah beach in Normandy, where the United States 4th Division landed.

Nearly 50,000 British sailors crewed about 4,000 landing craft and landing ships, ranging from small assault boats, carrying 22 men, to large tank transporters.

FLAGS OF COOPERATION

The D-Day operation required close cooperation between the Allied countries.

Courtesy of The D-Day Story.

41

THE BEACHMASTER'S STICK

Beachmasters had the job of keeping things moving on D-Day as troops and tanks started coming ashore.

Courtesy of The National Museum of the Royal Navy.

This is the famous Shillelagh stick that was used by Captain Colin Maud on Juno beach for pointing people in the right direction and as an unusual symbol of his authority. Along with directing the movement of troops and supplies, he had to oversee the evacuation of casualties and prisoners of war. Already highly decorated before D-Day, he was awarded a bar to his Distinguished Service Order for his work under fire.

The stick was immortalised when it featured in the film 'The Longest Day' with actor Kenneth More playing Captain Maud.

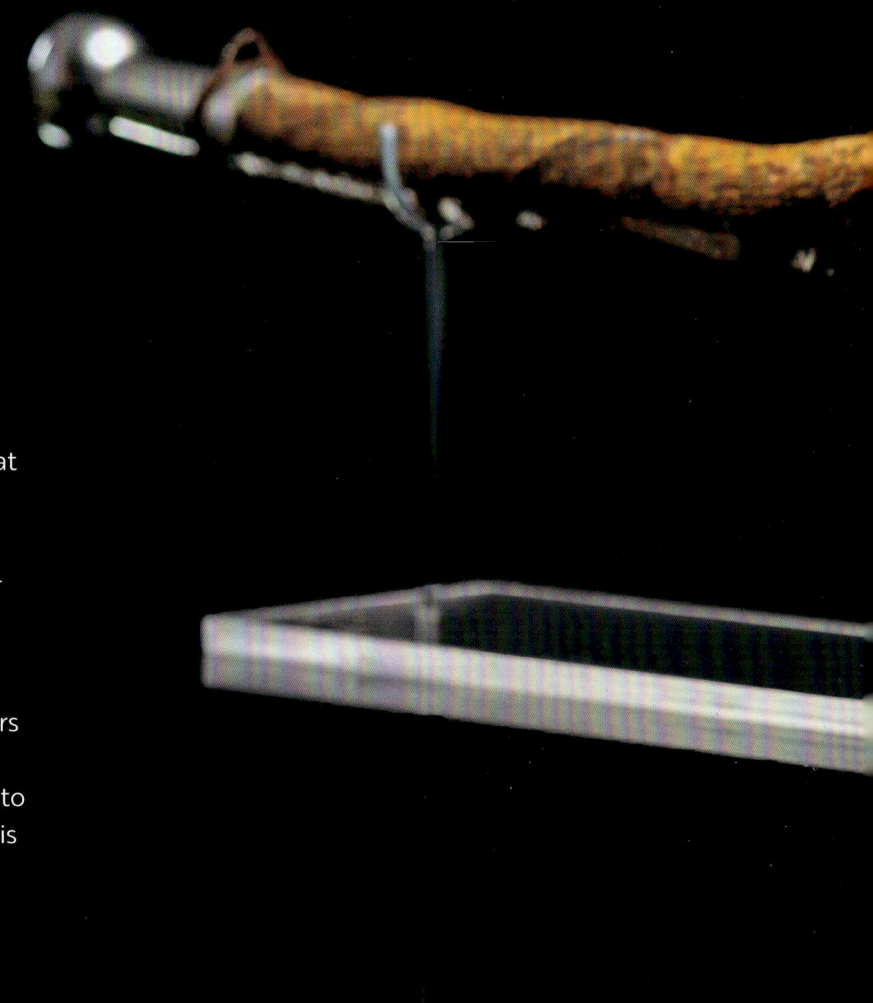

57

Les Calvados
Fonds de Roches
Roche de la Valette
Fonds de Roches
les Iles de Bernières
les Essarts de Langrune
Embouchure de la Seulles
le Hamel
Asnelles sur Mer
Meuvaines
Ver-sur-Mer
le Buisson
la Valette
Graye sur Mer
Courseulles sur Mer
Bernières sur Mer
St. Aubin sur Mer
Langrune sur Mer
Crépon
Banville
Camp Romain
Bazenville
Reviers
Tailleville
Tierceville
Colombiers-sur-Seulles
Villiers le Sec
la Délivrande
Douvres
le Manoir
Creully
Amblie
les Planches
Bény sur Mer
Moulineaux
St. Gabriel
Fontaine-Henry
Pierrepont
Basly
Brécy
Lantheuil
Anguerny
Thaon
le Fresne Camilly
Colomby sur Thaon
Barbière
Cully
Camilly
Cazelle
Coulombs
Anisy
Mathieu
Cairon
Villons les Buissons
Lieu Maillot
Secqueville en Bessin
Lasson
les Buissons
Loucelles
Vieux Cairon
Rots
Bray
Galmanche
Bronay
Putot en Bessin
Bretteville l'Orgueilleuse
Buron
Épron
Gruchy

42

The arrows on the map indicate landing areas on Gold, Juno and Sword beaches. The map was collected by Captain Colin Paxton, who served in the Royal Army Service Corps.

The bad weather, which had made the timing of the landings so difficult for the Allies, also meant the Germans were caught off-guard. They did not think an invasion would be possible at that time. Hitler and his generals were also convinced the main Allied attack would come later, in the Pas de Calais area.

THE GERMAN VIEW

This German map of the Normandy coast has pencil markings, apparently added on D-Day, showing where British and Canadian troops had landed and where they were moving inland.

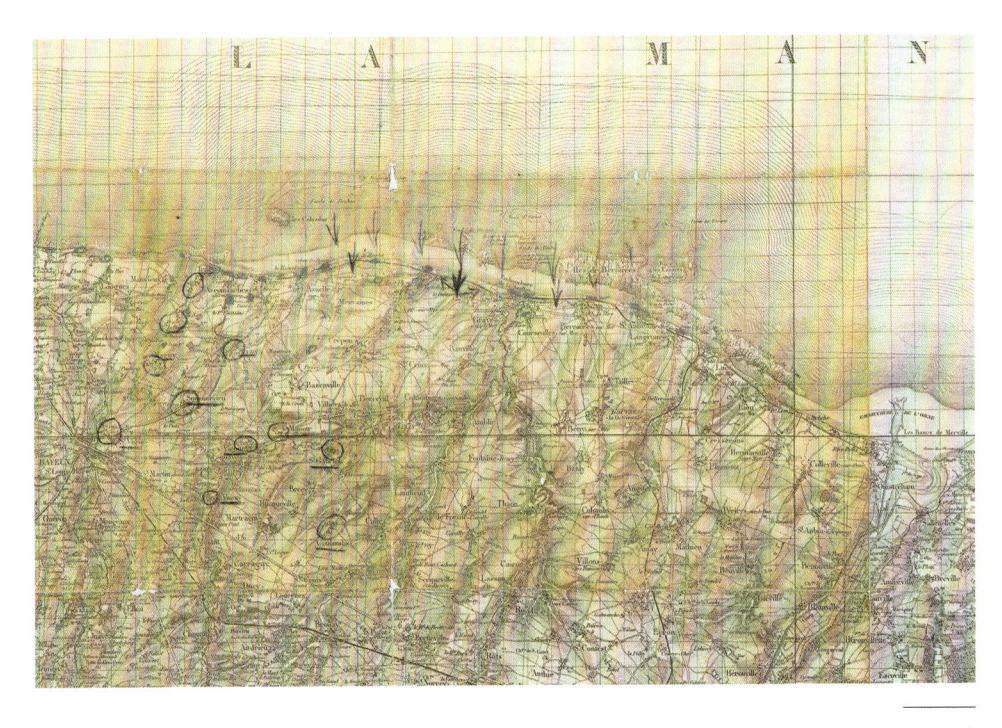

Courtesy of The D-Day Story.

This life preserver was found after D-Day on Omaha beach by Les Eastwood who served on Landing Craft Tank 7057. It consists of two separate tubes that can be inflated through a mouthpiece or by using two CO_2 gas cartridges.

Soldiers were instructed to wear the devices higher than the waist. Otherwise, there was a danger the weight carried on their shoulders might turn them upside down in the water, with the possibility they might drown.

43

OMAHA LIFESAVER

Amongst the equipment designed and manufactured for D-Day was this inflatable US life preserver for use by troops being transported to the Normandy beaches by landing craft.

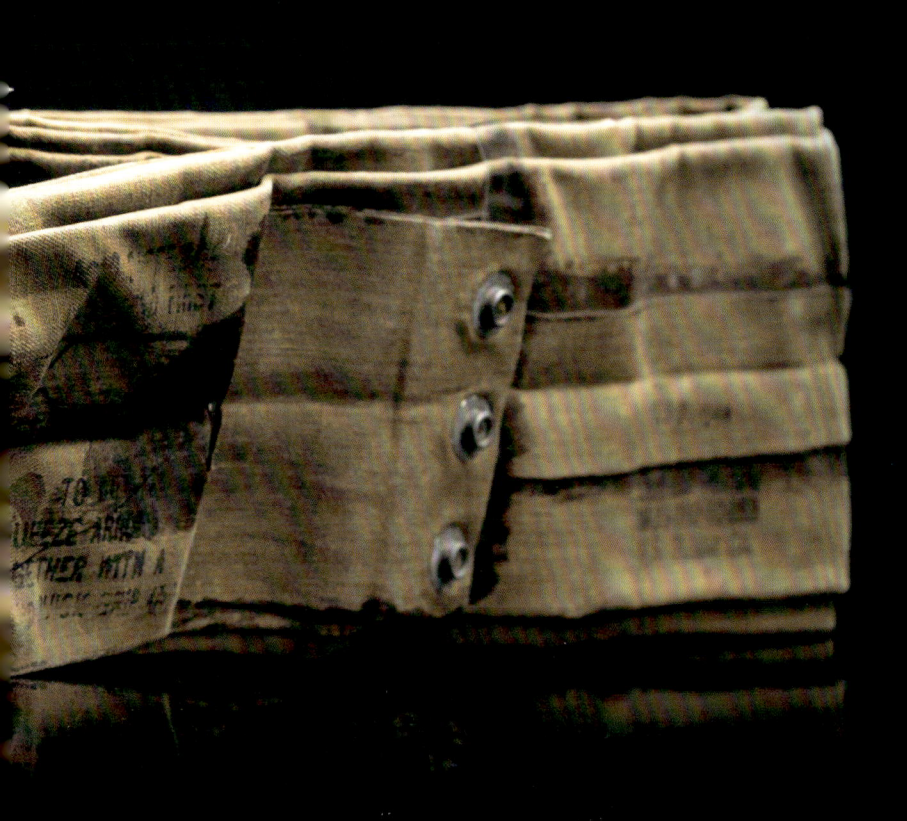

Courtesy of The D-Day Story.

44

URGENT MESSAGE

This leaflet was dropped from aircraft by the Allies, urging French people to evacuate the areas that were likely to become battle zones.

Courtesy of The D-Day Story.

The message from General Eisenhower was designed to minimise the number of deaths amongst French civilians. The leaflets were dropped just before the Allied bomber force went into action. French representatives in London had argued for advance warning to be given to people living in areas that were going to be the target for both air and naval bombardment. It is estimated nearly 20,000 civilians died during the fighting in Normandy, which took place between 6 June and 30 August 30 1944.

Message urgent

du Commandement Suprême des Forces Expéditionnaires Alliées

AUX HABITANTS DE CETTE VILLE

Afin que l'ennemi commun soit vaincu, les Armées de l'Air Alliées vont attaquer tous les centres de transports ainsi que toutes les voies et moyens de communications vitaux pour l'ennemi.

Des ordres à cet effet ont été donnés.

Vous qui lisez ce tract, vous vous trouvez dans ou près d'un centre essentiel à l'ennemi pour le mouvement de ses troupes et de son matériel. L'objectif vital près duquel vous vous trouvez va être attaqué incessamment.

Il faut sans délai vous éloigner, avec votre famille, pendant quelques jours, de la zone de danger où vous vous trouvez.

N'encombrez pas les routes. Dispersez-vous dans la campagne, autant que possible.

**PARTEZ SUR LE CHAMP !
VOUS N'AVEZ PAS UNE MINUTE A PERDRE !**

45

This is the blue ensign from the hospital ship H.M.H.S Lady Connaught, which served off the US beaches of Utah and Omaha. The ship was attached to the US naval forces and had American hospital staff and a British ship's crew.

The Lady Connaught was one of four British hospital ships which shuttled between the American beaches and Southampton. 54 large landing ships were also converted to transport casualties.

SEA HOSPITAL

The care of wounded troops was a high priority on D-Day and a fleet of ships were involved in providing immediate treatment and transporting casualties back to England.

Courtesy of The D-Day Story.

63

46

DECODING CLUES

To discover if the Allied invasion fleet had been spotted by the Germans, radio operators were carefully monitoring enemy frequencies and code-breakers were ready to quickly decode intercepted messages.

Courtesy of Bletchley Park Trust.

This message intercepted at 0430 on the morning of 9 June 1944, was one of the first to confirm the Germans were aware a major seaborne landing was underway. It says "Immediate readiness. There are indications that the invasion has begun."

It was sent to U-boats based in Bergen in Norway. It underlines the extent of German uncertainty about both the scale and the location of Allied operations. Bletchley Park took less than three hours to decode the message.

47

Frank Draper's landing craft was hit by a German shell, and he was mortally wounded, before setting foot on French soil.

He was taken to the troopship Empire Javelin. British sailor Bert Fuller did all he could to provide first aid for the dying man, but Frank passed away within a few minutes. Bert kept the binoculars as a reminder of D-Day for 60 years and then returned them to Frank's family in Virginia.

VALOUR IN FOCUS

American Frank Draper was carrying these binoculars as his landing craft approached Omaha Beach on D-Day.

Courtesy of The National D-Day Memorial Foundation, Bedford, Virginia.

48

LAYING THE FALLEN TO REST

An Army Chaplin's notebook underlines the suffering and sacrifice of the men who landed on the Normandy beaches to liberate occupied Europe.

Courtesy of Imperial War Museums.

Leslie Skinner was a chaplain in the British Sherwood Rangers, and he landed on Gold Beach on D-Day. During the Battle of Normandy, he went to great lengths to ensure any fallen soldier was given an appropriate burial, and that their relatives were informed.

He used the notebook to keep an accurate record of who had been buried and the location of graves, using sketches where necessary.

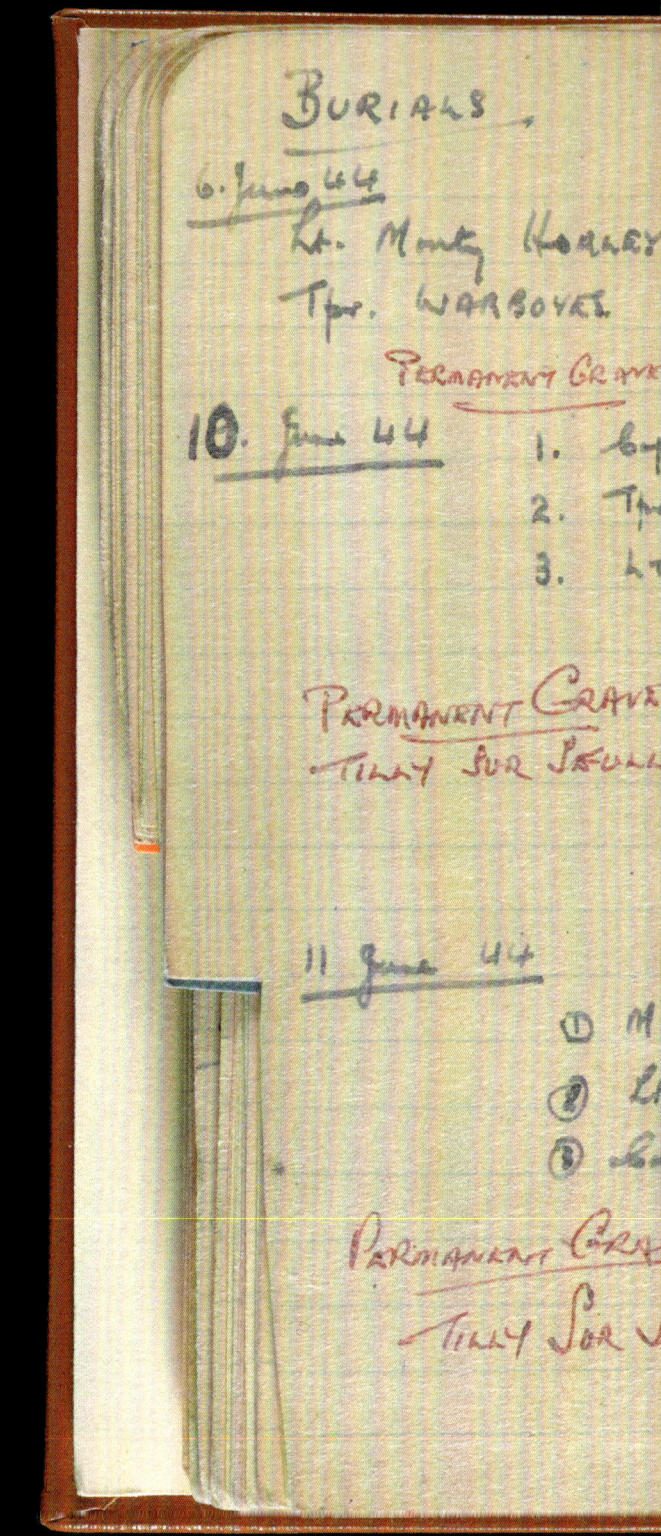

Buried by 25 B.D.S.
    Map. 37/18. Ref. 857872. (ASNELLES)
CEMETERY   NORMANDY

    Buried Map. 7F/1. Caen. Ref. 853704

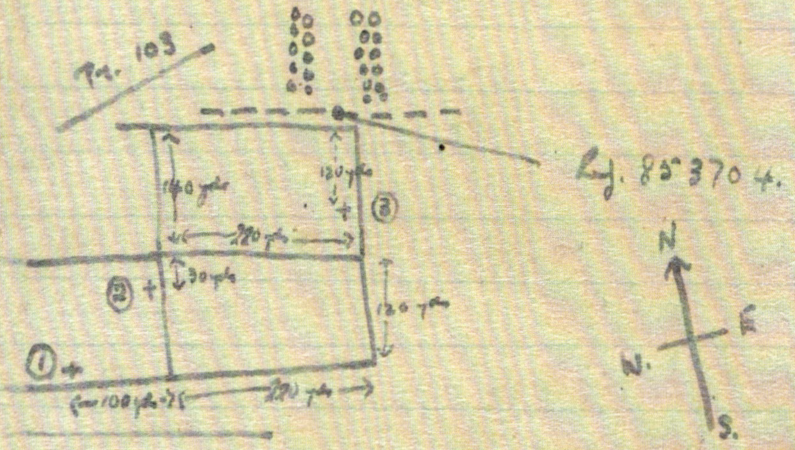

Pt. 103

Ref. 85 3704.

N
W — E
S

Buried. Map. 7F/1. Caen. [St. Pierre].
    Ref. 852691
ST. PIERRE.

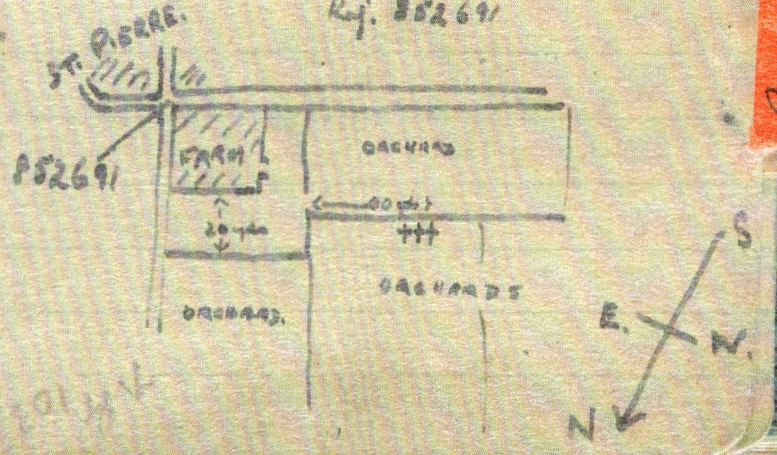

852691   FARM   ORCHARD
         ORCHARDS
ORCHARD

S
E — W
N

49

D-DAY GIANT

Quickly and cheaply made, most landing craft were scrapped soon after World War Two.

Courtesy of The National Museum of The Royal Navy.

This ship is a unique survivor. It is the last remaining Landing Craft Tank, a type of ship that delivered troops, tanks and other vehicles to the Normandy beaches.

LCT 7074 is now on display at the D-Day Story Museum in Portsmouth. It took 10 tanks to Gold Beach on 7 June 1944. It was used after the war as a floating mariners' club and then a nightclub in Liverpool. The LCT was rescued and restored by The National Museum of the Royal Navy, and opened to the public in 2020.

69

LUCKY LANDING CRAFT

In this letter to his 'darling wife' Petty Officer Engineer Albert Payne reveals his landing craft suffered 26 holes and had to be repaired after taking part in the D-Day landings.

Courtesy of The D-Day Story.

Writing home to his wife on 10 June 1944, Royal Navy sailor Albert Payne tells her, "… after 16 hours on French soil we went straight in dock with 26 gaping holes in our side and bottom." Part of the letter, that mentions the location of the landings, has been cut out by the censor.

Albert Payne joined the Royal

2014/544/2

THE SALVATION ARMY

"Keep in touch with the folks at home"

ON ACTIVE SERVICE
with the
CANADIAN FORCES

10 June 1944

HM LCT 720
GPO.

My Darling wife.

As the wireless told you we landed last Tuesday ▓▓▓▓▓▓▓ near ▓▓▓▓▓▓▓ & we got back on buckets & tow. with all trophy's flying from the mast — tin helmets, mine boards & Jolly Roger to boot. we were tired weary but oh boy were we happy to think our own crate had hammered Jerry like merry hell & then spent

Think *Any reference to shipping or troop movements will result in the delay or mutilation of this letter.*

51

The small town of Bedford in Virginia suffered the highest per capita D-Day loss of any community in the United States. Forty four soldiers, sailors and airmen from the town were in action on D-Day. Twenty lost their lives.

The bible was carried into battle by Raymond Hoback, who was one of the men from Bedford serving in A Company, 116th Infantry Regiment. Raymond and his brother, who had the Christian name Bedford, both died. Another soldier found the bible and returned it to the Hoback family.

BEDFORD BOY'S BIBLE

This bible belonged to one of the 20 men from a town in Virginia, who were all killed during the assault on Omaha Beach.

Courtesy of The National D-Day Memorial Foundation, Bedford, Virginia.

52

YOU'RE HAVING A LAUGH

Only a British Army officer would take part in the D-Day landings with a ventriloquist's dummy called Bertie packed in his kitbag.

Courtesy of The D-Day Story.

Bertie was a ventriloquist's dummy taken ashore on Juno beach by his creator, Captain Ted North of the Royal Warwickshire Regiment. During lulls in the fighting, Captain North and Bertie would entertain the troops. So he would not look out of place, Bertie had a special uniform and even some medals. Ted was a member of the Magic Circle and continued to use Bertie to entertain people after the war. Their last public performance was in 1985, about a year before Ted's death.

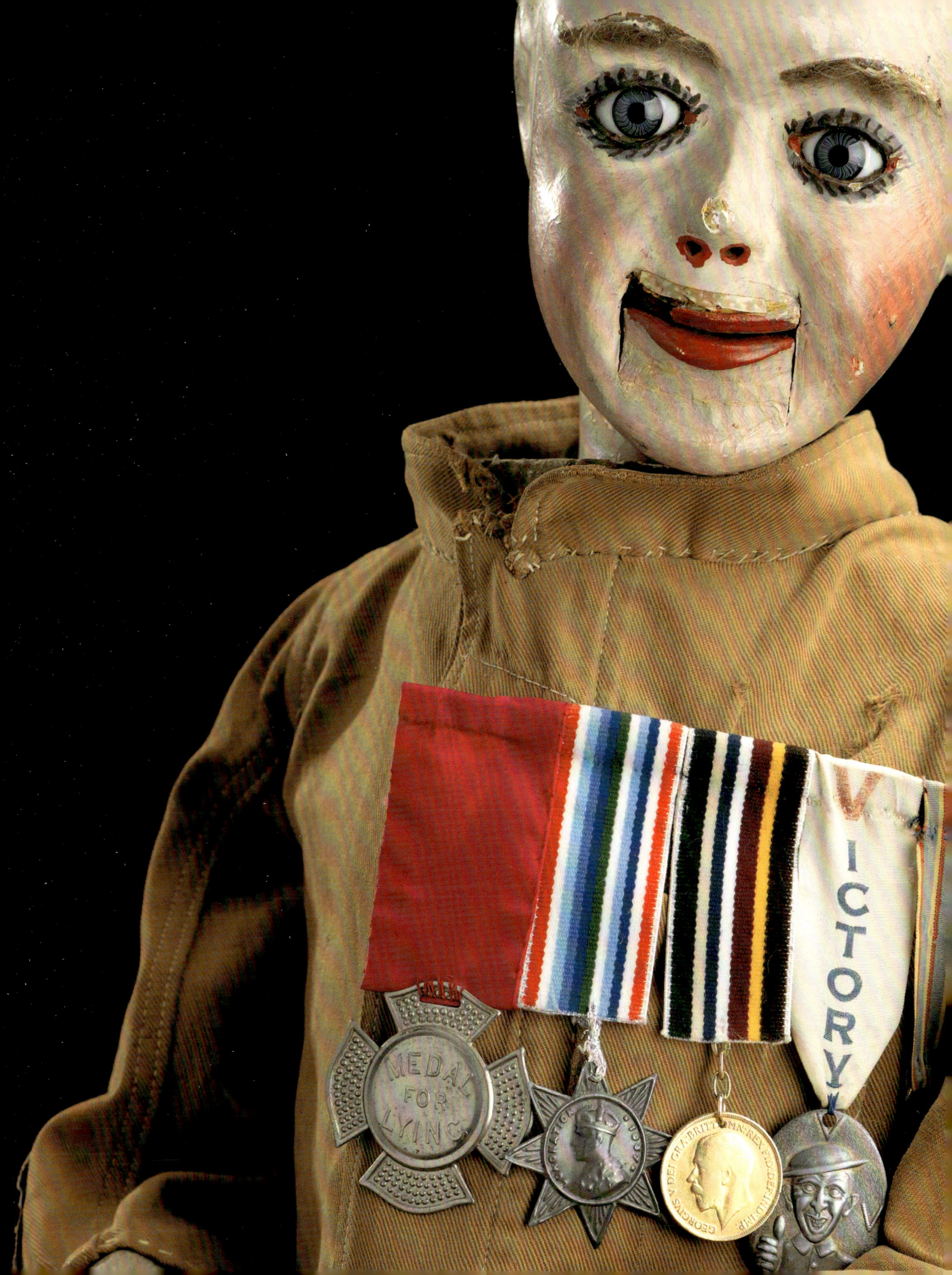
MEDAL FOR LYING
VICTORY

53

HEARTFELT CONDOLENCES

In this heartfelt letter, Lance Corporal Albert White writes to the mother of his friend, Private Wally Hansford, who has just died from the wounds he suffered while fighting in Normandy.

Courtesy of The D-Day Story.

In the letter, Lance Corporal Albert White tells Private Wally Hansford's Mum "... I was with him when he met his untimely end."

He also says "Ever since Wally came to France, he has been looked up to, by all of us, for his courage and his constant thought for his comrades." Albert explains that Wally was in a trench that received a direct hit.

54

Soldiers of the United States 320th Barrage Balloon Battalion landed on Omaha and Utah beaches on D-Day.

The standard winch they used to raise and lower their barrage balloons was too heavy for an assault landing craft, so a modified, lightweight device, was made. It was based on a winding mechanism for field telephone wires.

The men of the Barrage Balloon Battalion served for almost 150 days in Normandy. Three soldiers from the unit were killed and 17 were wounded.

THE BALLOON GOES UP

The first African American troops to go ashore in Normandy were members of a special unit that operated low altitude barrage balloons, which provided some protection from attacks by German aircraft.

Courtesy of The National WWII Museum.

55

KEEP YOUR HAT ON

Production of the famous American M1 steel helmet began in the summer of 1941 and by the end of the war twenty-two million had been produced.

Courtesy of Imperial War Museums.

This helmet was worn on D-Day by Pharmacist's Mate James Dale Jones, of the United States Navy who was on Landing Ship Tank 372. It anchored off Omaha Beach at about 2.30pm. After discharging its amphibious vehicles, the crew used small boats to pick-up troops who had been wounded in the beach landings. Towards the end of June 1944, James Jones served as a medic on a ship taking German prisoners of war from Normandy to the United States.

56

The Mulberry Harbours were created after a disastrous raid on Dieppe in 1942 had shown the Allies how difficult it would be to quickly capture a port in Normandy.

The structures consisted of large concrete sections that sat on the seabed, along with floating roadways and piers.

This part of the structure is called a 'Whale', one of the sections of floating roadway that linked the pierhead to the land. Large sections of the Mulberry Harbours can still be seen on the Normandy coast today.

HARBOURING A SECRET

The Mulberry Harbours were one of the big technological innovations of D-Day, designed to maintain a flow of troops and supplies as the invasion progressed.

Courtesy of Imperial War Museums.

57

COMFORT AND STYLE

Originally issued to airborne forces and commandos, the popular Denison smock was a much sought after item of clothing in the British Army during World War Two because of its comfort and style.

Courtesy of National Army Museum.

The Denison smock was worn by elite troops during the D-Day landings. Along with airborne forces and commandos, it was also issued to some reconnaissance and sniper platoons in front line infantry battalions. This smock was worn by Lieutenant Sydney Jary of the 4th Somerset Light Infantry. He landed in Normandy two weeks after D-Day, with the 43rd Wessex Infantry Division.

He wrote about his experiences as a young officer in Normandy in a best-selling book entitled "18 Platoon".

58

Troops with tanks and trucks were generally a little more comfortable during the Normandy campaign. They could carry tents, tarpaulins and bedding and often had better conditions than front line infantry, who could often find themselves living in slit trenches.

This photograph shows an improvised shelter that was rigged up at the back of a tank at Carpiquet near Caen. Trooper Dawson is getting his hair cut by Lance Corporal Johnnie Davies of 3rd County of London Yeomanry.

SHORT BACK AND SIDES

Living conditions for troops fighting in Normandy were often primitive but they always did what they could to make life more bearable.

Courtesy of National Army Museum.

59

WASHING DAY

Sergeant John Jenkins drew humorous cartoons, which he sent home to his wife and young daughter, so they would know what he was doing in Normandy.

Courtesy of The D-Day Story.

John Jenkins served as a Platoon Sergeant in the British Army's Pioneer Corps and landed on Gold Beach on D-Day. The series of cartoons he produced provide an amusing insight into the everyday life of soldiers in Normandy, including the need to do mundane tasks like washing clothes. John was given a standing ovation by world leaders, including HM The Queen and President Trump, at the commemorations to mark the 75th Anniversary of D-Day. John died in 2019 at the age of 100.

60

TICK TOCK SAVIOUR

Sergeant Roy Bishop had luck on his side during intense fighting in the village of Montchamp in Calvados in France on the 8 August 1944.

A piece of shrapnel went through his notebook and then through his wallet. But it was stopped by his fob watch, which he was carrying in the breast pocket of his shirt.

Sergeant Bishop served right through the fighting in France and Germany.

This is the Swiss fob watch that saved the life of Sergeant Roy Bishop of the Middlesex Regiment in Normandy.

Courtesy of National Army Museum.

61

DANGER MINES

Landmines laid by the Germans were a major challenge for the Allied forces landing In Normandy.

Courtesy of National Army Museum.

The Germans placed a variety of mines on the Normandy beaches and inland. Some were anti-personnel devices. Others were detonated by the weight of a truck or a tank.

This British Army mine detector was used during the D-Day landings. It could find mines made from metal, but it was not able to detect German mines made out of wood or glass. Special tanks with rotating flails were also used to clear a safe path across the beaches, by deliberately detonating landmines.

62

The breakwaters created by sinking old ships off the Normandy coast were called 'Gooseberries'. This humorous cartoon was drawn by Lieutenant William Hector Brereton of the Royal Navy. It shows the 'Gooseberry' he was in charge of setting up at Juno beach. Before the old ships set off for the French coast they were filled with concrete.

GOOSEBERRY CALMS THE SEA

To make things a little calmer for small boats and landing craft operating close to the D-Day beaches, some big old ships were sunk in lines just off the coast, to create artificial breakwaters.

Courtesy of The D-Day Story.

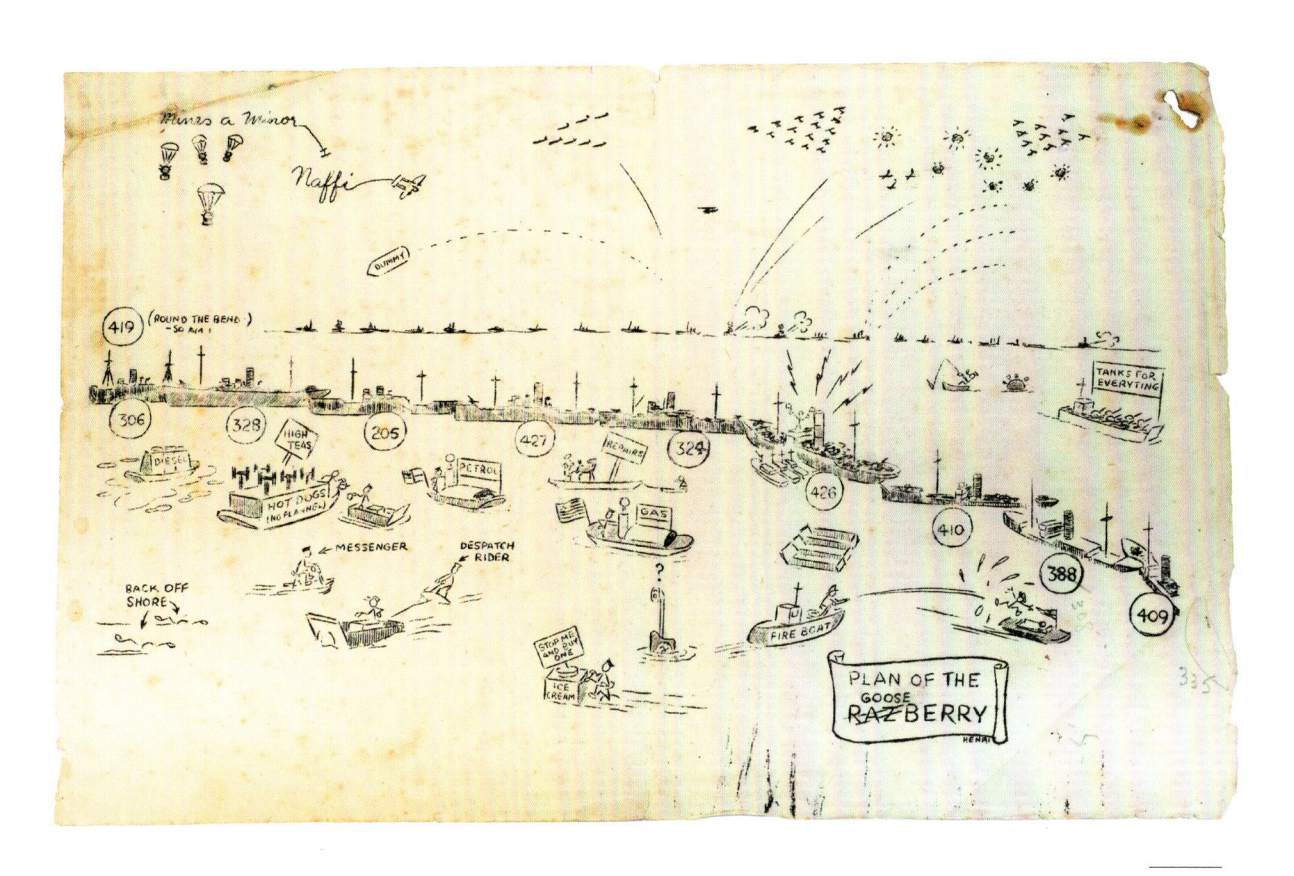

63

EYE IN THE SKY

British Army pilots flying small aircraft played a key role in directing artillery fire as the invasion force advanced through Normandy.

Denis Barnham, An Air Observation Post, 1944.

Courtesy of the RAF Air Historical Branch.

This painting by artist Denis Barnham shows the pilot of an Auster aircraft over a battlefield. The low speed and manoeuvrability of the Auster made it ideal for the job. If pilots encountered enemy fighters they would fly as low as possible. Using radios, the pilots would help the artillery hit targets by telling them where shells were landing.

Sixteen Air Observation Post Squadrons operated in World War Two. They were part of the Royal Air Force, but were largely manned by personnel from the Royal Artillery.

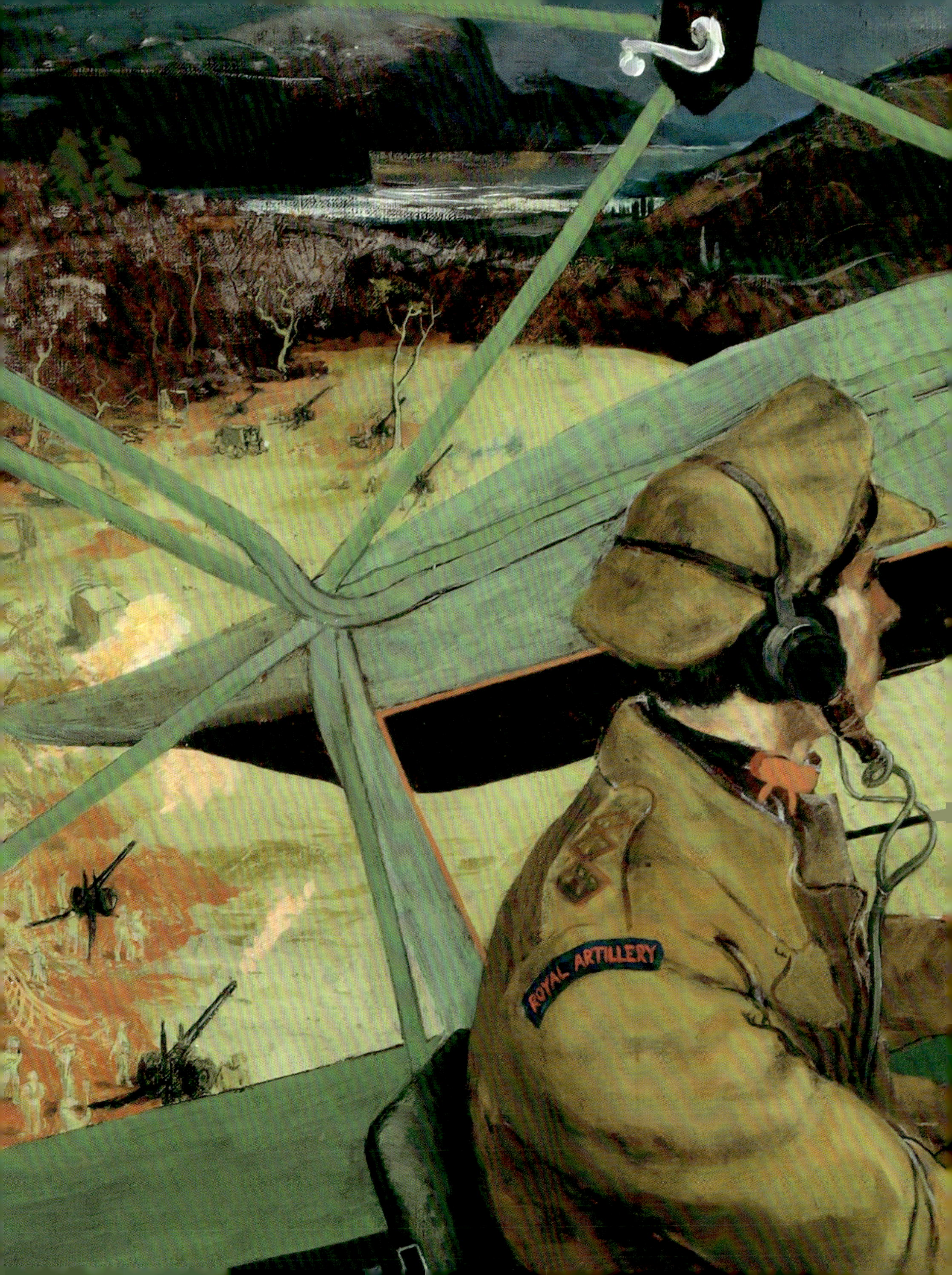
ROYAL ARTILLERY

64

TYPHOON TERROR

Hawker Typhoon aircraft equipped with rockets played a crucial role in the Normandy campaign by attacking German tanks, other vehicles and the railways.

Courtesy of Royal Air Force Museum.

A total of twenty six squadrons of rocket firing Typhoons were in operation at the time of the D-Day landings in June 1944. They worked very closely with troops on the ground.

RAF radio operators with VHF radios were embedded with front line units and could call up Typhoons to attack designated targets. The aircraft are credited with having a detrimental impact on the morale of German troops because of their firepower. In total, just over 3,300 Typhoons were built during World War Two.

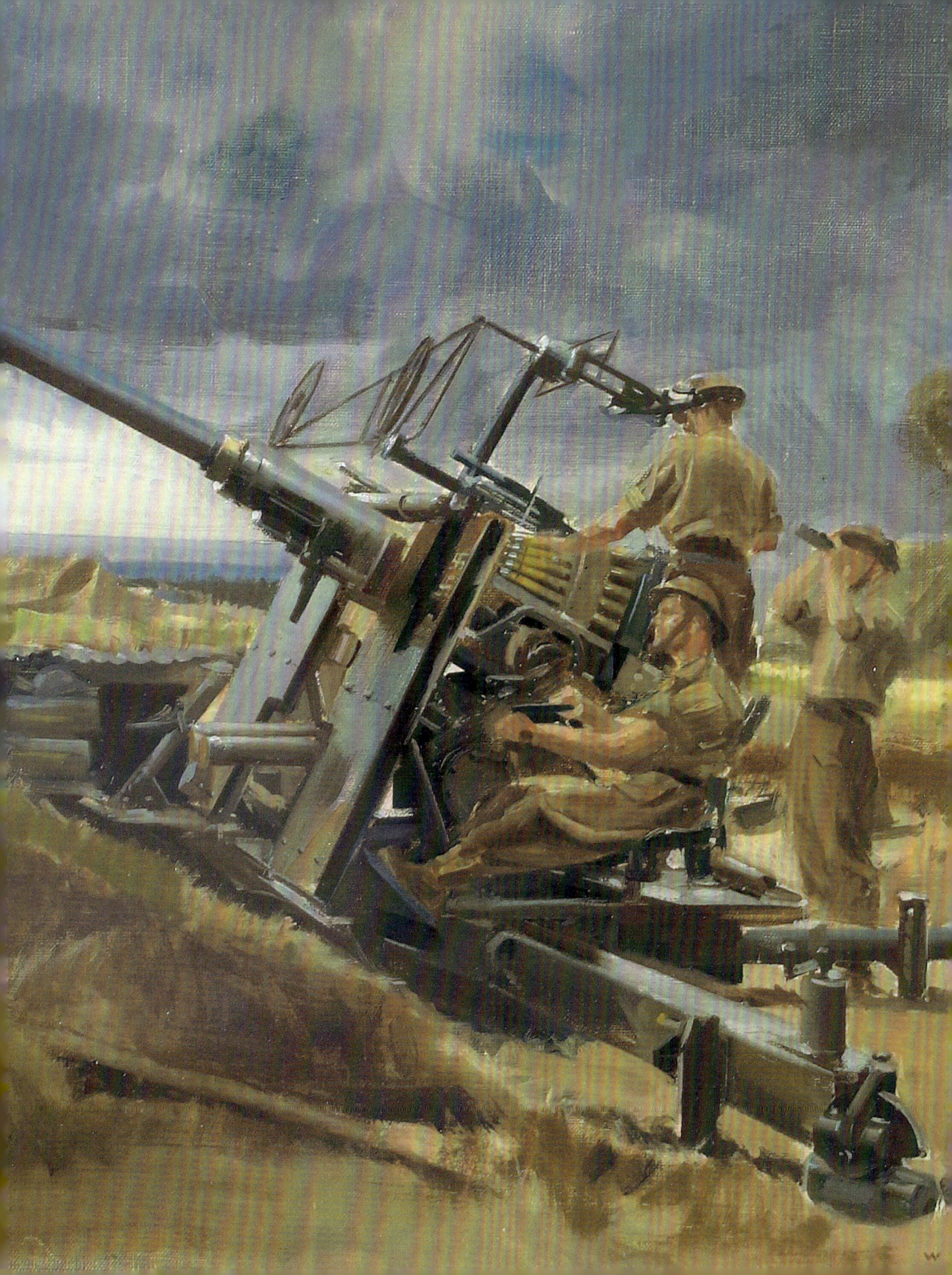

65

Within days of D-Day, the Allies were setting up airfields in Normandy, so planes could be refuelled and re-armed close to the front line. Artist Frank Wootton painted this picture of anti-aircraft gunners of the RAF Regiment, who had the job of protecting one of the brand-new Allied airfields. They are using a 40mm Bofors gun. Frank Wootton was an official war artist with the Royal Air Force throughout the Second World War.

PLANE PROTECTORS

This oil painting by war artist Frank Wootton shows anti-aircraft gunners of the RAF Regiment in action in Normandy.

Frank Wootton, Anti-Aircraft Gunners, No.219 Squadron, RAF Regiment, Normandy, 1944.

Courtesy of the RAF Air Historical Branch.

66

HUMAN TORPEDO

The Germans sank some Allied ships during the D-Day landings using a type of mini-submarine that was in essence a human torpedo.

Courtesy of The National Museum of The Royal Navy.

The 'Neger' was a torpedo with an electric motor, converted into a one-man semi-submersible with a range of about 50 miles. It had a conventional torpedo with an explosive warhead slung underneath. With its large bubble cockpit just above the surface of the water, the pilot would release the torpedo once

During the first few days of the invasion, these mini submarines sank or seriously damaged one cruiser, one destroyer and three minesweepers. It was not designed as a suicide weapon but it is estimated 80% of 'Neger' operators were killed.

67

Some of the BBC correspondents who reported on the D-Day landings were with military units that landed on the beaches. Others arrived by glider and parachute.

This dispatch was written by the BBC's Robert Dunnett, who was with American troops. He reports they are already six miles inland and describes the battle as being "... waged with machine gun, rifle and grenade, from tree to tree and ditch to ditch, and farm to farm."

HERE IS THE NEWS

A team of BBC reporters were amongst the British and American war correspondents who went to France with the Allied forces to provide eyewitness accounts of the fighting.

Courtesy of The D-Day Story.

68

MEDICAL CHEST

This is a type of medical chest used during the D-Day landings that includes a microscope and equipment for testing blood.

Courtesy of Imperial War Museums.

The medical chest was used by Surgeon Lieutenant Graham Airth, who served on a landing ship, which transported wounded troops from Normandy to the south coast of England.

As plans for Operation Overlord were being developed, Tank Landing Ships were identified as being the primary casualty transport for use in the early stages of the invasion. Some had small operating rooms, so treatment of seriously wounded men could begin as soon as possible.

69

The name 'Pluto' stood for 'Pipeline Under The Ocean' and involved the creation of two networks of special pipes. One was codenamed 'Bambi' and ran from Sandown on the Isle of Wight to Cherbourg. The other was called 'Dumbo' and was laid from Dungeness to Boulogne.

At the height of the operation, one million gallons of petrol a day was being pumped from England to France.

PLUTO FUELS LIBERATION

This is a section of the Pluto pipeline that was laid under the English Channel so crucial supplies of petrol could be pumped from England to France.

Courtesy of The D-Day Story.

70

RESISTANCE HEROES

The radio broadcast of a famous poem told members of the French resistance that the Allies were about to launch the D-Day invasion.

Courtesy of National Army Museum.

Resistance groups were active across France and made a vital contribution to the success of the Normandy landings by providing crucial intelligence and carrying out acts of sabotage.

Many resistance fighters sacrificed their lives to free their country from Nazi oppression. This photograph, taken in 1944, shows a group of resistance fighters marching behind a little girl, who is on her way to lay flowers on a local memorial. Her father had been killed by the Germans as they were driven from the town.

71

Mobile medical units arrived with the first waves of assault troops on D-Day. Major John Grice from Scotland was amongst the doctors deployed to Normandy in the aftermath of the landings. He was initially based at 34 Casualty Clearing Station.

His medical kit includes scalpels, clamps, scissors and forceps, along with cat-gut and silkworm ligatures.

In April 1945 Major Grice was sent to the recently liberated Belsen concentration camp to help with the relief effort. After the war he became a GP in Rochdale.

DOCTOR AT WAR

This medical kit was used by Major John Grice of the Royal Army Medical Corps who worked at a casualty clearing station during the Normandy campaign.

Courtesy of National Army Museum.

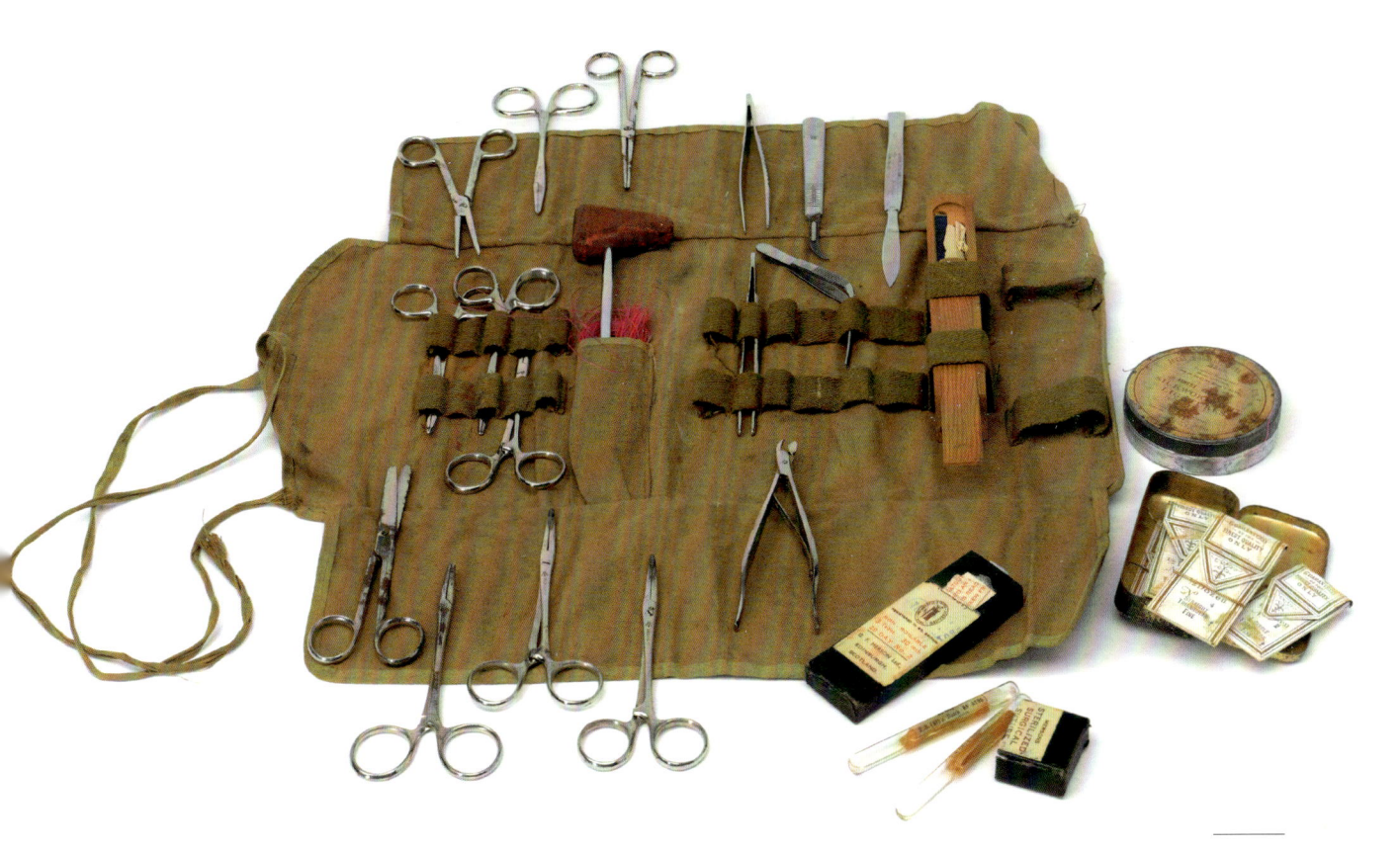

72

UNDERGROUND INTELLIGENCE

This armband, featuring the French flag, was used by Roger Moise, who was a member of one of the most successful and effective French resistance groups that was created during the Second World War.

Courtesy of The D-Day Story.

The Jade Amicol resistance network was set up in the south west of France in 1940 by British Intelligence. The group had strong support amongst members of the Catholic Church.

In late 1942, Jade Amicol moved its headquarters to Paris and the group was involved in the liberation of the French capital in late August 1944. Roger Moise, who wore this armband, served with them from March to September 1944.

73

CONCERT PARTY

This photograph shows Lorna Dean of an ENSA concert party getting some washing done during a break between performances in Normandy on 26 July 1944.

Courtesy of National Army Museum.

Entertaining the troops to boost morale was given a high priority by British forces during World War Two. Within a few weeks of the D-Day landings, entertainers were giving performances, close to the front line.

Lorna Dean was in a mobile concert party along with entertainers Billy Peters and June Worth. They were all part of ENSA, the Entertainments National Service Association, which was established in 1939.

74

POLISH STEEL

This is a badge from the 1st Polish Armoured Division, which had around 18,000 soldiers and fought during the final stages of the Battle of Normandy and all the way into Germany.

Courtesy of The D-Day Story.

Organised along the same lines as a British Division, the 1st Polish Armoured Division were equipped with Sherman and Cromwell tanks. This badge was worn by Jerzy Kobryner during the Battle of Normandy.

The Polish Division went to France in July 1944 and was in action early in August, achieving notable victories in the battles for Mont Ormel and Chambois, despite suffering considerable casualties.

The Poles were also amongst the Allied spearhead units involved in the liberation of Belgium and the Netherlands.

75

TELEGRAM TRAGEDY

It was telegram delivery boys who often had the unenviable task of handing over the messages that contained bad news about the fate of soldiers during World War Two.

Courtesy of The D-Day Story.

This brief telegram was sent to Corporal Rolly Quicke to tell him his school friend Andrew 'Dickie' Dickson had died on 7 June 1944.

It is one of so many tragic stories from the D-Day landings.

Dickson was serving as a Lieutenant in the East Yorkshire Regiment when he was wounded on Sword Beach on D-Day. He was then killed when the ship taking him back to England was bombed.

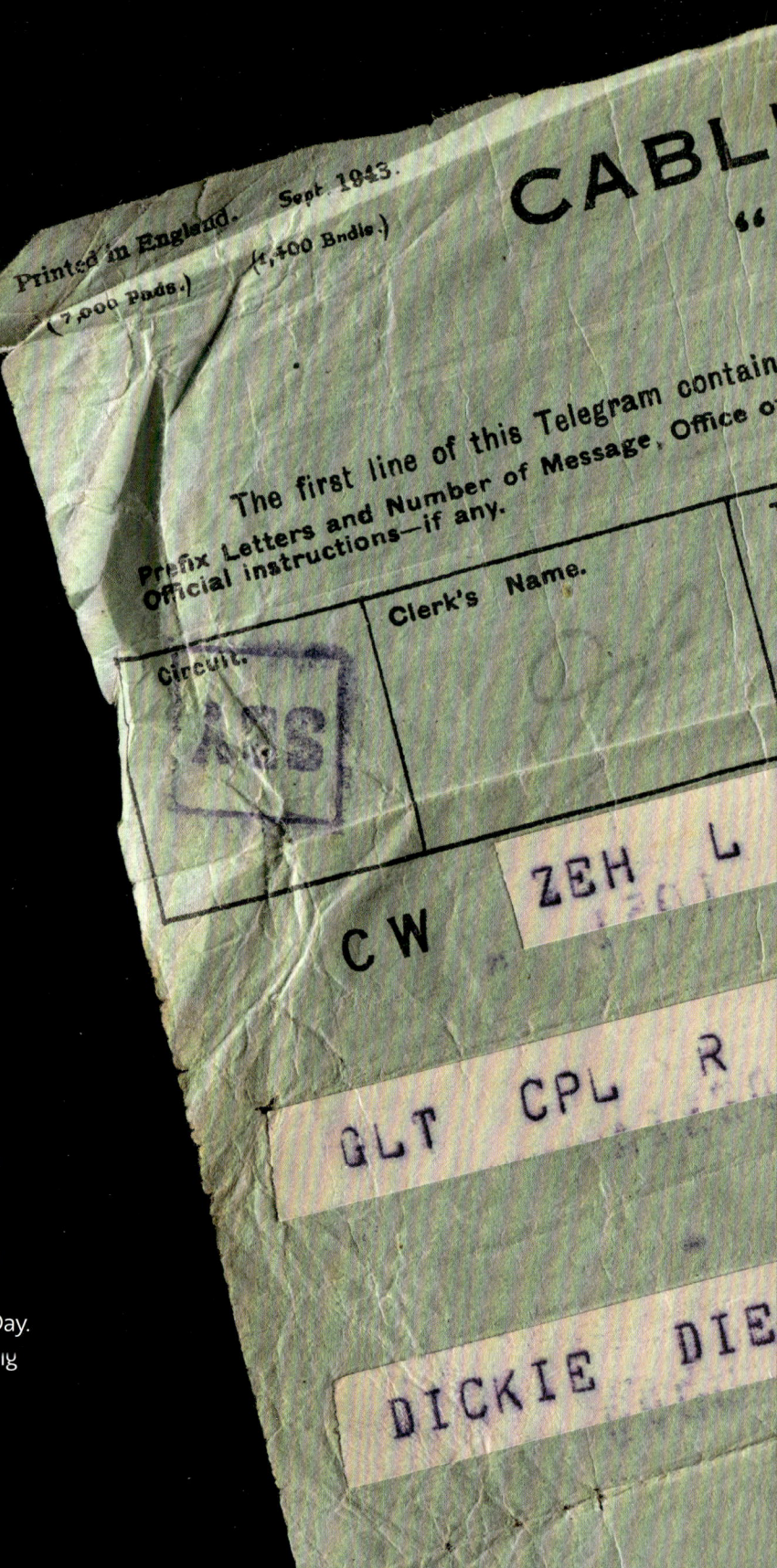

WIRELESS LIMITED
"Via Imperial"

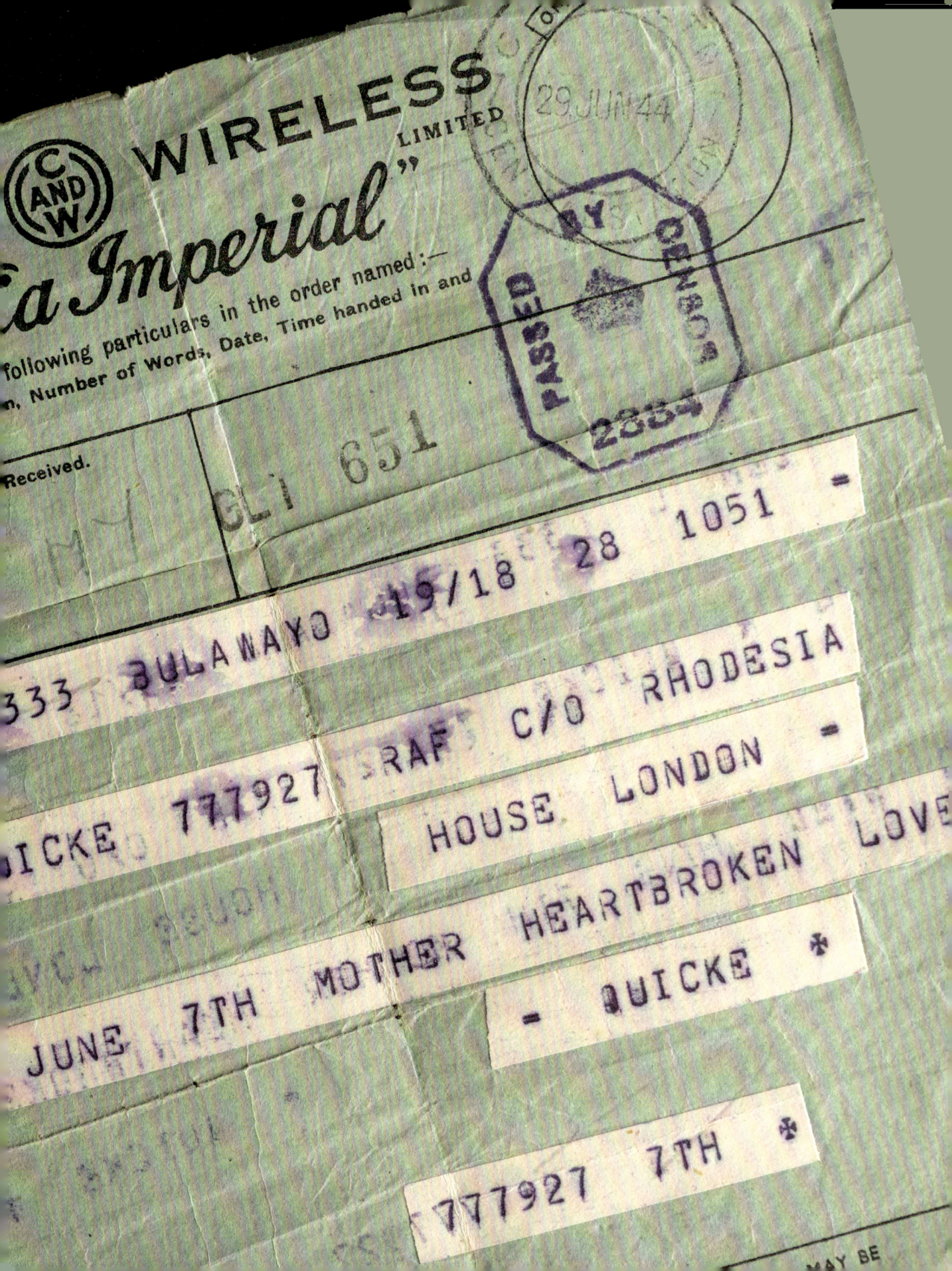

29 JUN 44

PASSED BY CENSOR 2884

CLT 651

333 BULAWAYO 19/18 28 1051 =

QUICKE 777927 SRAF C/O RHODESIA HOUSE LONDON =

JUNE 7TH MOTHER HEARTBROKEN LOVE - QUICKE *

777927 7TH *

102

76

The ring and the locket incorporate a photograph of Private Eric Harris of the 1st Battalion, Hampshire Regiment. The 24 year old from Milton in Portsmouth was killed on 11 August 1944 during the Battle of the Falaise Pocket. His mother had the items made and wore them every day until she died. Private Harris is buried at the Bayeux War Cemetery in Normandy.

NEVER FORGOTTEN

This ring and the locket show how some people had special items of jewellery made to provide a lasting and personal link to loved ones who were killed in battle.

Courtesy of The D-Day Story.

77

PEGASUS BRIDGE

Pegasus Bridge was captured by a small force of British troops in the first few minutes of D-Day, a full six hours before the beach landings started.

Courtesy of Mémorial Pégasus Museum.

181 men of the Oxfordshire and Buckinghamshire Light Infantry captured Pegasus Bridge over the Caen Canal along with another nearby bridge, which crossed the Orne River.

After taking off from Dorset, they landed at Ranville-Benouville in six Horsa gliders that had been towed across the English Channel by Halifax bombers. The commander of the force, Major John Howard, transmitted the code words 'Ham and Jam' to indicate both bridges had been captured. British forces held off fierce German counter attacks for many hours after capturing the bridges.

78

The flag was flown when members of the Portsmouth Branch of the Normandy Veterans Association gathered at parades, services and other ceremonies across the UK and during visits to Normandy. They also regularly gave talks to visitors to the D-Day Story Museum in Portsmouth.

The Association took part in the 70th anniversary of D-Day in June 2014. However, because the number of Normandy veterans was falling, the Association decided to disband in November 2014.

SERVICE NEVER FORGOTTEN

This is the flag of the Portsmouth Branch of the Normandy Veterans Association, which was set up to honour the memory of those who fought, and those who died, during the D-Day landings.

Courtesy of The D-Day Story.

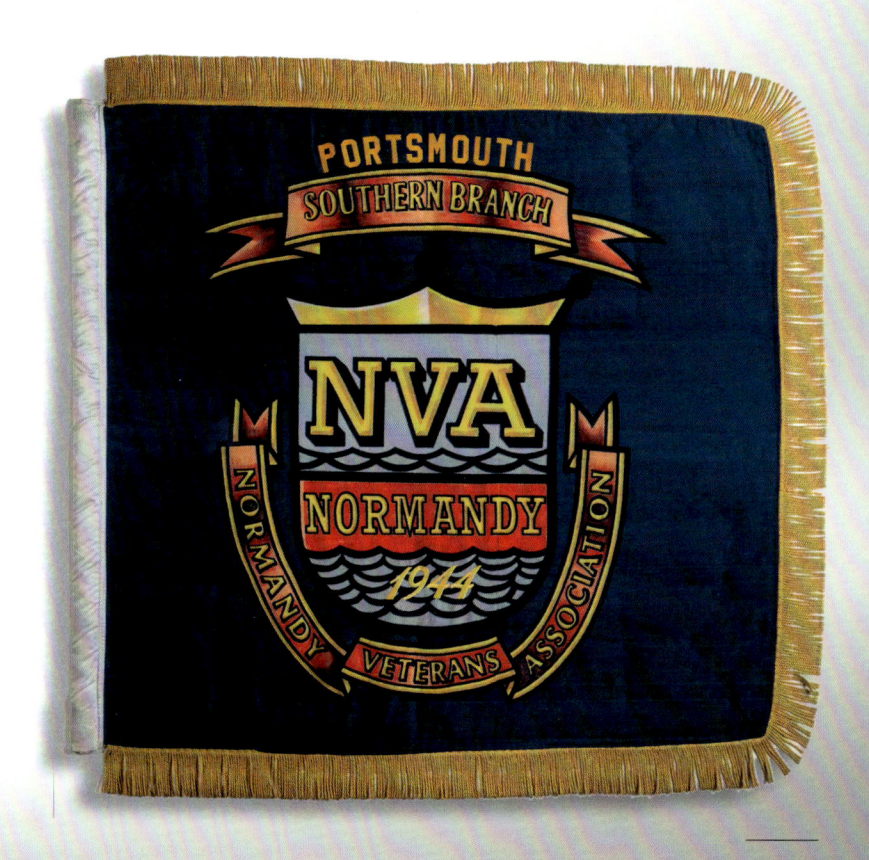

79

SYMBOLS OF GALLANTRY

These are the medals of Brigadier Peter Young, one of the highly experienced officers who took part in the D-Day landings, having already been awarded gallantry medals for his bravery in a series of battles during the war.

Courtesy of National Army Museum.

Brigadier Peter Young led 3 Commando during the D-Day landings. In 1940 he had been wounded during the evacuation of the British Expeditionary Force from Dunkirk, and then joined the commandos. He took part in a series of operations including the Dieppe Raid in 1942. He also participated in the invasion of Sicily. He was awarded the DSO for his role at Dieppe and the Military Cross three times for bravery between 1941 and 1943.

107

108

80

The Overlord Embroidery echoes some of the features of the Bayeux Tapestry, created to commemorate the Norman invasion of England in 1066.

The embroidery was made by the Royal School of Needlework and was designed by artist Sandra Lawrence. It tells the story of the preparations for the invasion and then shows images of ships crossing to Normandy, and the scenes on the beaches.

It was commissioned by Lord Dulverton and completed in 1974. It is on public display at the D-Day Story Museum in Portsmouth.

STITCHES IN TRIBUTE

This is the Overlord Embroidery which tells the story of the D-Day landings and the Battle of Normandy, in a hand-stitched design that is 83 metres long.

Courtesy of The D-Day Story and the Overlord Embroidery Trust.

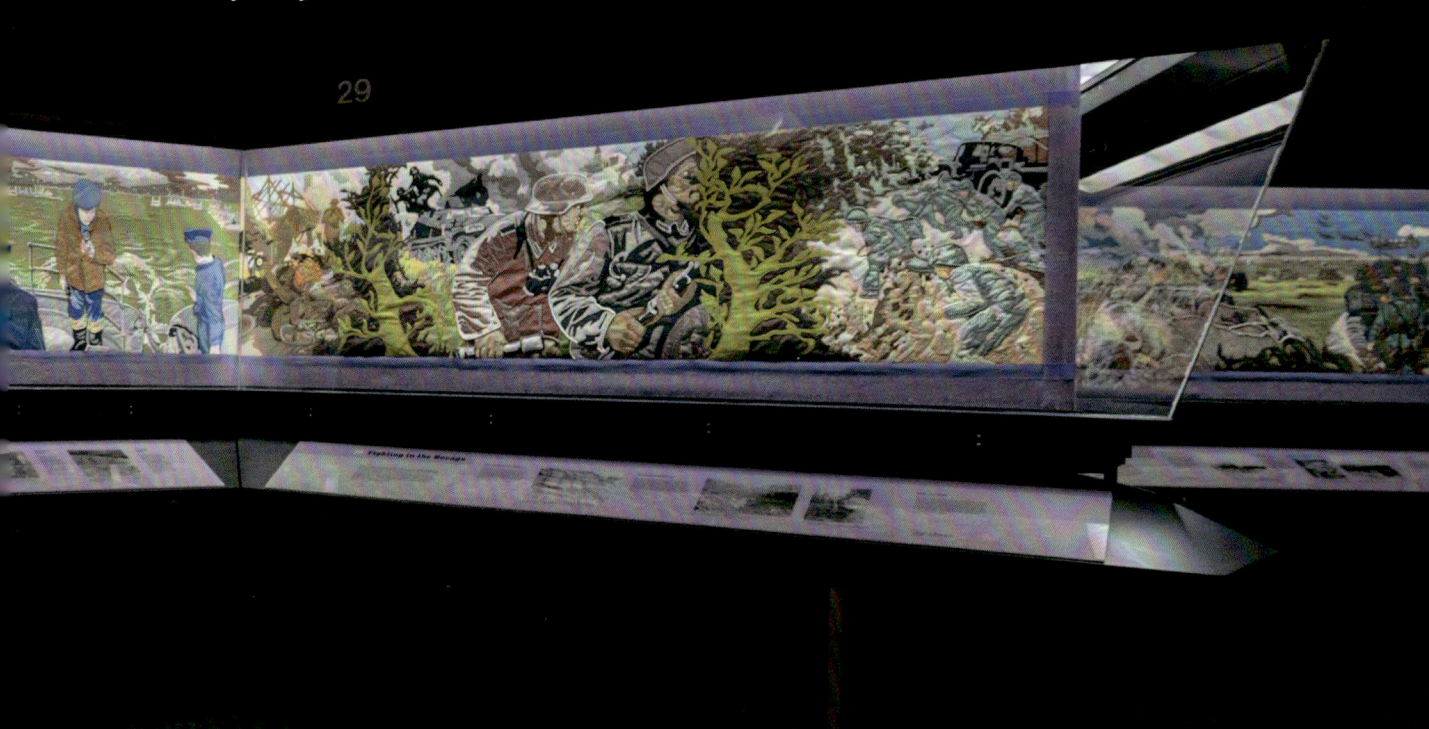

Sir Robert McALPINE **Wates**

THE D-DAY HARBOUR SECRET

Amongst the greatest triumphs of the D-Day campaign were the massive pre-fabricated Mulberry Harbours that allowed the Allies to quickly set up their own facilities to unload troops and supplies from ships on the Normandy coast.

The publication of this book has been supported by two companies who played a key role in the top secret project to design and construct the harbours, Sir Robert McAlpine and Wates.

The Mulberry Harbours were built because the Allies realised it would be extremely difficult to capture one of the heavily defended ports in Normandy in the early stages of Operation Overload.

Within hours of the first troops landing on the beaches, sections of the harbours were being towed across the English Channel. The Mulberry Harbours included sinkable breakwaters, floating pontoons, piers and roadways.

The Wates Group were heavily involved in the war effort building airfields, army camps and factories. The company constructed several large sections of the Mulberry Harbours including the piers, and pierhead pontoons.

The harbours were designed and built at yards across the country including Southampton and the West India Docks in East London before being assembled off the coast at Selsey in West Sussex and being towed across the Channel.

Another major construction company that played a leading role in the design and creation of the Mulberry Harbours was Sir Robert McAlpine.

It built part of the concrete breakwaters and 10 of the large caissons, each of them 200 feet long. Sir Malcolm McAlpine was chairman of the contractor's committee responsible for the design and supply of the breakwaters.

The Mulberry Harbour at Gold Beach was in use for 10 months after D-Day. Over two and a half million men, half a million vehicles and four million tonnes of supplies were landed before it was decommissioned. The Mulberry Harbour at Omaha Beach was severely damaged in a violent storm on 19 June 1944 and abandoned.

Sections of the Mulberry Harbours can still be seen on the Normandy coast and after the war parts of them were re-used to build bridges and to improve ports.

D-DAY IN NUMBERS

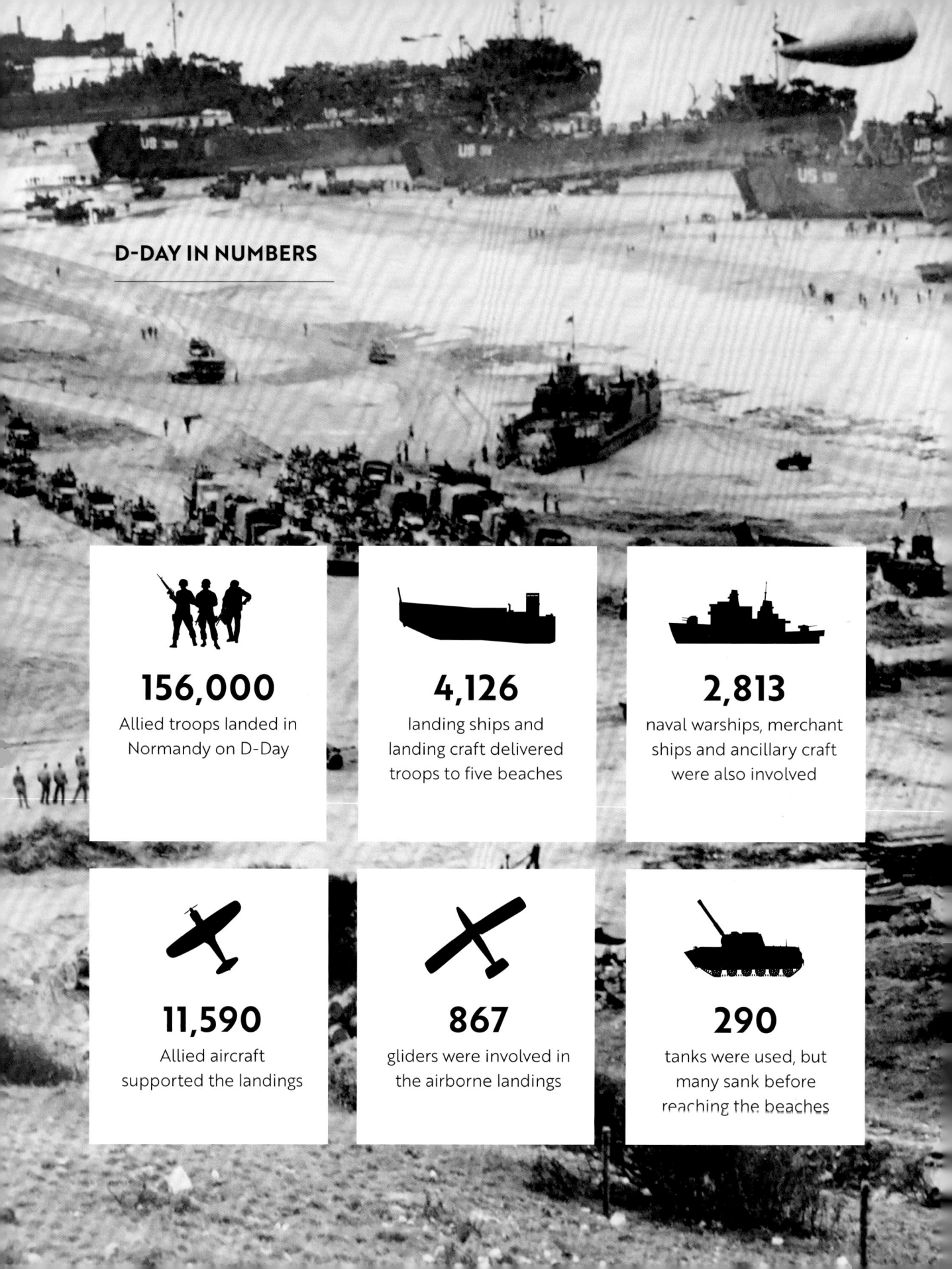

156,000
Allied troops landed in Normandy on D-Day

4,126
landing ships and landing craft delivered troops to five beaches

2,813
naval warships, merchant ships and ancillary craft were also involved

11,590
Allied aircraft supported the landings

867
gliders were involved in the airborne landings

290
tanks were used, but many sank before reaching the beaches

4,426
Allied personnel were killed on D-Day according to new research by The National D-Day Memorial Foundation, Bedford, Virginia

OVER 100,000
Allied and German troops were killed during the Battle of Normandy, from June 6 June 1944 to 30 August 1944

AROUND 20,000
French civilians died during the Battle of Normandy

875,000
Allied troops had landed in Normandy by the end of June 1944

A Sherman Firefly of 22nd Armoured Brigade, 7th Armoured Division comes ashore from an LST (Landing Ship Tank), Gold area, 7 June 1944.

MUSEUM OBJECT REFERENCES

1. **Letter from Private Jack Gollin**
   The D-Day Story
   DDS 2019/14/1

2. **Free French Recruiting Poster**
   Imperial War Museums
   IWM Art.IWM PST 3104

3. **Piece of Metal from USS Arizona**
   The National World War II Museum, New Orleans

4. **Biscuit Tin Radio**
   Imperial War Museums
   IWM COM 691

5. **Reconnaissance Suit**
   Imperial War Museums
   IWM UNI 3914

6. **Beach Postcard**
   Imperial War Museums
   IWM HU81693

7. **3-D Beach Model**
   Imperial War Museums
   IWM MOD 84.6

8. **Welder's Shield**
   The National World War II Museum, New Orleans

9. **'This is the Year' Poster**
   National Army Museum
   NAM 1990-06-153-1

10. **Map of Air Attacks**
    RAF Museum
    RAFM X004-6100

11. **General Montgomery's Plan**
    Imperial War Museums
    IWM Documents.20501/D

12. **Sexton Self-Propelled Gun**
    Royal Armouries,
    Fort Nelson XIX.527

13. **German Firing Diagram**
    The D-Day Story
    DDS 1996/89/1

14. **Armoured Recovery Vehicle**
    The D-Day Story
    DDS 1990/403

15. **Jeep Photograph**
    Imperial War Museums
    IWM B 5203

16. **Embarkation Map**
    The D-Day Story
    DDS 1995/69/1

17. **Women's Coat of Arms**
    The D-Day Story
    DDS 2003/1986

18. **Girl's Skipping Rope**
    Imperial War Museums
    IWM EPH10995

19. **Whittle Family Flag**
    The D-Day Story
    DDS 2005/708

20. **Soldier's Sick Bag**
    Imperial War Museums
    IWM EPH 4435

21. **Weather Report**
    RAF Museum
    RAFM AC71/9/26

22. **Betty White's Badges Jacket**
    The D-Day Story
    DDS 2010/51

23. **Southwick House Wall Map**
    National Museum of the Royal Navy/UK Government Art Collection

24. **Mine Sweeping Map**
    The D-Day Story
    DDS 1990/688

25. **White Ensign from Landing Craft**
    The D-Day Story
    DDS 2001/1332

26. **US Reserve Parachute**
    Imperial War Museums
    IWM EQU15131

27. **Douglas Dakota Cockpit**
    RAF Museum
    RAFM X002-9932

28. **Parachute Dummy**
    Imperial War Museums
    IWM FEQ 1389

29. **Eureka Radio Beacon**
    RAF Museum
    RAFM 2990/0272/R

30. **Royal Observer Corps Badge**
    RAF Museum
    RAFM X004-2050

31. **Sword Beach Map**
    The D-Day Story
    DDS 2019/15/3

32. **Carrier Pigeon Medal**
    The D-Day Story/
    Family of Frederick Jackson

33. **US Ranger's Boots**
    National D-Day Memorial Foundation, Bedford, Virginia

34. **Captain Wilson's Letter**
    The D-Day Story
    DDS 1986/24/1

35. **Focke Wulf 190 Aircraft**
    RAF Museum
    RAFM 1998/0214/A

36. **HMS Belfast Photograph**
    Imperial War Museums
    IWM MAR 555

MUSEUM OBJECT REFERENCES *continued*

37 **15 inch Shell**
National Museum of the Royal Navy
NMRN PH 2010/190

38 **Gold Beach Map**
National Army Museum
NAM 1984-06-153-5

39 **Sword Beach Photograph**
National Museum of the Royal Navy
NMRN RMM 1971/265/5

40 **Signal Flags**
The D-Day Story
DDS 2023/27/1-2

41 **Beachmaster's Stick**
National Museum of the Royal Navy
NMRN RNM 1980/176

42 **German Normandy Map**
The D-Day Story
DDS 2020/30/1

43 **US life Preserver Belt**
The D-Day Story
DDS 2016/537/2

44 **Warning Leaflet for French Civilians**
The D-Day Story
DDS 1997/3761

45 **Blue Ensign from Hospital Ship**
The D-Day Story
DDS 1989/511/1

46 **Note of Decoded German Message**
Bletchley Park Trust
BPT Archive BLEPK 0100.1.46

47 **US Soldier's Binoculars**
National D-Day Memorial Foundation, Bedford, Virginia

48 **Chaplin Leslie Skinner's Notebook**
Imperial War Museums
IWM Documents.10908

49 **Landing Craft Tank**
National Museum of the Royal Navy
NMRN/2015/1

50 **Albert Payne's Letter**
The D-Day Story
DDS 2014/544/2

51 **US Soldier's Bible**
National D-Day Memorial Foundation, Bedford, Virginia

52 **Ventriloquist's Dummy**
The D-Day Story
DDS 1987/ 451/1

53 **Albert White's Letter**
The D-Day Story
DDS 2021/102/25

54 **Barrage Balloon Winch**
The National World War II Museum, New Orleans

55 **US Medic's Helmet**
Imperial War Museums
IWM UNI 16204

56 **Mulberry Harbour 'Whale' Section**
Imperial War Museums
IWM FEQ 1828

57 **Denison Smock**
National Army Museum
NAM 1995-12-136-1

58 **Tank and Haircut Photograph**
National Army Museum
NAM 1975-03-63-18-124

59 **Cartoon Drawn by John Jenkins**
The D-Day Story
DDS 2015/53/6

60 **Roy Bishop's Watch**
National Army Museum
NAM 1992-10-97- 1 and 2

61 **British Army Mine Detector**
National Army Museum
NAM 1994-05-113-1

62 **Cartoon of Gooseberry Breakwater**
The D-Day Story
DDS 2016/221/1

63 **Painting of British Army Pilot Denis Barnham, An Air Observation Post, 1944**
RAF Air Historical Branch
RAFM L001-1868

64 **Hawker Typhoon Aircraft**
RAF Museum
RAFM 74/A/27

65 **Painting of Anti-Aircraft Gunners Frank Wootton, Anti-Aircraft Gunners, 1944**
RAF Air Historical Branch
RAFM L001-1917

66 **German Human Torpedo**
National Museum of the Royal Navy
NMRN PH 1993/1164

67 **Report by BBC Correspondent**
The D-Day Story
DDS 2016/541/13

68 **Graham Airth's Medical Chest**
Imperial War Museums
IWM FEQ 889

69 **Section of PLUTO Pipeline**
The D-Day Story
DDS 1995/83/1

Led by their piper, men of 7th Seaforth Highlanders,

MUSEUM OBJECT REFERENCES *continued*

70 **Photograph of French Resistance**
National Army Museum
NAM 1975-03-63-19-156

71 **John Grice's Medical Kit**
National Army Museum
NAM 2011-11-22-1

72 **French Resistance Armband**
The D-Day Story
DDS 2016/78/2

73 **Photograph of ENSA Performer**
National Army Museum
NAM 2006-12-98-27

74 **1st Polish Division Badge**
The D-Day Story
DDS 1993/27

75 **Rolly Quicke Telegram**
The D-Day Story
DDS 2004/3474

76 **Private Eric Harris Ring and Locket**
The D-Day Story
DDS 1995/104/1-2

77 **Photograph of Pegasus Bridge Memorial**
Pegasus Museum

78 **Portsmouth Normandy Veterans' Flag**
The D-Day Story
DDS 2016/16

79 **Brigadier Peter Young's Medals**
National Army Museum
NAM1988-11-9-1

80 **Operation Overlord Embroidery**
The D-Day Story/Overlord Embroidery Trust

A Sherman tank, probably of 13th/18th Royal Hussars, uses a Horsa glider as cover during fighting against German troops on 6th Airborne Division's drop zone near Ranville, 10 June 1944.

Photograph courtesy of Imperial War Museums.

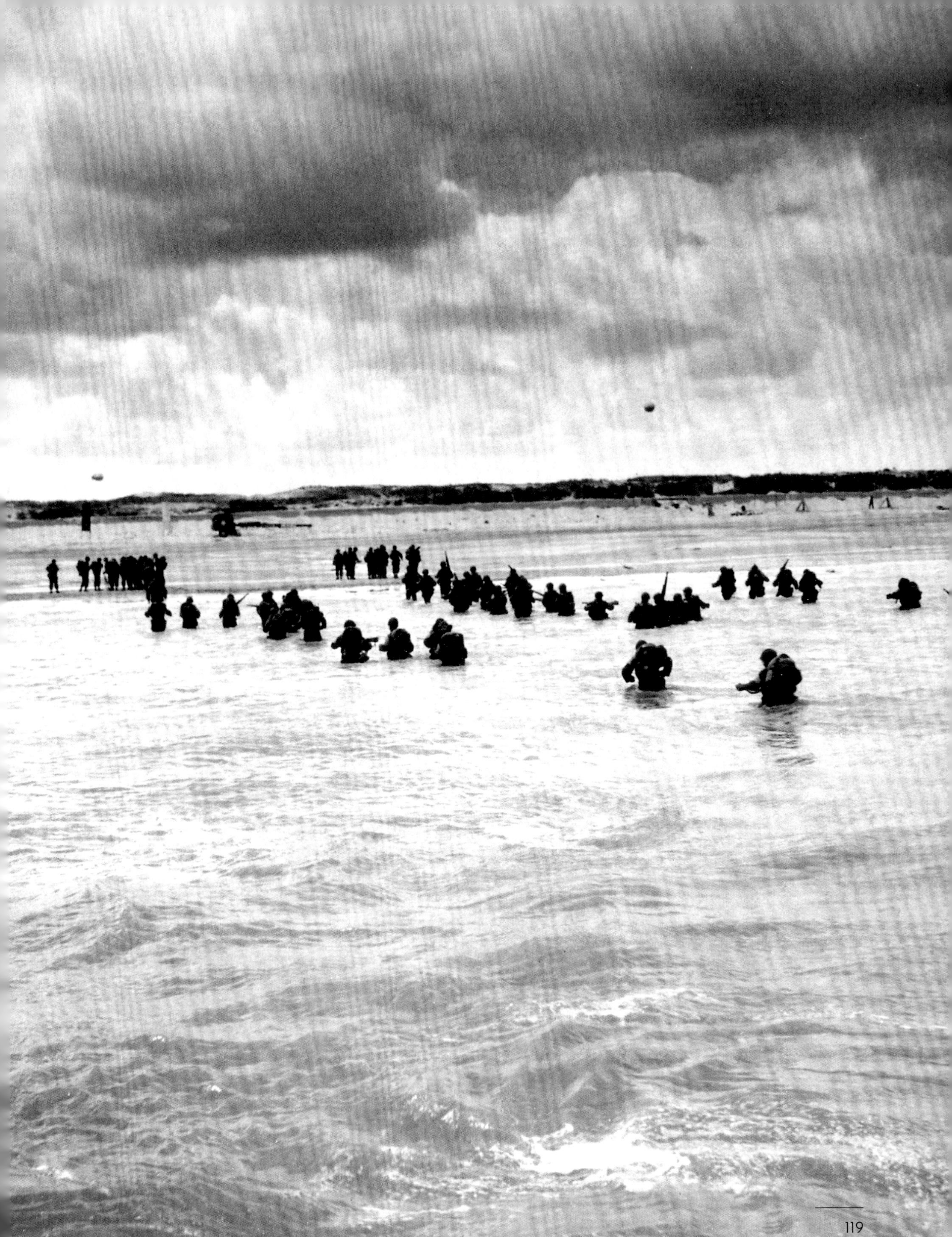

ACKNOWLEDGEMENTS

The book has been created as part of the D-Day in 80 Objects project to commemorate the 80th anniversary of D-Day. It could not have been possible without the support of our partners and sponsors.

Sponsor liaison, Marc Hanson, Portsmouth D-Day Museum Trust

Sponsors, Wates and Sir Robert McAlpine

Concept and Editor
Cathy Hakes, Portsmouth City Council

Written by Steve Humphrey

Designed by Janice Kalsi, StudioMoö Design

THANKS TO:

Imperial War Museums
James Bulgin, Rachel Donnelly, James Taylor
iwm.org.uk

The Royal Air Force Museum
Dr Harry Raffal
rafmuseum.org.uk

The National Museum of the Royal Navy
Trudie Cole, Will Heppa, Eileen Clegg, Sarah Ford, Louisa Blight
nmrn.org.uk

The National Army Museum
Melanie Marsh, Ian Maine
nam.ac.uk

The National WWII Museum, New Orleans, Louisiana
Kimberley Guise
nationalww2museum.org

The Overlord Embroidery Trust

The National D-Day Memorial Foundation, Bedford, Virginia
April Cheek-Messier, John D. Long
dday.org

The Royal Armouries, Fort Nelson
Richard Noyce
royalarmouries.org

Bletchley Park Trust
Erica Munro
bletchleypark.org.uk

Mémorial Pégasus
Nicholas Dumont
musee.memorial-pegasus.com

Southwick House
Fiona Sayer

PDSA
pdsa.org.uk

The family of Frederick Jackson

You can find out more about the 80 Objects by visiting **theddaystory.com**

Website content, object research, and creation by Andrew Whitmarsh & David Howells, Portsmouth City Council

The D-Day Story Museum is operated by Portsmouth City Council

Portsmouth CITY COUNCIL

NORTHERN LIMIT

G 13

G 11

FORCE BOUNDARY

J 12

MARCOUF

FORCE "A"
A

FORCE "G"
C

FORCE "K"
K

FORCE E

AUGUSTA

ANCON O

INTER TASK

BULOL G

HILAR

BAYFIELD

GOLD
G

G

JUNO
J

J

OMAHA

GRANDCAMP

VIERVILLE

PORT-EN-BESSIN

ISIGNY

ARROMANCHES COURS

B A

20 21 22 23 24 1 2 3 4

HIGH WATER STAND